Education's Epistemology

Education's Epistemology

Rationality, Diversity, and Critical Thinking

HARVEY SIEGEL

Oxford University Press is a department of the University of Oxford.
It furthers the University's objective of excellence in research, scholarship,
and education by publishing worldwide. Oxford is a registered trade mark of
Oxford University Press in the UK and certain other countries.

Published in the United States of America by Oxford University Press
198 Madison Avenue, New York, NY 10016, United States of America.

© Oxford University Press 2017

All rights reserved. No part of this publication may be reproduced, stored
in a retrieval system, or transmitted, in any form or by any means, without
the prior permission in writing of Oxford University Press, or as expressly
permitted by law, by license, or under terms agreed with the appropriate
reproduction rights organization. Inquiries concerning reproduction
outside the scope of the above should be sent to the Rights Department,
Oxford University Press, at the address above.

You must not circulate this work in any other form
and you must impose this same condition on any acquirer.

Library of Congress Cataloging-in-Publication Data
Names: Siegel, Harvey, 1952– author.
Title: Education's epistemology : rationality, diversity, and critical thinking / by Harvey Siegel.
Description: New York : Oxford University Press, 2017. | Includes index.
Identifiers: LCCN 2017003881 | ISBN 9780190682675 (hardcover)
Subjects: LCSH: Critical thinking. | Knowledge, Theory of. | Education.
Classification: LCC B105.T54 S525 2017 | DDC 128/.33—dc23
LC record available at https://lccn.loc.gov/2017003881

For Madeleine

Loving daughter and chocolatier extraordinaire

CONTENTS

Preface and Acknowledgments ix
Introduction xi

PART ONE RECENT STATEMENTS AND DEVELOPMENTS OF THE THEORY

1. Cultivating Reason   3

2. Education as Initiation into the Space of Reasons   20

3. Neither Humean nor (Fully) Kantian Be   33

PART TWO DISPOSITIONS, VIRTUES, AND INDOCTRINATION

4. What (Good) Are Thinking Dispositions?   49

5. "You Take the Wheel, I'm Tired of Driving; Jesus, Show Me the Way": Doctrines, Indoctrination, and the Suppression of Critical Dispositions   67

6. The Role of Reasons in Moral Education   76

7. Critical Thinking and the Intellectual Virtues   89

8. Open-Mindedness, Critical Thinking, and Indoctrination   108

PART THREE VALUES, RATIONALITY, AND THE VALUE OF RATIONALITY

9. Is "Education" a Thick Epistemic Concept?   123

10. Truth, Thinking, Testimony, and Trust: Alvin Goldman on Epistemology and Education   135

11. Rationality and Judgment   156

12. Epistemology in Excess?: A Response to a Heideggerian Reconceptualizing of Critical Thinking   172

PART FOUR RATIONALITY AND CULTURAL DIVERSITY

13. Multiculturalism and the Possibility of Transcultural Educational and Philosophical Ideals   197

14. Argument Quality and Cultural Difference   218

15. Multiculturalism and Rationality   238

16. Epistemological Diversity and Educational Research: Much Ado about Nothing Much?   258

17. How Should We Educate Students Whose Cultures Frown upon Rational Disputation?: Cultural Difference and the Role of Reason in Multicultural Democratic Education   280

Index   289

PREFACE AND ACKNOWLEDGMENTS

The chapters that follow have all been published previously; original publication details follow. Most have been only minimally edited; some have been modestly revised. I am grateful to the original editors and publishers for permission to use them here.

Chapter 1, "Cultivating Reason," was first published in R. Curren (ed.), *A Companion to the Philosophy of Education* (pp. 305–317). Oxford: Blackwell, 2003.

Chapter 2, "Education as Initiation into the Space of Reasons," first appeared in *Theory and Research in Education* 10.2 (2012): 191–202.

Chapter 3, "Neither Humean nor (Fully) Kantian Be," was published under the title "Neither Humean nor (Fully) Kantian Be: Reply to Cuypers," in *Journal of Philosophy of Education* 39.3 (2005): 535–547.

Chapter 4, "What (Good) Are Thinking Dispositions?," was published in *Educational Theory* 49.2 (1999): 207–221.

Chapter 5, "'You Take the Wheel, I'm Tired of Driving; Jesus, Show Me the Way': Doctrines, Indoctrination, and the Suppression of Critical Dispositions," appeared in L. F. Groenendijk and J. W. Steutel (eds.), *Analytisch Filosoferen over Opvoeding en Onderwijs: Liber Amicurum voor Ben Spiecker* (*Analytic Philosophizing about Upbringing and School Education: Festschrift for Ben Spiecker*) (pp. 129–138). Amsterdam: B.V. Uitgeverij SWP, 2004.

Chapter 6, "The Role of Reasons in Moral Education," was published in D. J. deRuyter and S. Meidema (eds.), *Moral Education and Development: A Lifetime Commitment (Festschrift for Jan Steutel)* (pp. 59–69). Rotterdam: Sense Publishers, 2011.

Chapter 7, "Critical Thinking and the Intellectual Virtues," first appeared in J. Baehr (ed.), *Educating the Intellectual Virtues: Essays in Applied Virtue Epistemology* (pp. 95–112). New York: Routledge, 2016.

Chapter 8, "Open-Mindedness, Critical Thinking, and Indoctrination," was published under the title "Open-Mindedness, Critical Thinking, and Indoctrination: Homage to William Hare," in *Paideusis* 18.1 (2009): 26–34.

Chapter 9, "Is 'Education' a Thick Epistemic Concept?," was published in *Philosophical Papers* 37.3 (2008): 455–469.

Chapter 10, "Truth, Thinking, Testimony, and Trust: Alvin Goldman on Epistemology and Education," appeared first in *Philosophy and Phenomenological Research* 71.2 (2005): 345–366.

Chapter 11, "Rationality and Judgment," was published in *Metaphilosophy* 35.5 (2004): 597–613.

Chapter 12, "Epistemology in Excess? A Response to a Heideggerian Reconceptualizing of Critical Thinking," first appeared under the title "Epistemology in Excess?: A Response to Williams," in *Journal of Philosophy of Education* 49.1 (2017): 193–213.

Chapter 13, "Multiculturalism and the Possibility of Transcultural Educational and Philosophical Ideals," was first published in *Philosophy* 74 (1999): 387–409.

Chapter 14, "Argument Quality and Cultural Difference," first appeared in *Argumentation* 13.2 (1999): 183–201.

Chapter 15, "Multiculturalism and Rationality," was published in *Theory and Research in Education* 5.2 (2007): 203–223.

Chapter 16, "Epistemological Diversity and Educational Research: Much Ado about Nothing Much?," first appeared in *Educational Researcher* 35.2 (2006): 1–10.

Chapter 17, "How Should We Educate Students Whose Cultures Frown upon Rational Disputation?: Cultural Difference and the Role of Reason in Multicultural Democratic Education," was published in Y. Raley and G. Preyer (eds.), *Philosophy of Education in the Era of Globalization* (pp. 7–14). New York: Routledge, 2010.

It is a pleasure to thank the friends, colleagues, and critics who commented on earlier versions of the chapters (and who are explicitly acknowledged in the chapters), and Peter Ohlin at OUP, whose advice was invaluable, and whose encouragement and good cheer were most welcome.

INTRODUCTION

In 1988 I published *Educating Reason: Rationality, Critical Thinking, and Education*, followed in 1997 by *Rationality Redeemed?: Further Dialogues on an Educational Ideal*. In both books I articulated and defended my "reasons conception" of critical thinking as an educational ideal, and in the second I responded to criticisms of the first as well. In the intervening years I have developed my view in both philosophical and educational directions and addressed still more criticisms. This volume collects seventeen of those more recent papers published between 1999 and 2017.

Part I collects three papers that set out and develop my positive view. Chapter 1 begins with a streamlined articulation of the *reasons conception*, briefly relates it to those of historically important philosophers and philosophers of education, and addresses challenges flowing from epistemological relativism, epistemic dependence, and feminist and postmodernist presuppositions. Chapter 2 contrasts my account with John McDowell's influential account of the development of mind, inspired by Wilfrid Sellars, that features "initiation into the space of reasons." Here I argue that my account is compatible with Sellarsian insights concerning the space of reasons, and with McDowell's (and R. S. Peters') idea that education is a matter of initiation, but that the Sellars/McDowell alternative does insufficient justice to the centrality, in my account, of the *epistemic quality* that is a fundamental requirement of critical thinking. Chapter 3 clarifies the relation between the "reason assessment" and "critical spirit" components of the reasons conception, the role of the Kantian principle of respect for persons in justifying it, the characters and roles of the normative and motivational forces of reasons in it, and the relation between the educational ideal of critical thinking and the complementary ideal of autonomy.

Part II includes five papers that deal with the *dispositions* and *virtues* that are central to the reasons conception, and with the proper characterization of *indoctrination*. Chapter 4 offers an account of thinking dispositions (including critical thinking dispositions), explains why they are central to critical thinking, and rebuts several extant criticisms of them. Chapter 5 amplifies that account and relates it to the avoidance of indoctrination—a fundamental issue for philosophy of education. Chapter 6 explores the role of reasons in moral education. Chapter 7 assesses the relationship between critical thinking and the intellectual virtues. It engages the virtue epistemology literature and argues against conceiving of critical thinking in solely virtue-epistemic terms. Chapter 8 explores further the character of indoctrination and assesses the relationship between critical thinking and a particular intellectual virtue, that of open-mindedness. Of these two, it is argued that critical thinking is the more fundamental.

Part III collects four papers that develop further the normative, epistemic dimension of critical thinking, particularly the nature of epistemic rationality, its place in the reasons conception, and the value of rationality so conceived. Chapter 9 serves as a bridge connecting Parts II and III by connecting the intellectual virtues considered in Part II to issues concerning rationality, epistemic normativity, and virtue epistemology more broadly. It argues that education is a "thick" concept in that it has both descriptive and normative dimensions, and that its value is both moral and epistemic. Chapter 10 systematically evaluates Alvin Goldman's claims that truth is both the ultimate epistemological value and the fundamental epistemic goal of education, and that critical thinking/rationality is of instrumental value only in that it helps us to achieve true beliefs. In it I argue against Goldman's claim that critical thinking is of instrumental value only. Rather, critical thinking and rationality are themselves of value independently of their instrumental tie to truth. Chapter 11 advances a view of rationality according to which it requires both rules and judgment, thus challenging both rules-only (the so-called Classical Account of Rationality) and judgment-only conceptions. These three chapters are epistemology-focused and illustrate the high degree of inter-relevance of epistemology and philosophy of education. Chapter 12 systematically responds to a Heidegger-inspired critique of this epistemological focus that argues that the reasons conception is deficient as an account of critical thinking precisely because is it overly focused on matters epistemological.

The five papers collected in Part IV address the contested connection between rationality and diversity. Chapter 13 defends the possibility, and actuality, of "transcultural," "universal" ideals from the criticism, made by Richard Rorty and many others, that all such allegedly universal ideals—such as that education should do its best to foster the abilities and dispositions of the critical thinker, or that education should strive to foster students' rationality—are not only deficient, but are also morally and politically noxious in that they illegitimately impose merely local ideals on hegemonically oppressed others. Chapter 14 examines the issue as it manifests itself in the context of argument evaluation, the suggestion here being that the quality of an argument is culture-relative in that a given argument may be good in one culture but bad in another. Chapter 15 continues the analysis by critically engaging with Stanley Fish's argument against the very coherence of multiculturalism, and with the cultural anthropologist Richard Schweder's case for the claim that critiques of culturally located values and ideals "from the outside" are illegitimate. In these chapters I defend the possibilities (and actualities) of objective, nonrelative argument evaluation, and of transcultural, universal ideals in both philosophy and education, in several ways—most fundamentally by showing that criticisms of these possibilities presuppose the very universality they hope to challenge. Chapter 16 addresses the same cluster of issues as they have been raised by educational researchers in terms of "epistemological diversity." Here, too, I argue that while such diversity is genuine, it has to be handled with care, and that its epistemological and educational ramifications are rather less than its defenders often suggest. Finally, Chapter 17 defends the thesis that in cases in which democratic values conflict with non- or antidemocratic cultural values in democratic multicultural societies, *democracy trumps cultural difference*: that is, while education in democratic multicultural states must honor and respect cultural difference as much as possible, it cannot and should not honor antidemocratic cultural values that conflict with the imperatives of democratic education themselves.

Together, the essays do several things. First, they further develop my "reasons conception" of critical thinking, and relate it to ongoing disputes in both epistemology and philosophy of education. Second, they continue to engage with critics and substantive criticisms. I am most grateful to my critics (including Harold Brown, Nicholas Burbules, Eamonn Callan and Dylan Arena, Stefaan Cuypers, Alvin Goldman, Trudy Govier, Chris Hanks, and Emma Williams) and to those whose work prompted my engagement and afforded the opportunity to develop my views further (including Jason Baehr, Paul Feyerabend, Stanley Fish, David Theo Goldberg, Alvin Goldman, William Hare, John McDowell, John Hardwig, Emily Robertson, Richard Rorty, David Shweder, Wilfrid Sellars, Ben Spiecker, and Jan Steutel). As should be clear from even a cursory reading, my positive stances have been refined, qualified, and occasionally corrected by that engagement.

Third, they further develop the epistemological side of philosophy of education—something I view as important in light of the subdiscipline's tendency to focus on moral/political matters. (The latter are important, of course; I have no wish to challenge their importance. But it is a mistake, I think, to lose sight of the fundamental epistemological dimensions addressed here.) Fourth, they demonstrate some of the ways in which epistemology can inform philosophy of education, as well as ways in which the latter can inform the former. Fifth, they engage a broad range of important work launched from a range of rival, too often antagonistic, traditions in philosophy, education, and anthropology, from classic figures to well-known and highly regarded contemporary philosophers, social scientists, public intellectuals, and social commentators. I continue to hold out hope for fruitful philosophical communication across rival traditions, and, in challenging popular "critiques of reason" emanating from some of those traditions, to have shown that honoring diversity is completely compatible with valuing rationality and critical thinking as fundamental philosophical and educational ideals.

The essays promulgate several theses: (1) that critical thinking is an important, and arguably the preeminent, educational ideal; (2) that it is best understood and most effectively defended in "reasons conception" terms, according to which the critical thinker has both the abilities required to evaluate reasons well and the dispositions, habits of mind, and character traits required to routinely engage in and be guided by such evaluations; (3) that evaluating reasons *well* is an epistemic matter, requiring the invocation of criteria of epistemic evaluation and, ultimately, epistemic rationality; (4) that rationality is best understood as fundamentally normative, both having and conferring value, and involving both rules and judgment; and (5) that cultural (and racial, gender, sexual orientation, ability, and other sorts of) diversity is crucially important, morally and sociopolitically, but is less significant epistemically than it is often supposed to be.

The chapters have been lightly edited, but appear in most respects as originally published. Changes of substance, few in number, have been indicated in the chapter endnotes. I have updated a few references where it seemed important to do so.

PART ONE

RECENT STATEMENTS AND DEVELOPMENTS OF THE THEORY

1

Cultivating Reason

1. Introduction

In the Western philosophical tradition, reason and rationality have long been regarded as important intellectual ideals. In the philosophy of education, their cultivation has been similarly esteemed as a central educational aim or ideal. Historically, philosophers of education whose positions otherwise diverge dramatically have consistently articulated, endorsed, and defended (with various qualifications) educational visions in which the cultivation of reason, or the fostering of rationality, has been central. Socrates is perhaps the clearest example of a philosopher who urged that education should encourage in all students and persons, to the greatest extent possible, the pursuit of the life of reason. Plato similarly venerated rationality, although he was a bit less sanguine concerning the degree to which the ideal could be successfully realized. Aristotle, too, championed rationality, both in theory and in practice, and he uttered remarkably modern-sounding ideas concerning education's duty to develop the character traits we now associate with the rational person. The great philosophers of the Middle Ages, no less than those of Antiquity, similarly championed an education aimed at the fostering and development of rationality, believing it to be requisite for a full realization of Christian faith. Descartes, Locke, Hume, Kant, Mill, and other great figures of the modern and Enlightenment periods also venerated rationality and praised it as an educational aim, the realization of which would enable humans to achieve their full potential as rational beings. More recently, Bertrand Russell extolled the virtues of an education in service of the cultivation of reason, and John Dewey developed a highly refined philosophy of education that placed his pragmatic conception of rationality at its center. More recently still, R. S. Peters and his British associates endorsed a version of the ideal of the cultivation of reason, placing reasons and rationality at the heart of their educational philosophy. The preeminent contemporary philosopher of education, Israel Scheffler, has similarly urged that rationality, reasons, and reasoned criticism be made basic to educational endeavors. Although no doubt an overly simple historical generalization, it seems clear that the overwhelming majority of philosophers of education, from Socrates to the present—despite sometimes dramatic differences in their overall views, and with various reservations and qualifications—have championed rationality and its cultivation as fundamental educational desiderata. No other proposed aim of education—knowledge, happiness, community, civic-mindedness, social solidarity, docility and obedience to authority, creativity, spiritual fulfillment, the fulfillment of potential, etc.—has enjoyed the virtually unanimous endorsement of historically important philosophers of education that reason and rationality have.

In contemporary discussions, the cultivation of reason continues to be defended by many as an important educational aim or ideal. Unlike some historical predecessors, contemporary advocates of the ideal do not understand reason as a special psychological "faculty"; in defending rationality, they do not align themselves with the historical movement known as Continental Rationalism, according to which knowledge is based on the perception or intuition afforded by such a faculty. Rather, what is advocated is that education should have as a fundamental aim the fostering in students of (1) the ability to reason well, that is, to construct and properly evaluate the various reasons which have been or can be offered in support or criticism of candidate beliefs, judgments, and actions; and (2) the disposition or inclination to be guided by reasons so evaluated, that is, actually to believe, judge, and act in accordance with the results of such reasoned evaluations. Students (and people generally) are rational, or reasonable, to the extent that they believe, judge, and act on the basis of (competently evaluated) reasons. Consequently, to regard the cultivation of reason as a fundamental educational aim or ideal is to hold that the fostering in students of the ability to reason well and the disposition to be guided by reasons is of central educational importance.

The two aspects of the ideal just mentioned deserve further comment. The first—the ability to reason well—presupposes an account of the constitution of good reasons upon which the ideal must inevitably rest. How do we determine that a proposed reason for some belief, judgment, or action is a good or forceful one (or not)? What are the guidelines, criteria, or principles in accordance with which the goodness of candidate reasons is to be ascertained? What is the nature of such principles? How are they themselves justified? These questions are epistemological in nature; they call for a general account of the relationship between a putative reason and the belief, judgment, or action for which it is a reason. Such an epistemological account will have to grapple with deep questions concerning the nature of epistemic justification, the relationship between justification and truth (and so the nature of truth), the relativity (or absoluteness) of principles of reason evaluation, and so forth. In this sense, the educational ideals of reason and rationality depend, for their own justification, on an adequately articulated and defended underlying epistemology. (Some of these questions are addressed below; see also Siegel 1988a, 1989a, 1997, 1998.)

The second aspect of the ideal mentioned above—the disposition or inclination to be guided by the results of the reasoned evaluation of reasons—has broader philosophical implications. Here, the ideal recommends not simply the fostering of skills or abilities of reason assessment, but also the fostering of a wide range of attitudes, habits of mind, and character traits thought to be characteristic of the rational or reasonable person (Scheffler 1989; Siegel 1988a). This extends the ideal beyond the bounds of the cognitive, for, so understood, the ideal is one of a certain sort of *person*. In advocating the fostering of particular dispositions, attitudes, and character traits, as well as particular skills and abilities, the proponent of this educational aim denies the legitimacy, or at least the educational relevance, of any sharp distinction between the cognitive and the affective, or the rational and the emotional. The ideal calls for the fostering of certain skills and abilities, *and* for the fostering of a certain sort of character. It is thus a general ideal of a certain sort of person—the sort of person it is the task of education to help to create. This aspect of the educational ideal of rationality aligns it with the complementary ideal of *autonomy*, since a rational person will also be an autonomous one, capable of judging for herself the justifiedness of candidate beliefs and the legitimacy of candidate values.

2. Critical Thinking

In the contemporary educational literature, these ideas are often discussed in terms of *critical thinking*. Advocates of efforts to foster critical thinking in the schools sometimes conceive this aim narrowly, in terms of imparting skills which will enable students to function adequately in their jobs, and in so doing to be economically productive. More often, however, proponents of the educational aim of critical thinking have in mind the broader view of critical thinking as more or less equivalent to the ideal of rationality. In any case, it is only when understood in this broad way that this educational aim can be adequately analyzed and defended (Siegel 1988a, 1997; Bailin and Siegel 2003). So understood, critical thinking is a sort of *good* thinking, so the notion of critical thinking is fundamentally a *normative* one. This distinguishes this understanding of critical thinking from those, common in psychology, which treat the notion as descriptive (Bailin et al. 1999).

To regard critical thinking as a fundamental educational aim is to hold that educational activities ought to be designed and conducted in such a way that the construction and evaluation of reasons (in accordance with relevant criteria) are paramount throughout the curriculum. As Israel Scheffler puts the point:

> Critical thought is of the first importance in the conception and organization of educational activities. (1989, p. 1)
>
> Rationality ... is a matter of *reasons*, and to take it as a fundamental educational ideal is to make as pervasive as possible the free and critical quest for reasons, in all realms of study. (p. 62, emphasis in original)
>
> The fundamental trait to be encouraged is that of reasonableness.... In training our students to reason we train them to be critical. (pp. 142–143)

To accord reasonableness central importance in education is not to say that other aims and ideals might not also be of serious importance, but rather that none outrank the primary obligation of educational efforts and institutions to foster critical thinking.

Why should the fostering of critical thinking be considered so important? There are at least four reasons. First, and most importantly, striving to foster critical thinking in students is the only way in which students are treated with *respect as persons*. The moral requirement to treat students with respect as persons requires that we strive to enable them to think for themselves, competently and well, rather than to deny them the fundamental ability to determine for themselves, to the greatest extent possible, the contours of their own minds and lives. Acknowledging them as persons of equal moral worth requires that we treat students as independent centers of consciousness, with needs and interests not less important than our own, who are at least in principle capable of determining for themselves how best to live and who to be. As educators, treating them with respect involves striving to enable them to judge such matters for themselves. Doing so competently requires judging in accordance with criteria governing the quality of reasons. Consequently, treating students with respect requires fostering in them the abilities and dispositions of critical thinking.

A second reason for regarding critical thinking as a fundamental educational ideal involves education's generally recognized task of preparing students for adulthood. Such preparation cannot properly be conceived in terms of preparing students for preconceived roles; rather, it must be understood to involve student self-sufficiency and self-direction. In this the place of critical thinking is manifest. A third reason for regarding the fostering of critical thinking as a central aim of education is the role it plays in the rational traditions which have always been at the center of educational activities and efforts (mathematics, science, literature, art, history, etc.). All these traditions incorporate and rely upon critical thinking; mastering or becoming initiated into the former both requires, and is basic to the fostering and enhancement of, the latter. A fourth reason involves the place of careful analysis, good thinking, and reasoned deliberation in democratic life. To the extent that we value democracy, we must be committed to the fostering of the abilities and dispositions of critical thinking, for democracy can flourish just to the extent that its citizenry is sufficiently critical (Siegel 1988a).

These four reasons can and should be spelled out at greater length, but they are sufficiently powerful to justify regarding critical thinking as a fundamental educational ideal. Efforts to foster critical thinking aim at the promotion of independent thinking, personal autonomy, and reasoned judgment in thought and action. These particular aims are themselves in keeping with broader conceptions of knowledge, reasons, and persons—for example, that all knowledge is fallible, that it is possible to objectively evaluate the goodness of reasons, and that personal autonomy is an important value (Bailin 1998).

These aims, and the broader conceptions in which they are grounded, are philosophically contentious; it is no surprise, then, that they—and the educational ideal of critical thinking itself—have been challenged. Several aspects of critical thinking are controversial. As already noted, while philosophers generally understand it normatively, psychologists and others often understand it descriptively. Philosophers debate its specifically epistemological dimensions (e.g., whether criteria of reason assessment should be understood as "absolute," or rather as relative to culture, context, or some other relativizing factor). Also contentious is the status of such criteria *as* epistemological, rather than political. A further, hotly debated controversy concerns the *generalizability* of critical thinking: Are the skills and abilities of critical thinking generalizable in that they apply across a variety of disciplines, problems, and contexts, or are they rather domain- or context-specific? Theorists also offer and debate the merits of conflicting accounts of key elements of critical thinking (e.g., concerning the nature of skills and dispositions). The place of subject-specific content knowledge in critical thinking is also controversial, as is the alleged distinction between critical and creative thinking. There is a large literature concerning all of this, which cannot be discussed here but is treated in Bailin and Siegel (2003).

Many approaches to teaching critical thinking have been developed. These, too, sometimes occasion controversy, consideration of which is not possible here. Worth mentioning in this context, though, is the Philosophy for Children program, pioneered by Matthew Lipman (1991). In this approach, classrooms become *communities of inquiry*, and students' critical thinking is developed through open discussion of fundamental philosophical issues (at age-appropriate levels of sophistication). In this and other programs, the close connections among critical thinking, rationality, and philosophy itself are made manifest.

Given the contentious nature of critical thinking, it is no surprise that the ideal of reason itself, and the desirability of its cultivation, also faces important challenges. I turn to some of them next.

3. Critiques of Reason
A. Relativism and the Philosophy of Science: The Case of Paul Feyerabend

Science is often conceived as the most impressive application and product of reason, and as the apex of rational activity. It is perhaps surprising, then, that some of the most pressing and important critiques of reason emanate from its philosophy. The last several decades of work in the philosophy of science have produced a range of challenges to science's claims to be the embodiment of rationality and the archetypical model of rational inquiry. These challenges include the critique of textbook models of "the scientific method" and of related accounts of the rationality of science; problems concerning the underdetermination of theory by data, the theory-ladenness of perception, and the rationality of theory choice; and various defenses of epistemological relativism. The literature on these matters is vast; I cannot do even minimal justice to it here (see Siegel 1985, 1987, 2004). Instead, I will address one of the most well-known critics of reason, both in science and more generally: Paul Feyerabend.

Feyerabend's book is called, provocatively enough, *Farewell to Reason* (1987). In it he argues that objectivity, rationality, and reason are false, destructive ideals which serve narrow and particular interests only, and which are valued by some traditions but by no means all (pp. 5 ff.); that "Reason" is without content, and is politically and culturally destructive because of its discouragement of diversity and its indefensible advocacy of "a right way of living" (p. 11); that reasons have no objective force that is binding on all; and that rationality is just a "tribal creed" masquerading as a general ideal—that "rationalists clamouring for objectivity and rationality are just trying to sell a tribal creed of their own" (p. 301). On Feyerabend's view, "It is time we bid it [i.e., Reason] farewell" (p. 17; see pp. 13, 319).

Is Feyerabend right that there are no such things as objective reasons; that rationality is but a "tribal creed"? These claims, though bold and in some ways intoxicatingly radical, are not well supported by Feyerabend's arguments. It is worthwhile to review those arguments in some detail, because doing so will reveal some general difficulties which plague any such attempt to criticize reason.

Consider Feyerabend's rejection of objective reasons:

> I assert that there exist no "objective" reasons for preferring science and Western rationalism to other traditions. Indeed, it is difficult to imagine what such reasons might be. Are they reasons that would convince a person, or the members of a culture, no matter what their customs, their beliefs or their social situation? Then what we know about

cultures shows us that there are no "objective" reasons in this sense. Are they reasons which convince a person who has been properly prepared? Then all cultures have "objective" reasons in their favour. Are they reasons referring to results whose importance can be seen at a glance? Then again all cultures have at least some "objective" reasons in their favour. Are they reasons which do not depend on "subjective" elements such as commitment or personal preference? Then "objective" reasons simply do not exist (the choice of objectivity as a measure is itself a personal and/or group choice—or else people simply accept it without much thought). (p. 297)

Note, first, that this passage runs roughshod over the is/ought distinction—the distinction between what people *do* do and what they *ought* to do—in its suggestion that reasons which fail in fact to convince people therefore ought not to convince them. But there are many clear cases in which people ought to be convinced by reasons, even though they in fact are not. For example, I should have been convinced by prior experience that I should have begun work on this chapter earlier than I did if I wanted to meet the deadline, although, regrettably and irrationally, I was not so convinced. Second, and more significantly, it presupposes that choices and judgments are necessarily "subjective" or nonobjective insofar as *subjects* (i.e., people with interests, attitudes, etc.) make them. Grant that choices and judgments are made by subjects and are in this sense "subjective." Does it follow that such judgments cannot be objective?

Obviously not. Consider a case: Alicia is a philosophy major about to graduate with her undergraduate degree; she has narrowed her options to the following: apply to graduate school in philosophy, apply to law school, or take a position with a local computer company. Does she have any objective reason to choose from among these options?

We can go two ways here. On the one hand, we can say that Alicia has perfectly objective reasons to (for example) apply to graduate school. Her intense love of the subject, the pleasure she takes in reading philosophy books and articles and in writing papers, her desire to be a publishing scholar and teacher of students like herself, her professors' encouragement and declarations of her likely success as a professional philosopher, and her dread of the prospect of a life in which she cannot spend time engaging in these activities all provide objective reasons for her applying. Her assignment of utilities to the alternative outcomes—that is, her valuing of the life of the philosopher more highly than those of the lawyer and computer company employee—may be subjective, but once those subjective utilities are assigned, the calculation of expected utility, and the choice of the future course which maximizes it, is as objective as can be. In this case, if she chose not to apply to graduate school despite her own valuations, she would be choosing irrationally. Her choice would not reflect the objective reasons she has to apply.

On the other hand, we can say that Alicia has no objective reason either to apply to graduate school in philosophy, to apply to law school, or to take the computer job. She has subjective reasons—her love of philosophy, her dread of law school and her worries about the glutted job market for lawyers, her mixed emotions about working with computers, etc.—and those are the only sort of reasons there are. If Alicia applies to graduate school, she acts on the basis of her reasons; if she applies to law school or takes the computer job, she likewise acts on that basis. All reasons are subjective, and all acts are subjectively reasonable.

This second response to Alicia's situation is Feyerabend's. But it is problematic. For, according to it, no judgment, choice, or action, however local, is better than any of its alternatives. All reasons are "subjective" and as good, subjectively, as their contraries; no one can be judged to have chosen or acted unreasonably. This is quite implausible, since examples of unreasonable actions and choices are, alas, all too common. But it is the bind one gets in when one insists that all reasons, because they involve human choice and judgment, are subjective, and therefore that all judgments, actions, and choices are subjectively reasonable.

The issue is not whether "subjective elements" accompany or are part of all judgment and choice—Feyerabend may well be right about that. The issue is rather whether some considerations have force, and ought to move judgers/choosers/actors, even when the judgers do not recognize those considerations as having such force. Given Alicia's attitudes toward her alternatives, however "subjective" those attitudes might be, her decision whether to apply to graduate school or not is as "objective" as can be. If the case is as I've described it, she has strong, perfectly objective reasons to apply to graduate school, and equally objective reasons not to apply to law school or take the computer job. Of course, the cases for each could be more equal in strength than I have presented them. That would make Alicia's choice more difficult, but not less objective.

In the end, this dispute turns on what is meant by "objective." Feyerabend takes it to mean something like "lacking subjective elements," and he argues that, so taken, no reasons are objective because reasons always function in ways that engage such subjectivity. But if "objective reason" is taken to refer rather to considerations that are relevant to, and ought to be taken into account and assigned due weight by, people making choices and judgments—and whose force ought to be recognized by those subjective choosers/judgers, even if they are not so recognized—then Feyerabend is mistaken in claiming that there are no objective reasons. Moreover, the defense, and so the consistency, of his position requires that there be reasons that are objective in just this sense. That is, his case that there are no objective reasons itself requires that there are such reasons—for if there are no such reasons supporting that case, we will have no objective reason to embrace his conclusion that there are none.

At bottom, Feyerabend has confused two quite different questions concerning the objectivity of reasons: whether they necessarily involve human subjectivity; and whether they might rightly be regarded as forceful, authoritative, and compelling even for those persons who are not convinced by them. The subjectivity issue is irrelevant to the objective forcefulness issue. Feyerabend has failed to provide any good reason to reject the claim that reasons can be objectively forceful. He has also failed to realize that his own positive view requires that some reasons have objective force. Thus, his claim that there are no objective reasons fails.

Is rationality but a "tribal creed" whose dictates have no force on the members of other tribes? Here we can be brief. Feyerabend is perhaps right that rationality may be regarded as a tribal creed, in the sense that only some people and cultures accept or respect it, while others do not. But that some people fail to be moved by or respect rational considerations in no way entails, as we have seen, that they ought not to be so moved. Feyerabend has failed to secure his contention that rationality is *just* another ideology or tribal creed.

In the end, then, Feyerabend's relativistic critique of reason and its cultivation fails to upend that ideal (Siegel 1989b). Other relativistic challenges face similar and additional difficulties (Siegel, 1987, 2001, 2004).

B. Epistemic Dependence

One prominent feature of education aimed at the cultivation of reason is its embrace of the complementary value of personal autonomy, in its insistence that students should come to be able to determine for themselves the worthiness of candidate beliefs, judgments, values, and actions. Many philosophers have questioned the *individualism* inherent in such a view. Critiques of individualism are many and varied; most relevant here are those which challenge the idea that students—and believers generally—are rightly thought to be able to "drive their own epistemic engines" and determine by themselves, from among candidate beliefs, which are worthy of embrace. Such *epistemic individualism* is challenged by advocates of what has come to be called *social epistemology*: the systematic study of the ways in which knowledge is irredeemably social, in large part because knowers are dependent on others for their knowledge. Because epistemic agents are *epistemically dependent* on others, epistemic individualism, it is argued, is a chimera.

Why think that we are epistemically dependent on others? The most important reason for thinking that we are so dependent is that most of our beliefs, including those that seem to qualify as knowledge, appear to depend upon the *testimony* of others, and require us to *trust* those others. It is clear enough that many of our beliefs *originate* in the testimony of others—the newspaper, the TV reporter, our parents, our teachers, etc.—and that these beliefs are overwhelmingly *sustained* by that testimony as well. It appears that relatively few, if any, of our beliefs are free from such dependence. Many of us believe, for example, that the sun is 93 million miles from Earth (on average), but how many have carried out that measurement themselves, or have any nontestimonial evidence for that belief? Similarly, many of us believe that the HIV virus causes AIDS, and that smoking tobacco increases one's risk of heart disease and stroke, though we have no familiarity with the relevant scientific evidence for these claims. A final example is the common belief (among citizens of the United States at the time I write, at least) that a particular person, Osama bin Laden, bears significant responsibility for the destruction of the World Trade Center in New York. What is our justification for this belief? Most of us have no direct evidence for these (and most other) beliefs, but rather believe them on the basis of the testimony of others. Our thoroughgoing reliance on the testimony of others, and our need to trust that testimony, has suggested to some that we must give up any pretense to epistemic individualism and to individual responsibility for belief, and so must reject the idea that getting students to think for themselves is an important educational directive. As John Hardwig puts it, our systematic epistemic dependence on others forces the conclusion that "it is sometimes *irrational* to think for oneself—that *rationality* sometimes consists in deferring to epistemic authority and, consequently, in passively and uncritically accepting what we are given to believe" (1985, p. 343, emphases in original).

It is controversial to say that we are as epistemically dependent on others, as Hardwig and others (e.g., Coady 1992, and various authors collected in Schmitt 1994) claim. Jonathan Adler, for example, claims that we are not, since those of our beliefs that are generated by the testimony of others are typically justified by our evidence concerning testimony's general reliability, and are moreover typically sustained and justified by being confirmed for us in ways that do not depend upon the testimony of others. Adler argues, first, that we each have overwhelming evidence for the general reliability of testimony conceived as a social process, since from our earliest days we have been recipients of testimonial reports, the vast majority of which have turned out to be correct. Our own evidence for the general reliability of testimony thus offers us a significant measure of epistemic *in*dependence, even concerning beliefs we accept solely on the basis of testimony. In addition, Adler discusses a variety of ways in which beliefs that originate in testimony can be nontestimonially confirmed, and argues that this kind of account can be given for a large majority of beliefs. For example, many of us believe that smoking tobacco increases one's risk of heart disease and stroke. Typically, we will have formed this belief on the basis of the testimony of others—reading it in a book or the newspaper, learning it in school, hearing it from a relative or friend, and so on. At the moment we acquire it, Adler argues, that belief is supported by our knowledge of the general reliability of such testimonial reports. However, it is typically subsequently confirmed for each of us routinely as we read both scientific and popular reports; speak with physicians, biologists, and others who do have direct familiarity with the details of the research; hear pronouncements on the matter from government officials; talk to our doctors; and even conduct relevant research ourselves. Because it is confirmed in these ways, each of us has nontestimonial evidence that justifies our belief, despite the fact that we first acquired it through testimony. In light of both our justified belief in the general reliability of testimony and the subsequent confirmation of specific beliefs that originate in testimony, Adler concludes that we are far less epistemically dependent as might appear at first glance (Adler 2002).

I find Adler's case against an overwhelming epistemic dependence compelling. But let us grant, for the sake of argument, that we are, as many authors claim, highly epistemically dependent upon others. What follows concerning the ideals of rationality and critical thinking? Does it follow from our alleged epistemic dependence that we should give up the commitment to epistemic individualism, and instead discourage students, and people generally, from thinking for themselves or exercising their reason?

It seems clear that this does not follow. For one thing, determining when we are in fact epistemically dependent and when not—when we should uncritically accept expert testimony and when we should endeavor to think for ourselves—itself requires critical thinking and the exercise of independent judgment. For another, we need to acknowledge a distinction between *rational* and *irrational* deference to the opinion of others, and to guard ourselves against the latter. Here, too, independent judgment and thinking for ourselves are necessary, and so the cultivation of reason is appropriate (Siegel 1988b).

The issues here are more complex than this brief discussion suggests, but I hope I've said enough to indicate why the phenomenon of epistemic dependence does not compromise the educational aim of cultivating critical rationality (cf. Hardwig 1985, Siegel 1988b, Coady 1992, Schmitt 1994, Goldman 1999, Adler 2002).

C. Feminist and Postmodernist Critiques

Deep challenges to the ideal of reason have been articulated by feminist critics, who argue that, as standardly conceived, the ideal harbors deep masculinist biases; and by postmodernist critics, who argue that the ideal is prototypically modernist and retains all the flaws associated with modernism. Central to these criticisms is the claim that reason, at least under dominant-culture conceptions of it, favors the values and practices of dominant groups in society and devalues those of groups traditionally lacking in power. Here, as earlier, the range of relevant literature and argument is enormous. I consider here only two challenges: the feminist complaint that reason privileges the perspectives and interests of men, and is biased against the perspectives and interests of women; and the postmodernist complaint that reason constitutes an objectionable "totalizing metanarrative" that reflects and advances the interests of culturally dominant groups, and marginalizes and oppresses members of non-dominant groups. (For further discussion of these and other challenges, see Bailin 1995; Siegel 1997; and Bailin and Siegel 2003.)

Is reason problematically "male"? Is the advocacy of its cultivation similarly "masculinist-ly" biased? Feminist writers frequently answer in the affirmative. The central contention is clearly articulated by Louise M. Antony and Charlotte Witt:

> Feminist challenges have, indeed, reached into the "'hard core' of abstract reasoning" itself, with charges that the most fundamental elements of the Western philosophical tradition—the ideals of reason and objectivity—are so deeply corrupted by patriarchy that they must be greatly transformed (if not utterly abandoned) by any philosopher committed to the development of conceptions of knowledge and reality adequate to the transformative goals of feminism. (Antony and Witt 1993, p. xiii, quoting Harding and Hintikka 1983, p. ix)

and by Sally Haslanger:

> [A] rational stance is itself a stance of oppression or domination, and accepted ideals of reason both reflect and reinforce power relations that advantage white privileged men. (Haslanger 1993, p. 85)

and, in a critical discussion of Catharine MacKinnon, by Elizabeth Rapaport:

> For MacKinnon, rationality is an enemy to be unmasked and destroyed. (Rapaport 1993, p. 129)

As MacKinnon develops the point:

> The *kind* of analysis that such a feminism is, and, specifically, *the standard by which it is accepted as valid*, is largely a matter of the criteria one adopts for adequacy in a theory. If feminism is a critique of the objective standpoint as male, then we also disavow standard scientific norms as the adequacy criteria for our theory, because the objective standpoint we criticize is the posture of science. In other words, our critique of the objective standpoint as male is a critique of science as a specifically male approach to knowledge. With it, we reject *male criteria for verification*. (MacKinnon 1987, p. 54, last two emphases added)

What follows from the rejection of "male criteria"? There seem to be only two possibilities: either that there are *no* criteria in terms of which theories can be evaluated, or that there are *different* criteria that should be appealed to in theory evaluation. The first of these is deeply problematic. If there are no criteria in terms of which we can legitimately evaluate theories, then the very possibility of evaluation is rejected. But this option is self-defeating: if evaluation in general is rejected, then we are unable to evaluate, or rationally prefer, the suggestions that male criteria should be rejected or that evaluation itself should likewise be rejected. But then we have no reason to accept these suggestions.

On the other hand, the rejection of "male" criteria of theory evaluation in favor of other, incompatible, "female" criteria, must itself—if the preference for the latter is to be itself defensible and non-arbitrary—rely upon (meta-)criteria in accordance with which these two rival sets of criteria can themselves be fairly evaluated. Standards and criteria of rational evaluation are in this way *required* for the conducting of any sort of serious scholarly endeavor, including that of criticizing particular conceptions of reason as problematically "male." In short, one cannot coherently embrace this particular feminist critique of reason and at the same time reject reason or rational standards entirely.

MacKinnon's specific rejection of the standards of science, and so science itself, as male implies an abandonment of the benefits of science, including benefits that accrue to the oppressed themselves. Noretta Koertge has argued in this connection that "science—even white, upperclass, male-dominated science—is one of the most important allies of oppressed people" (1981, p. 354). Martha Nussbaum has argued similarly with respect to reason and objectivity:

> Convention and habit are women's enemies here, and reason their ally. Habit decrees that what seems strange is impossible and "unnatural"; reason looks head on at the strange, refusing to assume that the current status quo is either immutable or in any normative sense "natural." The appeal to reason and objectivity amounts to a request that the observer refuse to be intimidated by habit, and look for cogent arguments based on evidence that has been carefully sifted for bias. (Nussbaum 1994, p. 59)

Of course, to say that standards are required for the rational defense of reason, or that rational standards are required for any sort of serious intellectual work whatever, is not to say that particular standards, or particular understandings of them, are themselves beyond critical challenge. On the contrary, one major sort of intellectual advance is precisely the sort that allows us to realize that our standards, or our interpretations of them, have in one way or another been defective and stand in need of criticism and improvement. Indeed, one of the main contributions of feminist scholarship has been precisely to establish that particular standards, or particular applications of them, have been problematically biased against women. But it cannot be wise, as Nussbaum points out (1994, pp. 60–61), to reject a standard on grounds of its misuse. We can debate the merits of particular standards and criteria, and particular understandings, interpretations, and applications of them, of course. But we cannot reject the standards and criteria of reason altogether—not, at least, if we wish to uphold the virtues of feminism and the value of women's perspectives.

Postmodernist challenges to reason and its cultivation are varied but equally fundamental. According to at least one version of this challenge, the cultivation of reason depends on a "totalizing" or "universalizing" conception of reason that both illicitly presupposes the perspective of dominant groups and denies the particularity of those who are members of other groups, thereby marginalizing and oppressing them. Accordingly, "reason" must be seen not as a universal form or criterion of proper thought, but rather merely the form in use, and favored, by dominant groups, whose power is enhanced by imposing it upon dominated others. Reason, that is, is not any sort of ultimate authority or arbiter, but is simply one ideology among others, which must be recognized as a source of unjust power and privilege rather than a legitimate source of epistemic authority; its cultivation among marginalized others must be seen as a political act of cultural hegemony rather than an effort to liberate, empower, and enhance the rational autonomy of all students and persons, including, in particular, those marginalized others.

This is clearly a very fundamental challenge. Like those already considered, however, it is not without difficulties, the most basic of which is that any such challenge to reason must, if it is to establish its case, itself be based on good reasons and provide good reasons for accepting its challenge as worthy. Consequently, the rejection of reason, to be epistemically forceful, must itself presuppose the legitimacy of reason (Siegel 1997, chs. 9–12).

The reader who has followed the discussion to this point will have noticed a recurrent theme, to which I turn next.

4. The Fundamental Reply to All Critiques of Reason

All critiques of the ideal of reason, like those just considered, can and should be considered on their own merits. But it is of considerable comfort to friends of the ideal that there is available a general reply to all attempts to reject the ideal, one that appears to be effective against them all, and which is manifested in the discussions of each of the specific critiques considered above. This reply, if successful, establishes *the impossibility of rationally rejecting reason—and so preserves the legitimacy of regarding its cultivation as an educational ideal*. I conclude this discussion by rehearsing the reply and assessing its effectiveness.

Reason can be rejected in two ways. First, it can be rejected without thought or argument—indeed, it can be rejected without the question of whether it *should* be rejected ever being recognized or addressed. Alternatively, it can be rejected on the basis of some reasoned challenge to it (e.g., that it fosters patriarchy, aids and abets oppression, depends upon a problematic individualism, rests on an inadequate conception of objectivity, or whatever). In the former case, rejection doesn't threaten the legitimacy of the ideal, since no challenge is made. It is the latter, philosophical sort of rejection that genuinely challenges the ideal's cogency.

But if such a challenge is made, it is forceful, and successful, just to the extent that it is based upon good reasons for rejecting the ideal. The challenger is arguing, in effect, that there is good reason to reject the ideal of reason. Any such argument against reason, if successful, will itself be an instance of the successful application of reason. That is, the reasoned rejection of the ideal is itself an instance of being guided by it. In this sense, the ideal appears to be safe from successful challenge, for any successful challenge will have to rely upon it, and any challenge that does not do so cannot succeed. While challenges to the ideal might succeed in refining our understanding of it, none can succeed in overthrowing it. Thus, the ideal cannot be successfully challenged.

Transcendental arguments like this one are notoriously controversial philosophically; I cannot provide a general defense of them here. But I should note that the argument does not prove too much. It does not suggest that other ideals are not important. Nor does it suggest that people cannot reject or live contrary to the ideal—though that they can (and do) does nothing to challenge its legitimacy, or the claim that they ought to be guided by it. The argument obviously will not persuade those who reject reason independently of an argument against it. But such an "argument-less rejection" fails as a critique, since it offers no criticism of the ideal or argument in favor of its rejection.

The proponent of rationality and its cultivation must, to be consistent, regard challenges to it as centrally important, and must regard the obligation to take such challenges seriously as integral to rationality itself. Hence, deep criticisms of the ideal, and reasoned consideration of both its praiseworthy characteristics and its indefensible ones, are exactly what the ideal itself recommends. Whether the ideal survives extant criticisms will always be, in some sense, an open question; such criticisms may well succeed in altering our understanding or defense of it. Nevertheless, there is a limit beyond which any proposed criticism of rationality cannot go without undermining itself. Hence, the ideal of rationality (at least in some formulation of it) cannot be coherently rejected (Siegel 1997, chap. 5, Epilogue).

References

Adler, J. (2002). *Belief's Own Ethics*. Cambridge, MA: MIT Press.
Antony, L. M., and C. Witt (eds.). (1993). *A Mind of One's Own: Feminist Essays on Reason and Objectivity*. Boulder, CO: Westview Press.
Bailin, S. (1995). "Is Critical Thinking Biased? Clarifications and Implications." *Educational Theory* 45.2: 191–197.
Bailin, S. (1998). "Education, Knowledge and Critical Thinking." In D. Carr (ed.), *Education, Knowledge and Truth: Beyond the Postmodern Impasse* (pp. 204–220). London: Routledge.
Bailin, S., R. Case, J. R. Coombs, and L. B. Daniels. (1999). "Conceptualizing Critical Thinking." *Journal of Curriculum Studies* 31.3: 285–302.
Bailin, S., and H. Siegel. (2003). "Critical Thinking." In N. Blake, P. Smeyers, R. Smith, and P. Standish (eds.), *The Blackwell Guide to the Philosophy of Education* (pp. 181–193). Oxford: Blackwell.
Coady, C. A. J. (1992). *Testimony: A Philosophical Study*. Oxford: Oxford University Press.
Feyerabend, P. (1987). *Farewell to Reason*. London: Verso.
Goldman, A. I. (1999). *Knowledge in a Social World*. Oxford: Oxford University Press.
Harding, S., and M. B. Hintikka (eds.). (1983). *Discovering Reality: Feminist Perspectives on Epistemology, Metaphysics, Methodology, and Philosophy of Science*. Dordrecht, The Netherlands: D. Reidel.
Hardwig, J. (1985). "Epistemic Dependence." *Journal of Philosophy* 82.7: 335–349.
Haslanger, S. (1993). "On Being Objective and Being Objectified." In Antony and Witt 1993, pp. 85–125.
Koertge, N. (1981). "Methodology, Ideology and Feminist Critiques of Science." In P. D. Asquith and R. N. Giere (eds.), *PSA1980: Proceedings of the 1980 Biennial Meeting of the Philosophy of Science Association*, Vol. 2 (pp. 346–359). East Lansing, MI: Philosophy of Science Association.
Lipman, M. (1991). *Thinking in Education*. Cambridge: Cambridge University Press.
MacKinnon, C. (1987). *Feminism Unmodified: Discourses on Life and Law*. Cambridge, MA: Harvard University Press.
Nussbaum, M. (1994). "Feminists and Philosophy." *New York Review of Books* 41.17: 59–63.
Rapaport, E. (1993). "Generalizing Gender: Reason and Essence in the Legal Thought of Catherine MacKinnon." In Antony and Witt 1993, pp. 127–143.
Scheffler, I. (1989). *Reason and Teaching*. Indianapolis, IN: Hackett. First published by Routledge & Kegan Paul, 1973.
Schmitt, F. F. (ed.). (1994). *Socializing Epistemology: The Social Dimensions of Knowledge*. Lanham, MD: Rowman & Littlefield.
Siegel, H. (1985). "What Is the Question concerning the Rationality of Science?" *Philosophy of Science* 52.4: 517–537.
Siegel, H. (1987). *Relativism Refuted: A Critique of Contemporary Epistemological Relativism*. Dordrecht, The Netherlands: Kluwer.
Siegel, H. (1988a). *Educating Reason: Rationality, Critical Thinking, and Education*. London: Routledge.
Siegel, H. (1988b). "Rationality and Epistemic Dependence." *Educational Philosophy and Theory* 20.1: 1–6.
Siegel, H. (1989a). "Epistemology, Critical Thinking, and Critical Thinking Pedagogy." *Argumentation* 3.2: 127–140.
Siegel, H. (1989b). "Farewell to Feyerabend." *Inquiry* 32.3: 343–369.
Siegel, H. (1997). *Rationality Redeemed?: Further Dialogues on an Educational Ideal*. New York: Routledge.
Siegel, H. (1998). "Knowledge, Truth and Education." In D. Carr (ed.), *Education, Knowledge and Truth: Beyond the Postmodern Impasse* (pp. 19–36). London: Routledge.

Siegel, H. (2001). "Incommensurability, Rationality, and Relativism: In Science, Culture, and Science Education." In P. Hoyningen-Huene and H. Sankey (eds.), *Incommensurability and Related Matters* (pp. 207–224). Dordrecht, The Netherlands: Kluwer.

Siegel, H. (2004). "Relativism." In I. Niiniluoto, M. Sintonen, and J. Woleński (eds.), *Handbook of Epistemology* (pp. 747–780). Dordrecht, The Netherlands: Kluwer.

2

Education as Initiation into the Space of Reasons

1. Introduction

A long tradition in the philosophy of education identifies education's most fundamental aim and ideal as that of the *fostering or cultivation of rationality*. In recent decades this aim has been advanced under the banner of *critical thinking*. Because this story is well known, I won't dwell on it in detail here. Instead, in what follows I will relate this tradition in philosophy of education to recent work, inspired by Wilfrid Sellars, on "*the space of reasons*." I will first offer a very brief overview of the tradition just mentioned. I will then briefly lay out Sellars' notion and discuss its place in the work of some of those influenced by Sellars, especially John McDowell. I will then address recent work in philosophy of education that suggests that there is a tension between Sellars' notion and the traditional educational ideal as I have developed and defended it in my own work, or that the Sellarsian view as developed by McDowell resolves outstanding difficulties with my version of the traditional view. I will argue that there is less tension than some of my critics suggest, and that the Sellarsian notion is in fact compatible with the traditional view as thus developed, but that it leaves out an important aspect of that view which should not be lost.

2. The Place of Reasons in Education: A Very Brief Overview

Throughout the history of Western philosophy, philosophical issues concerning education have enjoyed substantial attention. From Socrates' conversations with his fellow Athenians, Plato's *Republic*, and Aristotle's *Politics*, to the great philosophers of the Middle Ages, the Enlightenment, and the modern era, through to the twentieth century, issues concerning education, both epistemological and ethical/social/political, have loomed large on the philosophical scene. In this long history, there has been an unusual degree of agreement among the central figures in the philosophy of education concerning the place of reason, or the fostering of rationality, as the most fundamental aim of education.[1]

These days, the story is often told in terms of *critical thinking*. While there are a range of theories of critical thinking in the contemporary literature, and the usual amount of philosophical controversy, theorists are mainly agreed that critical thinking is best understood as involving two components: a *reason assessment* component involving the ability to evaluate the quality or epistemic strength of reasons, and a *critical spirit* component involving a range of dispositions, habits of mind, and character traits such that the critical thinker is actually disposed to engage in reason assessment and to be guided by it in belief, judgment, and action. On my own view of the matter, the ideal is justified by several considerations, but most importantly is compelled by our moral obligation to treat students, children, and indeed everyone with *respect as persons*. Failing to educate for critical thinking constitutes a failure to treat students with respect. On my view, the successful articulation and defense of the ideal requires as well a principled rejection of epistemological relativism, a non-epistemic conception of truth, an "internalist" conception of justification, and a "transcendental" justification of reason or rationality itself (Bailin and Siegel 2003; Siegel 1988, 1977, 2003, 2007b, 2010a; cf. Robertson 2009). These are, of course, highly contentious matters, and I cannot undertake a serious defense of them here. But I hope to have said enough to provide a proper background for the discussion of the "space of reasons" to follow. Several of them will be addressed further below.

3. Sellars and "The Logical Space of Reasons"

As is well known, Sellars' overarching project—and, according to him, the project of philosophy itself—was that of reconciling the "manifest image" of ourselves, as traffickers in the intentional contents of language and thought and the normative character of belief, judgment, and action, with a thoroughgoingly naturalistic, "scientific image" of human beings as complex but scientifically explicable denizens of the natural world.[2] Of special relevance here is Sellars' view of the "irreducibly normative character of epistemic discourse" (Rosenberg 2009, p. 10), and of thinking with/in terms of concepts itself:

> [A]nything which can properly be called conceptual thinking can occur only within a framework of conceptual thinking in terms of which it can be criticized, supported, refuted, in short, evaluated. To be able to think is to be able to measure one's thoughts by *standards of correctness*, of relevance, of evidence. (Sellars 2007, p. 374, emphasis added)

It is in the context of his celebrated critique of "the myth of the given" and his positive characterization of epistemic normativity and its incorporation in his "stereoscopic" reconciliation of the manifest and scientific images that Sellars introduced (in *Empiricism and the Philosophy of Mind*) the notion of "the logical space of reasons":

> The essential point is that in characterizing an episode or a state as that of *knowing*, we are not giving an empirical description of that episode or state; we are placing it in the logical space of reasons, of justifying and being able to justify what one says. (Sellars 1997, p. 76, emphasis in original)

The details of Sellars' view are complex and would require extended treatments of fundamental issues in the theory of meaning, the philosophy of language more generally, metaphysics and the philosophy of mind, and other core areas of philosophy. Such treatment would extend well beyond the present effort. Happily, for present purposes such an extended excursion is unnecessary. Our task here is to examine the relationship between Sellars' naturalistic view of the normativity of epistemic discourse, thought, and judgment as captured in his metaphor of the logical space of reasons and the traditional educational aim of the cultivation of reason.

4. Naturalism, Normativity, and Transcendence

Sellars' account of normativity is naturalistic; the scientific image is that given by the theoretical/explanatory sciences. What does Sellarsian "naturalism" come to? Perhaps as good an expression of Sellars' naturalism as any is this widely cited passage: "[I]n the dimension of describing and explaining the world, science is the measure of all things, of what is that it is, and of what is not that it is not" (Sellars 1997, p. 83).[3] This is enough to see that Sellars' naturalism is *metaphysical*: he takes the deliverances of the theoretical/explanatory sciences to be the final court of appeal with respect to questions concerning the constituents of the world ("of what is and what is not").

A central aspect of Sellars' project is that of reconciling the normativity of the manifest image with the naturalism of the scientific image.[4] That is, his stereoscopic combining of the manifest and scientific images aims to show, in part, that epistemic and other sorts of normativity can find their legitimate place in the scientific conception of the world. Such a reconciliation can be attempted in various ways, and recent decades have seen several such attempts. Quine is famously, though controversially, often understood to have championed the abandonment of normativity in favor of a thoroughgoing non-normative naturalism. Quine himself eventually explicitly rejected this interpretation of "Quinean" naturalism in favor of a version of instrumental efficacy (Quine 1986, p. 655); in any case it is untenable (Siegel 1984, 1995, 1996b). Sellars, of course, took normativity to be central; he was certainly not an advocate of its abandonment.

Another influential attempt, popular among both epistemologists and philosophers of science, goes under the banner of "normative naturalism." According to the normative naturalist (including the Quine of Quine 1986), epistemic normativity is a matter of instrumental rationality. On this view, cognitive ends or goals are presupposed or "given" and not criticizable on the basis of reasons; normativity is a matter of the judicious fitting of means to such "given" ends. This view, too, is open to serious criticism (Siegel 1989, 1990, 1996a, 1998, 2006). It is, in any case, not Sellars' view either.[5]

Rather, Sellars' view is that reason is "both naturalistic and nonreductive" (Hanks 2008, p. 204); that is, reason is a part of the natural world but nevertheless operates autonomously from it and cannot be reduced to it. This aspect of Sellars' view is developed at some length by both Robert Brandom and John McDowell;[6] I concentrate here on McDowell's discussion.[7] McDowell's effort to reconcile the "realm of law" (the realm in which Sellars' scientific image reigns supreme) with the "*sui generis* character of spontaneity" (the domain of the manifest image, in which human understanding, meanings, intentions, and rational relations are central) hinges on his effort to "rethink our conception of nature so as to make room for spontaneity" (McDowell 1994, p. 77). This "rethinking" is not an attempt to find some middle space between what McDowell calls "bald naturalism" and "rampant platonism" (pp. 72, 77; cf. 70–86); rather, it rejects the sharp distinction between them and builds on Aristotle's notion of "second nature" (p. 84), according to which we are "animals whose natural being is permeated with rationality" (p. 85), and in which we can "reconcile reason and nature" (p. 86) by noting how our understanding develops in the course of ordinary human experience. It is worth quoting McDowell at some length:

> Aristotle's picture can be put like this. The ethical is a domain of rational requirements, which are there in any case, whether or not we are responsive to them. We are alerted to these demands by acquiring appropriate conceptual capacities. When a decent upbringing initiates us into the relevant way of thinking, our eyes are opened to the very existence of this tract of the space of reasons. Thereafter our appreciation of its detailed layout is indefinitely subject to refinement, in reflective scrutiny of our ethical thinking. We can so much as understand, let alone seek to justify, the thought that reason makes these demands on us only at a standpoint within a system of concepts and conceptions

that enables us to think about such demands, that is, only at a standpoint from which demands of this kind seem to be in view. (McDowell 1994, p. 82)

There are several things to note about this passage. First, McDowell is clear that this account of how "our eyes are opened to the very existence of this tract of the space of reasons" is not limited to this "ethical tract":

> The point is clearly not restricted to ethics. Moulding ethical character, which includes imposing a specific shape on the practical intelligence, is a particular case of a general phenomenon: initiation into conceptual capacities, which include responsiveness to other rational demands besides those of ethics. Such initiation is a normal part of what it is for a human being to come to maturity, and that is why, although the structure of the space of reasons is alien to the layout of nature conceived as the realm of law, it does not take on the remoteness from the human that rampant platonism envisages. If we generalize the way Aristotle conceives the moulding of ethical character, we arrive at the notion of having one's eyes opened to reasons at large by acquiring a second nature. (McDowell 1994, p. 84)

McDowell's account is thus not limited to ethics, but is rather a general account of how our eyes are "opened to reasons at large." Second, the demands of reason are autonomous from and independent of us, in that the requirements and relations of reason "are there in any case, whether or not we are responsive to them." Third, acquiring an Aristotelian "second nature" is, on McDowell's account, very much a matter of education, broadly conceived; it is "a decent upbringing" that "initiates us into the relevant way of thinking." As McDowell also puts it, "ordinary upbringing can shape the actions and thoughts of human beings in a way that brings these [rational] demands into view" (p. 83). Fourth, such an education is clearly a matter of initiation into the space of reasons; it is, as McDowell says, "initiation into conceptual capacities, which include responsiveness to ... rational demands," which initiation is "a normal part of what it is for a human being to come to maturity."[8]

Let me note three points concerning McDowell's view. First, his proposed reconciliation of naturalism and normativity is accomplished by reconceiving of nature in such a way that the normativity of language and thought are built into the very nature of human beings who become aware of meanings, intentions, and rational relations during the course of their ordinary upbringing and coming to maturity as rational animals; their rationality is, so to speak, a central aspect of their natural character. Second, McDowell explicitly rejects the idea that mind, reason, or normativity "transcends" the natural world. On the contrary, such normativity is autonomous from nature in the sense that it is not determined by natural law, but it does not transcend nature in any metaphysically problematic way. As Chris Hanks characterizes McDowell's view, on it, "[w]e can acknowledge that humans are rational animals and hold that reason can be exercised autonomously without placing this process outside of nature and setting up a dualism between mind and world" (Hanks 2008, p. 207).

Third, and most importantly for present purposes, all this is completely compatible with the traditional view of the cultivation of reason as the fundamental aim of education and with my own development of the traditional view in terms of the fostering of rationality. The latter is completely in keeping with conceiving of education as initiation into the space of reasons. In particular, when we "acquire appropriate conceptual capacities" and are thus able to engage in what Sellars called "conceptual thinking," our thinking "is under a standing obligation to reflect about and criticize the standards by which, at any time, it takes itself to be governed" (McDowell 1994, p. 81). Such criticism and self-criticism are central to my accounts of critical thinking/rationality.[9]

5. Problems of Compatibility?

However, not all commentators agree that my view is compatible with the Sellars/McDowell reconciliation of naturalism and normativity. Why is my view thought to be problematic? The worry is that regarding epistemic criteria and standards of normative quality as reaching beyond or "transcending" particular reasoners and communities—so that, for example, reasoning in accordance with the gambler's fallacy is a mistake even in communities that regard it as a valid form of reasoning,[10] and slavery is morally objectionable even in communities that do not so regard it—forces me to abandon naturalism and thus to diverge from Sellars and McDowell. The worry is expressed most recently by Chris Hanks, who suggests that my view founders on its "relation of reason to the natural world" (2008, p. 194):[11]

> Siegel's notion of rationality stands, in a fundamental way, outside the empirical realm, populated as it is by particular circumstances, cultural traditions, and the messy contingencies of everyday life. His fallibilism wisely acknowledges that any specific application of critical thinking must take place under such conditions, but staunchly insists that rationality itself must involve criteria that stand independent of particular circumstances.... [He] adheres to the Kantian view that the grounding of philosophical (rational) truths must stand outside the causal, contingent realm of experience.... Siegel clings to a kind of Kantian transcendentalism.... Siegel maintains a commitment to rational

autonomy, which motivates him to argue for reason's transcendence of the natural frame. (pp. 199, 200, 204)

There is much to say in response to Hanks' complaint; I will do my best to be brief.

First, it is not true that on my view rationality itself "stands ... outside the empirical realm"—at least not as it is manifested in the reasoning, beliefs, judgments, and actions of actual agents—as Hanks acknowledges (p. 199). Does my "notion of rationality" stand outside that realm? It is not obvious how this question is best understood. On one way of reading it, lots of "notions"—numbers, arguments, ideals, etc.—"stand outside the empirical realm," in that they are abstract objects that, by their very nature, are not extended in empirical space. Of course, we could deny that the empirical realm is limited to the so extended, as McDowell does. So understood, insofar as the denizens of the space of reasons are in the empirical realm, my notion of rationality is as well. On yet another possible reading, such notions as these are *ours*, and so are in the empirical realm insofar as we ourselves are. So the claim that my notion "stands outside the empirical realm" is ambiguous—in some senses it is, in others it is not. But in no sense do I embrace or commit myself to any sort of *super*natural realm, a "realm" outside or beyond the ordinary, everyday world.

What about my "staunch insistence" that rationality involves criteria that are independent of particular circumstances? I certainly do insist on this—as does Hanks himself (pp. 210–211). Declaring that such criteria are "outside the empirical realm" is likewise ambiguous: the criteria are ours, put forward in our theorizing, and meant by us to extend beyond the boundaries of their articulation and acceptance. This is why we can say, for example, that reasoning that commits the gambler's fallacy is epistemically deficient independently of the context in which the reasoning occurs. Indeed, this is just McDowell's view, as we have seen: on his view, as on mine, the demands of reason are autonomous from and independent of us in that the requirements of reason "are there in any case, whether or not we are responsive to them." These demands, and the related criteria, are not "outside the empirical realm" on McDowell's view or on Sellars'—the domain in which they reside, the "space of reasons," is independent of/autonomous from the empirical realm, but not outside it. The same is true on my view.

Second, I have tried to be careful to distinguish stronger and weaker forms of "transcendence." I do offer a "transcendental" argument for justifying rationality (Siegel 1988, Postscript; 1997, ch. 5 and Epilogue), but here "transcendental" does not mean "outside the empirical realm," but rather refers to the argument form according to which something (in this case, rationality, or at least an acknowledgment of it and a commitment to it) is necessary if something else (in this case, the serious calling of rationality into question) is possible. When I say that epistemic criteria transcend local contexts, I do not thereby assign to criteria some special metaphysical status. Rather, I affirm just that what people in a given context say or think is criticizable on the basis of suitable criteria whose force is independent of and extends beyond the bounds of that context. This is more or less the same point Sellars makes when he says that "to be able to think is to be able to measure one's thoughts by standards of correctness," presuming, of course, that it is possible that one's thoughts might fail to measure up; and that McDowell makes when he says that our thinking "is under a standing obligation to reflect about and criticize the standards by which, at any time, it takes itself to be governed," presuming, again, that our thinking can fail to meet such standards—which they clearly can on McDowell's view, since according to it, "rational requirements ... are there in any case, whether or not we are responsive to them." "Transcendence" at my hands does not have the untoward metaphysical features that I join Sellars, McDowell, and Hanks in rejecting (Siegel 1997, 1999a, 1999b, 2001, 2007a, 2011).

I suspect that this tangle results from mistakenly insisting that my epistemological account of rationality/critical thinking be understood metaphysically, and by failing to distinguish epistemological and metaphysical naturalism. Like Sellars and McDowell, I too embrace metaphysical naturalism and reject all forms of supernaturalism. What I reject is *epistemological* naturalism, when that view is understood to involve or entail that "metaphysically naturalist" standing—i.e., something's standing as a thing that has "naturalistically emerged," e.g., by way of McDowell's "ordinary, decent upbringing," or its status as something genuinely in the world—guarantees positive epistemic standing.[12] The reason is simply put: The "natural" includes or gives rise to both the epistemically good and the epistemically bad, both truths and falsehoods, both justified and unjustified beliefs. So once we agree that everything arises or emerges naturally (i.e., as a result of natural processes), or is natural in that it is "in the world," the problem of distinguishing the good from the bad remains. Naturalist metaphysical status (i.e., being a product or a part of nature) is no indication of epistemic status or quality. Once we have agreed that minds generally, and the minds of critical thinkers in particular, emerge naturalistically and are part of the natural world, we need to deal with the fact that the minds of *uncritical* thinkers likewise so emerge and reside. Doing so requires the rejection of epistemological naturalism as here understood, but is of course compatible with metaphysical naturalism. Sellars, McDowell, Hanks, and I are agreed that critical thinking is embodied and that human nature is part of nature. We agree, further, that language, minds, ideas, and ideals all emerge naturalistically (i.e., from natural processes). However, we might disagree on what follows from that emergence. For the reason just rehearsed, I reject the claim that such naturalistic emergence or status establishes epistemic quality. Sellars, McDowell, and Hanks should agree, given their embrace of the independence and autonomy of the "space of reasons" from the "realm of law," and the "nonreductive" character of reason/rationality.

That is, my rejection of epistemological naturalism and my positive accounts of rationality and critical thinking are completely compatible with the metaphysical naturalism embraced by all four of us.[13]

6. A Key Missing Ingredient

While there is then no incompatibility between the two, there is something missing from the Sellars/McDowell view that is central to the traditional view with which we have been comparing it. Suppose that Sellars and McDowell are right about what is involved in humans becoming competent language users and conceptual thinkers. It does not follow that, as a matter of fact, competent language users/conceptual thinkers are *good* at making normative epistemic judgments. Epistemic discourse may be "irreducibly normative," as Rosenberg puts it; Sellars may be correct that "to be able to think is to be able to measure one's thoughts by standards of correctness." But one can "measure one's thoughts by standards of correctness" well or badly; one can, once one's "ordinary decent upbringing" opens one's eyes to the space of reasons and enables one to maneuver in that space, maneuver well or badly; one can be "initiated into the relevant way of thinking by a decent upbringing" and yet engage in such thinking either well or badly; and one can be a competent concept user and player of the game of giving and asking for reasons and yet play it either well or badly, epistemically speaking, in that one can, despite one's conceptual competence, judge badly the probative force of candidate reasons. If so, the ability to reason *well* is not guaranteed by an ordinary decent upbringing or the acquisition of appropriate conceptual capacities, unless having mastered a range of concepts somehow prohibits mistakes in reasoning or leads inevitably to epistemically high-quality thinking. This is, of course, not the case. Being "in" the space of reasons does not ensure that *good* reasoning will result. Every competent language user uses it in the space of reasons, yet not every such user is a critical thinker. More—in a word, *education*—is needed.[14]

Consequently, while the Sellars/McDowell view is compatible with the traditional ideal, that ideal requires more: it requires that ordinary decent upbringing and the acquisition of appropriate conceptual capacities—that is, normal human development as conceived by Sellars and McDowell—be supplemented by explicit educational interventions aimed at enhancing students' abilities to reason well. This is not surprising, since the mental life of every normal human being is lived "in" the space of reasons, but irrationality and uncritical thinking abound nonetheless. Simply acquiring appropriate conceptual capacities during the course of learning language (McDowell 1994, p. 125) is not enough, educationally speaking. At any rate, it is not enough once we are agreed that (1) one can learn a language yet reason badly, evaluate reasons badly, and/or fail to be disposed to believe, judge, and act in accordance with one's evaluation of the strength of candidate reasons; (2) we are obliged to treat students, as everyone, with respect as persons; and (3) so treating students requires doing our best to foster their rationality (Siegel 1988, 1997).

7. Conclusion: Education as Initiation into the Space of Reasons

R. S. Peters famously argued that education is fundamentally a matter of initiation.[15] I do not want here to defend Peters' view generally. But I do think that the idea that education importantly involves initiation is basically correct, and that it is readily adapted to the idea that education fundamentally involves the initiation of students into Sellars' space of reasons. Indeed, this seems to me to be essentially equivalent to the traditional claim that the central aim of education is the fostering of reason or rationality, except that initiation into the space of reasons, as Sellars and McDowell conceive it—by way of learning language and in that way acquiring appropriate conceptual categories—is, as we have seen, not by itself enough. Such an ordinary, decent upbringing needs to be supplemented with explicit educational interventions aimed at fostering students' critical thinking—that is, aimed at fostering their ability to evaluate reasons well and their dispositions to seek reasons, evaluate their power and convicting force competently, and be guided by the results of such evaluation.

There is thus no reason to think that there is any serious conflict between the traditional educational ideal concerning the fostering of rationality and the Sellars/McDowell view, contrary to Hanks' suggestion. Education can indeed be seen as a matter of initiation into the space of reasons. But such education, to satisfy the ideal, must do more than rest on ordinary decent upbringing and language learning. In particular, it must pay explicit attention to the fostering in students of sophisticated, epistemology-informed understanding of the criteria involved in reason assessment, so that students become good at assessing candidate reasons, and to the fostering of the suite of dispositions, habits of mind, and character traits constitutive of the critical spirit. Only thus enhanced will "initiation into the space of reasons" meet one of our deepest educational ideals.[16]

Notes

1. Even though philosophy of education has received short shrift in recent decades in philosophy departments in North America and much of Western Europe, the subject has historically enjoyed, and continues to deserve, an honored place. At least, so I have argued (Siegel 2009a). For a brief recap of the historical story, see Siegel 2003.

2. See especially Sellars 2007. Rosenberg 2009 is a helpful brief introduction to Sellars' thought; two book-length treatments are deVries 2005 and O'Shea 2007.
3. Readers will recognize the passage as playing on Aristotle's famous characterization of truth (cf. Aristotle *Metaphysics* 1011b).
4. O'Shea characterizes Sellars' view as "naturalism with a normative turn" (cf. O'Shea 2007, p. 3 and *passim*).
5. It is also possible simply to reject the project of reconciliation as an empty philosophical worry that is of no concern to the naturalist. For discussion, see Siegel 2010b.
6. This is an oversimplification. Both Brandom and McDowell offer their own distinct views, and do not just explicate Sellars' view. Nevertheless, in view of the clear and acknowledged way in which they each, in their own ways, develop the approach pioneered by Sellars—even including putting their views consistently in terms of "the space of reasons"—I hope the oversimplification can be forgiven.
7. While I don't discuss Brandom's view at length in what follows, I should note that his development of this aspect of Sellars' view is in important respects similar to McDowell's. In particular, on Brandom's view the normativity manifested in the space of reasons is independent of and autonomous from the scientific study of the realm of law, but is nevertheless a part of the natural world; such normative relations "are not studied by the *natural* sciences—though they are not for that reason to be treated as spooky and *super*natural" (Brandom 2000, p. 26, emphases in original).

    That said, I should also note that Brandom's concern—like Sellars'—is more a matter of linguistic than epistemic normativity; his inferentialist semantics and normative pragmatics primarily concern meaning, language, and linguistic practice, and focus centrally on his original theory of concept use/mastery in terms of inferential commitments and entitlements (see, e.g., Brandom 1994, pp. 600–601, 647, and *passim*; Brandom 2000, ch. 1, esp. pp. 1, 6, 10–11, 32; Brandom, 1997, p. 141). His understanding of rationality is similarly more linguistic than epistemic: rationality is a matter of playing the game of giving and asking for reasons well, where that in turn is a matter of proper deontic scorekeeping, i.e., of keeping track of commitments and entitlements (see, e.g., Brandom 1994, pp. 183, 253, ch. 9; Brandom 2000, pp. 31, 203–204). I suggest below that while this is good as far as it goes, it does not go far enough, in that one can play that game well, thereby establishing one's mastery of the relevant concepts, but nevertheless end up with epistemically deficient beliefs. There is more to rationality/epistemic normativity than proper concept use.
8. I have already quoted McDowell at too much length to add additional quotations here. But I want to recommend his closing section of the main text of the book (Lecture 6, section 8, pp. 124–126) for a very instructive overview of his view that also connects directly with a classic work in philosophy of education, Scheffler's "Moral Education and the Democratic Ideal" (1973).
9. I discuss this in several places; see especially Siegel 1988, 1997.
10. For discussion of this actual case, of logicians/probability theorists who regarded the gambler's fallacy as a legitimate form of reasoning, see Siegel 1992.
11. Hanks' discussion of what he sees as the problematic metaphysical character of my view takes place in the context of his treatment of the problem of indoctrination as it manifests itself in my dispute with Jim Garrison and his use of McDowell to overcome that dispute. I ignore most of Hanks' insightful paper here in order to focus on the relation between my view and McDowell's. I should acknowledge that Hanks is not alone in complaining about the metaphysics of my view; I regret I cannot undertake a systematic review of such complaints here.
12. Cf. Brandom's interpretation and endorsement of Sellars on this point: the "justificatory relation is not a natural one, but a normative one; it is not the empirical scientist, but the logician or epistemologist who has the final say about it" (Brandom 1997, p. 127; see also Brandom 2000, p. 117).
13. This paragraph borrows from and builds upon Siegel 2001.
14. This perhaps should not be surprising, since Sellars and McDowell are preoccupied with matters metaphysical—in particular, with what is required in order to have a mind at all,

and to "be rational" in that sense—and are not primarily concerned with the normative evaluation of the epistemic strength of candidate reasons. The preoccupation extends far beyond those two authors, of course, and is more or less universal in contemporary philosophy of mind. Special thanks to Randall Curren and Catherine Elgin for very helpful comments on this.

15. Cf. Peters 1972. The theme of education as initiation informs much of Peters' work. For helpful recent discussions, both of Peters and of education as initiation, cf. Scheffler 1995 and the essays in Cuypers and Martin 2009.

16. A version of this paper was presented at the Congress of the German Society of Philosophy (Deutscher Kongress für Philosophie), Munich, September 2011. I am grateful to Krassimir Stojanov for the invitation to participate in this event, and to him and its other participants, especially Randall Curren, as well as Jonathan Adler, Catherine Elgin, Israel Scheffler, and Amie Thomasson for very helpful comments, suggestions, and advice.

References

Bailin, S., and H. Siegel. (2003). "Critical Thinking." In N. Blake, P. Smeyers, R. Smith, and P. Standish (eds.), *The Blackwell Guide to the Philosophy of Education* (pp. 181–193). Oxford: Blackwell.

Brandom, R. B. (1994). *Making It Explicit: Reasoning, Representing, and Discursive Commitment.* Cambridge, MA: Harvard University Press.

Brandom, R. B. (1997). "Study Guide [to *Empiricism and the Philosophy of Mind*]." in Sellars 1997, pp. 119–181.

Brandom, R. B. (2000). *Articulating Reasons: An Introduction to Inferentialism.* Cambridge, MA: Harvard University Press.

Cuypers, S. E., and C. Martin (eds.). (2009). *Reading R. S. Peters Today: Analysis, Ethics, and the Aims of Education.* Oxford: Wiley-Blackwell.

deVries, W. A. (2005). *Wilfrid Sellars.* Chesham, UK: Acumen.

Hanks, C. (2008). "Indoctrination and the Space of Reasons." *Educational Theory* 58.2: 193–212.

McDowell, J. (1994). *Mind and World.* Cambridge, MA: Harvard University Press.

O'Shea, J. R. (2007). *Wilfrid Sellars.* Cambridge: Polity.

Peters, R. S. (1972). "Education as Initiation." In R. D. Archambault (ed.), *Philosophical Analysis and Education* (pp. 87–111). New York: Humanities Press.

Quine, W. V. (1986). "Reply to Morton White." In L. E. Hahn and P. A. Schilpp (eds.), *The Philosophy of W. V. Quine* (Library of Living Philosophers, vol. XVIII), pp. 663–665. La Salle, IL: Open Court.

Robertson, E. (2009). "The Epistemic Aims of Education." In H. Siegel (ed.), *The Oxford Handbook of Philosophy of Education* (pp. 11–34). New York: Oxford University Press.

Rosenberg, J. (2009). "Wilfrid Sellars." In *The Stanford Encyclopedia of Philosophy.* Edited by Edward N. Zalta. Stanford, CA: Center for the Study of Language and Information, Stanford University. https://plato.stanford.edu/archives/sum2011/entries/sellars.

Scheffler, I. (1973). "Moral Education and the Democratic Ideal." In *Reason and Teaching* (pp. 136–145). New York: Bobbs-Merrill. Reprinted 1989, Indianapolis: Hackett.

Scheffler, I. (1995). "The Concept of an Educated Person." In V. A. Howard and I. Scheffler, *Work, Education and Leadership: Essays in the Philosophy of Education* (pp. 81–99). New York: Peter Lang.

Sellars, W. (1997). *Empiricism and the Philosophy of Mind.* Cambridge, MA: Harvard University Press. Originally published 1956, in H. Feigl and M. Scriven (eds.), *Minnesota Studies in the Philosophy of Science*, vol. 1, pp. 253–329. Minneapolis: University of Minnesota Press.

Sellars, W. (2007). "Philosophy and the Scientific Image of Man." Reprinted in K. Scharp and R. B. Brandom (eds.), *In the Space of Reasons: Selected Essays of Wilfrid Sellars* (pp. 369–408). Cambridge, MA: Harvard University Press. Originally published 1962, in R. G. Colodny (ed.), *Frontiers of Science and Philosophy* (pp. 35–78). Pittsburgh: University of Pittsburgh Press.

Siegel, H. (1984). "Empirical Psychology, Naturalized Epistemology, and First Philosophy." *Philosophy of Science* 51.4: 667–676.

Siegel, H. (1988). *Educating Reason: Rationality, Critical Thinking, and Education*. London: Routledge.

Siegel, H. (1989). "Philosophy of Science Naturalized?: Some Problems with Giere's Naturalism." *Studies in History and Philosophy of Science* 20.3: 365–375.

Siegel, H. (1990). "Laudan's Normative Naturalism." *Studies in History and Philosophy of Science* 21.2: 295–313.

Siegel, H. (1992). "Justification by Balance." *Philosophy and Phenomenological Research* 52.1: 27–46.

Siegel, H. (1995). "Naturalized Epistemology and 'First Philosophy.'" *Metaphilosophy* 26.1/2: 46–62.

Siegel, H. (1996a). "Instrumental Rationality and Naturalized Philosophy of Science." *Philosophy of Science* 63.3 Supplement (PSA 1996 Proceedings, Part 1): 116–124.

Siegel, H. (1996b). "Naturalism and the Abandonment of Normativity." In W. O'Donohue and R. Kitchener (eds.), *The Philosophy of Psychology* (pp. 4–18). London: SAGE.

Siegel, H. (1997). *Rationality Redeemed?: Further Dialogues on an Educational Ideal*. New York: Routledge.

Siegel, H. (1998). "Naturalism and Normativity: Hooker's Ragged Reconciliation." *Studies in History and Philosophy of Science Part A* 29.4: 639–652.

Siegel, H. (1999a). "Argument Quality and Cultural Difference." *Argumentation* 13.2: 183–201.

Siegel, H. (1999b). "Multiculturalism and the Possibility of Transcultural Educational and Philosophical Ideals." *Philosophy* 74: 387–409.

Siegel, H. (2001). "Dangerous Dualisms or Murky Monism?: A Reply to Jim Garrison." *Journal of Philosophy of Education* 35.4: 577–595.

Siegel, H. (2003). "Cultivating Reason." In R. Curren (ed.), *A Companion to the Philosophy of Education* (pp. 305–317). Oxford: Blackwell.

Siegel, H. (2006). "Review of Hilary Kornblith, *Knowledge and Its Place in Nature*." *Philosophical Review* 115.2: 246–251.

Siegel, H. (2007a). "Multiculturalism and Rationality." *Theory and Research in Education* 5.2: 203–223.

Siegel, H. (2007b). "The Philosophy of Education." *Encyclopaedia Britannica Online*, September 2007. http://search.eb.com/eb/article-9108550.

Siegel, H. (2009a). "Introduction: Philosophy of Education and Philosophy." In Siegel 2009b, pp. 3–8.

Siegel, H. (ed.). (2009b). *The Oxford Handbook of Philosophy of Education*. New York: Oxford University Press.

Siegel, H. (2010a). "Critical Thinking." In P. Peterson, E. Baker, and B. McGaw (eds.), *International Encyclopedia of Education*, 3rd ed., vol. 6 (pp. 141–145). Oxford: Elsevier.

Siegel, H. (2010b). "Review of Penelope Maddy, *Second Philosophy: A Naturalistic Method*." *British Journal for the Philosophy of Science* 61.4: 897–903.

Siegel, H. (2011). "Epistemological Relativism: Arguments Pro and Con." In S. D. Hales (ed.), *A Companion to Relativism* (pp. 201–218). Oxford: Wiley-Blackwell.

3

Neither Humean nor (Fully) Kantian Be

1. Introduction

I am grateful to Stefaan Cuypers for his careful, detailed, and insightful explication and critique of my views on rationality and critical thinking (Cuypers 2004). Cuypers' analysis is accurate in most respects; however, it mistakenly attributes to me a Humean view of (practical)[1] reason that is not my own. I begin by setting the record straight on that. Cuypers' main critical point is that since I justify the claim that critical thinking is a fundamental aim of education on Kantian grounds, but that my account of practical reason is Humean rather than Kantian, my position lacks the resources to defend that basic claim—and that, further, there is a deep tension, or inconsistency, at the heart of my account. I address this criticism, and the alleged inconsistency, next. Central to this discussion will be Cuypers' treatment of (my treatment of) *autonomy*, which is not quite accurate. Independently of these matters, Cuypers' analysis raises deep issues about the motivational character of reasons; I close this reply by briefly addressing those issues.[2]

2. Is My Account Humean?

Cuypers claims that my "two-component theory of critical thinking ... turns out to be a version of the Humean conception of instrumental reason as normatively and motivationally powerless" (p. 75).[3] His claim is that my "two-component" account of critical thinking, consisting in the "reason assessment" component and the "critical spirit" component, "is, or comes close to, a Humean means-ends conception" of rationality (p. 83). According to Hume, "reason is, and ought only to be, the slave of the passions" (cited at p. 84). Reason is thus, on the Humean view, *instrumental* in that it serves the passions; our desires/passions provide our ends, and reason provides the means to attain those ends. Reason can tell us how best to achieve our ends, but not which ends to take as our own. Moreover, on the Humean view, reason cannot motivate action;

only passion and desire can so motivate. As Cuypers summarizes the Humean account: "On this instrumental conception, reason lacks robustly normative as well as robustly motivating power. The passions are the *sole* source of normative and motivational reasons" (p. 85, emphasis in original).

Contrary to Cuypers' claim, my account of critical thinking/rationality is not a Humean, means-ends, instrumental account. Rather, on my account, reasons provide normative support for candidate beliefs/judgments/actions, proportional to their quality, as determined by relevant criteria. Accordingly, on my view one ought to believe or judge that *p*, or perform some action *A*, just in so far as there are good reasons for doing so. Restricting myself here to practical reason, as Cuypers does, consider the case in which I have good reasons for *A*ing—say, helping a neighbor fix his broken fence. It may well be that my reasons for helping him are instrumental in that they further ends of mine (e.g., maintaining good relations with my neighbor, assuming that I value my neighborly relationship with him, and have as an end that those good relations be maintained). My account does recognize instrumental reasons as one sort of potentially good reason, and, as such, they deserve the due consideration of critical thinkers/rational persons. But, contrary to Cuypers, instrumental reasons are not the only sort of reason my account countenances.

Consider the following scenario: I am in my study, working on this paper, and am deeply engrossed in it. My strongest relevant desire is to continue to work on it. But I remember that I promised my neighbor that I'd help him fix his fence now. In this case, the act that would further my ends, and satisfy my desires, is that of continuing to work on the paper. This consideration gives me (or constitutes) an instrumental reason for doing so. But I have another reason that conflicts with that instrumental reason, one that urges a contrary action: namely, my promise to help gives me (or constitutes) a reason for leaving my computer and going to help my neighbor fix his fence. Now this second reason is not in the relevant sense[4] an instrumental one: I have no desire to help the old buzzard, for whom (let us suppose) I have no particular affection or desire to please; nor do I care about maintaining neighborly relations with him. Going to help him furthers no passion, desire, or end of mine. Nevertheless, my having promised to help him gives me a reason to go and help him, even though that act frustrates the satisfaction of my present desires.

Now I need not argue that the second reason trumps the first (though it well might, and I think in this case it would); I need to establish only that such a non-instrumental reason for action is possible, on my account. And it clearly is. My account does not limit itself to instrumental reasons, but rather acknowledges a broad range of sorts of reasons, including both instrumental and non-instrumental or "categorical" reasons (e.g., Siegel 1988, pp. 32–35, 129–131). So the charge that my account of critical thinking/rationality is Humean, or that the only sort of reason it countenances is that of instrumental reasons, fails.

Why does Cuypers think my account of rationality/critical thinking is, like Hume's, instrumental? First, on that account, there are two components, the reason assessment component and the critical spirit component, that are individually necessary and jointly sufficient for critical thinking, and, as Cuypers puts the point:

> This separation of the logico-epistemic dimension and the motivational dimension of reason mirrors the Humean distinction between the domain of "reason" and the domain of "the passions." Siegel's two-component structure of mental faculties repeats Hume's bipartite structure. The mere ability to assess reasons does not by itself imply the disposition actually to engage in reason assessment. So being appropriately moved by reasons requires more than "reason" alone: it also demands the critical spirit of "the passions." (p. 85)

As Cuypers correctly suggests, I do distinguish the two components, and regard the first, reason assessment component as insufficient to ensure critical thinking, for the straightforward reason that students (and persons more generally) may, and often do, have the ability to think critically but fail to exercise that ability. This seems a common enough phenomenon, especially in the educational context, to warrant inclusion of the second, critical spirit component as also a necessary component of a full account of critical thinking (Siegel 1988, pp. 39–42). So Cuypers is correct that my two-component view "mirrors" and "repeats Hume's bipartite structure." But, as explained further below, this "structural similarity" is insufficient to render my account an instrumental one.

But there is also a difficulty in the just-cited passage. Cuypers is correct that on my account "[t]he mere ability to assess reasons does not by itself imply the disposition actually to engage in reason assessment."[5] That is, a person can have the ability but fail to exercise it (either on a given occasion, or routinely). But it does not follow that "being appropriately moved by reasons requires more than 'reason' alone." The premise proclaims, rightly, that having the ability to assess reasons doesn't *guarantee* or *necessitate* either engaging in reason assessment on a given occasion or having the disposition to engage in such assessment. That is, the premise correctly proclaims that it is possible for a person to have the ability but both fail to exercise it on a given occasion and lack the disposition to do so. But it does not rule out the possibility that the ability, or the reasons resulting from its exercise, will generate the relevant action. Consequently, the conclusion does not follow: that p does not "imply" or guarantee q leaves open the possibility that p might nevertheless (either on occasion, or more generally) bring about q. In other words, that the ability to assess reasons does not "imply" or guarantee the disposition to act in accordance with such assessment is compatible with the ability's bringing about action in accordance with such assessment.

That is, contrary to Cuypers' reasoning here, "the reason assessment component" *can*, although it needn't, "motivate a person actually to believe and act in accord with his adequate reasons" (p. 85). Cuypers' reasoning here is of the form: *p* is not by itself sufficient to guarantee the occurrence of *A*; therefore *p* is incapable of bringing about *A*. But there are many counter-examples to this pattern of reasoning: stepping on the gas pedal is not by itself sufficient to guarantee the car's moving (the battery might be dead), but it might nevertheless bring about the car's movement on a given occasion; my thinking that I ought, all things considered, to go help my neighbor fix his fence is not by itself sufficient to guarantee my helping him (I might forget, or experience an episode of confusion brought about by an occasion of low blood sugar, or suffer a bout of *akrasia*), but it might nevertheless bring about my helping him on the occasion in question. One cannot, in short, argue from *p*'s insufficiency to "imply" or *guarantee* the occurrence of *A* to *p*'s inability to bring about *A*. I will return to this mistaken inference below.

Cuypers is correct that, on my account, the reason assessment component is not by itself sufficient, and the critical spirit component is also necessary, for a full account of critical thinking, insofar as the latter is rightly regarded as a fundamental educational ideal. But this does not commit me to a Humean account of practical reason, according to which reason is motivationally inert. On my account the critical spirit is a necessary component of a full account of critical thinking because the reason assessment component, as Cuypers correctly notes, does not *guarantee* appropriate movement by reasons. But that the reason assessment component does not guarantee, or "imply," appropriate movement does not render "reason"[6] motivationally inert or powerless. "Reason" *can* motivate, on my account, but it is not necessary that it does. That is why the critical spirit component is necessary for a full account of critical thinking, i.e., an account encompassing not just proper reason assessment but appropriate movement as well. Only an account of critical thinking involving the latter will suffice, if critical thinking is conceived as an educational ideal.

Cuypers' argument from "structural similarity"—in effect, an argument from analogy—thus overlooks relevant disanalogies between Hume's and my respective positions, one of which is that my view diverges from Hume's on the point just rehearsed: for Hume, as Cuypers depicts his position, reason *cannot* motivate; it is motivationally inert or powerless. Only desire or passion can motivate for Hume. On my view, by contrast, reason *can* motivate, and so is not necessarily motivationally inert. I might act solely because of my reasons for doing so (e.g., because I recognize that it is my duty to so act). In such a case I am motivated by my reasons, and so "reason" can (since it does) motivate.

Of course, this is not the only sort of possible case a full account of practical reason must address. I might, in another case, fail to act as "reason" directs, even when such a non-instrumental reason is the most forceful reason I have; my reasons for acting might fail to motivate me. Unlike the Kantian view, as Cuypers depicts it, on my view one's good reasons for acting might fail to motivate one to so act. That one's good reasons for acting *can* motivate the relevant action distinguishes my view from Hume's; that those reasons don't *necessarily* motivate that action distinguishes my view from Kant's (again, as Cuypers depicts their respective positions). I shall return to this issue of the motivational force of reasons in due course. For now, my point is this: Despite the "mirroring" and "structural similarity" that Cuypers correctly notes between my "two-component" view and "Hume's bipartite structure," my view is not Humeanly "motivationally powerless," in that it permits, while Hume's does not, that reasons can have motivational force. Nor is my view Kantianly "motivationally robust," in that it acknowledges, as Kant's does not, that reasons can fail to motivate and so do not guarantee action in accordance with their proper evaluation.[7]

Cuypers argues further that, on my account, the reason assessment component is not only motivationally inert, but is also *normatively* inert:

> [On Siegel's account,] reason is not only motivationally powerless but also normatively powerless. Reason itself does not constitute practical reasons; it only *assesses* them once they are given. Moreover, reason itself does not constitute specifically practical criteria of reason assessment; it only complies with such *given* criteria. Of course, reason can formally evaluate the epistemic soundness of, for example, moral reasons and the logical validity of moral arguments; yet it cannot be at the origin of the *content* of those reasons and those arguments' premises. That is to say, the reason component of critical thinking does not tell us what is intrinsically good (or bad) and what we ought (or ought not) to do. (p. 86, emphases in original)

I confess that I do not follow Cuypers' reasoning here; in any case the conclusion is false. It is not the case that on my view either specific practical reasons or specifically practical criteria of reason assessment are simply *"given"* and beyond critical scrutiny. Nothing is beyond such scrutiny. It is unclear to me what Cuypers means to refer to here by "origin," but it is not true that on my view the content of reasons or premises is beyond critical scrutiny. If *anything* "tell[s] us what is intrinsically good (or bad) and what we ought (or ought not) to do," it is "reason" (i.e., critical thinking/rationality) and the appropriate assessment of relevant reasons that does so. Desire/passion does not by itself do so, since we often desire things that are undesir*able*. Cuypers' claim that my view is normatively inert rests entirely on his misattributing to me the Humean view that is not my own. The normativity of reasons is at the heart of my account.

Cuypers is clear that the basis of his claim that my view is Humean is the "structural similarity" noted earlier:

> In the light of the structural similarity between Siegel's two-component theory of critical thinking and Hume's bipartite conception of practical reason, and in view of the Humean predicament of the reason assessment component as normatively and motivationally impotent, I conjecture that the conception of rationality underlying Siegel's theory of critical thinking is, or comes close to, a Humean means-end conception of rationality. (p. 86)

That is, Hume's view and mine share a common "bipartite structure"—Hume's is instrumental, therefore mine is instrumental. This is at best a quite weak argument from analogy: Hume's theory has property *P*, my account is "structurally similar" to Hume's theory, therefore my account also has property *P*. In any case, there is ample textual evidence that on my view epistemic normativity in general, and the normative forcefulness of practical reasons in particular, is entirely a matter of the quality of such reasons. It is simply a mistake to interpret my account of reasons—practical or otherwise—as either "normatively powerless" or "motivationally powerless." Consequently, Cuypers' attribution to my view of an instrumental conception of rationality is mistaken. The flaws of that conception mentioned in his discussion (86–88) are indeed flaws; on this Cuypers and I agree. The mistake is in attributing the instrumental view to me.

Cuypers seems aware that my account of rationality is not in fact Humean, as he cautiously qualifies his claim when he says that my position "is, or comes close to, a Humean, means-ends conception" (p. 83); that it "is, or comes close to, an instance of this Humean conception" (p. 84); that it "instantiates, or nearly exemplifies, a Humean instrumental conception" (p. 85); that it "is, at least in spirit, Humean" (p. 85); and that it "is, or comes close to, a Humean means-end conception" (p. 86). As we have seen, he also puts the point in terms of "the structural similarity between Siegel's two-component theory of critical thinking and Hume's bipartite conception of practical reason" (p. 86), on the basis of which he "*conjecture*[s] that the conception of rationality underlying Siegel's theory of critical thinking is, or comes close to, a Humean means-end conception of rationality" (p. 86, emphasis added). Yet, despite all these qualifying locutions—"is, or comes close to"; "instantiates, or nearly exemplifies"; "at least in spirit"; and so on—and despite the fact that what he identifies is but a "structural similarity" and his conclusion but a "conjecture"—Cuypers nevertheless concludes that my "two-component theory *is*, as demonstrated above, an instance of the Humean instrumental conception" (p. 86, emphasis in original). I trust it is clear that all these qualifying expressions, and the discussion above, suffice to indicate that Cuypers has demonstrated no such thing.

Cuypers rightly indicates that I have myself criticized means-ends, instrumental conceptions of rationality.[8] It is central to my more straightforwardly epistemological/philosophy of science discussions of rationality that a means-ends conception is inadequate. So Cuypers' claim is troublesome. If he were correct that my positive view of rationality is in fact, and despite myself, instrumental, I would have a lot of rethinking, and retracting, to do. But, as just indicated, he is not. My account of rationality, despite its "structural similarity" to Hume's account of practical reason, is not an instrumental, means-ends account.

3. Cuypers' Main Critical Claim

Cuypers' central criticism is that my account of practical reason is Humean—i.e., instrumental and both "normatively and motivationally powerless"—but that my Kantian defense of critical thinking as an educational ideal rests on the Kantian view of practical reason as non-instrumental and both "normatively and motivationally robust" (p. 75). The complaint is that, as a Humean, the Kantian justification is not available to me, and consequently that my account "lacks the theoretical resources to make the justificatory role of Kantian autonomy intelligible" (p. 76). Moreover, according to Cuypers' critique, that account harbors a deep tension, or inconsistency, in that it seems to require both a Humean and an incompatible Kantian account of practical reason: "There exists an irresolvable tension between Kant's robust conception of practical reason and Siegel's instrumental conception of critical thinking rationality" (p. 76). If successful, these criticisms would be damaging indeed, forcing both a new justification of critical thinking as an educational ideal (or the abandonment of the claim) and a substantial revision to avoid the inconsistency. Happily (for me), they are not successful.

I have already addressed the mistaken claim that my view is Humean. But is Cuypers right that my defense of the claim that critical thinking is a fundamental educational ideal is dependent on a robust Kantian view of practical reason that is unavailable to me? Cuypers is quite correct that my defense of that claim rests ultimately on an appeal to a Kantian moral principle of respect for persons, so if that principle requires a view of practical reason that is incompatible with the rest of my view, his objection remains. Does it?

The basic issue, I think, is this: How much of Kant's view of practical reason must I accept in order to embrace the Kantian principle of respect for persons? Cuypers argues that I have to accept pretty much all of it, since

> Kant's concept of the practical law is inseparable from a specific concept of practical reason and a specific concept of the person.... The person is not the empirical but the *noumenal* self, that is, the active self-determining agent with a rationally assertive point of view of his own.... As rationally autonomous agents, persons are not merely instrumental means but ends-in-themselves ...

> As a result, the Kantian principle of respect for persons, as respect for the practical law exemplified, is ultimately based on the *Kantian autonomy* of practical reason and the person. Accordingly, Siegel's justification of the critical thinking ideal on deontological grounds involves, in the final analysis, the acknowledgement of this Kantian conception of autonomy.... Siegel's implicit appeal to the Kantian autonomy of practical reason sharply conflicts with the over-all Humean character of his own two-component theory of critical thinking. That is to say, the justificatory appeal to Kantian autonomy is alien to the Humean means-end conception of rationality that ... constitutes the foundation of Siegel's reasons conception of critical thinking. If I am right about this, then Siegel cannot rationally justify the educational ideal of critical thinking on the basis of his own premises. (pp. 82–83, emphases in original)

As suggested above, I do not endorse the "Humean means-end conception of rationality" that Cuypers attributes to me. That is enough, I think, to escape the difficulty Cuypers sees with my effort to justify critical thinking as a fundamental educational ideal, since I could, being a non-Humean, simply accept the Kantian one. And it is worth pointing out that I do indeed embrace several core aspects of Kant's view, in particular his emphases on self-legislation, universal law, non-arbitrariness (see p. 82 for relevant Kant citations and Cuypers' explication), and of course the fundamental moral principle of respect for persons. But it is important to see that that overall view need embrace neither Kantian autonomy (as Cuypers depicts it) nor the Kantian view of practical reason in order to succeed.

First, I don't accept the Kantian view that practical reason always, or necessarily, "generates in us pertinent volitions and moves us all the way to action" (p. 82). As indicated above, on my view reasons, for action may, but need not, so move us. In this respect, at least, I part company with Kant.

Second, Cuypers is clear that Kant is talking about the practical reason of "noumenal" selves; I'm talking about students and other actual persons, who are not "noumenal" but rather are "empirical," that is, accessible to us and each other. It is such persons who, in my view, deserve to be treated with respect as ends-in-themselves, and not as mere means. I do not need to accept (as Cuypers acknowledges [pp. 83–84]) the Kantian metaphysical picture of the person and her autonomy in order to assert and accept the duty to so treat students and others; I am well within my rights in rejecting it. So Cuyper's *assumption*, that "Siegel eventually needs to appeal to Kantian autonomy in order rationally to justify critical thinking as an educational ideal" (p. 83), is incorrect.

But this claim of mine will surely seem to Cuypers to be mere counter-assertion rather than a direct response to his argument that, despite myself,

I am committed to Kantian autonomy. Thus, we must consider Cuypers' discussion of autonomy, and in particular his distinction between "two different conceptions of autonomy: the critically rational conception and the Kantian conception" (p. 76). I turn to this next.

On Cuypers' view, the *critically rational conception of autonomy*, to which I am claimed to subscribe, is one according to which "critical thinking is ... not only coextensive with rationality but also with autonomy" (p. 79). Cuypers is of course free to formulate any conception of autonomy he likes, but this one is not mine, since I do not regard critical thinking and autonomy as "the same educational ideal" (p. 79); nor does the passage Cuypers here cites from *Educating Reason* say that I do. Rather, my view is that autonomy is a *necessary but not sufficient condition* of critical thinking. Autonomy is a necessary condition of critical thinking because to the extent that the critical thinker is not autonomous, she is not "free to act and judge independently of external constraint, on the basis of her own reasoned appraisal of the matter at hand" (Siegel 1988, p. 54, cited by Cuypers, p. 79). It is not a sufficient condition of critical thinking because such reasoned appraisal might be of poor quality, and thus fail to satisfy the "epistemic quality" demands of the reason assessment component. Here, regrettably, Cuypers simply gets me wrong. He is right that, on my view, as in "our Western rationalistic intellectual tradition," "rationality has always been conceptually connected with freedom and autonomy" (p. 79). But there are many sorts of conceptual connection: "A is a necessary condition of R" is one such; "A is a sufficient condition of R" another; "A is coextensive with R" another; "A is identical to R" yet another. With A standing for *autonomy* and R for *rationality*, I endorse the first but not the second, third, or fourth of these.

On the basis of his failure to distinguish from among these different conceptual connections, Cuypers lumps rationality and autonomy together to create his "critically rational conception of autonomy": "Given the conceptual connection between rationality and autonomy, the educational ideal of critical thinking becomes indistinguishable from that of rational autonomy" (p. 79). He further explicates this conception by referring to R. S. Peters, Robert Dearden, and Stanley Benn, but this discussion (pp. 79–80) is too quick to tell if those authors actually require satisfaction of the reason assessment component, as I interpret it, as a necessary condition of autonomy. If they do, I part company from them, since it seems clear to me that one can reason, believe, judge, and act autonomously, but nevertheless badly, from the point of view of relevant criteria of reason assessment. (For example, the person who reasons, judges, or bets [epistemically] badly or irrationally—e.g., in accordance with the gambler's fallacy—might nevertheless reason, judge, or act perfectly autonomously.) In brief: I do not endorse the critically rational conception of autonomy, as Cuypers characterizes it.

Cuypers distinguishes the critically rational conception of autonomy from the *Kantian* conception, which is rehearsed in the long citation from Cuypers (pp. 82–83) near the beginning of this section. I have already indicated my rejection of certain strands of that conception. But Cuypers thinks that if I reject the Kantian conception of autonomy, I will be unable to justify critical thinking as a fundamental educational ideal, because I will have (in effect) eviscerated the Kantian principle of respect for persons, upon which that justification rests. Is this correct?

I don't think so. Cuypers is correct that for that justification to succeed, the Kantian principle must itself be justified; he is right as well that although I claim that it can be justified, I do not attempt to justify it myself (Siegel 1988, pp. 156–157, note 23; cited by Cuypers, p. 82). As I say in the cited note, my failure to attempt the justification is in part a function of my own limited competence as a moral philosopher: I consider myself to be an interested amateur, but far from expert, in this core area of philosophy. But as I also say in that note, it seems to me that the Kantian principle, sufficiently broadly interpreted, both admits of justification and "is widely acknowledged, in one form or another, by contemporary moral theorists of various persuasions" (Siegel 1988, pp. 156–157, note 23). Without citing chapter and verse or arguing the case in any detail, it seems to me that moral philosophers sympathetic to Kant (Korsgaard, O'Neill, Baron, Herman, Hill, etc.) offer highly plausible justifications of the principle of respect for persons that do not rely upon the (in my view) problematic aspects of Kant's metaphysical and action-theoretic views that I have rejected above. It also seems clear to me that many other (types of) moral theorists—e.g., consequentialists, contractarians, and virtue theorists—also typically endorse a Kant-like principle according to which persons *qua* persons are to be treated with respect, as ends-in-themselves, and never as mere means (though they of course derive their respective versions of the principle in un-Kantian ways). Thus, it seems to me that the principle is relatively uncontroversial, and that it might be secured by a variety of justificatory routes. So I do not regard this justificatory challenge as particularly pressing, though I immediately concede that I have not offered any deep justification of it myself. As just indicated, I think that the principle can be established without the Kantian baggage I have endeavored to shed. (It is perhaps misleading to call it a "Kantian" principle, however; I am happy to regard that as a label that serves mainly simply to honor the distinguished Königsberger, for whom the principle was basic.[9]) I do not read Cuypers as wanting seriously to challenge the principle, but only to argue that it can be established only by appealing to the Kantian conception of autonomy. But I do not see that he has established any such strong claim as this.[10]

For the reasons just given, I regard the principle of respect for persons as worthy of our embrace. While those reasons—important contemporary Kantian moral theorists offer plausible justifications for the principle that seem not to depend on the problematic aspects of Kant's own justification of it; other, non-Kantian moral theorists also endorse the principle; the principle is thus relatively uncontroversial; there seem to be a variety of justificatory routes to it—do not justify that principle directly, they do, I think, give us good (indirect)[11] reasons for thinking that it is so worthy. If this is right, then we are indeed justified in regarding critical thinking as a fundamental educational ideal, even without embracing the Kantian conception of autonomy.

This proposed justification is, of course, defeasible. Should all the given reasons collapse under critical scrutiny (the Korsgaardian, etc., reformulated Kantian justifications fail; the principle turns out to be more controversial than I've claimed; the alternative justificatory routes fail), I would then be faced with the following alternatives: offer a new justification of the principle that does not rely on Kantian autonomy, give up my reservations about some aspects of Kant's view and fully embrace Kantian autonomy, or give up the claim that critical thinking is a fundamental educational ideal. In this unhappy situation, I would presumably endeavor to embrace these alternatives in the order just listed. For now, it suffices to say that this unhappy situation is not the one in which we currently find ourselves. For the moment, at least, we have good reasons to embrace the principle of respect for persons, and, since (if my arguments succeed) the claim that critical thinking is a fundamental educational ideal follows from that principle, good reasons for embracing that claim. In other words, contrary to Cuypers' thesis, I have, despite his arguments, ample resources for the justification of that claim.

4. Are Reasons Intrinsically Motivating?

This is too large a question to treat fully here. But perhaps some very brief closing remarks are in order.

Must we choose between a Humean view of practical reason, according to which reasons for action are both normatively and motivationally inert, and a Kantian view, according to which they are in both respects forceful? I hope and think not, because, so understood, both views face deep difficulties. My view is, in this respect, neither Humean nor Kantian, although it embraces elements of each. On it, (good) reasons are normatively forceful, yet can be, and often are, motivationally inert. That is, they can settle the question of what we ought to do, and in that sense serve as a normative guide to action, and yet can nevertheless fail to move us to act.

On the views that Cuypers considers, the normative and motivational forces of practical reasons go together: such reasons have either both (Kant) or neither (Hume). I think an adequate account of reasons, both practical and theoretical, must pull them apart. On the view I favor, the normative force of reasons is determined wholly by their quality. But their motivating force is dependent on a wide range of considerations, including the degree to which the person whose reasons they are is disposed to act in accordance with them—i.e., on the degree to which that person has the "critical spirit." But I do not intend to defend that view further here. My point, rather, is simply to urge the pulling apart of the normative and motivational powers of practical reasons that Cuypers' Hume and Kant both join together.

There is obviously much more to be said about all this than I can say here.[12] I close by thanking Cuypers again for his careful and insightful treatment of my efforts to articulate and defend my conception of critical thinking as an educational ideal. While I am, in the end, not persuaded by his critical case, for the reasons given above, I am grateful for his sympathetic portrayal of my position, his careful attention to the details of my arguments, and the thoroughly professional spirit in which his case is prosecuted. I have learned much from his discussion.[13]

Notes

1. As Cuypers rightly notes (p. 80), my account of rationality is meant to apply to both sides of the theoretical/practical reason divide. So he is well within his rights to focus on that account as it applies to practical reason.
2. I happily and explicitly cede to Cuypers superior expertise in matters historical, and in what follows I take for granted his accounts of the Humean and Kantian positions. My interest is in showing that my position is free of the difficulties Cuypers alleges; whether or not that position is actually Humean or Kantian in any particular respect is not my concern here.
3. All page citations in the text are to Cuypers 2004, unless explicitly noted otherwise.
4. There is potential confusion here, as it could be thought that all actions have ends, in which case all practical reasons could be thought of as instrumental. For Kant the relevant distinction is between categorical and hypothetical imperatives, the latter issuing in "prudential" ends. I refrain from inserting that qualifier before the two occurrences of "end/ends" in this paragraph in order to maintain fidelity to the language with which Cuypers articulates his objection. Thanks to Walter Okshevsky for helpful advice here.
5. I leave aside the question of what sort of "implication" Cuypers might have in mind here. It seems clear enough that logical implication is not at issue.
6. I note in passing that I do not appeal to any "faculty of reason," nor do I speak of "reason itself." Rather, I follow Scheffler in treating "reason" as always implicitly plural (Scheffler 1989, p. 3).
7. Insofar as one is a perfect critical thinker, i.e., in full possession of both the reason assessment and the critical spirit components, one will perforce act in accordance with the normative force of relevant reasons. But no one is in fact perfect in this regard; being a critical thinker, and possessing the components, are matters of degree. (Moreover, as the saying goes, "the universe must cooperate.") Educationally, taking critical thinking as a fundamental ideal involves, in practice, aiming to maximize the probability of—but only ideally to guarantee—action in accordance with the dictates of competent reason assessment.
8. In addition to the criticism he discusses (pp. 84–88, discussing Siegel 1988, Postscript), he might as well have referred to Siegel 1985, 1990a, 1996, 1998, and/or 2000.
9. But see the further related remarks below, and my comments in Siegel 1990b, pp. 45–46.

10. Cuypers seems to allow the possibility of alternative justifications (p. 88), though his discussion here is too brief for me to be confident that I have interpreted it correctly.
11. For a brief discussion of the direct/indirect evidence distinction to which I here appeal, see Siegel 2004, p. 81.
12. I strongly recommend Robertson's "Practical Reasons, Authority, and Education" (1984), which, while somewhat dated now, remains the best discussion of which I am aware in the philosophy of education literature of the internalism/externalism controversy in the theory of action. Robertson's discussion not only incisively analyzes the philosophical issues concerning the motivational character of practical reasons; it also clarifies beautifully the educational relevance of the philosophical issue.
13. I am grateful to Walter Okshevsky and Michael Slote for very helpful criticisms, suggestions, and advice.

References

Cuypers, S. E. (2004). "Critical Thinking, Autonomy and Practical Reason." *Journal of Philosophy of Education* 38.1: 75–90.

Robertson, E. (1984). "Practical Reasons, Authority, and Education." In R. Roemer (ed.), *Philosophy of Education 1983: Proceedings of the Thirty-Ninth Annual Meeting of the Philosophy of Education Society* (pp. 61–75). Normal, IL: Philosophy of Education Society.

Scheffler, I. (1989). *Reason and Teaching*. Indianapolis: Hackett. Originally published in 1973 by Routledge & Kegan Paul.

Siegel, H. (1985). "What Is the Question Concerning the Rationality of Science?" *Philosophy of Science* 52.4: 517–537.

Siegel, H. (1988). *Educating Reason: Rationality, Critical Thinking and Education*. London: Routledge.

Siegel, H. (1990a). "Laudan's Normative Naturalism." *Studies in History and Philosophy of Science* 21.2: 295–313.

Siegel, H. (1990b). "Response to Mackenzie." *Educational Philosophy and Theory* 22.1: 45–47.

Siegel, H. (1996). "Instrumental Rationality and Naturalized Philosophy of Science." *Philosophy of Science* 63.3, Supplement (*PSA Proceedings*, Part 1): 116–124.

Siegel, H. (1998). "Naturalism and Normativity: Hooker's Ragged Reconciliation." *Studies in History and Philosophy of Science* 29.4: 639–652.

Siegel, H. (2000). "Naturalism, Instrumental Rationality, and the Normativity of Epistemology." In G Preyer and G. Peter (eds.), *The Contextualization of Rationality: Problems, Concepts and Theories of Rationality* (pp. 95–107). Paderborn, Germany: Mentis.

Siegel, H. (2004). "Faith, Knowledge and Indoctrination: A Friendly Response to Hand." *Theory and Research in Education* 2.1: 75–83.

PART TWO

DISPOSITIONS, VIRTUES, AND INDOCTRINATION

4

What (Good) Are Thinking Dispositions?

1. The Nature and Educational Importance of Thinking Dispositions

A wide range of educational researchers and theorists posit the existence, and investigate the character and educational relevance, of *thinking dispositions*. Philosophers of education investigating critical thinking typically conceive of it as involving both skills/abilities and dispositions (e.g., Crooks 1995; Ennis 1987; Lipman 1988; McCarthy 1993; McPeck 1990; Norris 1989; Passmore 1967; Paul 1990; Siegel 1988, 1997). When wearing their "educational researcher" in addition to their "philosopher" hats, some of these scholars investigate the complex ways in which critical thinking dispositions are relevant to educational research on testing for critical thinking, since explanations of, for example, poor test performance may reasonably appeal to lack of critical thinking dispositions rather than lack of abilities if it is granted that there are such dispositions (Ennis and Norris 1990, p. 33; Norris 1989, pp. 22–23; Norris 1995, p. 382; Norris 2003).[1] Moving beyond "critical" thinking to thinking more generally, some researchers have suggested that dispositions are essential not only to a proper conceptualization of thinking (and of intelligence), but to the design and implementation of educational interventions intended to improve thinking in everyday circumstances as well (Perkins, Jay, and Tishman 1993; Perkins et al. 2000). Developmental psychologists interested in education likewise argue that cognitive development depends importantly on thinking dispositions (Moshman 1998). All of this research, as already suggested, has direct implications for teaching: if inadequate learning results in part from failures of dispositions rather than of abilities or skills, instructional remediation efforts will have to be redirected, to some extent, from the latter to the former. More generally, the question of how best to foster desirable dispositions takes on practical and research importance once the relevance of dispositions to thinking performance is granted. The wide-ranging educational relevance of dispositions, in particular thinking dispositions, cannot be denied (Arnstine 1995, pp. 59 ff.), if it is granted that there are such things in the first place.

But should the "reality" of thinking dispositions, and thus their relevance to education, be granted? The answer depends upon the satisfactory quieting of legitimate doubts concerning the character, the explanatory ability, and, more fundamentally, the very existence of thinking dispositions. It is the purpose of this paper to quiet such doubts. So, how should we understand the educational and psychological theory and research just cited, which makes free use of the notions of dispositions in general, and thinking dispositions in particular? What *are* thinking dispositions? What is being claimed when it is said (for example) that Mary has the disposition (or is disposed) to think critically, that John is disposed to judge hastily, that Anne is disposed to assess critically what she hears or is told, or that Sam is disposed to reason fallaciously?

A common pair of answers to these questions—which, with some small qualifications and amplifications, I will defend in what follows—is that thinking dispositions are *properties of thinkers*, and that the thinkers mentioned have general *tendencies*, *propensities*, or *inclinations* to think in the ways attributed to them.[2] To say, for example, that Anne is disposed to assess critically what she hears or is told, is to claim that Anne, *as a matter of inclination*, considers the intellectual merits of what she hears or is told, the evidence for this claim typically being that she regularly and routinely acts in this way. She tends regularly (but not neurotically[3]) to ask, for example, whether what she hears or is told emanates from a reliable source, whether it conflicts with anything else she currently believes, whether she has any independent reason either to believe or to doubt it, and so on. Put negatively, to attribute this disposition to Anne is to claim that she generally does not accept what she hears or is told without first subjecting it to some measure of critical scrutiny and reflection.[4]

A thinking disposition, then, is a tendency, propensity, or inclination to think in certain ways under certain circumstances. But how are we to understand such tendencies and inclinations? To pursue these matters further, let us for the moment leave "thinking" behind, and concentrate on dispositions as such. In due course we will apply our findings concerning dispositions generally to those involving thinking in particular.

If a thinking disposition is a tendency, propensity, or inclination to think in certain ways under certain circumstances, then a disposition, more generally, is a tendency, propensity, or inclination to behave or act in certain ways under certain circumstances. Here the classic example in the philosophical literature[5] is that of sugar. Sugar, we say, is disposed to dissolve in liquid. This disposition is manifested countless times every day, as people prepare their coffee, tea, and other beverages: when put in liquid, the sugar actually dissolves.

But consider the sugar in Joe's sugar bowl. Joe does not take sugar in his coffee. He keeps a filled sugar bowl in his cupboard just in case company should call, but in fact Joe hardly ever has visitors, and when the rare visits take place, the visitors either don't have coffee or don't take sugar in theirs. So his sugar bowl sits, unused, year in and year out. Does the sugar in it have the disposition in question? The answer is, I trust, clear: the sugar in Joe's sugar bowl has the disposition to dissolve, even though it never actually dissolves. The disposition is a *counterfactual* property of the sugar: *had* it been placed in liquid, it *would have* dissolved.[6] This is so even in cases in which the sugar is never, in fact, so placed, and so never has the opportunity actually to dissolve, and so never actually dissolves. *Having* the disposition, that is, is independent of the behavior actually being manifested. It is in this sense that the disposition is counterfactual. Whether it is manifested depends upon the realization of the relevant enabling conditions: in the case of sugar, its being placed in a (nonsaturated) liquid solution (of an appropriate temperature).

How is this property to be understood? Is it something other than an "ordinary physical property"[7] of the entity that has it? With respect to sugar, it is clear that Quine is right to regard its disposition to dissolve as simply one of sugar's physical properties; our calling it a disposition, rather than a more "ordinary" property like mass, volume, or molecular structure, is just a matter of our way of identifying or (as Quine puts it) "specifying" it:

> I shall appeal freely to dispositions. We do so when we say what one *would* do, or what *would* happen, *if*. What then is a disposition? It is just one or another physical property, one or another trait of the internal structure or composition of the disposed object or related objects. The seeming difference between dispositions and other physical properties resides merely in our way of specifying them. We call a property a disposition if we specify it by citing a symptom, or test. The paradigm of dispositions, solubility in water, is a recondite matter of microscopic structure, but it is one we conveniently specify by just citing a symptom or test: the substance will dissolve on immersion. The disposition of an ape or bird to broadcast the appropriate signal is again a physical trait, something to do with the organization of the creature's neural network. (Quine 1995, p. 21, emphases in original)

We need not accept Quine's reductionism (according to which dispositions just *are* features of the internal structure of the disposed object), and so we needn't follow Quine all the way down the path of *physicalism*—according to which *all* (or all "scientifically respectable") properties are characterizable ultimately in terms of fundamental physical theory—in order to see that dispositions are not mysterious or metaphysically dubious entities, but rather are properties just like other properties. They differ from other properties only in the way in which we (sometimes) identify them. So, to take our earlier example—and to see that this account of dispositions applies to thinking dispositions as well as those which do not involve thinking—Anne's disposition to assess critically what she hears or is told is specified in terms of her characteristic reaction to hearing or being told something: her contemplating its source, its fit with other relevant beliefs of hers, etc. Presumably Anne's disposition to assess critically what she hears or is told, like Quine's example of "the disposition of an ape or bird to broadcast the appropriate signal," is (or supervenes upon), like the latter, "a physical trait, something to do with the organization of [Anne's] neural network." If we are optimists concerning science, we expect that in the fullness of time a fully adequate physical/neurophysiological characterization of Anne's disposition will be available to us.[8] But even if not, we are nevertheless free to regard her disposition as a genuine property of Anne's, on the basis of which we can explain her past thinking, and predict her future thinking, in standard counterfactual terms: *were* she to hear or be told something, in particular circumstances, she *would* react, other things being equal, in particular, specifiable ways.[9] Anne's disposition to assess critically what she hears or is told is a genuine, enduring feature of Anne, as real as her arm, her nervous twitch, her lively sense of humor, and the characteristic tone of her voice.[10]

2. Dispositions, Rules, and Behaviors

Some writers suggest that standard accounts of thinking dispositions, especially critical thinking dispositions, fail meaningfully to distinguish the disposition to think in particular ways from the formal rules to which such thinking must conform. Nicholas C. Burbules puts the charge as follows:

> I want to suggest ... that "reasonableness" refers to the dispositions and capacities of a certain kind of person, a person who is related in specific contexts to other persons—not to the following of formal rules and procedures of thought. Although a reasonable person is one who will tend to have, and offer, reasons to support his or her choices of belief and action, these are the manifestation of something more basic about this sort of person. A characterization solely in terms of "reason-giving" or "reason-following" confuses the symptom with the source of reasonable dispositions. A common trend, for example, in much current writing on critical thinking is to suggest the limitations of "logicality" as an approximation of what a critical thinker is and does; rather, we need to supplement the skills of logical reasoning with dispositions to apply them in contexts of practice. In some cases, unfortunately,

the characterization of these dispositions is rather thin: the difference between the logical rule "always test a syllogism for valid structure" and the "disposition to test syllogisms for valid structure" is hardly worth talking about. Similarly, the "rational passions" discussed by Israel Scheffler and others, such as a passion for rigor and clarity, are sometimes little more than the rephrasing of formal criteria in an emotive language. (Burbules 1995, pp. 85–86, notes deleted)[11]

Burbules is importantly right, I believe, to insist that the reasons that a reasonable person has and offers for her beliefs, judgments, and actions are "the manifestation of something more basic about this sort of person" than mere conformity with formal rules. What is this "more basic" thing? For the authors Burbules here criticizes—including me—the more basic thing is the disposition to evaluate well and be guided by reasons. This disposition is an important aspect of a person's character; as such, it is basic indeed. It is manifestly not reducible to a set of formal rules or criteria.

Why not? What is the disposition, other than conformity with formal rules? The answer should be clear from our earlier discussion: the disposition is a genuine tendency, propensity, or inclination to think in certain ways under certain circumstances. It is an underlying trait of a person, which exists even when not being manifested, and which underwrites predictions concerning future thinking. The disposition is the "animating motive"[12] which, if we have it, causes[13] us to think in conformity with such rules; it is what gets us actually to engage in such thinking (in the relevant circumstances). The formal rules concerning syllogistic validity are one thing; the ability to test a syllogism for valid structure is another, quite different thing; the disposition to do so is yet another. There is no reason to think that thinking dispositions of the sort being considered are nothing more than formal rules.[14] Indeed, how could they be, given that formal rules are not properties of persons, while thinking dispositions are?

Nor are dispositions merely behaviorally defined, such that anything we do on a regular basis is a disposition. Dispositions, as argued above, involve counterfactuality: if Mary has the disposition to challenge authority, we can predict that if she is confronted by an authority, other things being equal, Mary will challenge it. This is not a behavior; Mary has the disposition even when she is alone, asleep, and there is no authority in sight. Dispositions, then, are not simply regular behaviors. They are not behaviors at all. Rather, they are *tendencies to engage* in particular sorts of behaviors.

A further reason for thinking that dispositions are not just routinely performed behaviors is that the same disposition can prompt quite different behaviors. Consider again Mary's disposition to challenge authority. This disposition may manifest itself in a wide variety of ways, and these manifestations may systematically vary in various sorts of contexts. For example, when confronted by authorities, Mary may sometimes challenge them by shouting at them, sometimes by ridiculing them, sometimes by ignoring them, and so on. These are all ways in which authorities can be challenged, but they are different, behaviorally, from each other. They are all behaviors caused by the same disposition, but they are not instances of the same (type of) behavior. So dispositions cannot be regarded just as sets of routinized behavior, or as reducible to patterns of behavior. Rather, any given disposition can be manifested in a wide variety of ways. Dispositions cause us to act/behave in characteristic ways—for example, in ways that challenge authority—but they do not determine the precise form in which they are manifested, since they can be manifested in a wide variety of ways.[15]

I should briefly address one final issue before closing this section. Some readers may worry about all this loose talk of dispositions *causing* thought, behavior, and action. Is all our thinking and acting caused? Doesn't this deny our freedom, and reduce us to mere physical systems whose behaviors are no more conscious or self-directed than the paths of colliding billiard balls? I wish to make three points in response.

First, a disposition need not be, and typically is not, so strong as to *necessitate* any manifestation or behavior at all, let alone a particular one (as just noted). For example, I am disposed to engage in philosophical argumentation. It is a fairly strong disposition I have, as my family, friends, colleagues, and students will attest. But this disposition of mine can be, and often is, overridden—by fatigue, anger, frustration, sexual or gustatory desire, and so on. So not only is no particular manifestation of the disposition necessitated, but no manifestation at all is necessitated by the existence or possession of the disposition. (This is especially so in light of the range of strengths in which dispositions come: we may be strongly disposed, weakly disposed, etc. As noted above, having a disposition should not be conceived as an all-or-nothing affair.)

Second, regarding dispositions as causal does not necessarily rob us of our free will. The long-existing and frequently held metaphysical view called "compatibilism" (or "soft determinism") makes clear that our having free will is compatible with our actions having causes.[16]

The previous two points are metaphysical in nature. The third point is educational. Many, if not most, of the scholars interested in thinking dispositions are so interested because they see the fostering of dispositions as an important *educational* aim. Why is that? The idea is that if we manage to foster the relevant dispositions in students, their thoughts, judgments, and actions will be *changed*. For example, if students acquire the disposition to assess critically what they hear or are told, they will think and act in new ways. They will, for example, ask themselves questions concerning the reliability of sources, the possibility that the source in question has a vested interest in the matter, possible conflicts between what they have just heard or been told and other of their beliefs, and so on; and they will reject claims that they previously would have thoughtlessly accepted. That is to say, students' acquiring dispositions *affects* them—that is, *causally* affects them. If dispositions are not understood as having the potential to cause, i.e., "bring about," particular sorts of thought and action, what reason would there be to think it educationally important to foster them? Fostering dispositions can have an educational point only insofar as the dispositions we strive to foster can be understood as having the potential to influence—causally influence—students' thought, judgment, and action. It is that very causal influence that makes them the proper object of educational effort.[17]

I conclude that thinking dispositions are not reducible either to formal rules of thought or to particular behaviors or patterns of behavior. Moreover, regarding them as causal in nature does not commit us to unpalatable metaphysical results. So regarding them is required for any view which holds that the fostering of dispositions is an educationally important aim.

The educational importance of this conclusion is, I hope, clear. If thinking dispositions are taken to be reducible to either formal rules of thought or particular behaviors, teachers presumably would be well advised to endeavor to foster such dispositions in students by either teaching formal logic or conditioning such behaviors. But if thinking dispositions are understood as portrayed above, and thus as not reducible to either rules or behaviors, then the educational task of fostering students' thinking dispositions cannot fruitfully be conceived solely along either of those lines. Rather, educational efforts aimed at fostering students' thinking dispositions will need to focus on increasing student *sensitivity* to occasions in which such dispositions are appropriately exercised (Perkins, Jay, and Tishman 1993; Perkins et al. 2000), and to creating conditions in educational settings favorable to their development and exercise (Arnstine 1991; Arnstine 1995; Burbules 1995). The need for further educational research on these matters is clear.[18] Even clearer is the practical educational significance—for teaching, and for the design of learning environments—of taking the view of thinking dispositions defended here seriously.

3. The Explanatory Power of Dispositions[19]

To many, the idea that dispositions can figure in genuine explanations is unproblematic. Robert Brandon (1990, p. 15), for example, writes that "[i]t should be clear that we can explain the actual behavior of an object in terms of its abilities, capacities, or propensities," and he offers examples from physics and biology of such dispositional explanations. Among educational researchers, Perkins and Tishman (1997, ms. p. 8) write that "the notion of dispositions is an explanatory construct that addresses the gap between ability and performance by hypothesizing broad characterological traits that dispose some people more than others to marshal their abilities." But some writers question the ability of dispositions to explain. The worry is well articulated by David R. Olson and Nandita Babu:

> [A]lmost a half-century of psychology has gone into disabusing us of the explanatory value of such notions as traits, abilities, and dispositions. Nothing is added by the term "skill" in the phrase "critical thinking skill"; this is mere hypostatization—creating an entity by adding the noun "skill." Consequently, critical thinking is not explained by saying that someone has critical thinking abilities or dispositions. It is not an explanation of why someone took the money to say that he is larcenous or has a disposition to larceny. Furthermore, the theory of dispositional traits has been found to be ungeneralizable; whereas an observer may be tempted to describe another's missing the train by saying that the person is tardy or slothful, the subject of the description usually rejects the description, pointing rather to situational factors such as inability to find an umbrella. (Olson and Babu 1992, p. 182)

Consider again our running example of a thinking disposition: Anne's disposition to assess critically what she hears or is told. Is regarding this as a disposition a case of "mere hypostatization"? Is it erroneously "creating an entity" where none exists? Is an explanation of Anne's thinking in terms of the alleged disposition manifestly devoid of explanatory content or force, like "explaining" Jim's thievery in terms of his larcenous disposition (or, to take the standard example of an empty explanation, like "explaining" the pill's ability to put Jim to sleep in terms of the pill's "dormitive powers")? Finally, is the "ungeneralizability" of attributions of dispositional traits problematic? Let me take up these challenges in turn.

A. Hypostatization

Are we pointing to something that is not there when we speak of Anne's disposition to assess critically what she hears or is told? Are we "creating" this entity, otherwise nonexistent, by committing the sin of hypostatization? I do not see why we should think so. As argued above, Anne's disposition is a real, enduring feature of Anne. Absent a more direct challenge to the standard view, related above, of the reality and scientific respectability of dispositions, we should remain unperturbed by the charge of hypostatization, for the charge is false. We do not "create" dispositions by calling them so. Rather, they are real, enduring properties of people and other objects.

Indeed, this charge seems to rest on a conflation of *properties* and *entities*. I have been suggesting throughout that dispositions are properties, not entities, and that thinking dispositions are properties of thinkers. The charge of hypostatization seems clearly enough to amount to the charge that to regard dispositions as real is to regard them as (phony, nonexistent) entities, as objects or things of some sort. I agree that dispositions are not, in this sense, entities; here Olson and Babu are, I believe, correct. But that dispositions are not entities does not suggest that they are not genuine properties of entities. Once we distinguish between entities and properties, and regard dispositions as the latter, the charge of hypostatization is met: a particular thinking disposition is a real property of a particular person in just the way that a particular shade of red is a real property of a particular apple. No entities are thereby created.[20]

B. Explanatory Emptiness

Are explanations in terms of dispositions explanatorily empty? Are they necessarily or inevitably so? When we explain Anne's thinking or acting on a particular occasion, or the general pattern of her thinking or acting across many occasions,[21] in terms of her disposition to assess critically what she hears or is told, is our explanation doomed to emptiness and (hence) failure?

The answers to these questions will depend, of course, on one's account of explanation and explanatory adequacy. Philosophers and others who worry about such matters disagree about them (as philosophers will) and offer alternative theories of explanation; it is beyond the scope of this paper to delve deeply into these theories.[22] But it is not necessary to so delve in order to answer our questions. For it can readily be seen that, given the account of dispositions given above, dispositions can indeed explain.[23] Let us see why.

Consider first a dispositional explanation (i.e., an explanation in terms of dispositions) of a particular episode of thinking. Bonnie tells Anne that the president is scheduled to make an important speech on foreign policy in Paris later this evening. Unlike some of the other people that Bonnie has told of the speech, Anne does not immediately come to believe this of the president. Instead, she first considers the claim, asking herself questions concerning both its content and its source. Is the president likely to make such a speech? Hasn't he just made such a speech? If so, why would he give two major speeches on foreign policy in such a short period of time? Is there some international or political crisis that might call for such a speech? Why would he give it in Paris? And what about Bonnie? Is she the sort of person who keeps close track of the presidential itinerary and speech-making schedule? Does she have some special interest in or relationship to either the president, Paris, or some other aspect of the claim that would render her especially reliable, or unreliable, with respect to it?

For present purposes, it does not matter how Anne answers these questions. It is her *asking* them that calls for explanation. And the proposed explanation is that she asked them because she is disposed to assess critically what she hears or is told. Is this proposed explanation necessarily empty? There is no reason to suppose that it must be. It would be empty, perhaps, if every act of critical assessment was thought to be, necessarily, a manifestation of that disposition. But this is not the case. Joe, for example, is not so disposed—he routinely simply believes (without engaging in critical assessment of it) what he hears or is told. However, when Bonnie told him about the president's speech, it occurred to him that Bonnie's claim conflicted with the morning newscaster's claim that the president was spending the weekend at Camp David. Joe became confused—he no longer knew what to believe concerning the president's whereabouts—and subsequently he began to ask the same questions concerning Bonnie's claim that Anne had asked. Here Anne and Joe manifested the same behavior—they both engaged in the process of critically assessing what they were told—but their behavior did not manifest, and indeed could not have manifested, a shared disposition to do so, because Joe does not have it. He is not disposed to so engage.

If this kind of case is possible—and I see no reason to doubt that it is—then attributing the disposition to Anne is not empty, explanatorily or otherwise. The suggestion that it is depends upon regarding every act of thinking as the manifestation of some relevant disposition. But for any given act of thinking, whether or not it manifests the disposition in question depends upon additional information concerning the thinker's general tendency to engage in such acts. In the case before us, Anne routinely so engages; Joe does not. Consequently, we cannot explain Joe's critical examination of what Bonnie told him in terms of his disposition to assess critically what he hears or is told, because by hypothesis he does not have this disposition—he is not so disposed. We explain it, if we can, in other ways—for example, in terms of the cognitive dissonance produced by his hearing both what Bonnie told him and what the newscaster said. Attributing the disposition to Anne, on the other hand, is not empty, precisely because we have additional reason, over and above her critical questioning on this occasion, to think that she is indeed so disposed—that is, that she has the general tendency, propensity, or inclination to assess critically what she hears or is told. And we explain her critical assessment in this case by noting that this is the way she usually thinks; i.e., that it is a manifestation of an underlying, enduring feature or trait of Anne (a trait Joe lacks). The charge of emptiness, then, stems from the illicit assumption that every episode of thinking that can be described in a particular way necessarily counts as one that manifests a disposition routinely so to think. Once this assumption is unmasked, the charge is defeated.[24]

If any further reason to doubt the emptiness of such explanations is called for, consider the point made earlier, that dispositions which explain can also be used in order to predict. We would predict that the next time Anne hears or is told something, she will engage in critical assessment of it. We would not predict this of Joe. This shows clearly enough that the attribution of a disposition is not always empty (or "mere hypostatization"). Because it is not, explanation of thinking in terms of dispositions is not always empty either.

Consider next the dispositional explanation, not of individual episodes of thinking, but of general patterns of thinking. One may grant that the disposition to assess critically what she hears or is told explains why, in a particular case, Anne engages in such critical assessment, but yet doubt that that disposition can explain the long-term pattern of Anne's thinking (in such circumstances)—i.e., the pattern consisting of occasion$_1$, in which Anne critically assessed what she heard or was told; occasion$_2$, in which Anne critically assessed what she heard or was told, ... occasion$_n$, in which Anne critically assessed what she heard or was told. After all, one might think, that pattern just is the full manifestation of the disposition. How then can the disposition *explain* it? How can it be its own explanation?

This is a serious question, but it admits of a ready answer. Consider two alternative explanations of the pattern: (1) Anne's thinking manifested that pattern because she had the disposition to assess critically what she hears or is told, and (2) Anne's thinking manifested that pattern because in all the episodes of thinking included in the pattern, Anne's critical thinking instructor was observing Anne, and Anne did not want to disappoint her. These are, I hope it is clear, two alternative explanations of the pattern. To the extent that we have good reason to regard (2) as a plausible explanation—Anne's instructor was present, Anne really wanted not to disappoint her, etc.—we may doubt that Anne actually has the disposition. Of course, it may be that both (1) and (2) contribute to the explanation of the pattern; perhaps the episodes that make up the pattern are even, as philosophers sometimes put it, "causally overdetermined," in that both the disposition and the desire not to disappoint her instructor are individually sufficient to cause, and explain, the episodes that constitute the pattern. But to the extent that we have reason to doubt (2) (perhaps on many of the occasions in question, Anne's instructor was not in fact present, or we have evidence that Anne did not have that attitude toward her instructor), we think that there are no other plausible explanations of the pattern, and we have evidence that Anne really is so disposed, then we may with perfect propriety explain the overall pattern in terms of Anne's underlying disposition to assess critically what she hears or is told. The disposition is an underlying feature or property of Anne. As such, it can explain both the individual episodes of Anne's thinking which make up the pattern and the pattern as a whole.[25]

C. Ungeneralizability

Are dispositions "ungeneralizable," in that "whereas an observer may be tempted to describe another's missing the train by saying that the person is tardy or slothful, the subject of the description usually rejects the description, pointing rather to situational factors such as inability to find an umbrella"? Here it will suffice to make three brief points.

First, this is a claim not about dispositions, but about the *attribution* of dispositions. Clearly we must grant that a person may reject my attributing to her the disposition to behave slothfully. Of course if she *justifiably* rejects my attribution, we have no good reason to think that she is in fact slothful—in which case we obviously cannot explain her behavior in terms of her (nonexistent) disposition to so behave. But this is neither here nor there with respect to the current analysis. A person's being slothful is independent of her acknowledging that she is. Consequently, her rejection of the claim that she has the disposition shows neither that she doesn't have it, nor that her behavior cannot be explained in terms of it.

Second, the point is put in terms of *description*, whereas the serious question concerns not description but *explanation*. Of course, if the description is inaccurate, it is a mistake to attribute the disposition to her; and if it is a mistake to attribute the disposition to her, then one clearly cannot successfully explain the behavior (missing the train) in terms of the (nonexistent) disposition. Granted, descriptions can be inaccurate, and when they are inaccurate they cannot explain. Hence, people's descriptions of behavior, and attributions of dispositions, will differ. But none of this even begins to suggest that dispositions cannot explain.

Third, even if the attribution is justified—that is, if we have good reason to believe that the person really is slothful—it may nevertheless be the case that the correct explanation of her missing the train on this occasion does not involve her slothfulness but rather her inability to find an umbrella, as the cited passage suggests. This is actually a stronger point than the one made in that passage, since it doesn't depend upon the controversiality of the attribution of the disposition. But what it suggests is simply that having a disposition is not always sufficient for explaining a belief or an action, since the behavior on this occasion might be otherwise correctly explained. Granted. But this in no way challenges the thesis that dispositions can indeed contribute to successful explanations. For these three reasons, "ungeneralizability" fails to undermine the possibility of dispositional explanation.

I conclude that these three challenges to the possibility of dispositional explanation fail. There is ample reason to think that attributions of dispositions have content, and that when those attributions are justified and the dispositions are genuine, they can contribute to successful explanations of behavior, action, and thought. Thinking dispositions are not exceptions to this general claim; they too can explain.[26]

4. Conclusion

Genuine thinking dispositions, I have argued, are real tendencies, propensities, or inclinations people have to think in particular ways in particular contexts. As such, they are not the same as, or reducible to, either formal rules of good thinking or specific behaviors or patterns of behavior. They can, moreover, contribute to genuine explanations of both episodes of thinking and long-term patterns of thinking.

If this is so, our title questions are answered. The preceding paragraph summarizes what thinking dispositions *are*. To the question, "What good are they?," at least one answer is clear: thinking dispositions are good to the extent that they cause or bring about good thinking. They do their job when they constitute the "animating force" that causes thinkers to think well.[27, 28]

Notes

1. This research not only suggests that that the design of critical thinking tests must pay attention to dispositions; it also provides some empirical evidence that dispositions (and their lack) affect test scores.
2. Norris (1992b, 1993) helpfully regards disposition terms as referring to "underlying traits" of the entities that have the traits/dispositions the terms pick out. This is completely in keeping with the "standard" (Quinean) account of dispositions considered below. Brief comments on Norris' discussion may be found in Ennis 1993, McPeck 1993, and Siegel 1993.
3. In this essay I use Anne's disposition to assess critically what she hears or is told as a running example of a thinking disposition. I have assumed that this is a good or desirable disposition for a thinker to have, and that, other things being equal, a thinker who has it is a better thinker than a thinker who does not. However, in presenting the paper recently, I was brought up short by the criticism that a thinker who has this disposition might very well be neurotic, and that the desirability of the disposition is quite open to challenge. I would like to make two points in response. First, my intended contrast was between a thinker who is disposed to assess critically what she hears or is told and one who simply uncritically accepts the messages that come her way. The latter, I would have thought, is obviously excessively gullible; I was assuming that one task of education is to curb that sort of gullibility. As I acknowledge below, dispositions can often be overridden for good reasons—and so I was conceiving of the disposition as falling short of neurotic excess. I agree with my critics that *excessive* assessment is not a good thing. Second, though, it is important to see (as my critics did) that the desirability of this disposition is neither here nor there with respect to the overall argument. The account of dispositions offered is meant to apply to both desirable and undesirable dispositions. If you dislike this particular example, please substitute another of your own choosing. Thanks to Pamela Courtney-Hall and Michael Zlotnick for their challenging objections to the example.
4. To attribute a disposition is also, consequently, to make a *prediction* concerning future behavior, thought or action. On this point see Arnstine 1991, Arnstine 1995, and Siegel 1991.
5. See, for example, Quine 1960, pp. 33ff, 134, and 222–223, where he characterizes dispositions as real, and as indicative of (or equivalent to) "built-in, enduring structural traits" (p. 223). See also Quine 1974, Part One, where this view of dispositions is developed

further. Brandon (1990, p. 23), agreeing with Quine, argues that "a dispositional property is to be identified with its causal basis." Mills and Beatty (1979, p. 272) also regard dispositions as "ontologically real." Philosophers of science generally, and in particular, philosophers of the special sciences (physics, biology, etc.), whose work concerns dispositions and dispositional properties, embrace this standard view of dispositions as real properties of entities. The sugar example was (I think) introduced into the literature by Ryle (1949).

6. I am here ignoring the distinction, important for the analysis of conditionals but irrelevant for present purposes, between counterfactual and subjunctive conditionals.
7. I put this expression in scare quotes because it must be admitted that "ordinary physical properties" are themselves typically dispositional; consequently, it cannot be established that dispositions are not mysterious or metaphysically dubious simply by pointing out that they are just like typical ordinary physical properties. I hope, however, that this discussion will suffice to establish that dispositions of the sort being considered are not any more mysterious or dubious than other physical properties. Thanks here to the incisive criticism of Israel Scheffler (1963, pp. 162–178), who sheds important light on the scientific legitimacy of disposition terms, and to Donald Arnstine.
8. In which case the disposition term serves as a "promissory note for an eventual description in mechanical terms" to be cashed in by future scientific advances (Quine 1974, p. 14).
9. As Quine puts it, Anne's disposition "is a present passive physical state of [Anne's] nervous system, however little understood, and whether or not activated or otherwise detected" (Quine 1995, p. 76).
10. I hope it is clear that I am not arguing that there is no difference at all between the dispositions of thinking beings and the dispositions of inanimate objects. I am arguing only that the former can be understood along the lines of the latter to the extent indicated in the text. This is completely compatible with acknowledging, for example, that beliefs, attitudes, and values can be relevant to persons having and exercising dispositions (and to the explanation of their having and exercising them)—and thus that the fostering of dispositions in educational contexts will typically involve engaging students' beliefs, attitudes, and values, and will be quite unlike (say) chemically re-engineering molecules in order to render a given substance soluble. My claim is that thinking dispositions are *real*, not that they are always or necessarily "mechanical" or noncognitive. Here I am indebted to the suggestions of Donald Arnstine, Nicholas Burbules, and Stephen Norris. It is important to note that having/not having a thinking disposition is a matter of degree; one can have a strong or a weak disposition, for example, to assess critically what one hears or is told. Having a thinking disposition is not, typically, an "all or nothing" matter. Regarding thinking dispositions as admitting of degrees of strength is completely compatible with regarding them as real. See here the empirical work on strength of dispositions in Perkins, Jay, and Tishman 1993 and Perkins et al. 2000. Finally, to call such dispositions "enduring" is not to say they are necessarily unchanging. If they were, there would be no educational point to attending to them.
11. I agree with much of what Burbules says here, particularly his suggestion that "'reasonableness" refers [in part] to the dispositions and capacities of a certain kind of person"; indeed, this is just the view put forward in Siegel 1988. Burbules goes on in the cited paper to argue for a characterization of reasonableness in terms of "virtues" rather than dispositions; for further discussion of Burbules' view, see Siegel 1997, ch. 7. In what follows I do not address Burbules' overall view, but rather just the specific complaint that thinking dispositions—in particular, the dispositions involved in thinking rationally or critically—usually are not (cannot be?) distinguished from "formal rules" of thought. It should be noted that "always test a syllogism for valid structure" is hardly a "logical rule." Here I am indebted to Risto Hilpinen.

I must in fairness note that Burbules does not actually deny that logical rules and dispositions can be distinguished; he claims, rather, that the distinction between them is "hardly worth talking about." But I do not see how to interpret this claim other than the way I interpret it in the text, as calling the distinction itself (or its point) into question.

12. I owe this phrase—and much else—to Nick Burbules, with whom I have discussed these issues at length. I am grateful to him for his incisive conversation and criticism.
13. The cause of an action or thought, as I am here understanding it, is just whatever it is that brings that action or thought about.

14. Nor can thinking dispositions be understood simply as thinking which conforms to formal rules, since, as just noted, the thinking (and its conformity with such rules) is one thing, the disposition to engage in it another.
15. This is not to say that the precise manifestation is not caused at all, but only that it is not caused solely by the disposition. Other causal factors—the agent's mood, the amount of sleep he had last night, the level of testosterone in his blood, the attitude of his culture to alternative behavioral manifestations of it, etc.—all can contribute causally to the determination of the precise behavioral manifestation of the disposition on a particular occasion.

    To anticipate the next section: dispositions (e.g., to challenge authority) are "theoretical" in the sense that they can unify lower level "phenomenological" descriptions of behavior (e.g., shouting, ridiculing, and ignoring). This ability to unify might also be understood as part of the explanatory contribution dispositions can make. Thanks to Risto Hilpinen for this observation.
16. For a recent defense of compatibilism see Erwin 1997, ch. 1.
17. I hope it is clear that my aim has been to establish *that* dispositions can and do sometimes cause. *How* they cause is an important further issue that I have not addressed here. There are many different sorts of dispositions, ranging from "mechanical" ones such as sugar dissolving to more "cognitively charged" ones such as challenging authority; the manners by which they cause seem obviously to encompass a similarly wide range.
18. Existing research is instructively summarized in Perkins et al. 2000.
19. In Siegel 1991 (p. 31, note 3), I suggested—as I now see it, mistakenly—that dispositions might not be able to contribute to explanations either of particular actions or thinking episodes, or of patterns/tendencies of action or thought. In what follows I reject that earlier suggestion, and argue that dispositions can indeed explain.
20. Thanks here to Edward Erwin, Risto Hilpinen, and an anonymous reviewer.
21. This distinction, between particular *acts* or *episodes* of thinking/acting, on the one hand, and general patterns of thinking/acting, on the other, is an important one that is addressed further below.
22. The interested reader should consult Kitcher and Salmon 1989.
23. For further discussion of dispositions and their ability to explain, see the essays in Tuomela 1978. This collection contains several classic discussions of dispositions, including selections from Ryle, Carnap, Hempel, Goodman, and Quine. A more recent examination of the philosophical issues may be found in Armstrong, Martin, and Place 1996.
24. Of course, the charge (that dispositional explanations are empty) might also stem from the conviction that dispositions are not real, but are "mere hypostatizations." However, if the preceding discussion is correct, this conviction has been discredited.

    Parallel remarks to those just made apply to the case of explaining Jim's thievery in terms of his disposition to larceny. Contrary to the suggestion of the cited passage, the attribution of a larcenous disposition to Jim is not necessarily empty; if Jim's disposition to larceny is genuine, then it can contribute to the explanation of a given instance of his stealing. The success of any such explanation depends upon the further filling out of the case, but it isn't doomed to failure at the outset. (Similarly for the "dormitive powers" case.)

    Finally, it may be claimed that dispositional explanations are empty because they are tautological. But as the Anne/Joe case demonstrates, this needn't be so. Indeed, it is quite difficult to formulate an explanatory claim that is tautological. Here, and throughout, I am indebted to the excellent suggestions of Edward Erwin.
25. Christine McCarthy (1993) insightfully distinguishes between "episodic" and "dispositional" senses of "critical thinking"; in drawing the distinction in the text between episodes or acts of thinking and general patterns of thinking, I am leaning heavily on McCarthy's distinction. For discussion of the latter see Siegel 1993.

    I should acknowledge here that "disposition" is systematically ambiguous: it is sometimes used to refer to a long-term pattern of behavior, and sometimes to refer to whatever it is that prompts, or brings about, the elements of the pattern. In the first sense, the pattern cannot be explained in terms of the disposition, since they are the same thing. But it is the second sense that has been in play throughout, and is the intended sense here; it is in this sense that (I am claiming) the disposition can explain the pattern. Moreover, as Jerrold Coombs pointed out to me, understanding "disposition" in the first sense, as equivalent to the pattern, has the effect of implicitly denying the counterfactual character of dispositions; this provides an independent reason for understanding the term in the second way. My thanks to Coombs for this insight, and to Donald Arnstine and Israel Scheffler, whose comments prompted this note.

26. It may be that Olson and Babu take the view they do because they regard thinking dispositions (or, in their view, what passes for such) as a different sort of phenomenon, property, or entity than other sorts of dispositions: thinking (or "mental"?) dispositions are one thing; physical/chemical/biological/everyday dispositions are another. If so, they need to explain and justify such a distinction.

27. As such, they constitute a wholly legitimate and important focus for educational research of the sort cited above, which promises a deeper understanding of their cognitive character, an increased grasp of their role in the design of tests of thinking, and promising new approaches to fostering their development in the classroom.

Needless to say, my main focus here has been to say something about what thinking dispositions are. I have not seriously addressed the pedagogical question concerning how best to foster thinking (and other desirable) dispositions. On that question I am largely in agreement with the suggestions of Arnstine (1991), Arnstine (1995), Burbules (1995), Perkins, Jay, and Tishman (1993) and Perkins et al. (2000). Future research promises important insights into this pedagogical question.

28. I am grateful to Donald Arnstine, Nicholas Burbules, Edward Erwin, Risto Hilpinen, Stephen Norris, Israel Scheffler, Shari Tishman, and those who heard it presented at the University of Ljubljana in 1997 for insightful criticisms of and good suggestions concerning an earlier draft. A plan to present the paper at a meeting of the South Atlantic Philosophy of Education Society (SAPES) meeting in September 1998 was frustrated by Hurricane Georges, whose path threatened Miami and forced the cancellation of my flight. Nevertheless, I am grateful to SAPES for inviting me to present the paper; to Peter Carbone, who delivered the paper in my absence; to my commentators—Jim Garrison, Peter Hessling, Beatrice Sarlos, and Lynda Stone—from whose comments I have benefitted; and to Robert Heslep, for his insightful criticism and suggestions. The paper was presented at a meeting of the Northwest Philosophy of Education Society, Vancouver, January 1999; my thanks to those in attendance on that occasion for their stimulating comments. Finally, I am indebted to the anonymous referees.

References

Alexander, H. A. (ed.). (1993). *Philosophy of Education 1992: Proceedings of the 48th Annual Meeting of the Philosophy of Education Society*. Urbana, IL: Philosophy of Education Society.

Armstrong, D. M., C. B. Martin, and U. T. Place. (1996). *Dispositions: A Debate*. Edited by T. Crane. New York: Routledge.

Arnstine, B. (1991). "Rational and Caring Teachers: How Dispositional Aims Shape Teacher Preparation." In Ericson 1991, pp. 2–21.

Arnstine, D. (1995). *Democracy and the Arts of Schooling*. Albany: State University of New York Press.

Brandon, R. (1990). *Adaptation and Environment*. Princeton, NJ: Princeton University Press.

Burbules, N. C. (1995). "Reasonable Doubt: Toward a Postmodern Defense of Reason as an Educational Aim." In Wendy Kohli (ed.), *Critical Conversations in Philosophy of Education* (pp. 82–102). New York: Routledge.

Crooks, S. (1995). "Developing the Critical Attitude." *Teaching Philosophy* 18.4: 313–325.

Ennis, R. H. (1987). "A Taxonomy of Critical Thinking Dispositions and Abilities." In J. B. Baron and R. J. Sternberg (eds.), *Teaching for Thinking* (pp. 9–26). New York: W. H. Freeman.

Ennis, R. H. (1993). "Critical Thinking: What Is It?." In Alexander 1993, pp. 76–80.
Ennis, R. H., and S. P. Norris. (1990). "Critical Thinking Assessment: Status, Issues, Needs." In S. Legg and J. Algina (eds.), *Cognitive Assessment of Language and Math Outcomes* (pp. 1–42). Norwood, NJ: Ablex.
Ericson, D. P. (ed.). (1991). *Philosophy of Education 1990: Proceedings of the 46th Annual Meeting of the Philosophy of Education Society*. Normal, IL: Philosophy of Education Society.
Erwin, E. (1997). *Philosophy and Psychotherapy: Razing the Troubles of the Brain*. London: Sage.
Kitcher, P., and W. Salmon (eds.). (1989). *Scientific Explanation*. Minneapolis: University of Minnesota Press.
Lipman, M. (1988). *Philosophy Goes to School*. Philadelphia: Temple University Press.
McCarthy, C. (1993). "Why Be Critical? (Or Rational, or Moral?): On the Justification of Critical Thinking." In Alexander 1993, pp. 60–68.
McPeck, J. (1990). *Teaching Critical Thinking*. New York: Routledge.
McPeck, J. (1993). "Underlying Traits of Critical Thinkers: A Response to Stephen Norris." In Alexander 1993, pp. 58–59.
Mills, S. K., and Beatty J. H. (1979). "The Propensity Interpretation of Fitness." *Philosophy of Science* 46.2: 263–286.
Moshman, D. (1998). "Cognitive Development beyond Childhood." In D. Kuhn and R. Siegler (eds.), *Handbook of Child Psychology*. Volume 2, *Cognition, Perception, and Language* (pp. 947–978). 5th ed. New York: Wiley.
Norris, S. P. (1989). "Can We Test Validly for Critical Thinking?" *Educational Researcher* 18.9: 21–26.
Norris, S. P. (ed.). (1992a). *The Generalizability of Critical Thinking: Multiple Perspectives on an Educational Ideal*. New York: Teachers College Press.
Norris, S. P. (1992b). "Introduction: The Generalizability Question." In Norris 1992a, pp. 1–15.
Norris, S. P. (1993). "Bachelors, Buckyballs, and Ganders: Seeking Analogues for Definitions of 'Critical Thinking.'" In Alexander 1993, pp. 49–57.
Norris, S. P. (1995). "Format Effects on Critical Thinking Test Performance." *Alberta Journal of Educational Research* 41: 378–406.
Norris, S. P. (2003). "The Meaning of Critical Thinking Test Performance: The Effects of Abilities and Dispositions on Scores." In D. Fasko (ed.), *Critical Thinking and Reasoning: Current Research, Theory, and Practice* (pp. 315–330). Cresskill, NJ: Hampton Press.
Olson, D. R., and N. Babu. (1992). "Critical Thinking as Critical Discourse." In Norris 1992a, pp. 181–197.
Passmore, J. (1967). "On Teaching to Be Critical." In R.S. Peters (ed.), *The Concept of Education* (pp. 192–211). London: Routledge & Kegan Paul.
Paul, R. W. (1990). *Critical Thinking: What Every Person Needs to Survive in a Rapidly Changing World*. Edited by A. J. A. Binker. Rohnert Park, CA: Center for Critical Thinking and Moral Critique, Sonoma State University.
Perkins, D. N., E. Jay, and S. Tishman. (1993). "Beyond Abilities: A Dispositional Theory of Thinking." *Merrill-Palmer Quarterly* 39: 1–21.
Perkins, D. N. and S. Tishman. (1997). "Dispositional Aspects of Intelligence." Paper presented at the Second Spearman Seminar, "Intelligence and Personality: Bridging the Gap in Theory and Measurement," University of Plymouth, Devon, England, July 1997.
Perkins, D. N., S. Tishman, R. Ritchhart, K. Donis, and A. Andrade. (2000). "Intelligence in the Wild: A Dispositional View of Intellectual Traits." *Educational Psychology Review* 12.3: 269–293.
Quine, W. V. (1960). *Word and Object*. Cambridge, MA: MIT Press.
Quine, W. V. (1974). *The Roots of Reference*. LaSalle, IL: Open Court.
Quine, W. V. (1995). *From Stimulus to Science*. Cambridge, MA: Harvard University Press.
Ryle, G. (1949). *The Concept of Mind*. New York: Barnes and Noble.
Scheffler, I. (1963). *The Anatomy of Inquiry: Philosophical Studies in the Theory of Science*. Indianapolis: Bobbs-Merrill.
Siegel, H. (1988). *Educating Reason: Rationality, Critical Thinking, and Education*. New York: Routledge.

Siegel, H. (1991). "Fostering the Disposition to Be Rational." In Ericson 1991, pp. 27–31.
Siegel, H. (1993). "On Defining "Critical Thinker" and Justifying Critical Thinking." In Alexander 1993, pp. 72–75.
Siegel, H. (1997). *Rationality Redeemed?: Further Dialogues on an Educational Ideal*. New York: Routledge.
Tuomela, R. (ed.). (1978). *Dispositions*. Dordrecht, The Netherlands: D. Reidel.

5

"You Take the Wheel, I'm Tired of Driving; Jesus, Show Me the Way"

Doctrines, Indoctrination, and the Suppression of Critical Dispositions

1. Ben Spiecker on Indoctrination

According to Ben Spiecker's important account of it, indoctrination involves *the inculcation of doctrines*, which itself involves the *suppression of critical dispositions, intellectual virtues, and rational emotions*. All of these expressions require some explication.

Doctrines, in Spiecker's view, are "a special class of beliefs [that] relate to issues that are considered to be of the utmost importance to us, like the nature and ultimate destination of mankind and the way in which a just society is to be organized" (1991, p. 16)[1]. They "are those systems of belief that to a large extent determine the doings and dealings of the adherents" (p. 17). It is a sufficient condition of indoctrination that a doctrine be inculcated (p. 16).

Such *inculcation*, and so indoctrination, "is always associated with the suppression of a critical attitude" and with "the hampering of intellectual virtues and rational emotions" (p. 16). Doctrines are "screened ... from criticism, from questions about their *validity*"; they "persist by virtue of non-critical attitudes" (p. 17, emphasis in original). On Spiecker's view, then, a victim of indoctrination has a non-critical attitude. The indoctrinator "willfully" (p. 17) suppresses the development of students' critical attitudes and dispositions.

The suppression of a critical attitude and of critical dispositions is importantly connected by Spiecker (along with long-time collaborator Jan Steutel) to the suppression of *intellectual virtues* (open-mindedness, respect for evidence and for the considered arguments of others, impartiality, intellectual honesty, consistency, tolerance towards rival views, intellectual modesty, etc.) and *rational emotions* (love of truth, valuing of reasons and evidence, concern for accuracy, contempt for lying, evasion and distortion, etc.).[2] Spiecker and Steutel's (1997) penetrating analysis of intellectual virtues and rational emotions is of the first importance in its own right; it also enhances Spiecker's account of indoctrination, by clarifying the virtues and emotions that indoctrination suppresses.

2. Indoctrination and Liberal Civic Education

Spiecker and Steutel relate the critical attitudes and dispositions that are central to critical thinking (and that sharply contrast with the attitudes and dispositions of the indoctrinated) to the intellectual virtues and rational emotions just noted. They argue, further, that this complex of critical attitudes and dispositions, intellectual virtues, and rational emotions—which I will call the *critical complex*—is fundamental to *liberal civic education*, i.e., education for citizenship in a liberal state, and that indoctrination is therefore antithetical to such education.[3] Their idea is that the very attitudes, dispositions, intellectual virtues, and rational emotions that indoctrination suppresses are those that enable a liberal state to function and flourish, and that citizenship in such a state requires. Consequently, indoctrination is antithetical to liberal civic education.

Spiecker and Steutel are, in my view, completely correct about the centrality of the critical complex to liberal civic education. Moreover, Spiecker's account of indoctrination, of which a central aspect is the suppression of critical dispositions—and by extension, the suppression of the critical complex—is an important attempt to relate indoctrination to a far broader range of educational issues than is usually the case. Philosophers of education typically discuss indoctrination as it relates to individual students. But Spiecker (and Steutel) make(s) clear that the matter has important social, moral educational, and political ramifications. In this respect, their contributions seem to me to be both highly important and almost entirely correct.

3. Three Problems for Spiecker's Account of Indoctrination

I am in considerable sympathy with Spiecker's account of indoctrination in terms of the suppression of a critical attitude and critical dispositions; my own account runs along these same lines (Siegel 1988, ch. 5). I also have great sympathy for Spiecker's (and Steutel's) relation of indoctrination to the broader themes of intellectual virtues, rational emotions, and liberal civic education. However, I have three reservations concerning Spiecker's account, which I develop next. The most important of these is his limiting of the *content* of doctrines, and thus indoctrination, to those systems of belief that "to a large extent determine the doings and dealings of the adherents" (p. 17). By limiting doctrines to (basically) moral, political, and religious beliefs, the account fails to acknowledge that students can be indoctrinated in a far broader way; namely, that students can be led to non-critical attitudes and dispositions generally, and that these can affect all their beliefs, including their scientific beliefs. These three problems can, I think, be easily resolved by modest, judicious revisions, which keep intact the core idea that indoctrination is fundamentally a matter of protecting beliefs from critical scrutiny.

A. The Relation between Doctrines and Indoctrination

Spiecker holds that it is a necessary condition of something counting as a doctrine that it be "screened from criticism, from a critical attitude" (p. 17). But while Spiecker is correct (in my view) to think that such "screening" is a necessary condition of indoctrination, it does not seem right to regard it as a necessary condition of a belief or a belief system's constituting a doctrine, for if it is, whether or not a given belief or system counts as a doctrine will depend, counterintuitively, upon the way in which it is believed. Consider a given belief or belief system *BS*. Whatever its content, whether political, religious, literary, scientific, or whatever, it will be possible for one person, "Mineke the Critical Thinker," to hold it on the basis of critical reflection, and for another, "Hans the Indoctrinated," to hold it because he has been prevented from subjecting it to critical scrutiny. In this case, *BS* would count (on Spiecker's account) as a doctrine for Hans, but would not count as a doctrine for Mineke. But whether or not *BS* is a doctrine should not depend on the way it is believed by different believers. Rather, a belief system ought to count as a doctrine on the basis of its formal characteristics and its content (e.g., that it is sufficiently broad, internally consistent, and capable of determining "the doings and dealings of the adherents") independently of its (not) having been screened from criticism. Consequently, the "screening from criticism" that Spiecker points to seems to me to be better understood as a necessary condition not of doctrines, but rather of indoctrination. Hans' uncritical embrace of *BS* is a mark not of *BS*' status as a doctrine, but rather of Hans' having been indoctrinated.

B. The Possibility of Non-indoctrinating Belief Inculcation

Is it correct that "inculcating doctrines is always associated with the suppression of a critical attitude," and thus that the inculcation of doctrines always involves indoctrination? (p. 16). Given Spiecker's account of "doctrine," this appears to be true by definition. Even so, there are other sorts of belief inculcation that are not obviously indoctrinating—indeed, are obviously non-indoctrinating—in that they do not involve the suppression of a critical attitude or disposition. A good teacher (or parent) can inculcate beliefs in her students, concerning (for example) arithmetic, science, politics, religion, history, or government, while at the same time fostering in those students the critical attitudes and dispositions that Spiecker rightly prizes, even with respect to the very beliefs inculcated. We should not infer, from the claim that the inculcation of doctrines always involves indoctrination, the much stronger claim that all belief inculcation necessarily constitutes indoctrination. The inculcation of beliefs might, but need not, involve indoctrination. Consequently, an account of indoctrination should not preclude the possibility of non-indoctrinating belief inculcation.[4]

Spiecker does not claim that non-indoctrinating *belief* inculcation is impossible; his claim is rather that non-indoctrinating *doctrine* inculcation is impossible. Nevertheless, his account comes dangerously and unnecessarily close to precluding the possibility of non-indoctrinating belief inculcation, because on his view the inculcation of doctrines always involves indoctrination; the possibility of non-indoctrinating belief inculcation exists on his account only because of his sharp distinction between doctrines and other beliefs. In the next section I criticize that distinction. If that criticism succeeds, the possibility in question disappears from Spiecker's account. That account can be saved by denying that distinction (as I will urge below), or by relaxing the alleged necessary connection between the inculcation of doctrines and indoctrination (as I have urged above), or both. The point here is that Spiecker wants and needs to allow the possibility of non-indoctrinating belief inculcation, but is unable to do so except by holding both that a sharp doctrine/non-doctrinal-belief distinction can be drawn and that the inculcation of doctrines always involves indoctrination. But these are both problematic. I have criticized the latter in the previous section; I turn to the former in the next.

C. The Scope of "Doctrines" and "Indoctrination": The Allegedly Limited Domain of Indoctrination

The main problem for Spiecker's account, I believe, is its limitation on the *scope* of "indoctrination" to what is in the end an arbitrary subclass of beliefs and belief systems. On Spiecker's view, students are in general not subject to indoctrination in particular subjects—he mentions science and mathematics (p. 17)—that are not "considered to be of the utmost importance to us" (p. 16), and/or do not "to a large extent determine the doings and dealings of the adherents" (p. 17). There are two problems with this limitation. First, it is unclear how to distinguish systematically between those subjects "of the utmost importance to us," that "to a large extent determine [our] doings and dealings," and those of less importance, that do not so determine. Second, so limiting indoctrination is in tension with the fundamental idea that indoctrination is marked by the suppression of critical dispositions. I develop these in turn.

i. Which subjects, beliefs, or belief systems are "of the utmost importance to us"? There does not seem to be a univocal answer to this question. What I judge to be of the utmost importance, you might well judge to be of less importance, or indeed of no importance at all. Similarly, what "to a large extent determines [my] doings and dealings" might determine your doings and dealings to a far lesser extent. You might be guided mainly by your religious beliefs, while I might be guided mainly by my political or philosophical or scientific beliefs. In other words, the singling out of a special subclass of our beliefs as subject to indoctrination seems in the end arbitrary, in that there does not appear to be any non-arbitrary way to do this. In any case, doing it in terms either of specific subject matter content, perceived importance, or action-guiding influence seems clearly not to work.

Spiecker offers *science* as an example of a subject normally not subject to indoctrination. Is it true that scientific beliefs are not subject to indoctrination? Consider the fundamentalist Christian who rejects evolution in favor of "creation science." Is it not even possible that instances of this rejection be rightly understood as a matter of indoctrination? Why not? Suppose that Johan attends Bob Jones University, and while there is indoctrinated into a fundamentalist Christian belief system. At that "university," Johan takes the required biology class, during which the students are instructed in the Bob Jones view, according to which evolutionary theory is a front for "secular humanism," and "scientific" creationism is the only legitimate account of all matters biological. As a result of Johan's experience in that class, he comes to embrace the creationist belief system and embraces those beliefs in the uncritical way that Spiecker so well describes. Would it not be perfectly straightforward to describe this case as one in which Johan is indoctrinated into a "creationist biological" belief system? Examples like this make it clear that scientific beliefs can be indoctrinated just as readily as can religious, political, or other beliefs, and moreover that scientific belief systems cannot be systematically distinguished from religious or other belief systems, since Johan's biological belief system has a clear religious component. Neither subject matter, perceived importance, nor action-guiding significance will suffice to distinguish a subclass of beliefs that are subject to indoctrination from the remainder of the class of beliefs that are not.[5]

ii. The point becomes more clear when we consider that aspect of indoctrination about whose importance Spiecker and I are agreed: the suppression of critical attitudes and dispositions. Let us agree that such suppression is a key feature of indoctrination. Should we think that it can occur only with respect to particular beliefs? What reason do we have for so thinking? As far as I can see, we have no such reason. On the contrary, critical attitudes and dispositions can be suppressed generally, and in egregious cases this is exactly what happens: no matter what subject matter or belief is under consideration, the indoctrinated (e.g.) Marxist, Maoist, or Christian will determine his or her own belief by consulting the canonical texts, or their *BS*-authoritative interpreters; asking "What would Jesus (or Karl or Mao or Jerry Falwell) think?"; and believing accordingly. The indoctrinated believer, that is, may have his or her critical attitudes and dispositions suppressed *generally*, and not just with respect to some particular subset of subjects or beliefs. Indeed, this seems likely, given the difficulty, just noted, of picking out a subset from the larger set of beliefs as that subset alone subject to indoctrination. Thus, the idea that indoctrination is restricted to a particular class of doctrines, which is itself a subclass of the larger class of subjects, beliefs, or belief systems, is in tension with the idea that indoctrination is fundamentally a matter of the suppression of critical attitudes and dispositions. My proposal is that the tension be resolved by giving up the former and maintaining the latter.

In thus tweaking Spiecker's account so as to avoid or resolve these three problems—by dropping the ideas that a belief system's counting as a doctrine is a matter of the way in which it is believed (rather than its formal characteristics and content), that all belief/doctrine inculcation is necessarily indoctrinating, and that only certain sorts of beliefs/belief systems are subject to indoctrination—I mean to be merely strengthening it around the edges, rather than pointing out any basic flaw. This is because I think that Spiecker's account, according to which indoctrination fundamentally involves the suppression of critical attitudes and dispositions, and the concomitant suppression of intellectual virtues and rational emotions, is essentially correct.[6]

4. The Remedied Account Defended: A Lyrical Test Case

I propose now to offer as a test case of Spiecker's account the lyrics of a recent country/bluegrass/gospel song, "The Wheel."[7] The lyrics are as follows:

> *Verse 1*: I left home at seventeen,
> Coast to coast and everywhere between,
> Looking for trouble, came so easy to me.
> I was going nowhere, moving too fast,
> Every day could be my last,
> I'm at the end of the line, good Lord help me please.
>
> *Verse 2*: Rolling down a rocky road,
> On this life of sin I'd chose,
> Out of control, I was running blind.
> Now I'm pulling over, changing drivers,

> I'm gonna be a soul survivor,
> Leaving all those wicked ways behind.
>
> *Chorus*: You take the wheel, I'm tired of driving,
> You take the wheel, I'm tired of driving,
> You take the wheel, I'm tired of driving,
> Jesus, show me the way.

It is admittedly something of a stretch to look for philosophical wisdom in this sort of popular music, which is not, after all, noted for its intellectual sophistication or depth. Nevertheless, these lyrics raise questions concerning the putative value of the critical complex, and by implication the putative disvalue of indoctrination, in a particularly pointed way. So, is the sincere singer of this song either a victim or an advocate of indoctrination? Let us briefly consider how Spiecker's account deals with this question.

It should be noted, first, that the singer—whom I assume is singing the song sincerely (i.e., he genuinely wants to "hand the wheel over to Jesus")—is asking, in effect, for a permanent vacation from the tasks associated with autonomous thinking and deciding. Is so asking a sign of indoctrination? Spiecker's account correctly says "no," since the singer's request could result from a critical assessment of his current state and ability to cope with life's demands. However, it seems clear that the singer is *advocating* his own indoctrination, since he is seeking to be freed from his presumed critical dispositions and protected from "the shafts of impartial evidence" (Russell 1957, p. vii). And here Spiecker's advice is clear: this is *not* a good thing to advocate, for oneself or for others, for the reasons his account provides.

Can one choose, autonomously and critically, to give up one's autonomy and critical thinking? As the example suggests, as a matter of psychological fact it seems clear that one can. In asking Jesus to take the wheel and relieve him of the burden of utilizing the critical complex and thinking for himself, the singer is perhaps not yet indoctrinated. But he is in effect asking, desiring, and choosing to be indoctrinated. What does Spiecker's account say about this?

As Spiecker notes (p. 19), so choosing suggests a psychological weakness or deficiency. The issue here is one of psychological health. If the absence of psychological health is a potentially powerful obstacle to the exercise of critical thinking, as Spiecker and I both believe, then the singer's plaintive refrain might be best understood not as a mark of indoctrination, but rather as an indication of psychological fragility, an inability to accept responsibility, and perhaps a sign of clinical depression.

In the narrow, Anglo-American sense of "education," according to which education is largely a matter of schooling, it is somewhat unclear what responsibility education has for the provision of psychological health. In the broader, European sense of childrearing (*opvoeding* in Dutch), education's responsibility concerning such health is clear. Spiecker wisely embraces this responsibility, urging that education strive to foster psychological health as a precondition of critical thinking and its requirements concerning critical attitudes and dispositions. In this way his account acknowledges psychological reality and education's need to address it, while simultaneously affirming its aim of fostering critical thinking and its duty to avoid indoctrination.

The example also highlights the distinction between the *capacity* for critical thinking and its *exercise*. The singer manifests the capacity in his request to Jesus, but desires not to exercise it, preferring instead to let Jesus "take the wheel." This is an important distinction that acceptable accounts of critical thinking and indoctrination must recognize. It is well marked by Spiecker's emphasis on critical dispositions, since on his account one can possess the skills and abilities of, and so the capacity for, critical thinking, without having the disposition to exercise that capacity.

The issues raised by these lyrics are fundamental ones that I have only superficially addressed. But it seems clear that Spiecker's account can handle them without undo difficulty. Moreover, a clear strength of the account is its forceful treatment of the psychological dimensions of indoctrination, a matter to which most accounts of indoctrination do not attend. Whether or not Spiecker's account of indoctrination and the critical complex satisfactorily resolves them— a matter too complex to resolve definitively here—it is a sign of the depth of that account that it very plausibly addresses them. Spiecker has provided an important account of indoctrination, and of several related topics, that students of philosophy of education are well advised to subject to critical scrutiny. I predict that it will survive such scrutiny largely intact.[8]

Notes

1. All untethered page references to Spieker are to his "Indoctrination: The Suppression of Critical Dispositions" (1991).
2. Spiecker 1991, pp. 18–20; cf. Spiecker and Steutel 1995, p. 392–393; Spiecker and Steutel 2001, p. 303; Steutel and Spiecker 1999, p. 62; Steutel and Spiecker 1997, p. 59 and *passim*.
3. Spiecker and Steutel 1995; Steutel and Spiecker 1999; Spiecker and Steutel 2001.
4. I have defended both the possibility and the educational importance of non-indoctrinating belief inculcation in Siegel 1988, ch. 5.
5. Spiecker acknowledges the point about creationism, but in effect denies that it challenges this aspect of his view (p. 20; see also pp. 17, 21).
6. My own account, according to which indoctrination is marked by a *non-evidential style of belief* (Siegel 1988, ch. 5), is very similar to Spiecker's account as just adjusted, although it should be emphasized that his account is put to far broader use than mine in his and Steutel's extension of it to liberal civic education.

7. "The Wheel," written by T. Villanueva, R. Ellsworth Carter, and B. Carter, recorded by The Derailers on their CD *Genuine* (2003: Sony Music Entertainment Inc.).
8. Thanks to Jan Steutel and Leendert Groenendijk for inviting my participation in this project and for their helpful advice and criticisms of an earlier draft.

    I owe Ben Spiecker a large debt, and am happy to have the opportunity to publicly acknowledge that debt here. I first met Spiecker in the fall of 1990 when I was spending a semester at the University of Amsterdam. We spent a fair amount of time (along with Jan Steutel and Wouter van Haaften) getting to know each other philosophically and struck up a friendship that still endures: one of my favorite activities remains "roddeling" with Spiecker about the various movements of the denizens of the philosophy of education world. During that semester, Spiecker suggested that I apply for a newly advertised position in the Department of History and Philosophy of Education at the Rijksuniversiteit Groningen. The eventual occupant of the position, Jeroen Dekker, very generously invited me to the RuG to serve as a visiting professor. Thanks to Spiecker's suggestion and Dekker's generosity, my family and I spent five summers in Groningen, a delightful period that we all remember with fondness. The position gave us a marvelous opportunity to get to know Europe, and it gave me the chance to solidify relationships with European philosophers and philosophers of education. It remains a singularly important period in my life, one that I would not have experienced but for Spiecker. It is a great pleasure to thank him in this Festschrift that celebrates his philosophical contributions. Dank je wel, Ben!

References

Russell, B. (1957). *Why I Am Not a Christian and Other Essays*. London: George Allen & Unwin Ltd.

Siegel, H. (1988). *Educating Reason: Rationality, Critical Thinking, and Education*. London: Routledge.

Spiecker, B. (1991). "Indoctrination: The Suppression of Critical Dispositions." In B. Spiecker and R. Straughan (eds.), *Freedom and Indoctrination in Education: International Perspectives* (pp. 16–29). London: Cassell.

Spiecker, B., and J. Steutel. (1995). "Political Liberalism, Civic Education and the Dutch Government." *Journal of Moral Education* 24.4: 383–394.

Spiecker, B., and J. Steutel. (2001). "Multiculturalism, Pillarization and Liberal Civic Education in the Netherlands." *International Journal of Educational Research* 35.3: 293–304.

Steutel, J., and B. Spiecker. (1997). "Rational Passions and Intellectual Virtues: A Conceptual Analysis." In H. Siegel (ed.), *Reason and Education: Essays in Honor of Israel Scheffler* (pp. 59–71). Dordrecht, The Netherlands: Kluwer.

Steutel, J., and B. Spiecker. (1999). "Liberalism and Critical Thinking: On the Relation between a Political Ideal and an Aim of Education." In R. Marples (ed.), *The Aims of Education* (pp. 61–73). London: Routledge.

6

The Role of Reasons in Moral Education

1. Reasons: What Are They?

Most generally, and in a slogan, reasons are *considerations that purport to support* candidate beliefs, judgments, and actions. That is, *p* is a reason for *q* if *p* is a consideration that, if good, favors or counts in favor of some specific belief, judgment, or action *q*. Let us call the beliefs, judgments, and actions that reasons purport to support *targets*. Some examples are given in Table 1.

The items in the left-hand column are reasons for the corresponding items in the right-hand column. What is the significance of calling them "reasons"? Most fundamentally, calling them reasons indicates that, if they are any good, they provide *support* for their corresponding targets; that is, they are considerations that count in favor of their targets, and, at least to some extent, render their targets *worthy* of belief, judgment, or action.

The italicized slogan stands in need of qualification. Strictly speaking, reasons are not the sort of thing that can purport anything, so the slogan should not be taken literally. The important aspect of the slogan is not "purport" but "support": reasons—if they are good reasons—stand in supportive relations to the things for which they are reasons. I use "purport" in the slogan in order to acknowledge that not all reasons in fact support their intended targets: bad reasons, non-reasons, pseudo-reasons, etc., may be offered in support

Table 1 **Examples of reasons and the targets they support**

Reasons	Targets
The ground is wet.	It has rained here recently.
She is intelligent, thoughtful, and socially adept.	She is a strong candidate for the position.
Hitting him will hurt him.	You should not hit him.

of some *q* but fail to provide the support in question. It is the support that is key. (For example, someone may offer "the ground is *dry*" as a reason for believing that "it has rained here recently," in a modified version of the first example above, but the offered reason provides no support for that belief.) In saying that reasons "*purport* to support," I mean to indicate just that candidate reasons can fail to support their targets, being either bad reasons or non-reasons.

There are many different kinds of reasons. Philosophers distinguish between *theoretical* and *practical* reasons. The former involve reasons for *belief*; the latter, reasons for *action*. They distinguish as well between *instrumental*, means-ends reasons and *categorical* reasons. The former involves the conduciveness of means to the efficacious achievement of particular goals or ends ("If you want to do well on the exam, study hard"); the latter involves reasons not aimed at or limited to any particular ends ("Whatever your practical ends, you owe it to yourself to do your best on the exam"). There are deep, important philosophical issues concerning these and related distinctions and types of reasons, but I will pass over them here. For our purposes, the key feature of reasons is just their tendency (or failure) to provide the requisite support for their targets.

So understood, reasons are at the heart of the educational ideal of *critical thinking*. Many educational philosophers/theorists, myself included, regard critical thinking as a fundamental educational ideal, central to curriculum, policy, and practice. To regard critical thinking as a fundamental educational ideal is to hold that educational activities ought to be designed and conducted in such a way that the construction and evaluation of reasons (in accordance with relevant criteria) are paramount throughout the curriculum. What is critical thinking? While there are a range of theoretical accounts of it, with varying emphases and the usual helping of philosophical controversies, most accounts understand it as involving both (1) a *reason assessment* component, encompassing the skills and abilities needed to create, recognize, and evaluate candidate reasons; and (2) a *critical spirit* component, usually understood to involve a host of dispositions, habits of mind, and character traits, such as a propensity to seek and evaluate candidate reasons, a willingness to subject one's beliefs and values to critical scrutiny, open-mindedness, fair-mindedness, and intellectual modesty or humility. It is in the context of the critical spirit that the education of the *intellectual virtues* finds its natural home (Steutel and Spiecker 1997, 1999).

Much more can and should be said about the proper articulation of the ideal of critical thinking and the place of reasons within it, but saying so would distract us from the present topic. Here we must be content to note that that topic is importantly connected to that concerning the identity and character of our most fundamental educational ideals.[1]

2. Moral Education: What Is Its Aim?

Moral education is one of the most contentious areas of educational endeavor. What are we trying to accomplish when we engage in the moral education of our children and/or students? Are we trying to pass on to them our own moral beliefs? Are we trying rather to enable them to make their own moral judgments? To make them particular kinds of people? No doubt the answers to these questions will depend upon who "we" are. But another set of questions is perhaps more tractable. These questions concern the aspects or dimensions of our children and students that we ought to be trying to influence when we engage in moral education: Ought we to try to influence their *actions*, their *beliefs*, their *thinking/reasoning*, their *habits*, their *character*, and/or their *sentiments*? Let us consider each in turn.

A. Actions

This is perhaps the most obvious thing we want our moral education efforts to affect. Consider the parent of a small child telling him not to hit his little sister or take her toys without first asking for and receiving her permission. Normally, the parent wants the child, first and foremost, to behave properly. That is, the parent wants the child not to hit his sister or take her toys. More generally, we don't want only that the small child believe that he shouldn't hit his little sister, we want him actually not to hit her. Action, then, seems to be a proper target of moral education—*prima facie*, moral education has a proper *action-guiding* aim.

B. Beliefs

When we engage in moral education, should we try to guide, shape, or otherwise influence the beliefs of our children, students and/or peers? It seems undeniable that most of us in fact do so try. Should we?

Often, at least, we should. Consider again the parent of a small child telling him not to hit his little sister or take her toys without asking first. Normally, the parent wants the child not only to behave properly, but to believe properly, too. That is, the child should come to believe that it is wrong to—and so he should not—hit his sister or take her toys.

Belief figures in the moral education of older children and adults, too. When teenagers and college students behave badly, we want not only to correct their behavior, but their beliefs as well. ("It's wrong to, and so you should not, text while driving; it puts innocent people at risk.") And in political discussions concerning moral matters—for example, whether the state has a moral obligation to provide health care for all its citizens, or whether, and if so under what conditions, immigrants should be extended certain benefits—we want to affect our interlocutors' beliefs as well as their political allegiances. We could debate whether the latter example should be counted as an example of moral education. But since the intended end result of such discussions is at least often the bringing about of a change of opinion concerning moral matters, it seems appropriate to call this too a matter of moral education. (Consider: "After our conversation I realize that I have a moral obligation to give more to charity than I have been giving." In such a case, shouldn't we count the conversation as an episode of moral education? Moral education needn't take place only in homes or schools, and it needn't involve children.)

Belief change, then, seems also to be a proper aim of moral education. At least one of the things we hope our moral education efforts will affect is the beliefs of our children, students and peers. So it appears that moral education also has a *belief-guiding* aim.[2]

C. Thinking/Reasoning

While it seems true that moral education rightly aims at influencing both the beliefs and the actions of the morally educated, we must be careful to acknowledge important constraints on the practice of moral education. We cannot impart beliefs or foster actions in our students willy-nilly. As moral educators, we have no alternative but to impart beliefs to young children, and to encourage them to act in particular ways, before they are able to reason about the standing of those beliefs and actions. But we want our students to be able, eventually, to consider for themselves the reasons for and against those beliefs and actions. ("Why shouldn't I take my sister's toys?"; "Why should I give to charity?") We don't want to *indoctrinate* students into any particular set of moral beliefs, or provoke them into thoughtlessly or irrationally acting in morally evaluable ways. (I concentrate next on belief, setting aside action for the moment, in order to focus briefly on the threat of indoctrination and its proper avoidance.)

How we can impart beliefs *sans* reasons while avoiding indoctrination is a tricky matter. Certainly, part of the story involves fostering students' *autonomy*, their ability to *think critically*, and their *critical dispositions*, so that they can eventually judge competently for themselves the strength of the reasons for imparted (and other candidate) beliefs.[3]

More generally, whatever we want to say about indoctrination and its avoidance, an important aim of moral education is the enhancement of students' abilities to *think well* about moral matters. Our moral education would not be successful, or of high quality, if we got students to believe and act in accordance with our own views about moral matters, but left them at the end of their moral education unable to say or understand why their beliefs and actions are/have been worthy, or to think intelligently about objections and alternatives to them. If this is right, then the ability to *reason well* concerning moral matters is also a proper aim of moral education. That is to say, moral education has a *reason-guiding* aim.[4]

D. Habits

Aristotle famously argued that the development of proper habits is an important aim of moral education: "The virtues arise in us ... through habit.... We become just by doing just actions, temperate by doing temperate actions, brave by doing brave actions" (Aristotle, *Nicomachean Ethics*, 1103a-b). Many other thinkers, including Dewey and R. S. Peters, have agreed with Aristotle's dictum. One can question whether the development of habits is an intrinsic aim of moral education, or whether it is only instrumental for the achievement of virtue or one of the other noted aims of moral education. Resolving this question is not essential here, so long as it is agreed that in some guise the development of proper habits is a legitimate aim (whether intrinsic or instrumental) of moral education. So, with this qualification in hand, let us grant the point: an important aim of moral education is the development of proper habits. That is, moral education has a *habit-guiding* aim.

E. Virtue/Character

Aristotle is also associated with the view that an important aim of moral education is the development in students of *moral virtues*, or *traits of character*. Traits such as honesty, empathy, sympathy, fair-mindedness, and so on are generally thought to be both important virtues and virtues that it is the proper function of moral education to foster. The parent wants her small child not just to not hit his little sister, but to develop a virtuous, morally praiseworthy character that disposes him not to do such things. Let us grant that moral education also has a *virtue-* or *character-guiding* aim.

There are many deep questions to be asked concerning such virtues/character traits. For example: Are intellectual virtues a subclass of moral virtues, or are these distinct sorts of virtues? If distinct, is the task of moral education the fostering of both kinds of virtue or only the moral ones? Steutel and Spiecker (1997) offer a penetrating analysis of both sorts of virtue and of the relations between them; I regret that space precludes consideration of their complex and instructive discussion here.

F. Sentiments

Closely related to, or perhaps a species of, habit and virtue/character views are those that focus on *feelings* or *sentiments*. Nel Noddings (1984) has famously argued for the fundamentality of *caring* to moral education. Michael Slote has developed an account of moral education that draws not only on the work of Noddings and Carol Gilligan, but also on the sentimentalist moral theories of Hume, Hutcheson, and others, as well as recent psychological work by Martin Hoffman on the character and development of *empathy*. An important feature of Slote's view is that the development of empathy is best understood not as a matter of reason, reasons, reasoning, or rationality, but rather as a psychological process involving the fostering of certain *feelings*. On his view, moral norms are based in human feeling and emotion rather than reason or rationality, and "being moral amounts to being (fully) empathically caring with others" (Slote 2010b, p. 131). An important benefit of the view, Slote argues, is that it offers a better account of moral motivation than do its rationalist alternatives: if the child anticipates *feeling badly* about hitting his sister, he will be less likely to hit her. So an important part of the view involves the "inductive" processes that give rise to such feelings studied by Hoffman.

Slote's account is summarized in his 2010 article "Sentimentalist Moral Education"; I commend it to the reader's attention, along with his books *The Ethics of Care and Empathy* (2007) and *Moral Sentimentalism* (2010a), referred to therein, and the critical essays responding to it published alongside it. In one of them, Noddings endorses much of Slote's view:

> I strongly agree with Slote that moral education should help to cultivate the moral sentiments. We should encourage children to feel good about treating others well and bad about hurting them.... No care theorist would argue against the claim that emotion is more basic to morality than reasoning. (Noddings 2010, p. 148)

At the same time, Nodding raises important questions about various aspects of this view, insisting—as does Slote—that reasons and reasoning nevertheless have an important place in moral education. The just-cited passage continues:

> As Slote explains, that assertion does not imply that reasoning is unimportant in care ethics. On the contrary, care ethics demands a well-developed capacity for reasoning because it does not depend on axiomatic rules and principles. Carers must think well in order to assess and to respond appropriately to the expressed needs of the immediate cared-for while considering the likely effects of their decisions on the wider web of care and on the caring relation itself. Both reflective and instrumental reasoning are required. But feeling motivates our action and moral reasoning at every step. (p. 148)

All of this deserves more attention than I can give it here. For now, let us grant the plausibility of the basic sentimentalist idea, and grant that moral education has a *feeling-, emotion-,* or *sentiment-guiding* aim as well as the others identified thus far. Let us also note that the emotion/reason contrast often used to distinguish sentimentalist from "rationalist" approaches to moral education should not be overdrawn: as the most recently quoted passage makes clear, sentimentalist theories do not reject reason; rather, they find an important, though subordinate, place for it in their theories. I shall return to this point below.

3. The Role of Reasons in Moral Education

Philosophers, psychologists, and moral educators have argued about the legitimacy of the place of each of our six ingredients in a properly conceived and executed moral education. Aristotle and many others have emphasized the importance for moral education of the development of proper habits. Many parents, concerned that their children carry on their moral tradition, take belief to be central, holding that moral education should see to it that their children's moral beliefs mirror their own. Developmental psychologists such as Lawrence Kohlberg, as well as moral philosophers in the broadly Kantian tradition such as Richard M. Hare, Richard S. Peters, and Kurt Baier, take reason/reasoning to be the key to moral education (Curren 2001). Many philosophers have insisted upon the centrality to moral education of the fostering of particular virtues and/or traits of character. Those in the broadly Humean, sentimentalist tradition, in particular Noddings and Slote, have (as just described) argued for the centrality of the development of particular psychological traits or sentiments, especially those of caring and empathy. Almost everyone thinks that moral education ought to result in morally appropriate action. So it appears that all six of our listed ingredients arguably have some legitimate role to play in moral education.

We should acknowledge that these several views of moral education are in various ways at odds with one another, so perhaps we should not concede too quickly that all six of our proposed ingredients are in fact important ingredients of moral education. We should also acknowledge that our six ingredients do not necessarily or obviously exhaust the range of ingredients; room might be made for others. Moreover, almost everything said thus far can be—and most of it in fact has been—challenged by moral philosophers, moral psychologists, or moral educators. That said, I propose to adopt a pluralistic view of the matter here, and assume that moral education properly aims at all six ingredients. That is, it aims to foster morally appropriate belief and action, skilled moral reasoning, morally appropriate habits, morally praiseworthy virtues and character traits, and desirable moral sentiments.

If beliefs, actions, thinking/reasoning, habits, virtues/character traits, and sentiments all have a proper role to play in moral education, how should we understand the role of reasons in moral education? The picture is complicated, because the role, relevance, and influence of reasons vary across our six ingredients: reasons and reasoning appear to be relevant to some, central to others, and perhaps irrelevant to others. Let us consider them in turn.

A. Action

Actions, especially the actions of small children, clearly *can* be influenced by factors other than reasons. For example, we can be guided by fear, a desire to please, and a host of other emotions, as well as by threat, intimidation, force, and other "external" influences. But we can also be guided by reasons, as the practices and studies of "practical reason" and "instrumental reason" indicate: one may act because of, and be guided by, one's reasons. Reasons and reasoning, then, are at least potentially relevant to the guiding of action, but they are not necessary for it. How relevant they are will generally depend on the practices of moral education in play: if we want and try to get small children to not speak unless spoken to, reasons will likely play little role; if we want them to think about how they would feel if someone did something (some particular action that is the focus of the moral education episode) to them, and to guide their own action accordingly, there seems to be a larger action-guiding role for reasons. It seems that reasons needn't, but can, have a role to play in moral education's effort to guide action.

B. Belief

Similar remarks apply to moral education's practices of belief-guidance. Beliefs clearly can be guided by factors other than reasons. For example, they can be guided by practices that indoctrinate, as well as by a range of feelings and emotions. But like actions, beliefs can be guided by reasons as well, and in fact many moral education efforts focus on this sort of belief-guidance. So, as with actions, how relevant reasons and reasoning are to such guidance depends on the practices of moral education in play. If the parent in our earlier example wants her small child to believe that it's wrong to hit his little sister, she can foster this belief by giving reasons ("imagine how you would feel if your big brother did that to you"), or by issuing threats, creating fear, and a variety of other non-reason-involving techniques. So, as with action, it seems that reasons needn't, but can, have a role to play in moral education's effort to guide belief.

C. Thinking/Reasoning

Here, reasons and reasoning are, more or less by definition, central. Insofar as thinking and reasoning are proper dimensions of moral education and their influence is a proper aim of moral education, there must be a place for reasons and reasoning in it.

D. Habit

Habits seem clearly to be the sorts of things that can be developed independently of reasons and reasoning. Practice and drill seem key to their development, and while reasons can, in principle, be utilized in order to motivate such development ("if you don't develop this habit, you'll never win the tournament/become valedictorian/win his/her love"), feelings and emotions can as well. As noted earlier, Aristotle famously urged the importance of the cultivation of habits as important for moral education; interestingly, he is often understood to have championed the habituation of rational understanding rather than emotional response or mindless reaction.[5] Be that as it may, it seems clear that while the development of habits can be influenced by reasons and reasoning, they can readily be developed in non-reasoning ways. As with actions and beliefs, how relevant reasons and reasoning are to the fostering of habits will depend on the practices of moral education in play.

E. Virtue/Character

As with actions, beliefs, and habits, reasons and reasoning needn't, but can, play roles in the fostering of particular virtues and character traits. They can be developed with the aid of reasons and reasoning ("here's why honesty is important"), but they can just as well be developed with the help of appeal to particular emotions or feelings. Here, too, how relevant reasons and reasoning are to the fostering of virtues and character traits will depend on the practices of moral education in play.

F. Sentiment

Sentimental moral education, perhaps exemplified by moral education focused on caring, is often articulated by contrast with reasons and reasoning. But, as we have seen, both Noddings and Slote accept that the latter have a legitimate role to play, even in moral education efforts that are explicitly aimed at the fostering of appropriate sentiments. So even those, like Noddings and Slote, who hold that emotion is more basic to morality and moral education than reasoning find an important (though not dominant) role for reasons and reasoning in moral education. As with actions, beliefs, habits, and virtues, particular sentiments can be developed or enhanced by the use of reasons and reasoning, but can also be fostered in non-reasoning ways. As with the other just-mentioned ingredients, how relevant reasons and reasoning are to the fostering of morally desirable sentiments will depend on the practices of moral education in play.

It seems, then, that of our six ingredients, only one—thinking/reasoning—requires the use of reasons for its development. Reasons needn't, but can, have a role to play in the fostering of the other five in the course of moral education. There is room to argue for an expansive role for reasons in the fostering of those five, but there is equally room to argue for a diminished role. Different approaches to moral education will assign a greater or lesser role to reasons, both in terms of their use in the fostering of those five and in terms of the centrality of the sixth.

4. The Status of the Required Ingredient

I have not offered anything like proper arguments for the legitimacy of each of our six proposed ingredients. The legitimacy of the place of all six can, will, and should be debated by teachers and other educators, including moral educators, and by philosophers, parents, and citizens as well. Nevertheless, each seems plausible enough that the wise course still seems to be the pluralistic one that accepts the proper influence of each as a legitimate aim of moral education.

Supposing that the proper influencing of all six are legitimate dimensions of moral education efforts, it is undeniable that reasons have a place in moral education, for thinking/reasoning is one of the six. But this seems too easy. Can anything more be said by way of establishing a substantial and ineliminable role for reasons in moral education?

I see four considerations that favor such a role. First, there is the prima facie case made above for the place of the fostering of children's/students' abilities to reason about moral matters in moral education and the undeniable role of reasons therein. Second, there are the prima facie cases made for the role of reasons/reasoning in the development of the other five ingredients; while the size and relative importance of that role will vary across the five, it seems clear that reasons will have at least some minor role to play in most, if not all, of them, and might well have a quite substantial role in several, and possibly even all, of them. Third, there is the case (discussed above) made by Noddings and Slote for the important, if subordinate, role of reasons even in moral education conceived along sentimentalist lines. These three considerations seem to me to be collectively quite substantial, and together to establish a strong case for there being some substantial role for reasons in any viable conception of moral education.

Fourth, there is an argument that I have offered elsewhere for the central role of reasons in education generally, in the context of the effort to establish the centrality to education of the ideal of critical thinking.[6] The basic idea is that we are obliged to foster children's/students' critical thinking, because doing so is required by our obligation to treat them with *respect as persons*. The idea that all persons ought to be treated with respect as persons is a Kantian one. As applied to moral education, the claim is that a moral education that fails to foster students' ability to think critically about morality fails to treat them with respect as persons, because, whatever beliefs it imparts, actions it encourages, habits or sentiments it fosters, etc., students so educated will be unable to determine for themselves the worthiness or otherwise of those very beliefs, actions, habits, and so on. Treating students with respect, in other words, requires that we do our best to enable them to decide skillfully for themselves the desirability of candidate beliefs, actions, etc.; to foster their dispositions to exercise their ability to do so; and to invite and encourage that exercise—however threatening to our own beliefs and values it might be. Otherwise, however desirable the outcomes of moral education are, they will have been imposed on students from without, rather than having been embraced from within, on the basis of the students' own independent judgment. In short, we are obliged to treat everyone, including children and students, with respect as persons; doing so requires that we foster and respect their own critical thinking and independent judgment; such thinking and judgment centrally involves the competent assessment of reasons; consequently, insofar as we are engaged in moral education at all, the meeting of this obligation requires that reasons play a significant role in it. Any moral education that has no such role for reasons fails to meet our obligation to treat children and students with respect as persons.[7]

5. Conclusion

As we have seen, there is no quick, easy answer to the question, "What is the role of reasons in moral education?" That said, the four considerations just rehearsed seem to me to establish that that role is both necessary and substantial, although its exact character remains somewhat elusive because of the difficulty in specifying its contributions to the fostering of our five proposed non-reasoning ingredients. (Further considerations in favor of the important role of reasons and reasoning in moral education are given in Musschenga 2011.)

This somewhat imprecise conclusion may well strike readers as unsatisfying. It strikes me that way. What the imprecision shows, I think, is that in order to pin down the role of reasons in moral education with more precision, we have first to resolve more fundamental controversies concerning rival theories of moral education, the place of our six ingredients within them, and the role of reasons in the development of the other five.[8]

Notes

1. For more on the nature of reasons and their place in an adequate conception of critical thinking, see Bailin and Siegel 2003; Siegel 1988, 1997, 2003.
2. There are nevertheless some limits to the legitimacy of education's aim to influence student belief. For one thing, there are limits of *manner*: it is not acceptable to guide student belief by way of indoctrination or brainwashing (cf. Siegel 1988, ch. 5). For another, it is important

to respect and foster student *autonomy*, and this generally requires leaving students' beliefs to their independent judgment. For a discussion of the limits on the legitimate guidance of student belief in the context of science education, see Laats and Siegel 2016, ch. 7. Having noted them here and in the next section of the text, I otherwise leave such limits aside in what follows.
3. Cf. Siegel 1988, ch. 5; Siegel 2004; Steutel and Spiecker 1997, 1999.
4. Cf. Scheffler 1989; Siegel 1988, 1977, 2003.
5. Cf. Slote 2010b, p. 141, n. 6.
6. First spelled out in Siegel 1988, ch. 3.
7. The claim made here does not concern the teaching of the five other ingredients, but rather the need to foster students' capacity to submit such teachings to independent critical scrutiny, however taught. It can be seen as a kind of meta-obligation: however we foster the other five ingredients—whatever role reasons play in that fostering—we are obliged to foster students' capacity to subject what is taught to their independent critical judgment.
8. It is my great pleasure to be a part of this effort to honor my friend and philosophical colleague Jan Steutel, whose work, widely admired for its clarity, depth and good judgment, stands as a model for us all. My sincere thanks to the editors, Doret de Ruyter and Siebren Meidema, both for the opportunity to participate in this Steutel-honoring effort and for their helpful suggestions on the penultimate draft.

References

Aristotle. (1985). *Nicomachean Ethics*. Translated by T. Irwin. Indianapolis: Hackett Publishing Company.
Bailin, S., and H. Siegel. (2003). "Critical Thinking." In N. Blake, P. Smeyers, R. Smith, and P. Standish (eds.), *The Blackwell Guide to the Philosophy of Education* (pp. 181–193). Oxford: Blackwell.
Curren, R. (2001). "Moral Education." In L. C. Becker and C. B. Becker (eds.), *Encyclopedia of Ethics* (2nd ed., pp. 1127–1131). New York: Routledge,
Laats, A., and H. Siegel. (2016). *Teaching Evolution in a Creation Nation*. Chicago: University of Chicago Press.
Musschenga, B. (2011). "Teaching Moral Reasoning." In D. J. deRuyter and S. Meidema (eds.), *Moral Education and Development: A Lifetime Commitment* (Festschrift for Jan Steutel) (pp. 71–84). Rotterdam: Sense Publishers.
Noddings, N. (1984). *Caring: A Feminine Approach to Ethics and Moral Education*. Berkeley: University of California Press.
Noddings, N. (2010). "Moral Education and Caring." *Theory and Research in Education* 8.2: 145–151.
Scheffler, I. (1989). "Moral Education and the Democratic Ideal." In *Reason and Teaching* (pp. 136–145). Indianapolis: Hackett. First published Indianapolis: Bobbs-Merrill (1973).
Siegel, H. (1988). *Educating Reason: Rationality, Critical Thinking, and Education*. London: Routledge.
Siegel, H. (1997). *Rationality Redeemed?: Further Dialogues on an Educational Ideal*. New York: Routledge.
Siegel, H. (2003). "Cultivating Reason." In R. Curren (ed.), *A Companion to the Philosophy of Education* (pp. 305–317). Oxford: Blackwell.
Siegel, H. (2004). "'You Take the Wheel, I'm Tired of Driving; Jesus, Show Me the Way': Doctrines, Indoctrination, and the Suppression of Critical Dispositions." In L. F. Groenendijk and J. W. Steutel (eds.), *Analytisch filosoferen over opvoeding en onderwijs: Liber amicorum voor Ben Spiecker* (pp. 129–138). Amsterdam: B. V. Uitgeverij SWP.
Slote, M. (2007). *The Ethics of Care and Empathy*. London: Routledge.
Slote, M. (2010a). *Moral Sentimentalism*. New York: Oxford University Press.
Slote, M. (2010b). "Sentimentalist Moral Education." *Theory and Research in Education* 8.2: 125–143.

Steutel, J., and Spiecker, B. (1997). "Rational Passions and Intellectual Virtues: A Conceptual Analysis." In H. Siegel (ed.), *Reason and Education: Essays in Honor of Israel Scheffler* (pp. 59–71). Dordrecht, The Netherlands: Kluwer.

Steutel, J., and Spiecker, B. (1999). "Liberalism and Critical Thinking: On the Relation between a Political Ideal and an Aim of Education." In R. Marples (ed.), *The Aims of Education* (pp. 61–73). London: Routledge.

7

Critical Thinking and the Intellectual Virtues

1. Introduction

What is the relation between critical thinking (henceforth CT) and intellectual virtue? Is CT an intellectual virtue or a cluster of such virtues? Is there anything more to CT than the intellectual virtues it involves? In what follows I hope to answer these questions by addressing three clusters of issues: (1) Are the dispositions, habits of mind and character traits constitutive of the "critical spirit" rightly conceived as intellectual virtues? What is gained or lost by so conceiving them? (2) Do the intellectual virtues include abilities as well as dispositions, or are abilities something separate? (3) Should we be "reliabilists" or "responsibilists" with respect to the intellectual virtues? That is, must the intellectual virtues, in order to be virtues, reliably secure the truth? Or might they rather be "excellences" or "perfections" that needn't secure the truth, or be reliable generators of it, in order rightly to be considered virtues? Finally, I will address a more specific question: (4) What is the connection between *virtue* and *reason*? More specifically still: Is a virtuous intellect *eo ipso* a rational one? My discussion of the first three clusters of issues will, I hope put, me in position to offer a direct answer to the fourth. I will argue that (unless the former is defined as requiring the latter) a virtuous intellect is *not* necessarily a rational one, and that in addition to the intellectual virtues, rational abilities—those captured by the *reason assessment* component of critical thinking—are required. I support educational efforts aimed at fostering the intellectual virtues, including in particular those dispositions, habits of mind, and character traits constitutive of the "critical spirit," and have argued for this aim *ad nauseam*, but that is only part of our proper educational task if we are concerned to help students become intellectually virtuous critical thinkers.

2. Are the Components of the Critical Spirit Rightly Conceived as Intellectual Virtues?

In *Educating Reason* (Siegel 1988) I defended a two-component account of critical thinking, according to which a critical thinker has mastered both the *reason assessment* and *critical spirit* components of critical thinking. On my account, these components are individually necessary and jointly sufficient for being a critical thinker. (There are many refinements of and qualifications to the account that I will not discuss here.[1])

The reason assessment component, as its name suggests, concerns the skills and abilities required to evaluate reasons well, i.e., in ways that properly reflect appropriate epistemological criteria concerning the probative force of proffered reasons and evidence. Central to the reason assessment component is the requirement that *epistemic criteria be met*. That is, to assess reasons well is to assess them in terms of relevant epistemic criteria, properly understood and applied. For example, if a candidate reason fails to support a target proposition or candidate for belief (henceforth *target*), the assessment must judge it to be a failed reason that in fact offers no evidential support to the target. Likewise, if the reason does provide some degree or amount of support to the target, the assessment must assess it as providing just that much support. This relation of support is an epistemic or evidential relation between the reason and the target; it is what it is (that is, the reason/evidence in question entails or provides conclusive/strong/some/weak/no support for the target), and provides what support that it does, *independently of the character, dispositions, or virtues of the assessor.*[2] This component, though an essential component of the account, will not occupy us unduly here. Most relevant for present purposes is the critical spirit component, to which I turn next.

The critical spirit component includes a cluster of attitudes, dispositions, and character traits, many of which could equally be thought of as intellectual virtues. Among them are (1) the dispositions to seek reasons and evidence, to demand reasons and justifications for claims advanced, to query and (when appropriate) investigate proffered but unsubstantiated claims, and to engage in open-minded and fair-minded reason assessment; (2) a willingness and inclination to conform belief, judgment, and action to epistemic principle, especially those concerning the proper normative evaluation of reasons and evidence; (3) a cluster of related attitudes and character traits, including a rejection of partiality and arbitrariness, a commitment to the objective evaluation of relevant evidence and to the sympathetic and impartial consideration of interests, and the valuing of good reasoning, intellectual honesty, justice to evidence, objectivity of judgment, and impartiality with respect to epistemic evaluation generally, even when it runs counter to self-interest; and (4) habits of mind consonant with all these. They overlap in complex ways, and I do not presume any sharp distinctions among the mentioned attitudes, dispositions, character traits, and habits of mind. The critical spirit involves, fundamentally, *caring* about reasons and their quality, reasoning, and living a life in which they play a fundamental role.[3]

These attitudes, dispositions, and character traits can be manifested or exercised well or badly from the epistemic point of view; their exercise does not require or guarantee the meeting of relevant epistemic criteria. For example, I can be disposed to seek reasons and evidence but be bad at finding them; I can try my best to conform belief, judgment, and action to epistemic principle but be unsuccessful at so conforming them; I can strive to assess reasons in accordance with appropriate epistemic criteria but have only the dimmest grasp of relevant criteria and their application, and so evaluate the strengths of proffered reasons badly. To borrow a useful distinction from an earlier philosophical time, these components of the critical spirit are couched in terms of *task* verbs rather than *achievement* verbs: one can seek reasons but fail to find them; demand reasons but misevaluate them; query and investigate claims ineffectively; assess reasons open-mindedly and fair-mindedly but inappropriately from the epistemic point of view; etc. It is because one can have the critical spirit but be terrible at reason assessment that the latter component is required. It is because one can be good at reason assessment but too often fail to engage in it that the former component is required. That is why the two components are individually necessary but only jointly sufficient for being a critical thinker.

These several dimensions of the critical spirit overlap substantially with recent presentations of the intellectual virtues, which include such things as inquisitiveness, diligence, perseverance, resourcefulness, ingenuity, attentiveness, thoughtfulness, open-mindedness, fair-mindedness, intellectual patience, intellectual courage, carefulness, thoroughness, intellectual charity, intellectual conscientiousness, intellectual humility, intellectual generosity, and caring pro-attitudes toward intellectual ends such as knowledge, rationality, and understanding (cf. Baehr 2011; Roberts and Wood 2007; Zagzebski 1996). Many, and perhaps all, of these virtues have a proper place in a complete account of the critical spirit.[4]

Are the constituents of the critical spirit best thought of as intellectual virtues?

There are some reasons for thinking so—that is, there are advantages to conceiving of the several constituents of the critical spirit as intellectual virtues. First, doing so enables us to build detailed characterizations of their structure and character, as William Hare and Jason Baehr have done for open-mindedness[5] and Baehr, Robert C. Roberts and W. Jay Wood, and Linda T. Zagzebski have done for several others of the intellectual virtues, but that CT theorists generally have not. Second, they are *good*; some dispositions/character traits (e.g., intellectual sloth) are not. Calling them "virtues" marks this.[6] Third, the CT theorist stands to learn much from the virtue epistemologist, who offers the potential for (a) more detailed accounts of the dispositions/traits/virtues, (b) deeper understanding of the desirability/normative standing of the dispositions/traits, and (c) deeper understanding of the "characteristic psychology" of the intellectually virtuous person and the desires from which the intellectual virtues flow[7] (Baehr 2011, pp. 6–16). Finally, it must be emphasized that the terminological question is secondary, if important at all. These attitudes, dispositions, and character traits are important, characterologically and educationally, whatever they're called.

One drawback of regarding the constituents of the critical spirit as intellectual virtues is that doing so brings to the fore several philosophically controversial matters that the critical spirit (as I've articulated it) does not. Virtue talk immediately brings to mind Aristotle and the host of issues that philosophers wrestling with the Aristotelian virtue tradition have routinely faced, including the causes of the virtues, the explanation of some particular person's possession of some particular virtue, the nature and necessity of the motivational character of the virtues, the goodness or "personal worth" of the virtues and the character and justification of this particular sort of normativity, etc.[8] I am not suggesting that these issues are not philosophically worthy; of course they are. But they complicate our educational theorizing in ways that CT does not. In particular, as I will argue below, conceiving the constituents of the critical spirit as intellectual virtues unnecessarily complicates the justification of CT as an educational ideal along the Kantian lines that Israel Scheffler and I have articulated. This is not to say that they are not intellectual virtues, but rather that so conceiving them is an unnecessary complication if our aim is to establish the educational centrality of the ideal of CT. A further drawback, discussed next, concerns the relation between the reason assessment component of CT and the intellectual virtues, a relation that is more complex and problematic than the relation between that component and the critical spirit.

3. What Are the Relations between CT Abilities and (a) CT Dispositions and (b) Intellectual Virtues?

Whether or not we regard the features constitutive of the critical spirit as intellectual virtues, how should we understand their relation to the abilities that together constitute the *reason assessment* component of CT? My account, like most extant accounts, sharply distinguishes between those abilities and the critical spirit/intellectual virtues, but some theorists regard the abilities as a necessary part of the virtues, in that one cannot have the virtues without having at least a modicum of the abilities. For example, Shari Tishman, Eileen Jay, and David N. Perkins seem to draw the same sharp distinction between abilities and dispositions that CT theorists typically draw:

> Can you play the piano? *Do* you play the piano? These are different questions, and your answer may well be "yes" to the first and "no" to the second. The first question asks about ability: If you sat down in front of a piano, could you play a tune? The second tacitly asks much more—it goes beyond ability and asks about inclination: Are you disposed to play the piano? Do you like to play? Do you play regularly?
>
> Playing the piano is like higher order thinking in at least this respect: In both cases, ability alone is not enough to ensure ongoing performance. Just as having the ability to play the piano does not guarantee the disposition to do so, having certain thinking skills does not mean that one will use them. In fact, research shows that students often fail to use the thinking skills they are taught. For example, research on reasoning and argument shows that, when explicitly asked, people can easily give many reasons opposite their favored side of the case—that is, they have the ability. But typically they fail to do so—that is, they lack the disposition. (Tishman, Jay, and Perkins 1993, p. 147, emphasis in original)

Tishman, Jay, and Perkins are clear that the relevant abilities and dispositions are distinct, that one can have the former but not the latter, and that it is educationally important to foster both. In the same paper these authors suggest that thinking dispositions "include abilities but go beyond them," and that such dispositions "are comprised of three elements: abilities, sensitivities, and inclinations.... Abilities refer to the capabilities and skills required to carry through on the behavior. Sensitivities refer to an alertness to appropriate occasions for exhibiting the behavior. Inclinations refer to the tendency to actually behave in a certain way" (p. 148, reference omitted).

This tripartite distinction between abilities, sensitivities, and inclinations is salutary; I welcome the inclusion of sensitivities into the mix. But it is worth noting that "disposition" is defined in such a way as to render "inclination" a necessary but insufficient condition: if I'm inclined to A (e.g., play the piano or consider reasons contrary to my own point of view), I may or may not have the disposition to A: to have it I need not just that inclination, but also the relevant sensitivity and ability. This is contrary not just to ordinary usage, but also to the lengthy citation above, in which "disposition" and "inclination" seem to be used synonymously. In any case, "disposition" is here understood as something that includes abilities as a necessary but insufficient condition. Tishman, Jay, and Perkins (1993) are clear that, on their view, while one cannot have a disposition without the relevant ability, one can have the ability without the relevant disposition. They are importantly right that "abilities alone are not enough" (p. 148), and for the reason they give: one can have the ability but not exercise or utilize it, and we want our students not just to be able to think critically or conduct themselves in intellectually virtuous ways, but actually to so think and conduct themselves. In order to keep this educational directive before us, the abilities/dispositions distinction seems both appropriate and necessary.

One might agree that some distinction like this is needed while also holding that particular abilities are constitutive and necessary components of particular dispositions.[9] Below I will offer some considerations that weigh against this latter claim. But it is worth emphasizing here that, aside from a disagreement about the character of dispositions—that is, does having one require having the corresponding abilities or not?—this disagreement is not of much educational moment. Tishman, Jay, and Perkins (who think that having the disposition requires having the associated abilities, the latter being a constitutive component of the former) and I (who thinks that having the associated abilities is not necessary for having the disposition) are agreed that possession of both the abilities and the dispositions is educationally crucial. Whether or not having the ability, though distinguishable from the disposition, is nevertheless a constitutive component of it, such that without the ability one does not have the associated disposition, all sides are agreed that educationally we must do our best to foster both. So this dispute concerning the nature of dispositions, however important it is philosophically, is not significant educationally.

Tishman, Jay, and Perkins are not alone in building abilities into dispositions, so that to have the disposition is *eo ipso* to have the ability (and conversely, to lack the ability is to lack the disposition). Ron Ritchhart defines dispositions as "[a]cquired patterns of behavior that are under one's control and will as opposed to being automatically activated.... They are dynamic and idiosyncratic in their contextualized deployment rather than prescribed actions to be rigidly carried out. More than desire and will, *dispositions must be coupled with the requisite ability. Dispositions motivate, activate, and direct our abilities*" (Ritchhart 2002, p. 31, emphasis added). Here dispositions must be "coupled with" relevant abilities, but the latter need not be partly constitutive of the former. Elsewhere, however, Ritchhart writes that "[d]ispositions are about more than a desire or inclination to act. They consist of a general inclination consisting of values, beliefs, and underlying temperaments; an awareness of occasions for appropriate action; motivation to carry out action; and *the requisite abilities and skills needed to perform*" (p. 51, emphasis added). Here the abilities are built into the dispositions.

As we have seen, both Tishman, Jay, and Perkins and Ritchhart reject a sharp abilities/dispositions distinction, regarding abilities both as something a person can have without any disposition to enact or engage, and also as a constitutive component of dispositions, necessary for their exercise. Since I want to maintain the distinction and reject its rejection, I am concerned to challenge the "abilities are built into dispositions" view of their relationship. Ritchhart is clear that he is writing from "the psychological perspective" (2002, p. 20), as are Tishman, Jay, and Perkins.[10] Is the tendency to conceive of dispositions as including abilities a disciplinary matter, with psychologists but not philosophers including the former as necessary constituents of the latter?

As it turns out, some philosophers also regard abilities as necessary constituents of dispositions, in that if one lacks the relevant ability one cannot possess the associated disposition. Hare, for example, offers his well-known account of open-mindedness in ways that reflect both theses just noted. He agrees, in some passages at least, that abilities can be had without any disposition or inclination to exercise them; and, although he sometimes treats open-mindedness as involving just the willingness and disposition to revise belief in the face of new evidence, at other times he regards it as requiring at least minimal competence with respect to the abilities of reason assessment as well.[11] In the former, the ability is not a necessary constituent of the disposition; in the latter, it is—although only in a minimal way, since only minimal competence with respect to the ability is needed in order to have the disposition. Baehr embraces the latter view as well, holding that having the intellectual virtues requires having at least some ability to pursue appropriate epistemic ends in epistemically respectable ways:

> If I desire to get to the truth but am incompetent at asking good questions, assessing evidence, taking up alternative points of view, and so on, then, all my good epistemic will notwithstanding, my claim to intellectual virtue will be weak indeed. (Baehr 2016, p. 91)[12]

So the different views we have been considering concerning the relationship between dispositions/virtues and abilities do not seem to divide along disciplinary lines.

However plausible the "possessing the disposition/virtue requires possessing and manifesting the relevant epistemic abilities" view might be, the alternative view—that a sharp distinction is appropriate—seems to me preferable for two reasons. First, as the long citation above from Tishman, Jay, and Perkins makes clear, it is clearly possible for a person to possess a given ability without possessing even a smidgen of a disposition to utilize the ability, and as these authors note, psychological research seems to establish that people are in fact like this: they can and do sometimes have the ability (e.g., to play the piano or consider reasons contrary to their own points of view) but lack the disposition. This is reason enough, I think, to retain the sharp distinction in question. Educationally, this point is important because it forces us to acknowledge and address the educational task of fostering dispositions as well as abilities in our students, along with the educational deficiency of imparting the latter but not the former.[13]

More importantly, all the abilities that mark the execution (and so the possession) of the virtues—taking up alternative points of view, judging open-mindedly and fair-mindedly, attending to important details, asking thoughtful questions, etc.—can be done well or badly from the epistemic point of view: One can judge open-mindedly but irrationally, attend to important details but misevaluate their evidential significance, ask thoughtful but irrelevant questions, etc. Consequently, the manifestation of the abilities Baehr mentions, while perhaps indicators of possession of the virtues, won't indicate anything about the quality of thought the virtues are supposed to secure. As noted earlier, the abilities alleged to be constitutive of the virtues are couched in terms of task rather than achievement verbs. But what we want, educationally, is achievement. More specifically, we want students to get it right not only in the sense of having the right kind of character, but also in the sense of reasoning, judging, and exercising their intellectual virtues in ways that reflect relevant epistemic criteria. Consequently, conceiving virtues as excellences of character will not suffice to secure the satisfaction of the reason assessment component of CT.

I have argued, in agreement with all the authors so far discussed, that one can have the ability but not the disposition. The question dividing us concerns the claim that the former is a necessary, constitutive component of the latter. Is this right? Can one have the disposition but not the ability?

It is clearly possible for a person to be disposed to *A* while being very bad at *A*-ing. For example, one can be disposed to do the crossword puzzle every day while also being very challenged in one's ability to solve a crossword puzzle. Similarly for driving, cooking, *and thinking*: Sam can love to read novels and be strongly disposed to read them at every available moment while failing to grasp even the most rudimentary plot twists and character development; Jane might be strongly disposed to read science blogs but understand precious little of what she reads and manifest very little critical ability concerning the bits she does understand; Bob can be disposed to seek the truth but be terrible at discerning it despite his best efforts. Can these worthies be *completely* devoid of ability while still being disposed/virtuous? As we've seen, Baehr says no, that without at least some competence/ability, one cannot possess the virtue. As we've also seen, Tishman, Jay, and Perkins and Ritchhart agree. But the latter are talking about dispositions, not virtues, as are the CT theorists who discuss the matter, while Baehr is talking about intellectual virtues.

There are several points to note here. First, we should not conflate "disposition" and "intellectual virtue." I have been treating them thus far as if they were two terms referring to the same thing, but we now have reason to distinguish them: perhaps one can have a disposition without the accompanying abilities, but nevertheless one cannot have the related intellectual virtue without the abilities. For example, Baehr (2013, p. 152) might be right that having the virtue of open-mindedness requires having some ability to detach from or transcend a default cognitive standpoint in order to take up alternative standpoints, while having the disposition to be open-minded might be had without any such ability: John might have the disposition and yet be exceedingly bad at seeing things from other points of view.

Second, intellectual virtues, at least on Baehr's "personal worth" conception of them, are more complex and demanding than dispositions: to have a given intellectual virtue, one needs not only the relevant disposition but also the right motivation, affect/attitude, competence, and judgment[14] (Baehr 2016). These latter four components of intellectual virtues may be highly desirable, but they are both philosophically and educationally ambitious: philosophically because alternative accounts of the virtues do not require them;[15] educationally because they seem obviously enough to be harder to foster than the dispositions alone. For example, do we really have to ensure that students *take pleasure in* the exercise of the virtues in order to have succeeded educationally? (Baehr 2016). Supposing that Baehr is right about the necessity of the appropriate affect/attitude toward the exercise of the virtues in order to have them—a virtuous person must take pleasure in their exercise—is the person who exercises the right dispositions out of duty rather than pleasure an educational failure? *Must* we side with Aristotle rather than Kant here in order to succeed educationally?

Third (to extend the first point above), the conflation of "dispositions" and "intellectual virtues" creates unnecessary and perhaps illusory problems. Baehr says, contrary to my view that a person could have a critical-spirit-constitutive disposition but be incompetent at execution and so fail to have mastered the reason assessment component of CT, that "the possession of certain skills/abilities/competences is *part of what it is* to possess an intellectual virtue."[16] But my view is not about the possession of an intellectual virtue, but rather of a disposition. My claim is that a person can (and many people in fact do) have a critical-spirit-constitutive disposition even though she lacks the relevant ability. For example, she might be disposed to seek reasons, evaluate evidence, submit her reasoning to suitable criteria, etc., but also be very bad at these things, thus satisfying the critical spirit component but not the reason assessment component of CT. Baehr may well be right about "certain skills/abilities/competences" being *"part of what it is* to possess an intellectual virtue"—whether he is will depend on the deliverances of intellectual virtue theory. But is he right that the possession of skills/abilities/competences is part of what it is to have a disposition? As a general matter, this seems wrong: the eager but dull student might well have the disposition to seek relevant evidence concerning his term paper's thesis but be very bad at finding it. Likewise, he might have the disposition to evaluate what evidence he does find but be thoroughly incompetent at evaluating it. Here it seems quite crucial to distinguish claims made about dispositions from parallel claims made about intellectual virtues.

Perhaps I am being too cavalier here. Can the eager but dull student be *completely* lacking in the skills and abilities of reason assessment but nevertheless have the dispositions constitutive of the critical spirit? Here we come to a fourth point. Baehr says that one must be *competent* with respect to the abilities for one to have the relevant intellectual virtue (Baehr 2016; cf. Baehr 2011, p. 152). Hare says that to have the virtue of open-mindedness (and presumably other intellectual virtues as well), one must be *at least minimally competent* with respect to reason assessment (cf. Siegel 2009 for references). This raises an obvious question: What degree of competence is required for possessing a given intellectual virtue? How often or frequently must one manifest these virtues in order to have them? I don't see how such a line can be non-arbitrarily drawn. If the line is to be drawn at competence, we'll need both a way to measure it and a cut-off point below which the person lacks competence and so lacks the virtue.[17]

Moreover, once again we should be careful not to conflate virtues and dispositions. Supposing that competence is required for possession of the virtue, is it likewise required for possession of the related disposition? That is, can one have some meaningful measure of the critical spirit without *any* ability to assess reasons? It seems to me possible in principle. Baehr might respond by distinguishing between (merely) natural virtues and genuine or full virtues (2011, pp. 28–29). But this would be again to conflate virtues and dispositions.

Further, while it may be acceptable to virtue theorists to measure possession of a virtue by the frequency of its manifestation in a person's behavior, it seems a mistake to measure possession of a disposition in this way, because dispositions needn't be manifested in order to be (and be known to be) possessed (Siegel 1999).

For these several reasons I resist both the conflation of virtues and dispositions and the claim that abilities are necessary constituents of dispositions.

4. Reliabilist versus Responsibilist Accounts of the Intellectual Virtues

A well-known divide among intellectual virtue theorists separates them into *reliabilist* and *responsibilist* camps. Roughly, reliabilists take candidate intellectual virtues to be genuine intellectual virtues because their exercise reliably produces true belief; they are *faculties, abilities,* or *powers* that are part of our natural biological endowment—e.g., our perceptual mechanisms, memory, and natural reasoning abilities. The virtues are virtues because of their tendency actually to produce true belief; this is what makes them virtues (cf. Baehr 2011, ch. 4; Sosa 1991, 2007, 2009). Responsibilists, on the other hand (and again roughly), take candidate intellectual virtues to be genuine intellectual virtues because they are *excellences* or *perfections*; the virtues are virtues not because they reliably produce truth (or anything else) but because their exercise manifests a suitable excellence.[18]

I will not enter here into a serious treatment of this controversy, but I want to register some reasons for preferring the responsibilist view, the most important of which is that it is the view most in keeping with the most appropriate and defensible epistemology *of education*.

Catherine Z. Elgin offers several considerations that count heavily against the reliabilist view: Whether or not the exercise of a candidate virtue reliably yields true belief is an empirical question, and we only rarely have such evidence; whether or not such an exercise reliably yields true belief typically depends upon the exercise of related virtues, so truth-conduciveness is not usually ascribable to particular virtues, but rather to clusters of them; truth-conduciveness alone cannot be enough to secure virtue status because it is too easy to generate trivial truths, in which case the exercise of the virtue is not virtuous; truth-conduciveness is an inappropriate measure of virtue because in both hostile epistemic environments (e.g., demon worlds) and hospitable ones the scrupulous inquirer is more virtuous than the fickle one, even if the former does not reliably produce truths (Elgin 2013, pp. 137–139). As she concludes: "Truth conduciveness seems neither necessary nor sufficient for epistemic virtue" (p. 139).

I think Elgin is right about all this. Another consideration that seems to me equally compelling takes its cue from the fact that our interests here are not just (purely) philosophical, but *educational* as well. In education, results alone are not enough. Teachers want their students not just to believe truths, but to believe for the right reasons and appreciate the justification those reasons confer; not just to get the right answer, but to get it in the right way (e.g., by using appropriate methods/procedures) and to appreciate the rightness of that way. That is, educators are concerned that students utilize their critical intellects, and so see their task as involving, in part, the development of those intellects and the fostering of the dispositions to use them. To put this point another way: in education, we must be internalists about justification.[19] For the same reasons, in education we must be responsibilists rather than reliabilists about the intellectual virtues. Whether or not our students believe truly is not entirely up to them; as the saying goes, in order for their justified beliefs to be true, "the universe must cooperate." But if they (gather and) evaluate evidence well—that is, in accordance with appropriate epistemic criteria concerning the probative force of reasons and evidence—and, further, are disposed to do so, they will be educational successes. Truth is an epistemic good, of course. But so are rationality and justified belief, and so is CT. From the educational point of view, the student who, by virtue of her CT, has justified but false beliefs is a superior student to her counterpart who has unjustified but lucky true ones (Robertson 2009; Siegel 2005). Insofar as we are concerned to connect this point to the nature of intellectual virtue, we should understand it in the responsibilist rather than the reliabilist way.[20]

5. The Relation between Virtue and Reason

We are at last in position to answer the final questions with which we began, concerning the connection between virtue and reason. Is the intellectually virtuous person, in virtue of that virtuousness, rational? Can an intellectually virtuous person be so and yet be deficient from the point of view of reason? Can she be seriously lacking in or even completely without CT abilities?

These questions are not equivalent. Moreover, there is quite a bit of imprecision in them, because being intellectually virtuous and being rational are matters of degree, because it is unclear whether competence is required for possession of the intellectual virtues (as opposed to the relevant dispositions), and because it is unclear, if some competence is required for possession of a given virtue, how much competence is required. So let us consider the various possibilities, beginning with the last question just listed.

1. *Can an intellectually virtuous person be completely without relevant cognitive/intellectual/reason assessment*[21] *abilities?* As we have seen, both Baehr and Hare say no: on their views, an intellectually virtuous person must have at least some abilities. For my own part, I'm prepared to concede the point as it involves intellectual virtues, but not as it concerns CT dispositions: a person could, I think, have the requisite dispositions but none of the ability. For example, Joe could be strongly disposed to base his beliefs on relevant reasons and evidence, and yet be completely lacking in ability to do so—he consistently infers badly, fails to recognize the epistemic significance of candidate reasons, etc. Here, as earlier, much will depend on avoiding the virtue/disposition conflation.

2. *How much is enough?* Granting that, so long as we're talking about intellectual virtues rather than CT dispositions, some minimum competence/ability is required for possession, this minimal ability is not enough. Suppose Joe has the minimum ability required for possession of the requisite virtues, along with whatever else is required. He then counts as intellectually virtuous, at least with respect to the particular virtues in question. But he would be sadly lacking from the point of view of CT, precisely because he is very bad, or only minimally good, at reason assessment. That is, the virtue approach, understood as requiring just minimal ability, places insufficient emphasis on the reason assessment component of CT.

3. *Can an intellectually virtuous person be so, and yet be deficient from the point of view of reason?* Since one can be rational but still "deficient from the point of view of reason"—that is, being rational does not require being *perfectly* rational—we should say the same of the intellectually virtuous person: she can

be intellectually virtuous while still being less than perfectly rational, and in that sense being deficient from the point of view of reason. As far as I can see, this is uncontroversial and agreed to by all intellectual virtue and CT theorists.

This brings us to the most crucial question:

4. *Is the intellectually virtuous person, in virtue of that virtuousness, rational?* That is, does being intellectually virtuous entail, or guarantee, being rational? While this is, I think, the most crucial question before us here, I think it is fairly easily and uncontroversially addressed. To the extent that possessing an intellectual virtue requires meeting some adequate threshold of competence with respect to the abilities captured by the reason assessment component of CT, we should answer affirmatively: meeting this threshold entails being rational. Of course, to the extent that possession of an intellectual virtue does not require meeting the threshold, possessing the virtue does not entail being rational. Everything depends upon the threshold. For Hare, it is minimal—possessing the virtue requires some *minimal* ability (cf. Siegel 2009). For Baehr, it requires *competence*, but he does not precisely specify the degree of competence required (Baehr 2013, 2016).

So being intellectually virtuous ensures being rational, so long as being rational—that is, being as competent (with respect to the abilities needed for possession of the virtue) as is required for the possession of the virtue—is built into the requirements for (i.e., is a necessary condition of) having the virtue. This condition trivially secures the "virtue entails reason" relation.

Notice, though, that the competence required for possession of a given intellectual virtue varies from virtue to virtue; neither singly nor conjointly do they amount to mastery of the reason assessment component of CT. First, on the "virtue entails reason" view now being considered, competence with respect to the abilities required for possession of a virtue will vary from virtue to virtue: for open-mindedness, the ability to see things from the other point of view will be required; for intellectual courage, that one won't be required, but other abilities—perhaps the ability to maintain one's belief or pursue some intellectual good in the face of the threat of harm to oneself (Baehr 2011, p. 177)—will be. The abilities required for being generally intellectually virtuous will be something of a motley collection. It would be convenient for the intellectual virtue theorist if all the various abilities required for possession of the intellectual virtues could be collected under the umbrella of the abilities constitutive of the reason assessment component of CT, such that insofar as they are abilities required for the possession of the intellectual virtues, they will be aspects of that component. I don't take this to be a particularly important point, but if true this would provide a theoretical unity to an otherwise apparently motley collection.

More pressing is that the competence required for possession of given intellectual virtues is not the same as competence with respect to the reason assessment component of CT. Rather, it is competence with respect to whatever is required for the proper exercise of the several virtues. These can clearly diverge. For example, Maria might be competent at taking another's point of view, and so be competent with respect to that aspect of open-mindedness, and so (to that extent at least) have the virtue of open-mindedness, yet be very bad or only minimally good at reason assessment, and so fail to be competent with respect to the reason assessment component of CT. If this is the case generally, as I think it is— one can have the virtues of open-mindedness, intellectual courage, intellectual conscientiousness, etc., and yet still be an incompetent assessor of reasons— then having the several competences required for possession of the intellectual virtues on Baehr's account will not ensure that the intellectually virtuous person has sufficiently mastered the reason assessment component of CT. In this respect, CT is more demanding an ideal than that of fostering the intellectual virtues, since one could in principle achieve the latter while failing to achieve the former. So if being rational involves epistemically competent reason assessment, being intellectually virtuous does not entail or guarantee being rational.

6. CT, Intellectual Virtues, and the Aims of Education

It is worth reminding ourselves why all this is worth pondering. Why are we concerned with CT, the intellectual virtues, and the relation between them?

The concern with CT is justified, I think, by its importance as an educational ideal. The ideal is in turn justified by several considerations, including its role in helping students to become self-sufficient and prepared for adulthood, its place in the rational traditions into which we seek to initiate students during their education, and its important role in democratic life. Most importantly, it is justified by our duty to treat students (and everyone else) with *respect as persons*. An education guided by the ideal of CT is the only one that so treats students, because it acknowledges, respects, and strives to foster their autonomy, independent judgment, and right to question, challenge, and demand reasons for what is taught (including CT itself). This is, of course, a big claim, one I have defended elsewhere and so will not defend here. If correct, it establishes the educational centrality of the ideal (Siegel 1988, ch. 3 and *passim*, 1977, 2003, 2010; cf. Scheffler 1989).

How does CT connect to the intellectual virtues? I think Baehr is right that the latter "manifest themselves in critical thinking" but that the two are not identical.[22] Is there any reason to think that the fostering of the intellectual virtues is also an important, even a more important, educational ideal?

We can all agree that students who are intellectually virtuous are to be preferred to those who are not, just as are students who are morally virtuous, smart, imaginative, sensitive, courageous, caring, etc. There are many good things that students can be. But are these all rightly thought of as educational ideals? I hesitate, only because if we are serious about treating students with respect, then what they become and what dispositions and virtues they value, possess, and manifest is importantly *up to them*. While we strive to foster CT abilities and dispositions in our students, we also (if we are doing it right) invite them to evaluate for themselves the worthiness of these things and submit our arguments for that worthiness to their independent scrutiny and judgment.[23]

It is unclear to me that the intellectual virtues, however excellent they are, can be justified in the same way. Rather, they must be justified in other ways, most of which I cannot consider here. But perhaps I might be allowed a brief word about one such way, one that enjoys a distinguished history in the tradition of scholarship on the virtues; namely, to justify them along broadly Aristotelian lines, in eudaimonistic terms. This seems to me far more controversial and problematic than the Kantian justification I favor. Our educational obligation is not to deliver our students to flourishing lives (or happy ones), but rather to prepare them to consider for themselves (among many other things) the virtuousness of the virtues and their place in their own lives. In this respect, educating for intellectual virtue is more ambitious, and contentious philosophically, than educating for CT. On Baehr's view, "intellectual virtues just are character traits that make their possessor good or excellent in the relevant intellectual-cum-personal way. They are 'personal intellectual excellences'" (2011, p. 93). But one person's excellence is all too often another person's vice. Consider, e.g., the 2012 Platform of the Republican Party of Texas, which states:

> We oppose the teaching of Higher Order Thinking Skills (HOTS) (values clarification), critical thinking skills and similar programs that are simply a relabeling of Outcome-Based Education (OBE) (mastery learning) which focus on behavior modification and have the purpose of challenging the student's fixed beliefs and undermining parental authority.[24]

While their targets are HOTS, OBE, and CT, it is clear that the endorsers of this platform plank reject the intellectual virtue of open-mindedness, since they reject educational programs that "have the purpose of challenging the student's fixed beliefs." Defending CT from this complaint, in terms of respect for students as persons, is I think straightforward. But the endorsers are in effect advocating *not* treating the students of Texas with respect as persons—indeed, they are rejecting the very idea that students should be so treated—and this view is open to obvious and powerful challenge.[25] However, the argumentative path to defending the virtue of open-mindedness, in those terms, from those who reject it, seems (to me at least) more demanding and daunting: it would require the resolution of all the large issues at the heart of virtue theory we have seen: What are the relevant virtues, i.e., "excellences" or "perfections"? How are they individuated and justified? Why think there is a unified account of "flourishing" on offer? Here the Texas Republicans seem on firm dialectical ground: if they don't antecedently agree that "challenging fixed beliefs" is a good thing—which they don't—what can be said that will demonstrate the error of their view, short of a thoroughgoing articulation and defense of virtue theory? And how successful is such a defense likely to be, given their very different conception of human flourishing?[26]

All this is just to say in other words what I said above: establishing the fostering of the intellectual virtues as a fundamental educational ideal is more ambitious and philosophically daunting than establishing the ideal of CT. This is, of course, not to say that the fostering of the intellectual virtues is not a legitimate ideal. But it is to say that the ideal of CT (1) gets us at least most of what we want; (2) captures at least much of what is of value concerning the intellectual virtues; and (3) enjoys a more established, less contentious, justificatory path.

7. Conclusion

It is well past time to draw this discussion to a close. I have argued that CT is not simply an intellectual virtue or a cluster of such virtues: it is less than the virtues in that its critical spirit component involves dispositions, habits of mind, and character traits, but that these needn't amount to full-blown virtues; and it is more than the virtues in that its reason assessment component involves all the abilities required to assess reasons in epistemically respectable ways, which the intellectual virtues do not. While there are some reasons for regarding the constituents of the critical spirit as intellectual virtues, noted above, there are also reasons for not doing so, also noted above. I have also offered reasons for maintaining the distinction between abilities of reason assessment, on the one hand, and dispositions/intellectual virtues, on the other; warned against the conflation of "dispositions" and "virtues"; and argued that we should be responsibilists rather than reliabilists about the intellectual virtues, especially insofar as education is concerned. Finally, I have argued that a virtuous intellect need not be a rational one, unless competence with respect to reason assessment is built into possession of the virtues, in which case the inference from virtue to reason is trivial. Rather, if we are concerned to educate so as to promote reason as well as virtue, we must foster the abilities captured by the reason assessment component of CT in addition to fostering the intellectual virtues. If we are concerned to help students become intellectually virtuous critical thinkers, our proper educational task includes more than fostering the intellectual virtues.[27]

Notes

1. For example, mastery of the components, and thus being a critical thinker, is a matter of degree: no one is in fact a perfect critical thinker or a perfectly uncritical thinker. In

this respect, critical thinking is an *ideal*: it is to be strived for even though destined to be achieved at best only to some degree or other. The ideal, moreover, is importantly epistemological, in that relevant epistemic criteria are central to its articulation and achievement. Its status as an educational ideal is justified by several considerations, most importantly by the moral imperative to treat students/children with *respect as persons* (for discussion of these several points and others, see Siegel 1988, 1997, 2003, 2010; Bailin and Siegel 2003).

2. I presume here that support is a matter of degree. There are many epistemological niceties lurking here concerning alternative conceptions and accounts of belief, justification, support, etc., that I cannot address systematically here. The present point—that the reason assessment component involves meeting epistemic criteria, and that meeting/failing to meet them is a matter of the evidential relation between the target and its proffered reasons/evidence, a matter that is independent of the character or virtue of the assessor—can I think be sustained without picking sides in those large epistemological disputes. For more on the evidential support relation, cf. Leite 2008, pp. 421–422.

3. This brief characterization is distilled from Siegel 1988, pp. 39–42. Cf. Scheffler 1989, pp. 28–29, 60–64, 75–79 and *passim*, and Scheffler 1991, pp. 4–5, for the dimensions of character central to a proper conception of the critical spirit in particular, and of critical thinking as an educational ideal more generally. I am happy to acknowledge once again my deep indebtedness to Scheffler's pioneering work.

4. I recommend Baehr's categorizing of intellectual virtues in accordance with their places in challenges to successful inquiry (2011, pp. 17–22).

5. Hare's account of open-mindedness extends across many publications, beginning with his seminal *Open-Mindedness and Education* (1979). For chapter and verse, see Siegel 2009; cf. also Baehr 2011, ch. 8.

6. Thanks to Jason Baehr for highlighting this point, and for his consistent support and encouragement with respect to this project.

7. I here note but do not address a general unease I have concerning the philosophical appropriateness of such armchair psychologizing, which is especially rampant in moral psychology and philosophy of mind in contemporary analytic philosophy. Indeed, I side with Catherine Z. Elgin in doubting that particular intellectual virtues have a characteristic psychology (Elgin, personal communication).

8. See here Baehr 2011, pp. 22–29, for an initial discussion of some of them, and Baehr 2013 for a detailed account of the explanation of possession of a virtue.

9. Thanks again to Jason Baehr for insightful criticism.

10. I should note that Ritchhart's discussion of "intellectual character," and in particular his detailed, nuanced, and psychologically informed account of how to educate students so as to have it, is rich, suggestive, and plausible; I commend it to interested readers.

11. Hare's position is discussed in detail in Siegel 2009; see esp. p. 32, note 9.

12. Baehr calls this the "competence component" of an intellectual virtue, and holds that all such virtues include it, such that without the competence one lacks the virtue. Cf. Baehr 2016, pp. 91–92; Baehr 2013, pp. 7–10; and, with respect to the abilities required for open-mindedness, Baehr 2011, pp. 152–153.

13. This point is very familiar in the CT literature; Sharon Bailin, Robert Ennis, Stephen Norris, Richard Paul, Israel Scheffler, and many others beside myself have made it. For (incomplete) references, see Siegel 1997, pp. 65–67.

14. In "The Cognitive Demands of Intellectual Virtue" (2013, p. 113), Baehr describes the latter as involving a "rationality constraint" on the possession of an intellectual virtue; it is a constraint required by his "personal worth" conception of the intellectual virtues (roughly, to have the virtue, the person's efforts must be attempts to achieve what she has good reason to believe is good), rather than that a given belief meet epistemic criteria, as required by the reason assessment component of CT.

15. See here Baehr's discussions of rival theories of the intellectual virtues (2011, ch. 7), as well as those of Battaly (2015), Roberts and Wood (2007), and Zagzebski (1996).

16. Personal e-mail communication, June 4, 2013, emphasis in original, quoted with permission.

17. Baehr acknowledges that establishing "the minimal demands of an exercise of a character trait or virtue" is "very difficult" (2011, p. 154).
18. Baehr 2011. Battaly (2015, ch. 1) provides a helpful summary of the different positions. Linda Zabzebski's (1996) "hybrid" view, according to which virtues must be both reliably truth-conducive and excellences of character, demands more detailed treatment than I can give it here.
19. Here I am indebted to Emily Robertson (cf. Robertson 2009).
20. Elgin's advocacy of a "reflective endorsement" account of the intellectual virtues is both highly plausible and very much in keeping with the present point. As she puts it, an autonomous believer/critical thinker/epistemically virtuous agent "filter[s] deliverances ... through a critical sieve, accepting only those she considers worthy of her reflective endorsement.... [H]is beliefs are products of his reflective endorsement. He is willing to stand behind them because they satisfy his standards" (Elgin 2013, p. 141–142). Her defense of the fostering of autonomy and critical thinking and of the importance of treating students with respect (pp. 148–150) is also completely in keeping with the view defended here.
21. Notice that this introduces yet another imprecision into our current problem. I will not pursue it further here.
22. Personal communication, May 8, 2012.
23. Cf., e.g., Siegel 1997, pp. 24–25, 73–87.
24. 2012 Platform of the Republican Party of Texas, Report of Platform Committee and Rules Committee, accessed June 13, 2013, at http://a.tfn.org/site/DocServer/2012-Platform-Final.pdf?docID=3201.
25. Not least: it is self-defeating.
26. Elgin makes the same point concerning the adjudication of the dispute between Aristotle and Christians concerning the status of humility—for Aristotle it's a vice, for Christians a virtue—and other controversial cases as well (Elgin 2013, p. 136).
27. This paper originated with an invitation from Jason Baehr to speak at a conference on "Educating for Intellectual Virtues" at Loyola Marymount University in June 2013. I am grateful to the good suggestions offered by the conference participants, in particular Baehr, Heather Battaly, Marvin Berkowitz, Kate Elgin, and Emily Robertson, and to Benjamin Hamby and especially Baehr for detailed and very helpful criticisms and suggestions on the penultimate draft. Baehr's good advice saved me from several substantial errors. I regret my inability to quiet all his doubts.

References

Baehr, J. (2011). *The Inquiring Mind: On Intellectual Virtues and Virtue Epistemology*. Oxford: Oxford University Press.
Baehr, J. (2013). "The Cognitive Demands of Intellectual Virtue." In T. Henning and D. P. Schweikard (eds.), *Knowledge, Virtue, and Action: Putting Epistemic Virtues to Work* (pp. 99–117). London: Routledge.
Baehr, J. (2016). "The Four Dimensions of an Intellectual Virtue." In C. Mi, M. Slote, and E. Sosa (eds.), *Moral and Intellectual Virtues in Western and Chinese Philosophy: The Turn toward Virtue* (pp. 86–98). New York: Routledge.
Bailin, S., and H. Siegel. (2003). "Critical Thinking." In N. Blake, P. Smeyers, R. Smith, and P. Standish (eds.), *The Blackwell Guide to the Philosophy of Education* (pp. 181–193). Oxford: Blackwell.
Battaly, H. (2015). *Virtue*. Boston: Polity Press.
Elgin, C. Z. (2013). "Epistemic Agency." *Theory and Research in Education* 11.2: 135–152.
Hare, W. (1979). *Open-Mindedness and Education*. Kingston, ON: McGill-Queen's University Press.
Leite, A. (2008). "Believing One's Reasons Are Good." *Synthese* 161.3: 419–441.
Ritchhart, R. (2002). *Intellectual Character: What it Is, Why it Matters, and How to Get it*. San Francisco: Jossey-Bass.

Roberts, R. C., and W. J. Wood. (2007). *Intellectual Virtues: An Essay in Regulative Epistemology*. Oxford: Oxford University Press.

Robertson, E. (2009). "The Epistemic Aims of Education." In H. Siegel (ed.), *The Oxford Handbook of Philosophy of Education* (pp. 11–34). New York: Oxford University Press.

Scheffler, I. (1989). *Reason and Teaching*. Indianapolis: Hackett. First published 1973 (London: Routledge and Kegan Paul).

Scheffler, I. (1991). "In Praise of the Cognitive Emotions." Reprinted in Scheffler, *In Praise of the Cognitive Emotions* (pp. 3–17). New York: Routledge. Originally published in *Teachers College Record* 79.2 (1977): 171–186.

Siegel, H. (1988). *Educating Reason: Rationality, Critical Thinking, and Education*. London: Routledge.

Siegel, H. (1997). *Rationality Redeemed?: Further Dialogues on an Educational Ideal*. New York: Routledge.

Siegel, H. (1999). "What (Good) Are Thinking Dispositions?" *Educational Theory* 49.2: 207–221.

Siegel, H. (2003). "Cultivating Reason." In R. Curren (ed.), *A Companion to the Philosophy of Education* (pp. 305–317). Oxford: Blackwell.

Siegel, H. (2005). "Truth, Thinking, Testimony and Trust: Alvin Goldman on Epistemology and Education." *Philosophy and Phenomenological Research* 71.2: 345–366.

Siegel, H. (2009). "Open-Mindedness, Critical Thinking, and Indoctrination: Homage to William Hare." *Paideusis* 18.1: 26–34.

Siegel, H. (2010). "Critical Thinking." In P. Peterson, E. Baker, and B. McGaw (eds.), *International Encyclopedia of Education* (3rd ed., vol. 6, pp. 141–145). Oxford: Elsevier.

Sosa, E. (1991). *Knowledge in Perspective*. New York: Cambridge University Press.

Sosa, E. (2007). *A Virtue Epistemology: Apt Belief and Reflective Knowledge*. Vol. 1. Oxford: Oxford University Press.

Sosa, E. (2009). *Reflective Knowledge: Apt Belief and Reflective Knowledge*. Vol. 2. Oxford: Oxford University Press.

Tishman, S., E. Jay, and D. N. Perkins. (1993). "Teaching Thinking Dispositions: From Transmission to Enculturation." *Theory into Practice* 32: 147–153.

Zagzebski, L. T. (1996). *Virtues of the Mind: An Inquiry into the Nature of Virtue and the Ethical Foundations of Knowledge*. Cambridge: Cambridge University Press.

8

Open-Mindedness, Critical Thinking, and Indoctrination

1. Introduction

It is an honor to join in the celebration of Bill Hare's retirement. For several decades Hare has set the standards for clarity, precision, argumentative rigor, and educational relevance of work in philosophy of education, in Canada and beyond. His work on open-mindedness, and on teaching and other matters of educational practice, is of the first importance and will influence the field for decades to come. I can only hope that the freedom from teaching and committee meetings that retirement brings will enable him to make further exceptional contributions to our collective effort to shed philosophical light on education. His work will remain a model for us all.

In this paper I focus on Hare's work on open-mindedness, an ideal that Hare has clarified and defended powerfully and tellingly. It is not an exaggeration to say that Hare's work put open-mindedness on the philosophy of education map. I will not challenge this work; on the contrary, I find Hare's account of the character and importance of open-mindedness compelling and completely persuasive. However, it raises a question that has not received much attention: What is the relation between open-mindedness and other important educational aims and ideals? In particular, what is its relation to the ideal I myself have defended, that of critical thinking?

I was stimulated to think about this question by a paper by Eamonn Callan and Dylan Arena. In their paper "Indoctrination" (2009), Callan and Arena develop an account of indoctrination according to which the fundamental feature of the phenomenon is the resulting close-mindedness and close-minded belief of the indoctrinated student: "[T]he inculcation of close-minded belief is indoctrination" (p. 116).[1] This contrasts with my own view, according to which the mark of the indoctrinated student is rather the non-evidential style with which she holds her indoctrinated beliefs, which is itself a failure of critical thinking.[2]

Hence the question concerning the relation between close-mindedness and critical thinking.

Callan and Arena's discussion is exemplary in several respects. First, it embraces an "outcome" approach to indoctrination, according to which indoctrination is best understood in terms of its effects on student learning and beliefs. (Full disclosure: I have defended this approach myself, in Siegel 1988, ch. 5.) Second, it explains convincingly both the attractions and the weaknesses of the three traditional accounts of indoctrination, according to which indoctrination is to be understood in terms of the intention of the teacher, the methods employed by the teacher, or the doctrinal nature of the subject matter. Third, it emphasizes the important points that indoctrination and close-mindedness (a) are matters of degree, and needn't be thought of as all-or-nothing affairs; and (b) are not necessarily permanent conditions, in that an indoctrinated person can overcome her indoctrination and close-mindedness over time.

While I am generally quite sympathetic with the account of indoctrination in terms of close-mindedness articulated and defended by Callan and Arena for the reasons just rehearsed, one question bothered me: is close-mindedness the fundamental feature of the indoctrinated mind, or is it rather a manifestation of a more fundamental feature of such minds—namely, a non-critical or non-evidential style of belief? Since I have argued for just such an account myself (Siegel 1988, ch. 5), this question was one I quickly decided to pursue. I do that next. But the question can be pursued more generally, i.e., without reference to indoctrination: given that both open-mindedness and critical thinking are important educational aims—we rightly want our students to be open-minded, and to be critical thinkers—what is the relation between these two worthy aims? Is one logically or conceptually more fundamental than the other? Is either a necessary or sufficient condition of the other? I pursue these questions in the following section.

2. Close-Mindedness, Non-evidential Style of Belief, and Indoctrination

While Callan and Arena (2009) plump for the fundamentality of close-mindedness to the correct account of indoctrination, their account actually depends on the victim of indoctrination having a non-evidential style of belief as much as it does close-mindedness:

> Insufficient regard for evidence is essential to an adequate conception of indoctrination, or so we shall argue. (p. 109)

> [E]xcessive resistance to [belief] revision does seem to be symptomatic of the indoctrinated mind, as we intuitively understand that condition. (p. 110)

> Those whom we suspect of being indoctrinated may devote themselves to winning converts and exposing the errors of all who disagree with them, and that cannot be done without heeding relevant evidence. But when belief is held regardless of the evidence, its maintenance has been divorced from consideration of the evidence, however extensive that consideration may be for other purposes, such as proselytizing. This condition of non-evidential maintenance, like unshakable belief, is also redolent of the intellectual rigidity we intuitively associate with being indoctrinated. (p. 110)

> [T]he effect of indoctrination has to do ... with some illicit breach between conviction on the one hand and the assessment of the evidence on the other. (p. 110)

This certainly sounds as though the mark of the indoctrinated mind is its non-evidential style of belief—just the view I favor. Indeed, the situation is even more complex, in that Callan and Arena's account of close-mindedness seems itself to depend upon a failure of critical thinking, and, more specifically, upon a non-evidential style of belief:

> To believe Proposition P close-mindedly is to be unable or unwilling to give due regard to reasons that are available for some belief or beliefs contrary to P because of excessive emotional attachment to the truth of P. (p. 111)

On this account of the matter, being close-minded with respect to a given belief P is a matter of believing that P non-evidentially, coupled with a particular causal explanation of the non-evidential style (i.e., caused by "excessive emotional attachment to the truth of P"). Callan and Arena argue that that causal explanation is, along with lack of due regard to reasons, a further necessary condition of close-mindedness:

> What also seems necessary is a special emotional investment in the truth of some belief that an open mind regarding that belief would threaten: the belief has become integral to the individual's understanding of who she is and why her life matters so that seriously considering evidence contrary to the belief is threatening to her very identity. (p. 111)

Callan and Arena's discussion of this threat, its psychological dimensions, the related intellectual vices of intellectual cowardice and intellectual arrogance, and the distinction between the psychological depth and breadth of close-mindedness (pp. 111–112) is a suggestive bit of moral psychology, although I would not myself want to rule out other causal paths to close-mindedness—some of which Callan and Arena acknowledge elsewhere (e.g., pp. 113–114). However, the point I want to pursue concerning the relation between close-mindedness and non-evidential style of belief can be pursued independently of this causal question, so I will set that question aside.

Callan and Arena's main reason for thinking that close-mindedness offers a better account of indoctrination than non-evidential style of belief is that close-mindedness, unlike disregard of the evidence, need not be total:

> So if we are trying to make sense of indoctrination as a practice that warrants moral disapproval, then the concept of close-mindedness, which admits varying degrees, seems better suited to capture the full range of relevant outcomes than [belief held regardless of the evidence]. (p. 111)

I agree that close-mindedness admits of degrees. But a disregard of relevant evidence, and a non-evidential style of belief more generally, also admit of degrees. If so, this point is not enough to favor close-mindedness over non-evidential style of belief as the key to indoctrination.[3]

I think the key question is this: Does giving "due regard to reasons" in Callan and Arena's account of close-mindedness involve just acknowledgement of and attention to available reasons, or the competent evaluation of such reasons as well?[4] If the former, one can be open-minded and yet fail to think critically; if the latter, the open-minded person is guaranteed to be a critical thinker because critical thinking is built into open-mindedness. To put the matter slightly differently: Is the open-minded person, in virtue of her open-mindedness, automatically or necessarily a competent evaluator of reasons? Does open-mindedness, that is, include the reason assessment component of critical thinking? To pursue these questions, we must set aside issues involving the proper account of indoctrination, and turn directly to the relations between open-mindedness and critical thinking.

3. Open-Mindedness, Style of Belief, and Critical Thinking: Multiple Relationships and the Question of Fundamentality

I suggested above that the fact that close-mindedness admits of degrees is not enough to favor close-mindedness over non-evidential style of belief as the key to indoctrination. I now want to move beyond indoctrination and argue that we should not favor open-mindedness over critical thinking as the fundamental epistemic ideal of education. On the contrary, it is critical thinking that is more fundamental.

The main reason for thinking so is that open-mindedness appears not to have anything to do with the *quality* of open-minded thinking and the beliefs that result from it. Rather, it seems clear that an open-minded person can be open-minded and yet think and believe *badly*: she can give "due regard to reasons" and yet assess those reasons incompetently or mistakenly; she can pay full attention to reasons, evidence and argument—give them "due regard"—and yet handle them badly from the epistemic point of view, and so believe open-mindedly but incompetently.

Is this right? Can a person think and believe open-mindedly yet badly? Here we must examine in more detail the character of open-mindedness as articulated by its most well-known and well-respected advocate, William Hare.

Hare's classic account of open-mindedness, *Open-Mindedness and Education* (1979), opens with a very brief gloss: open-mindedness essentially involves "a willingness to revise and reconsider one's views" (p. x). A bit more expansively, he writes that "a person must be both willing *and* able to revise his own position if he is to be open-minded" (p. 8, emphasis in original), and that "an open-minded person is one who is willing and able to revise his beliefs." More expansively still, he says,

> We do not want to make imagination, cleverness, or creativity necessary conditions of open-mindedness. Thus it is not the case that the ability to get results is a necessary condition of open-mindedness, but it is necessary that the person should not have been made incapable of the activity of giving consideration to such objections as others raise.
>
> A person who is open-minded is disposed to revise or reject the position he holds if sound objections are brought against it, or, in the situation in which the person has no opinion on some issue, he is disposed to make up his mind in the light of available evidence and argument as objectively and as impartially as possible. (pp. 8–9)

The mention of "sound objections" suggests that open-mindedness requires recognizing actually sound objections *as* sound—that is, evaluating the objections accurately or correctly—thus making open-mindedness depend not just on the ability and willingness to revise beliefs, but on the epistemic *quality* of revision as well. And I must acknowledge that other passages in Hare's work suggest this as well.[5] But the idea that the quality of belief-maintenance and -revision is a necessary condition of open-mindedness seems to contradict the clear majority of Hare's glosses on the latter notion, including his explicit declaration, just cited, that "it is not the case that the ability to get results is a necessary condition of open-mindedness." Rather, Hare's official account of the notion seems to be that the necessary conditions of open-mindedness do not include the quality of belief revision, but rather just the willingness and ability to revise beliefs, along with the disposition to "objectively and impartially"— but not necessarily epistemically correctly—consider "available evidence and argument." A further citation lends weight to this interpretation of Hare's view of the matter:

> [I]n saying that [a] person is open-minded, we reveal our assessment of how we think the person *would* act should objections be raised to his view. He would give attention to the objections, he would make revisions in a certain context, he would give up a view altogether. In short, we judge that he is disposed to reconsider. (p. 9, emphasis in original)

This interpretation is further supported by Hare's discussion of rationality (p. 11–14) Tellingly, he writes,

> [A] person may fall short of rationality by offering an argument which is invalid; let us say that he commits the fallacy of affirming the consequent. He asks that we accept that if p then q. Then he points out that q. He concludes by affirming p. We, of course, will rightly charge that this is irrational, that it does not follow. But we are not at all entitled to say that he is not open-minded just because he has committed a fallacy. In the light of our reply, we may see at once that he is disposed to withdraw the argument. A person not very adept at logic might even *tend* to commit fallacies of this sort yet deserve the ascription open-minded on the basis of his disposition to withdraw such fallacious arguments when the flaw is pointed out. (pp. 11–12, emphasis in original)

It seems clear that if this person can rightly be declared open-minded, even though his reasoning and subsequent beliefs are irrational, then quality of reasoning and belief cannot be a necessary condition of open-mindedness. Rather, as Hare says later on this page, "the open-minded attitude is precisely that of being willing to form and revise our views in the light of relevant and pertinent considerations" (p. 12). Thus, at least in his classic early account of it, open-mindedness is, on Hare's view, a matter of having the ability to revise beliefs in the face of new evidence and argument, a willingness to do so, and, more strongly, the disposition to do so. It involves the *attitude* of "willing[ness] to revise one's views in the light of counter-evidence" (p. 129; see also p. 60). It does not, however, require that the open-minded person's consideration of the evidence and argument be of high epistemic quality. I'm open-minded if I attend to the new evidence and arguments that come my way, however badly I reason with and about them. Hare's summary of his chapter-length analysis is completely in keeping with this interpretation:

> [T]he trait of open-mindedness qualifies a person's activities in thinking, chiefly his ability and willingness to form and revise his views in the light of evidence and argument. This will be unpacked into a variety of dispositions such as a willingness to consider objections, to subject his own views to critical scrutiny, to seek out objections to his own position, and so on. The context will determine which of these more specific criteria are demanded. (p. 20)

Hare reiterates this account in his subsequent *In Defence of Open-Mindedness*:

> [O]pen-mindedness involves a willingness to form and revise one's views as impartially and as objectively as possible in the light of available evidence and argument. (Hare 1985, p. 3)

> [The] fundamental commitment to rational appraisal ... is the hallmark of open-mindedness. (p. 97)

Hare's more recent discussions echo these earlier accounts:

> Properly understood, open-mindedness is a fundamental intellectual virtue that involves a willingness to take relevant evidence and argument into account in forming or revising our beliefs and values, especially when there is some reason why such evidence and argument might be resisted by the individual in question. (Hare 2003b, p. 76)

> Open-mindedness is an intellectual virtue properly ascribed when an individual or a community is disposed to take into account all that is relevant to forming a sound judgment and likewise disposed to reconsider judgments already made, or in formation, in the light of emerging difficulties, especially when it is tempting to avoid acting in these ways. (Hare 2003a, p. 4)

On the basis of these several citations, it seems clear that, on Hare's account of it at least, open-mindedness involves the ability, willingness, and disposition to reconsider one's beliefs in the light of new (to the believer) evidence, arguments, and potentially countervailing considerations. It does not require the ability to assess these new considerations correctly or well. From the epistemic point of view, it is quite possible to reason open-mindedly but badly, and to believe open-mindedly but unjustifiably, incompetently, and even irrationally. I think Hare is right about this—open-mindedness is one very good thing; evaluating reasons, evidence, and arguments competently is another.

If this point is correct, what should we say about the relationships obtaining between open-mindedness and critical thinking? We should say at least the following:

a. *Open-mindedness is a necessary (but not sufficient) condition of critical thinking.*

Can one be open-minded and yet an uncritical thinker/believer? Yes, one can believe open-mindedly but fail to master (or lack the disposition to believe, judge, and act in accordance with) the reason-assessment component of critical thinking. That is, one can think, reason, and believe open-mindedly but badly. So open-mindedness is not a sufficient condition of critical thinking; that is, being open-minded does not insure that one's thinking or believing meets relevant standards of epistemic quality.

But one cannot be a critical thinker without being open-minded, because open-mindedness—the ability and disposition to seek reasons and evidence, and to believe in accordance with their proper evaluation—is a central aspect of the critical spirit component of critical thinking. If one is not open-minded, one lacks the critical spirit, and so lacks a central, necessary component of critical thinking. So open-mindedness is a necessary condition of critical thinking.[6]

Putting these two points together: open-mindedness is a necessary but not a sufficient condition of critical thinking.

b. *Critical thinking is a sufficient (but not necessary) condition of open-mindedness.*

Can one be a critical thinker and yet be close-minded? No. If one is a critical thinker, one has the critical spirit—which includes a willingness and ability to reconsider one's beliefs in the light of new reasons and evidence—and so is open-minded. So being a critical thinker is sufficient for being open-minded.

On the other hand, one can be open-minded but not a critical thinker—as we have just seen—if, for example, one fails to evaluate candidate reasons and evidence in epistemically appropriate ways. That is, one can reason and believe open-mindedly but badly. So being a critical thinker is not a necessary condition of open-mindedness.

Putting these two points together: critical thinking is a sufficient but not a necessary condition of open-mindedness.

If open-mindedness is necessary but not sufficient for critical thinking, and critical thinking is sufficient but not necessary for open-mindedness, then

c. *Critical thinking is the more fundamental educational ideal.*

The achievement of open-mindedness leaves us, if we are to be critical thinkers, still needing to master the several epistemic ingredients of the reason assessment component of critical thinking—mastering the many (general and subject-specific) principles of reason assessment, as well as the general theoretical understanding of what might be called the *epistemology of reasons*,[7] along with that portion of the critical spirit that goes beyond open-mindedness. To put the point in perhaps misleadingly temporal terms: one's becoming open-minded is part of the journey toward becoming a critical thinker—not the other way around. When one is a critical thinker, one is *eo ipso* open-minded. Open-mindedness is a component of the overarching ideal of critical thinking.[8]

4. Conclusion: On Educational Aims and Ideals, and Another Brief Look at Indoctrination

It is worth noting that Hare's view is not that open-mindedness is either the only or the most fundamental epistemic aim of education, but only that it is a necessary aim:

> [T]he claim is not that open-mindedness is the sole aim of education. It is claimed here that it is a necessary aim of education. (Hare 1979, p. 63)

My own view, that critical thinking is "first among equals" among educational aims and ideals, because any claim in support of the fundamentality of any other ideal would depend upon critical thinking itself for its vindication (Siegel 1988, p. 137), is in this respect more ambitious. But Hare and I are agreed that open-mindedness is not only an important aim, but a necessary one, for any education worthy of the name. Indeed, I have not offered here a single substantive criticism of Hare's work on open-mindedness, which I continue to think correct and to regard with great admiration. It was not Hare's many discussions, but rather Callan and Arena's treatment of indoctrination, that prompted my concern about the relationship between open-mindedness and critical thinking.

So what should we say about that treatment? Are Callan and Arena right that teaching is best seen as morally objectionable indoctrination just when it results in close-mindedness, rather than a non-evidential, and so non-critical, style of belief?

I confess to conflicting intuitions here. If I inculcate student beliefs in such a way that their credulity and sloth, which my teaching has fostered, render them unable to think critically about those beliefs, and so results in the students believing them non-evidentially, have I not indoctrinated them? It seems to me that I have, although I am happy to grant that my teaching has not rendered them close-minded. But I can see the force of Callan and Arena's point: my students' indoctrinated states are not the result of close-mindedness, but rather (in this example) of my teaching's rendering them credulous or intellectually slothful. My inclination now is to think that one could go either way here, but that the case for the fundamentality of critical thinking made above extends to our understanding of indoctrination, and also lends support to the claim that indoctrination is better seen as a matter of non-evidential style of belief rather than close-mindedness. Going this way would give us a more unified overall theoretical understanding of education, by connecting our account of fundamental ideals with that of indoctrination. This sort of theoretical unification is not nothing. But neither is it determinative; it is just one additional point in favor of understanding indoctrination in terms of non-evidential style of belief. So I would welcome, and be open to, additional argument in support of Callan and Arena's account of indoctrination in terms of close-mindedness.

It is perhaps worth pointing out that the issue separating us is a relatively small one. The question is, are open-minded but non-evidential believers possibly victims of indoctrination? Callan and Arena answer in the negative: if the believers are open-minded, they haven't been indoctrinated, no matter what other intellectual vices their teachers' teaching has saddled them with. My own answer is that if those other vices render them such that they believe non-evidentially, then they can and should be regarded as having been indoctrinated. I acknowledge Callan and Arena's helpful distinction between close-mindedness and other vices, including those of credulity and sloth. But I am not persuaded, by appeal either to intuitions or ordinary usage, that open-minded but non-evidential believers cannot rightly be described as victims of indoctrination. The only reason for preferring the account that I have offered is that of theoretical unification, and I concede that this reason is not sufficient to settle the matter. I look forward to further exploration of the issue by both Callan and Arena and others.

I end in praise of both open-mindedness and critical thinking. More importantly, I close with praise for Bill Hare's sterling contributions to our understanding of open-mindedness and its place in education, his important work on teaching and on the virtues, and his remarkable impact on his many students. And I look forward to his further contributions to education and its philosophy.[9]

Notes

1. I must acknowledge that I have quoted this sentence misleadingly; it appears simply as the antecedent of a conditional statement. It is actually difficult to find a straightforward,

unqualified statement of Callan and Arena's positive view—that indoctrination is teaching that brings about close-minded belief—in their paper. Still, there is no question that that is their positive view. So I hope I can be forgiven this misleading quotation. It is worth noting that their view echoes Hare's: "[T]o be indoctrinated is to have a closed mind" (Hare 1979, p. x).

2. "[I]ndoctrination, insofar as it is a matter of fostering a non-evidential style of belief, is anti-critical. There is a deep, although obvious, connection between style of belief and critical thinking. A person who has an evidential style of belief has a disposition to seek reasons and evidence, and to believe on that basis; and this, we have seen, is a central component of critical thinking. A person with a non-evidential style of belief, on the other hand, lacks this key feature of critical thinking" (Siegel 1988, pp. 87–88).

3. Callan and Arena gently chastise me (pp. 120–121, note 7) for urging that "[i]ndoctrination may be regarded as the collection of those modes of belief inculcation which foster a non-evidential, or *non-critical*, style of belief" (quoting from Siegel 1988, p. 80, emphasis in original), on the grounds that some such modes may result in defects other than close-mindedness: "Credulity and intellectual sloth may prevent critical inquiry and nourish non-evidential styles of belief, but they are not the same as close-mindedness, and therefore, the teaching that produces them is not the same as indoctrination" (p. 34). I certainly agree that credulity and intellectual sloth are different intellectual vices than that of close-mindedness, and am happy to grant that point. But its bearing on the question at issue—i.e., whether indoctrination is best understood in terms of close-mindedness or critical thinking/non-evidential style of belief—is unclear, and it should be pointed out that as it stands the point seems clearly enough to presuppose, rather than constitute an independent reason for, their view that indoctrination is a matter of close-mindedness. I return to this matter below.

4. In the language of the account of critical thinking put forward in *Educating Reason*, chapter 2, does it include mastery of the "reason assessment" component of critical thinking? That is, does it involve the ability "to assess reasons and their ability to warrant beliefs, claims and actions *properly*" (Siegel 1988, p. 34, emphasis added)? It is also worth pointing out that critical thinking involves not just the competent evaluation of reasons already available, but also the dispositions to so evaluate, and to seek and produce further reasons, evidence, and arguments relevant to candidate beliefs. I won't develop this point further here.

5. Several of Hare's discussions do in fact suggest that at least some minimal competence in reason assessment is necessary for open-mindedness (see, e.g., Hare 1979, p. 79; Hare 2001, p. 42; Hare 2003, p. 79; Hare 2007, p. 22). I am grateful to Hare for his help and usual insightfulness on this and related matters.

6. Hare makes a closely related point—that open-mindedness is a necessary condition of "a concern for truth"—in Hare 1979, pp. 60–61.

7. See, e.g., Siegel 1988, p. 37. I have referred only to *Educating Reason* here. Many of the points mentioned thus far are further developed in Siegel 1997 and other publications.

8. The previous several pages have proceeded from my reading of Hare as holding that open-mindedness is not dependent on matters of epistemic quality; that one can believe open-mindedly but badly. Suppose this reading of Hare, and this understanding of open-mindedness, is mistaken. Suppose, that is—as was suggested by several commentators, notably Christopher Higgins and Hare himself—that in order to reason and believe open-mindedly, one's reasoning and believing must comport at least minimally with relevant epistemic standards, so that open-mindedness involves at least partial mastery of the reason assessment component of critical thinking?

This understanding of open-mindedness is at odds not only with Hare's standard account of the notion, but with ordinary usage as well, since we do in fact (in English, at least) routinely attribute open-mindedness to people independently of their ratiocinative abilities and inclinations. Hare's groundbreaking analysis seems to establish this clearly and compellingly.

In conversation and correspondence after the presentation of an earlier version of this paper (see note 10 below for details), Hare has effectively reminded me that on his considered view, open-mindedness requires at least a minimal competence with respect to reason assessment. (See references in note 5 above.) Indeed, on Hare's considered view, open-mindedness and at-least-minimal-competence-with-respect-to-reason-assessment are necessary conditions of each other, and are "importantly intertwined" (as I have described the interrelationship between rationality and objectivity in Siegel 1999 and (with Alven Neiman) somewhat more expansively in Neiman and Siegel 1993). I have no serious objection to this way of looking at the relation between open-mindedness and critical thinking. But I would point out that as long as the competence involved is genuinely minimal, my claim that critical thinking is the more fundamental ideal seems to stand, in that one could, on this view of the matter, be fully open-minded and yet only minimally competent as a critical thinker, thus meeting the first but failing to meet the second. I would also point out that building minimal reason assessment competence into the definition of open-mindedness seems a fairly substantial change from what I above called Hare's "official account" of the notion. Thanks to Higgins and especially Hare for correspondence that prompted this note.

9. I was fortunate to present a version of this paper at the recent conference in honor of Hare's retirement, "Open-Mindedness and the Virtues in Education: Conference Celebrating the Work of Professor William Hare," at Mount Saint Vincent University, Halifax, Nova Scotia, October 2–4, 2008. I am grateful to the audience members for their helpful questions, comments, and suggestions, and to Bill Hare for his insightful reactions and exceptional grace.

References

Callan, E., and D. Arena. (2009). "Indoctrination." In H. Siegel (ed.), *Oxford Handbook of Philosophy of Education* (pp. 104–121). Oxford: Oxford University Press.
Hare, W. (1979). *Open-Mindedness and Education*. Kingston, ON: McGill-Queen's University Press.
Hare, W. (1985). *In Defence of Open-Mindedness*. Kingston, ON: McGill-Queen's University Press.
Hare, W. (2001). "Bertrand Russell and the Ideal of Critical Receptiveness." *Skeptical Inquirer* 25.3: 40–44.
Hare, W. (2003a). "The Ideal of Open-Mindedness and Its Place in Education." *Journal of Thought* 38.2: 3–10.
Hare, W. (2003b). "Is It Good to Be Open-Minded?" *International Journal of Applied Philosophy* 17.1: 73–87.
Hare, W. (2007). "What Is Open-Mindedness?" In William Hare and John P. Portelli (eds.), *Key Questions for Educators* (pp. 21–25). San Francisco: Caddo Gap Press.
Neiman, A., and H. Siegel. (1993). "Objectivity and Rationality in Epistemology and Education: Scheffler's Middle Road." *Synthese* 94.1: 55–83.
Siegel, H. (1988). *Educating Reason: Rationality, Critical Thinking, and Education*. London: Routledge.
Siegel, H. (1997). *Rationality Redeemed?: Further Dialogues on an Educational Ideal*. New York: Routledge.
Siegel, H. (1999). "Review of Nicholas Rescher, *Objectivity: The Obligations of Impersonal Reason*." *Ethics* 109.4: 917–919.

PART THREE

VALUES, RATIONALITY, AND THE VALUE OF RATIONALITY

9

Is "Education" a Thick Epistemic Concept?

1. Introduction

I begin by noting two doubts about this effort. First, I am leery of "concept talk" and the concept of "concept," a concept which has itself resisted analysis.[1] Second, I share the worries expressed by Samuel Scheffler (1987) concerning the viability of the thick/thin distinction as applied to concepts: can the distinction be sharply drawn at all? If not, does that render the aim of this exercise—to explore the benefits to be gained by pursuing epistemology "thickly"—pointless or doomed to failure? Since I think the answers to these questions are "no" and "no," I will mainly set these worries aside, and in what follows I will take "thick" and "thin" to be poles on a continuum, presuming that concepts manifest them (or not) to varying degrees.

Despite those worries, the project here pursued nevertheless seems to me worth pursuing for several interrelated reasons. First, epistemologists generally neglect education—as central a knowledge-oriented human practice as there is—in their epistemological efforts. But education is not only rich in epistemological content and relevance; specific epistemological issues—for example, those concerning ultimate epistemic aims and values, and the evidential status of testimony—are helpfully viewed in the context of education, such that thinking about education promises substantial benefit for the pursuit of standard epistemological questions.[2] This is especially true in the current epistemological climate, in which both *virtue* epistemology and *social* epistemology are high on the epistemological agenda. Both philosophers of education and virtue epistemologists are keen to understand epistemic virtues and the desirability of fostering them. (More on this below.) And education is arguably the social practice most concerned with the development and transmission of knowledge; it is, consequently, or at least should be, of primary interest to the social epistemologist (Siegel 2004a). Finally, if, as I suggest below, education is rightly viewed as a "thick" epistemic concept, it might illustrate the benefit of pursuing epistemology "thickly."

Supposing the concept of "concept" legitimate and the thick/thin distinction sufficiently viable, at least when viewed as a difference in degree, our questions are: (1) Is "education" an epistemic concept at all? (2) If it is, is it thick or thin?

2. The "Thick/Thin" Distinction, in Ethics and Epistemology

Bernard Williams famously introduced the distinction between "thick" and "thin" ethical concepts in his *Ethics and the Limits of Philosophy* (1985). On Williams' account, thin ethical concepts are general and abstract; they are not "world-guided." That is, their application is not dependent on the way the world is (p. 129). Williams' examples of thin ethical concepts include "good," "right," and "ought" (p. 128). Thick ethical concepts, by contrast, are more specific, less abstract, and world-guided; they are also "action-guiding." That is, they typically provide one with (defeasible) reasons for action (p. 140). Williams' examples of thick ethical concepts include "treachery," "promise," "brutality," and "courage" (p. 129).

Samuel Scheffler's well-known essay review of Williams' book (Scheffler 1987) raises some deep difficulties with the distinction, arguing of specific ethical concepts—Scheffler gives as examples five "clusters" of three concepts each, and suggests of the resulting fifteen concepts (justice, fairness, impartiality, liberty, equality, freedom of expression, privacy, self-respect, envy, needs, well-being, interests, rights, autonomy, and consent)—that "it is impossible confidently to classify various of the concepts ... as either thick or thin" (p. 417). He offers several reasons for thinking so (pp. 417–418), the details of which need not detain us here. His ultimate suggestion that is relevant to the present effort is that "any division of ethical concepts into the two categories of the thick and the thin is itself a considerable oversimplification" (p. 418).

I worry whether the notion of "world-guidedness," assuming that it makes sense in the ethical context, can be transposed neatly to the epistemological context, since (a) many epistemic concepts are not directly connected to action in the way that ethical concepts are, and (b) epistemologists contest the degree to which the application of many epistemic concepts (e.g., "... is a good reason for ...") depends upon the way the world is. Waiving such worries here, I think the best way forward is to give up the idea that the thick/thin distinction (assuming that it makes sense in the epistemological context) is a sharp one, and, as suggested above, instead regard it as a matter of degree. Doing so allows us to pursue our question as follows: In what respects, and to what degree, is "education" a thick epistemic concept; and in what respects, and to what degree, is it rather a thin epistemic concept? I pursue these questions below.

3. Education: A Genuinely Epistemic Concept?

"Education"—that is, the concept associated with the social practice—has a wide range of epistemological dimensions; insofar, it seems clearly enough to qualify as a specifically epistemic concept. I briefly review some of those dimensions next.

A. Epistemic Aims of Education

First, and most importantly, there are fundamental aims of education that are epistemological in nature. It is widely held by education scholars, as well as by educators, policymakers, and concerned citizens, that the fostering of *critical thinking* is a fundamental educational aim, and indeed that critical thinking is an overridingly important educational ideal (Bailin and Siegel 2003; Scheffler 1989; Siegel 1988, 1997, 2003). Since critical thinking is best understood in terms of *rationality*—indeed, as the "educational cognate" (Siegel 1988, p. 32) of rationality—and since rationality is in turn a central epistemological notion, related as it is to *reasons* and *justification*—it seems clear enough that at least in this respect "education" counts as an epistemic concept.

There is considerable philosophical controversy concerning the epistemic aims of education. Alvin Goldman (1999, ch. 11), for example, argues that the ultimate epistemic aim of education is truth—more exactly, the learning/teaching of truths and the fostering of the abilities to discern/discover truths and to distinguish truths from falsehoods—and that the fostering of the skills, abilities, and dispositions relevant to critical thinking and rational belief are merely instrumentally valuable in terms of their ability to advance the ultimate aim of truth. Others, including Emily Robertson (2009) and myself (Siegel 2005), while not denying the legitimacy of the aim of truth, argue to the contrary that critical thinking and rational belief are educationally fundamental, and are of more than (merely) instrumental value. Catherine Z. Elgin (1999) takes the fundamental epistemic aim of education to be understanding. It is possible that some combination of these is ultimately the best account of the epistemic aims of education—that is, that there is a plurality of such aims rather than a single overriding aim[3] (Siegel 2005). There is no need to delve deeply into this matter here (although I will return to it briefly below).[4] The fact that the aim or point of education is tied up with central epistemological concerns lends credence to the claim that "education" is a genuine epistemic concept.[5]

B. "Being Educated" and the Educated Person

Much has been written, especially in the heyday of the ordinary language strain of analytic philosophy of education, about the concept of the "educated person."[6] Israel Scheffler provides a helpful summary statement of the overall character of both the concept and this literature, which draws on previous work of R. S. Peters, Michael Oakeshott, John Passmore, and Scheffler himself:

> [W]e have described the learning [an educated] person acquires as worthwhile and significant, as broad rather than narrow, as involving understanding rather than mere information or trained skill. We have emphasized the cognitive perspective afforded by such learning, incorporating knowledge that is active, principled, and transformative of perception. We have further required that the knowledge acquired be supplemented by care, producing some form of passion or engagement. We have stressed the development of an individual point of view free of cliché and the ability to articulate it in exchange with others. Finally, we have emphasized membership in a critical community and participation within various traditions of imaginative thought. (Scheffler 1995, p. 90)

This general characterization of the concept of the educated person has been subjected to serious criticism, some of which Scheffler responds to in the pages following this passage (pp. 90–99; see also Phillips 2008). I do not wish to endorse this or any other particular analysis of the concept "educated person" here. Still, it seems clear that any such account will centrally involve knowledge, understanding, cognitive perspective, and virtues[7]/dispositions/character traits/habits of mind that are largely epistemological in character.

Is the converse also true? If the analysis of "educated" will centrally involve epistemological notions, is a complete analysis of knowledge also likely to mention "education" or "being educated?" Consider the following questions.

i. *Is education a necessary condition of knowledge or justified belief?* That is, must persons have been educated in order to be knowers or justified believers?

Here it is important to distinguish between "education" and "schooling." It is obvious enough that persons don't need to have participated in formal schooling activities in order to know or justifiably believe things. But can persons know or justifiably believe anything without having been educated in some more general sense?

Much depends here upon the detailed formulation of the question, and upon other contentious philosophical matters. For example, if one thinks that knowing or justifiably believing requires at least some linguistic facility, that language-learning is an essentially social phenomenon, and that what goes on when a very young child learns a first language counts as "educative," then one might think that knowing does indeed require having been educated. All these theses are controversial. One might think that some knowing is pre- or nonlinguistic (e.g., the knowledge that animals or pre-linguistic infants have, or the knowledge furnished by simple perceptual experiences), thus rejecting the first thought just mentioned. One might reject Wittgenstein's private language argument and hold out for the intelligibility of private language, thus rejecting the second thought mentioned. Finally, one might reject the idea that speaking to and in the presence of pre-linguistic infants counts as educating them, thus rejecting the third thought mentioned. And obviously, much more would have to be said about the concepts of "education" and "being educated" than has been said thus far.

I think it must be granted that these matters are sufficiently controversial philosophically that it would require quite a lot of philosophical work to establish that having been educated is a necessary condition of being a knower or justified believer.[8] Insofar, we have seen no reason to think that being educated does constitute such a necessary condition. And there seems to be no problem imagining (or pointing to actual) people who become, through their own efforts, able to know and justifiably believe as well as those who have been educated. So the case for the thesis that being an educated person, or having been educated, is a necessary condition of being a knower or justified believer is far from being made. On the contrary, it seems not to be such a condition.

ii. *Is "being educated" an epistemic virtue?*

Even if it is correct that a person might know or justifiably believe that *p* without having been educated—that is, even if it is correct that education is not a necessary condition of knowledge or justified belief—it remains nonetheless that education and educative experiences aim to transmit knowledge (and at least sometimes succeed in this), as well as the reasons and evidence that justify such knowledge. Education also helps students to develop the skills and abilities required to understand the relationships obtaining among items of knowledge and the reasons and evidence that support(s) them, to discover or create new items of knowledge, and to assess competently the myriad knowledge claims that come one's way. Finally, education also helps to foster the many dispositions, habits of mind, character traits, and epistemic virtues that characterize critical thinkers, rational and justified believers, and knowers. In this respect, education, though perhaps not necessary for knowledge or justified belief, is as fundamental to the cultivation of these desirable epistemic states as can be. It thus makes sense to think of "being educated" as itself an epistemic virtue.[9]

iii. *Should all people be educated?* That is, is it a norm of some sort (moral, epistemic, or social/political) that people be educated?[10]

I think the answer here is clearly "yes," for at least three (sorts of) reasons. First, and most importantly, we are obliged to treat students with *respect as persons*, and so treating them requires doing our best to foster in them the abilities and dispositions characteristic of the critical thinker, which is itself a paradigmatically educational task.[11] If correct, this would be a *moral* reason for endorsing this norm.

Second, educating students is in fact fundamental to the cultivation of the desirable epistemic states mentioned above. This is a contingent empirical claim, of course, but it seems clearly enough to be true in the actual world: the desirable epistemic states do not in general emerge, at least to a satisfactory extent, without specific educational interventions. If correct, this would be an *epistemic* reason for endorsing this norm.

Third, education has an important role to play in readying students for full participation in civic, especially democratic, society. Many historical and contemporary figures have argued both for the importance of this aim and for the centrality of educational efforts in achieving it. If correct, this would be a *social/political* reason for endorsing this norm.

If all this is correct, then while education is not a necessary condition of knowledge, it will nevertheless play an important role in our broad understanding of knowledge and knowers.

C. Education and the Fostering of Epistemic Virtues

I just mentioned "virtues." I might well have begun with them. Although we should not lose sight of the difficulties concerning virtues discussed in the previous chapter, on a sufficiently loose and liberal understanding of the term, the fostering of virtues generally—and of epistemic virtues in particular—is central to education, on almost all extant philosophical accounts of it.

The work of philosophers of education who focus on education's epistemological dimensions, and of virtue theorists in epistemology, overlaps considerably. Among the former, theorists of critical thinking (Sharon Bailin, Robert Ennis, Matthew Lipman, John McPeck, Richard Paul, Emily Robertson, Israel Scheffler, and yours truly, among many others) emphasize the central educational task of the fostering of specific dispositions, habits of mind, and character traits in students, many of which correspond, at least roughly, to the fostering of specific epistemic virtues. The dispositions emphasized by philosophers of education include those of seeking truth; seeking, respecting, and valuing reasons; judging in accordance with the strength of reasons; evaluating such strength competently and fair-mindedly; imagining (and competently assessing) new possibilities; putting oneself in the place of one's interlocutors and seeing things from their perspective; taking seriously the possibility that one might be mistaken; etc. Specific character traits so emphasized include fair-mindedness, open-mindedness, thoughtfulness/reflectiveness, intellectual humility, etc.[12] This overlaps substantially with the work of epistemological virtue theorists.[13]

Consider, as an example, the dispositions to seek and evaluate reasons, and to be guided in belief, judgment, and action by such evaluations. These have been central to the characterization of critical thinking in the philosophy of education literature, and are closely associated with or (partly) constitutive of the virtue of *reasonableness*. The latter is of interest to virtue epistemologists, and I focus on these dispositions and the associated virtue briefly in order to illustrate the ways in which the intellectual virtues on which that literature concentrates overlaps with, and perhaps sheds light on, the virtues of concern to virtue epistemologists.

It would be a mistake to suggest that the many theorists of critical thinking are agreed on all matters of substance; of course they are not. Still, there is a fair degree of agreement on the following points. First, it is crucial that the dispositions be understood as genuine dispositions (and so the large literature on the metaphysics of dispositions comes into play in the characterization of the virtue[14]); it won't do if students are able to seek and evaluate reasons and be guided by such evaluations, but do so only intermittently, sporadically, when the mood takes them, or when their own interests aren't at stake. Such intermittent reason-seekers/evaluators would be deficient from the points of view of both critical thinking and the virtue of reasonableness. The abilities in question are insufficient without the associated dispositions. Second, these dispositions must be more than casual behavioral "add-ons," but must rather be deeply ingrained in and integral to the *character* of the critical thinker/reasonable person. Accordingly, being a critical thinker/reasonable person requires intellectual virtues that are closely associated with or partly constitutive of *character traits* that are epistemologically and educationally (and morally) fundamental (Burbules 1995; Siegel 1988, 1997, 2003).

One might go further here and urge that virtue epistemology itself describes the aims of education, since virtue epistemology aims to tell us what good knowers should be like, and education aims, in part, to turn children into good knowers.[15] There is considerable insight in this suggestion, though I think it must be handled with caution. For one thing, the remit of education is far broader than the epistemic, involving dimensions of character, moral training, sociality and civic participation, and so on, all of which go beyond the epistemic. Even if the suggestion is limited to epistemic matters, such that virtue epistemology describes only the epistemic aims of education, it is still, I think, overly general, in that these aims plausibly include (as we have seen above) understanding and a kind of cognitive perspective, both of which seem to go beyond the requirements of "good knowers." Finally, education is subject to constraints of manner—a teacher may aim to get her students to know that *p*, but only certain ways of getting them to know it are acceptable, educationally. For example, brainwashing and indoctrination are at least arguably ways of getting students to know, but these ways are unavailable to the educator.[16] It is not clear that the simple question of whether someone knows something is subject to the same constraint. For these reasons I am hesitant to cede to virtue epistemology the entirety of the task of describing the epistemic aims of education—to do this well, I think, attention must be given not only to the virtues possessed by good knowers, but also to other virtues that are arguably epistemic but that go beyond those possessed by such knowers, as well as to the character of educational activities and the constraints under which they must be carried out. Moreover, as urged in chapter 7 above, there are some daunting problems with conceiving of the aims of education in virtue terms. Nevertheless, since, on a sufficiently broad understanding of "virtue," the fostering of specific epistemic virtues is a central task of education, there is undoubtedly a close connection between the work of virtue epistemologists and that of philosophers who endeavor to articulate the epistemic aims of education.[17]

Work in virtue epistemology is of course complex, multilayered, and multiply contentious, and I cannot engage it seriously here. Still, there is no question that—again, suitably broadly understood—the fostering of specific epistemic virtues is a central task of education, and this also lends credence to the claim that "education" is a genuine epistemic concept.[18]

I offer the three sets of considerations just (far too briefly) sketched—i.e., those concerning the epistemic aims of education, what is involved in being educated and the related concept of the "educated person," and education's task of fostering epistemic virtues—as reasons for regarding "education" as a specifically epistemic concept. The concept has other dimensions or aspects than the epistemological, and no doubt other epistemological dimensions than the three mentioned thus far. In any case, I shall proceed on the assumption that the case has now been made that "education" is indeed an epistemic concept. The question to be addressed next is whether it is thick or thin.

4. "Education" as a "Thick" Epistemic Concept

There are several respects in which "education" appears to be a "thick" epistemic concept, or at least thicker than other standard epistemic concepts such as "knowledge." Compare these two. Standard theories of knowledge analyze the concept in terms of some combination of necessary and sufficient conditions, in the familiar way on which many of us cut our philosophical teeth. The concept remains general and the analyses relentlessly abstract. The application of the concept is not, in general, "world-guided," and epistemologists are generally more interested in furthering their analyses by way of consideration of imaginative examples than by examining either the world or the knowers in it.[19] "Education" and "being educated," by contrast, seem in general less abstract, and more dependent on real world descriptions, depictions, values, and social practices. Whether or not an activity or social practice counts as educative, or a person as educated, seems to depend, similarly, on nuanced understandings of real world practices. For example, are a person's knowledge of local history, her ability to add and subtract numbers with facility, her curiosity about the worlds of things and ideas and her corresponding inclination to seek information and inquire, or her tendency to challenge the declarations of her teachers and political leaders indicators of her having been educated? The answers to these questions will depend upon a variety of real world descriptions of different sorts: in particular, of the detailed characterizations of the knowledge, ability, and inclinations in question, and of the educational practices of the local community.

The answers to these questions will also depend on local educational values (both proclaimed and in fact advanced) and practices—in some contexts, her knowledge, abilities, and inclinations will count in favor of her being educated; in others, they will be indicators of flaws that would have been eliminated, or at least mitigated, if only she had been educated. This highlights the important fact that "education" and "being educated" are culturally mediated or culturally dependent concepts, in a way that "knowledge" (as treated by most epistemologists at any rate) is not. By this I mean that what counts as an educational practice, and who counts as an educated person, is at least to some degree culturally specific. (Think of cultures that are more or less traditional, more or less open to critical questioning and the challenging of elders and authority figures (including teachers), more or less governed by unchallengeable sacred texts, etc.) The need to negotiate such cultural matters forces philosophers of education—even those, like me, who seek to establish culturally independent educational ideals—to treat key concepts, including "education" itself, more "thickly" than epistemologists are generally obliged to treat "knowledge."[20]

Whether someone is "educated" or whether some social practice counts as "education" is not solely a question of description or of value; it is at once a matter of description and of value, and as such the concept seems to have the dual character that Williams (1985) thinks holds for thick ethical concepts (like "courage").

5. Conclusion: Pursuing Epistemology "Thickly"

I hope to have made plausible the claim that "education" is a genuine epistemic concept. While I remain somewhat ambivalent about the legitimacy and helpfulness of the thick/thin distinction, at least as applied to specifically epistemic concepts, I hope to have made plausible the claim that, to the extent that the distinction is viable, "education" is more thick than thin. Along the way I hope to have clarified the relationship between virtue epistemology and the epistemological aspects of philosophy of education, as well as the sense in which and the degree to which being educated is itself an epistemic virtue. Elsewhere I have urged social epistemologists to turn their attention to epistemological questions concerning education (Siegel 2004a). I close by urging virtue epistemologists in particular, and epistemologists more generally, to do the same. The philosophy of education can only benefit from such attention—as, I hope, will epistemology itself.

Notes

1. For example, Timothy Williamson, in his absorbing and sophisticated recent defense of "armchair philosophy" (Williamson 2007), mentions and discusses several accounts (or conceptions) of the concept of "concept," including (a) "what synonymous expressions ha[ve] in common" (p. 13), (b) "the constituents of thought" (p. 15), "modes of presentation, ways of thinking or speaking, or intellectual capacities" (p. 15), the denizens of "the realm of sense or thought" (p. 17), "meanings" (p. 29), and "mental or semantic representations" (p. 30). This is quite an array of accounts of what is usually taken to be a single concept.
2. At least, so I have argued—e.g., in Siegel 2004a and 2005 and the Introduction to Siegel 2009. The latter also discusses the unhappy separation of philosophy of education from general philosophy and urges their reunification, in epistemology and more generally. Notable exceptions to the blanket charge of neglect just leveled are also acknowledged therein.
3. In the years since this paper was first published, important work defending the ideal of the fostering of the intellectual virtues appeared, in particular that of Jason Baehr and Duncan Pritchard. See chapter 7 for discussion and references.
4. For a highly informative and nuanced survey and discussion of the domain, see Robertson 2009.
5. I hasten to note that there are other aims of education besides the epistemological ones just mentioned. Some concern the fostering of individual moral and other virtues and character traits; others are more social/political in nature. Acknowledging these, it is clear, does not jeopardize the epistemic aims that constitute one reason for regarding "education" as a genuinely epistemic concept. Acknowledging them rather makes clear that it is not a *solely* epistemic concept.
6. For a brief, helpful survey, see Phillips 2008, sec. 2.
7. I have in this chapter used "virtue" very generally as a near-synonym for "character trait," in ways that do not reflect a serious engagement with the virtue epistemology literature. In the previous, more recently written chapter I register my concerns with the term and with the idea that the fostering of the intellectual virtues is an important epistemic aim of education.
8. This also suggests the degree to which philosophical questions concerning education are intertwined with questions in other areas of philosophy, including in the present instance the philosophies of language and mind. For more on this theme see the Introduction to Siegel 2009.
9. Thanks here to Ben Kotzee.
10. Here it is important to keep in mind the distinction between education and schooling. Even if it is correct, as I argue next, that all people should be educated, it does not follow

that all people should be required to participate in formal school activities. That is, "All people should be educated" leaves open *how* they should be educated. Formal schooling is but one option here. I am not an opponent of formal schooling by any means. I want only to insist that requiring it for all would require far more argument than has been given thus far.

11. This is a big claim that I cannot defend here. See Siegel 1988, ch. 3.
12. For summaries and references to the relevant literature, see Bailin and Siegel 2003; Siegel 1988, 1997, 2003. On open-mindedness, see Hare 1979, 1985.
13. See, e.g., the papers in Axtell 2000; Fairweather and Zagzebski 2001; Brady and Pritchard 2003; Sosa 2007; and the literature discussed in the previous chapter. The literature here is large and growing fast, and these references are only meant to pick out the tip of the iceberg. For further critical discussion, cf. chapter 7 above.
14. On dispositions in general, see Kistler and Gnassounou 2007. For educationally relevant thinking dispositions in particular, see Siegel 1999b.
15. This idea was suggested by Ben Kotzee. I am grateful to Kotzee not only for the invitation to contribute to this special issue of *Philosophical Papers*, but also for his many stimulating suggestions concerning the thickness/thinness of "education" and "being educated," including this one. Cf. chapter 7 above, written several years after this one, for more detailed consideration.

    One might also think, as Kotzee suggests, that the link between the philosophy of education and virtue epistemology might provide an argument for doing philosophy of education as well as epistemology "thickly," by "thinking about the virtues that a good education fosters rather than by analyzing the concept of education." While sympathetic, I would resist the dichotomy. Surely philosophers of education should (and do) "think about the virtues that a good education fosters," but such thinking will also be informed (if anything is) by conceptual considerations. My earlier reservations about "concept talk" were not meant to suggest that philosophy could do without any attention to concepts at all, but rather only to note some difficulties with the concept of "concept." Again, thanks to Kotzee for the suggestion.
16. There is a very large literature on such matters; a good place to start is Scheffler 1989.
17. For further discussion, see Robertson 2009.
18. I apologize to the reader for the repeated qualifications. For the reasons why, see chapter 7.
19. Although "naturalized" accounts of knowledge are exceptions to this generalization. For a powerful defense of philosophical methodology as "a subtle interplay of logic and the imagination," see Williamson 2007 (cited passage from p. 19).
20. This is not to suggest or endorse any sort of cultural relativism. For my own take on these matters, see Siegel 1997, 1999a, 2004b.

References

Axtell, G. (ed.). (2000). *Knowledge, Belief, and Character: Readings in Virtue Epistemology*. Lanham, MD: Rowman & Littlefield.
Bailin, S., and H. Siegel. (2003). "Critical Thinking." In N. Blake, P. Smeyers, R. Smith, and P. Standish (eds.), *The Blackwell Guide to the Philosophy of Education* (pp. 181–193). Oxford: Blackwell.
Brady, M., and D. Pritchard (eds.). (2003). *Moral and Epistemic Virtues*. Malden, MA: Blackwell.
Burbules, N. C. (1995). "Reasonable Doubt: Toward a Postmodern Defense of Reason as an Educational Aim." In Wendy Kohli (ed.), *Critical Conversations in Philosophy of Education* (pp. 82–102). New York: Routledge.
Elgin, C. Z. (1999). "Epistemology's Ends, Pedagogy's Prospects." *Facta Philosophica* 1: 39–54.
Fairweather, A., and L. Zagzebski (eds.). (2001). *Virtue Epistemology: Essays on Epistemic Virtue and Responsibility*. Oxford: Oxford University Press.

Goldman, A. I. (1999). *Knowledge in a Social World*. Oxford: Oxford University Press.
Hare, W. (1979). *Open-Mindedness and Education*. Kingston, ON: McGill-Queen's University Press.
Hare, W. (1985). *In Defence of Open-Mindedness*. Kingston: McGill-Queen's University Press.
Kistler, M., and B. Gnassounou (eds.). (2007). *Dispositions and Causal Powers*. Aldershot, UK: Ashgate.
Phillips, D. C. (2008). "Philosophy of Education." In E. Zalta (ed.), *The Stanford Encyclopedia of Philosophy*. Stanford, CA: Center for Study of Language and Information, Stanford University. http://plato.stanford.edu/entries/education-philosophy/.
Robertson, E. (2009). "The Epistemic Aims of Education." In H. Siegel (ed.), *The Oxford Handbook of Philosophy of Education* (pp. 11–34). New York: Oxford University Press.
Scheffler, I. (1989). *Reason and Teaching*, Indianapolis: Hackett. Originally published in 1973 by Routledge & Kegan Paul.
Scheffler, I. (1995). "On the Idea of an Educated Person." In V. A. Howard and I. Scheffler, *Work, Education, and Leadership: Essays in the Philosophy of Education* (pp. 81–100). New York: Peter Lang.
Scheffler, S. (1987). "Morality through Thick and Thin." *Philosophical Review* 96.3: 411–434.
Siegel, H. (1988). *Educating Reason: Rationality, Critical Thinking, and Education*. London: Routledge.
Siegel, H. (1997). *Rationality Redeemed?: Further Dialogues on an Educational Ideal*. New York: Routledge.
Siegel, H. (1999a). "Multiculturalism and the Possibility of Transcultural Educational and Philosophical Ideals." *Philosophy* 74: 387–409.
Siegel, H. (1999b). "What (Good) Are Thinking Dispositions?" *Educational Theory* 49:2: 207–221.
Siegel, H. (2003). "Cultivating Reason." In R. Curren, ed. *A Companion to the Philosophy of Education* (pp. 305–317). Oxford: Blackwell.
Siegel, H. (2004a). "Epistemology and Education: An Incomplete Guide to the Social-Epistemological Issues." *Epistéme* 1:2: 129–137.
Siegel, H. (2004b). "Relativism." In I. Niiniluoto, M. Sintonen, and J. Woleński (eds.), *Handbook of Epistemology* (pp. 747–780). Dordrecht, The Netherlands: Kluwer.
Siegel, H. (2005). "Truth, Thinking, Testimony and Trust: Alvin Goldman on Epistemology and Education." *Philosophy and Phenomenological Research*, 71.2: 345–366.
Siegel, H. (2007). "The Philosophy of Education." In *The Encyclopaedia Britannica Online*. http://search.eb.com/eb/article-9108550.
Siegel, H. (ed.) (2009). *The Oxford Handbook of Philosophy of Education*. New York: Oxford University Press.
Sosa, E. (2007). *A Virtue Epistemology: Apt Belief and Reflective Knowledge*. Vol. 1. Oxford: Oxford University Press.
Williams, B. (1985). *Ethics and the Limits of Philosophy*. Cambridge, MA: Harvard University Press.
Williamson, T. (2007). *The Philosophy of Philosophy*. Malden, MA: Blackwell.

10

Truth, Thinking, Testimony, and Trust

Alvin Goldman on Epistemology and Education

1. Introduction

Despite both the central importance of education in the work of many of the major figures of the Western philosophical tradition and the deep philosophical issues raised by the practice of education, contemporary philosophers have not always regarded philosophy of education as an important, or even a legitimate, area of philosophy.[1] As he has done on many other philosophical fronts, Alvin Goldman has challenged this conventional view by paying considerable attention to education in his recent work on social epistemology. Especially noteworthy are his views of the place of truth, and of testimony and trust, in an adequate characterization of the aims of teaching and of education.

Goldman's aim, in *Knowledge in a Social World* (1999),[2] is nothing less than the articulation and establishment of a new discipline. He calls his proposed discipline *veritistic* (i.e., *truth-linked*) *social epistemology* (VSE): the study of the social processes that facilitate or inhibit our collective efforts to obtain or increase *knowledge*. Knowledge is understood, in turn, in the "weak" sense of *true belief*. VSE is motivated by the truth of Aristotle's dictum that "All men by nature desire to know" (p. 3)—that is, desire accurate or true information, in contrast with misinformation (false belief) and lack of information (ignorance)—both for its own sake and to facilitate our other practical concerns. Social epistemology is *social* in its focus on social paths to knowledge and the practices of social groups in the pursuit of knowledge. *Truth*, though, is the key notion of VSE, and its key question is which social processes help (or hinder) us in the pursuit of knowledge (i.e., true belief). In the book, Goldman examines a wide range of social practices—both "generic" practices involving testimony, argumentation, communication, and speech regulation, and practices in the specific domains of science, law, democracy, and education—always focusing on the extent to which these practices conduce to true belief. While his entire discussion is worthy of attention, I here restrict myself to his treatment of education.

Goldman's veritistic approach to social epistemology gives pride of place to truth as both the highest epistemic value and the fundamental aim of education.[3] Equally noteworthy is his emphasis on the social dimensions of educational epistemology, in particular the roles of testimony and trust in appropriate teacher-student interactions. I agree with Goldman on many points, in particular his (broad) embrace of veritism and his critique of "veriphobia," his criticism of the postmodern rejection of truth, his stress on the compatibility of veritism and the centrality to education of the aim of fostering critical thinking, his thesis that (non-"radical" or -degenerate forms of) multiculturalism is (are) compatible with (Goldman's nonessentialist brand of) veritistic epistemology, and his insistence that both truth and expertise are relevant to curricular decisions and his discussion of ways in which nonexperts can accurately appraise expertise in curricular contexts. Despite all this agreement, there are, I think, two points on which Goldman's account is problematic: the relation of truth to critical thinking, and the roles of testimony and trust in education and its epistemology. I address these two in what follows.

2. Truth and Thinking

Goldman's chapter on education begins with a declaration:

> The fundamental aim of education, like that of science, is the promotion of knowledge [i.e., true belief]. Whereas science seeks knowledge that is new for humankind, education seeks knowledge that is new for individual learners. Education pursues this mission in several ways: by organizing and transmitting pre-existing knowledge, by creating incentives and environments to encourage learning, and by shaping skills and techniques that facilitate autonomous learning and steer inquiry toward truth. This veritistic conception is a traditional picture of what education is all about, one aligned with an "Enlightenment" conception of epistemology. Despite popular critiques of the Enlightenment view, the veritistic model is still the best available, one that fits all stages of education from lowest to highest. Admittedly, knowledge and knowledge-dedicated skills are not the sole educational goals. Education in studio art or music performance, for example, is not primarily concerned with propositional knowledge or with skills for acquiring propositional knowledge. But propositional knowledge is, nonetheless, education's most pervasive and characteristic goal. (p. 349)

Like Goldman, I too defend an "Enlightenment" conception of epistemology, and have challenged popular but, in my view, misguided criticisms of it (Siegel 1997, 1998). So ours is an in-house dispute, carried on within the Enlightenment camp. My counterclaim is that *rational* belief is as entitled as is true belief to be regarded as "the crucial epistemic aim" (p. 363) of education; and that the fostering of the skills, abilities, and dispositions and habits of mind constitutive of *the critical thinker/rational person*[4]—in particular, those involved in *reason assessment*—is educationally fundamental (Siegel 1988, 1997). Following Goldman, I focus here primarily on the epistemic aim. So the issue before us is: is "the crucial epistemic aim" of education that of true belief, or rational belief (or both)? Are our educational efforts (insofar as they concern student belief) rightly regarded as aiming, fundamentally, at the production of *true* belief, or rather *rational* belief, or perhaps both, in our students?

On the view of "the crucial epistemic aim" that I favor, education should strive to foster, not (just) true belief, but (also) the skills, abilities, and dispositions constitutive of critical thinking, and the rational belief generated and sustained by it.[5] Goldman considers this alternative to his preferred, veritistic view, i.e., the position that "the crucial epistemic aim is not *true* belief, but warranted, justified, or rational belief" (pp. 362–363, emphasis in original). He does not challenge the educational value of critical thinking. He argues, rather, that it must be seen not as "an epistemic end in itself," but rather as "a useful *means* to the fundamental epistemic end of true belief" (p. 363; see also Goldman 1998, pp. 445–446). As Goldman articulates his view:

> I am very sympathetic to some form of critical-thinking approach, but this is not incompatible with veritism. Unlike many critical-thinking advocates (such as Siegel), I do not see critical thinking as an epistemic end in itself. Critical thinking or rational inference is a useful *means* to the fundamental epistemic end of true belief. It is a crucial skill that should be developed in cognizers to help them attain true belief. Acknowledging an important role for critical thinking in education, then, is no admission of any flaw in veritism. It can be seen as merely an elaboration of veritism's implications. (p. 363, emphasis in original)

Goldman and I are agreed that both the fostering of the skills and abilities of critical thinking, and the production of true belief, are legitimate educational aims. And, indeed, Goldman's later, extended comments concerning the educational importance of critical thinking (p. 366) are sufficiently forceful to warm the hearts of its advocates. Despite this agreement, however, questions remain. Is Goldman right that the former is of merely instrumental value, and that only the latter is rightly regarded as "the fundamental epistemic end" of education? Is education in this respect like the "great variety of human endeavors [that] are dedicated, quite properly and understandably, to the discovery and dissemination of truths" (Goldman 1998, p. 439)? Is it true that "the fundamental aim of education, that is, of schooling systems at all levels, is to provide students with knowledge [i.e. true belief] and to develop intellectual skills that improve their knowledge-acquiring abilities" (ibid.)?[6] If true, does this place educational activities aimed at enhancing critical thinking "on a deeper foundation" than they might otherwise enjoy (Goldman 1998, p. 445)? I argue next that all these questions should be answered in the negative. While I happily concede the instrumental value of critical thinking that Goldman emphasizes, I will argue that its value is not *merely* instrumental, and that critical thinking and rational belief are educationally fundamental, and the latter epistemically fundamental, for reasons independent of their instrumental tie to truth.[7]

A. Epistemic Aims of Education: One or Many?

It is worth noting, first, that Goldman's characterization of VSE—according to which social epistemology's focus is on the degree to which particular social processes produce knowledge, understood in the weak sense of true belief—threatens to force upon us a false dichotomy. Why think that there must be only *one* fundamental epistemic aim of education? It is easy to think that, since veritism is to be the organizing principle of social epistemology, truth must be the fundamental aim of all social epistemic practices, including educational ones. But from the fact that VSE takes as its central concern the study of the truth-conduciveness of such practices, it does not follow that those practices have truth as their fundamental aim. Still less does it follow that their aim is *solely* that of truth. In particular, the fundamental aim of education might be plural, encompassing both true and rational belief, thus rendering the weak sense of knowledge the inappropriate sense for education.[8]

Indeed, advocates of critical thinking will, with Goldman, regard the production of true belief as an important educational aim, for at least two reasons. First, teaching typically involves content presumed by the teacher to be true; thus, those advocates can and should embrace true (and not just rational) belief as a basic educational aim. Second, given the standard view among epistemologists (including Goldman, p. 133) of the relationship between truth and rationality or justification[9]—i.e., that the latter are *fallible indicators* of the former—it is clear that such advocates will regard true belief as a straightforward and welcome concomitant of the achievement of rational belief: we aim for our students to believe critically/rationally; if they do, they will (if that standard view is correct) perforce typically believe truly as well.

But it is difficult to conceive of *mere* true belief, i.e., belief held independently of critical thinking and/or without rational support, as itself the fundamental epistemic end of education. Consider the teacher who takes p to be true and a suitable target of educational effort. That teacher endeavors to get her students to believe that *p*. But true belief that *p simpliciter* is not enough; if it were, many objectionable ways of achieving it—brainwashing, indoctrination, fabrication, deception, chemical manipulation, etc. —would be permissible. But they are not. As Israel Scheffler has long argued, teaching must be carried out under appropriate restrictions of *manner*: as teachers, we aim to get students to believe curricular content that we ourselves take to be true, for reasons that we take to be good reasons for regarding that content as true; we aim further that our students' resulting true beliefs will be held on the basis of those reasons:

> To teach, in the standard sense, is at some points at least to submit oneself to the understanding and independent judgment of the pupil, to his demand for reasons, to his sense of what constitutes an adequate explanation. To teach someone that such and such is the case is not merely to try to get him to believe it: deception, for example, is not a method or a mode of teaching. *Teaching involves further that, if we try to get the student to believe that such and such is the case, we try also to get him to believe it for reasons that, within the limits of his capacity to grasp, are our reasons*. Teaching, in this way, requires us to reveal our reasons to the student, and, by so doing, to submit them to his evaluation and criticism. (Scheffler 1960, p. 57, "our" emphasized in original; cf. pp. 57–59; Scheffler 1965, pp. 11–13; Scheffler 1989, p. 62)

If something like Scheffler's view here is correct, as I believe, students' true belief *simpliciter* cannot be a suitable epistemic aim either of teaching in particular or of education more generally. Rather, the aims of true belief and rational belief (as well as that of fostering students' informed and independent judgment) are tightly intertwined, and equally necessary, in any education worthy of the name. Rational belief and the critical thinking on which it typically depends are not then merely instrumentally valuable in light of their tie to true belief; rather, they are as fundamental, as epistemic aims of education, as is true belief. Consequently, we err if we saddle ourselves at the outset with the weak sense of knowledge. We limit the reach of social epistemology unduly as well by limiting ourselves to the weak sense. As far as the social practices of education are concerned, it is the strong sense that is most relevant. As Scheffler puts the point:

> Since teaching that Q presupposes that the teacher takes "Q" to be true (or at least within the legitimate range of truth approximation allowable for purposes of pedagogical simplification and facilitation) and since the activity of teaching appeals to the free rational judgment of the student, we might say that the teacher is *trying to bring about knowledge, in the strong sense*. . . . The teacher does not strive merely to get the

student to learn that Q, but also to get him to learn it in such a way as to know it—i.e. to be able to support it properly. (Scheffler 1965, p. 12, emphasis added)[10]

In this section I have urged two points. First, if the epistemic aim of education is to be couched in terms of knowledge, it is the strong rather than the weak sense of knowledge that is the more appropriate aim. We should not let VSE's focus on the propensities of social processes to promote true belief mislead us into thinking that the fundamental aim of all such processes is such promotion. This is especially true in the case of education. Second, we ought not allow ourselves to be forced to choose between true belief and rational belief as the fundamental aim of education, on the ground that there is or can be only one such aim. On the contrary, both are equally legitimately regarded as "fundamental." If so, then the value of rational belief (and so critical thinking) is not *merely* instrumental.

B. "Bare Difference," Lucky True Belief, and Educational Success

A good way to see whether critical thinking and rational belief have value independently of their instrumental tie to truth is to imagine cases in which the only difference between otherwise identical beliefs is that one is rationally held, on the basis of the exercise of critical thinking, while the other is not—that is, cases in which everything is held constant (including truth value) except rational or justificatory status. If the one is epistemically more valuable than the other, we have a reason to think that the value of that which distinguishes between the two is not merely instrumental with respect to truth.[11]

So consider Maria and Mario, both of whom truly believe that p. Maria's belief is rational in that it was generated and is sustained by her critical thinking, while Mario's is not—Mario's is a lucky true belief. It is uncontroversial that, as a general matter, Maria's belief is more valuable epistemically than Mario's: the former is better justified, more rational, more epistemically responsible, more satisfying of legitimate epistemological obligation, and more epistemically praiseworthy than the latter (Feldman 2002). The matter is even clearer if we imagine that Maria and Mario are students, and that p is a bit of curricular content. Both Maria's and Mario's answers on the relevant exam affirm that p, but as their teachers we judge only Maria's answer adequate. Indeed, responsible teachers will construct their exams in such a way as to distinguish between Maria's and Mario's answers, if only by requiring that students show their work, present their evidence, or give their reasons. But the only difference between Maria's and Mario's answers, and their associated beliefs, is their justificatory status: Maria's belief is rational, and its being so is dependent upon her exercise of critical thinking, while Mario's is not. The superior epistemic value of Maria's belief is a function of that difference. That superior value is independent of the belief's instrumental tie to truth, since, by hypothesis, both Maria's and Mario's beliefs are true.

A moment's reflection reveals that the same valuation obtains in the case in which p is false. Again, both Maria's and Mario's beliefs have the same truth value; again, we judge Maria's superior to Mario's. Whether p is true or false, Maria's belief that p is epistemically superior to Mario's. Holding everything constant (including truth value) except justificatory status, the bare difference argument strongly suggests that rationality/justification has value independently of its instrumental tie to truth.

C. Access to Truth

We don't in general have "direct access" to truth; if we want our beliefs to be true, we typically have no option but to reason evidentially. That is, we have to *judge whether p* is true, and, if we're rational, we do this on the basis of reasons and evidence. This is the case generally; it is especially important in the context of education: we want students to estimate or judge the truth competently, and that means being able and disposed to reason well, evaluate evidence well, search for evidence well, construct and evaluate arguments well, etc. Given the elusiveness of truth and the difficulty of discerning it, justification-conferring critical thinking skills and abilities are central to the lives of truth-seeking epistemic agents, and so to their education. This point deserves further development.

Because we lack direct access to truth, we have no choice but to approach truth by way of justification. The point is made by many contemporary epistemologists. As Nicholas Rescher puts it, "we have no way of getting at the facts directly, without the epistemic detour of securing grounds and reasons for them" (Rescher 1988, p. 43). Roderick Firth puts it as follows: "To the extent that we are rational, each of us decides at any time t whether a belief is true, in precisely the same way that we would decide at t whether we ourselves are, or would be, warranted at t in having that belief" (Firth 1981, p. 19).[12] As Laurence BonJour articulates and explains the point:

> What makes us cognitive beings at all is our capacity for belief, and the goal of our distinctively cognitive endeavors is *truth*: we want our beliefs to correctly and accurately depict the world. If truth were somehow immediately and unproblematically accessible ... so that one could in all cases opt simply to believe the truth, then the concept of justification would be of little significance and would play no independent role in cognition. But this epistemically ideal situation is quite obviously not the one in which we find ourselves. We have no such immediate and unproblematic access to truth, and it is for this reason that justification comes into the picture. (BonJour 1985, p. 7, emphasis in original)[13]

Such citations could by multiplied indefinitely. Tellingly, Goldman himself makes the point:

> The usual route to true belief, of course, is to obtain some kind of evidence that points to the true proposition and away from rivals. (p. 24)

What follows from this generally conceded point concerning our limited access to truth? Not that justification, rational belief, and critical thinking aren't instrumentally valuable in virtue of their fallible tie to truth. The point does not challenge that instrumental relationship—indeed, it strongly affirms it. In so far, Goldman's picture is correct.

So suppose that Goldman is right that the fundamental epistemic value is truth, and that, as he follows the just-cited passage, "the rationale for getting such evidence is to get true belief" (p. 24). It remains nonetheless that while we aim at truth, we determine truth value by engaging in inquiry and assessing justificatory status: Is there good reason to regard the proposition in question *as* true? As educators, we want students to become able and disposed to seek, find, and competently recognize/identify the truth, to the fullest extent that our fallible methods and abilities and limited evidence allow (as veritism acknowledges). If so, the basic *educational* aim should be seen not as the production of true belief, per se, but rather as that of enabling students to *judge or estimate wisely* the truth, and this sort of judgment just is judgment based on the proper evaluation of reasons and evidence. We aim to enable students "not to judge the truth infallibly but to estimate the truth responsibly" (Scheffler 1965, p. 54), and that is a matter of critical thinking. If this is correct, a fundamental aim of education must be the development in students of the ability to assess truth status skillfully and accurately. It is only through such assessment that students can hope, and be expected, to reach and recognize the truth they seek. Consequently, critical thinking, and its pursuit of justified belief, are at least as fundamental, *educationally*, as the aim of true belief. Here, as earlier, we should resist allowing ourselves to be forced to choose between true belief and rational belief as the fundamental epistemic aim of education. Granting that we want students to believe truly, and that we value critical thinking and rational/justified belief in part because of their instrumental tie to truth, it remains nonetheless that education, in virtue of our limited access to truth, has as a fundamental aim that of equipping students to judge or estimate the truth well by thinking critically about relevant reasons and evidence.

This is not to deny that such thinking is instrumentally valuable with respect to truth. It is to deny, rather, that this is its *only* value. Education is primarily concerned to foster not just true belief (i.e., knowledge in the weak sense), but also critical thinking, responsible believing, and justified belief, which are only fallibly tied to truth (and so, when true belief is achieved, knowledge in the strong sense). If so, from the educational point of view, critical thinking is fundamental, independently of its instrumental tie to truth.

D. Fundamental Epistemic Values: One or Many?—Considered Independently of Education

Most of the discussion thus far treats the status of truth and critical thinking/rational belief as fundamental epistemic aims *of education*; I have argued that we should regard both, independently, as such aims. But Goldman's case that rational belief is of merely instrumental value with respect to truth involves far more than education; we should consider his more general case.

In his "Unity of the Epistemic Virtues," Goldman "explore[s] the tenability of [the] doctrine . . . that the various epistemic virtues are all variations on, or permutations of, a single theme or motif" (2002b, p. 51).[14] In the version of "epistemic unitarianism" that Goldman defends, the "cardinal value, or underlying motif" in question is "something like true, or accurate, belief" (2002b, p. 52). He defends this view, which might be labeled "veritistic virtue-epistemological unitarianism" (VVEU), by arguing for its superiority with respect to the rival views that there is a plurality of epistemic virtues, with no underlying unity ("pluralism"), or that some epistemic value other than truth is the underlying motif or ultimate value. The key alternative epistemic value of interest to us here is that of justified belief or justificational value, so the main alternatives to VVEU to be considered are the pluralistic view according to which rational belief is virtuous independently of its tie to truth, and the rival unitarian view according to which rational belief is itself the underlying motif of the epistemic virtues. But since I have been defending the pluralistic view thus far, I will ignore the rival unitarian view and concentrate on Goldman's challenge to pluralism.

That challenge comes first in the form of a challenge to what he calls "deontological evidentialism" (DE), according to which "an agent should assign a degree of belief to a proposition in proportion to the weight of evidence she possesses." According to its proponents, "the requirement of proportioning is a purely deontological one, not derived from any consequentialist consideration, such as the thesis that proportioning leads to truth." It is rightly seen as "a rival to veritism [because] it would not rationalize proportionment as a means to true belief, error avoidance, or any other further end, but would treat it as an independent principle of 'fittingness'" (2002b, pp. 55–56).

Goldman's objection to DE is that it cannot "account for the virtues of evidence gathering" (2002b, p. 56). Since one can proportion belief to one's evidence, and so perfectly manifest these virtues, no matter how little evidence one has—even if one has no evidence at all, one can proportion belief appropriately by suspending judgment—one need never seek evidence. As Goldman puts it, DE "is perfectly content with investigational sloth!" (2002b, p. 56). But it is a virtue so to seek—especially in science (2002b, p. 56). Hence DE fails as an alternative unitarian view, Goldman argues: DE and its virtue of "fittingness," and the resulting justificational value stemming from belief proportioned to strength of evidence, cannot be the underlying motif of all epistemic virtues, since it cannot account for the virtues of evidence gathering.

There are a number of replies that might be made here. One is to argue that our specifically *epistemological* duty involves that relevant to *rational* or *justified* (rather than true) belief—if I do everything I can to believe rationally, I have done my epistemological duty, whether or not my belief turns out to be true (Feldman 2002). Another is to argue that DE can somehow account for the virtues of evidence gathering. Yet another is to argue that while Goldman's point is correct for science, in most other epistemic contexts the virtues of evidence gathering are less clearly virtues.[15] Still another is that "investigational sloth" and intellectual laziness can be criticized not just on epistemological grounds, but also as failures of *character* (see below). But the most important reply is also the most straightforward: Goldman's point challenges the alternative unitarian view that all epistemic virtues can be united by the underlying motifs of rational belief or belief proportioned to existing evidence, but it does nothing to impugn the pluralistic view that some epistemic virtues (e.g., those involving evidence gathering) are virtuous in light of their connection to true belief, while others (e.g., those involving proportioning belief to one's evidence) are virtuous in light of their connection to rational belief. That is, Goldman's point challenges the alternative unitarian view, but it does nothing to challenge the pluralistic view defended above.

This same criticism can be made of Goldman's further arguments in favor of VVEU. These arguments attempt to show that "epistemologists [who] would insist that justified belief, not true belief, is the primary epistemic value" (2002b, pp. 62–63) are mistaken, since justified belief, i.e., belief which accords with the evidence, is valuable instrumentally, with truth being the fundamental value toward which such belief aims. But even if correct, this cannot establish VVEU as superior to pluralism, but only to the alternative unitarian view according to which maximal justificational value is the underlying motif uniting the various epistemic virtues. The pluralism defended above, according to which true belief and rational or justified belief are independent basic epistemic virtues, is perfectly compatible with rational belief's instrumental value. It holds merely that such belief is also valuable, and virtuous, independently of its admitted instrumental tie to truth. So any argument that establishes that instrumental tie will fail to upend pluralism. To do that, the additional assumption that there is or can be only one "underlying motif" or ultimate epistemic virtue must be made. But that assumes rather than establishes unitarianism. As we saw above, however, there are good reasons to resist the assumption that there can be only one fundamental epistemic value or virtue.[16]

E. Further Reasons for Regarding Critical Thinking and Rational Belief as Fundamental Educational Aims, Considered Independently of Epistemology

Thus far we have been considering epistemology-related reasons for regarding critical thinking and rational belief as fundamental aims of education. However, it is worth noting briefly that there are epistemology-independent reasons for so regarding them as well.

First, we want students (and persons generally) to be *reflective* about their beliefs—to question their beliefs; to ask themselves: "I (don't) believe that *p*, but *should* I?"—and that education should help to foster this reflectiveness.[17] Such reflection takes our fallibility seriously. It is clear that it can in turn be justified in veritistic terms—we value it because it can help to weed out error and increase true belief. But it enjoys an integrity and non-instrumental value of its own. That a critical thinker is able and disposed to revise or correct her thought or action in light of criticism (by herself or others) is not just a mark of her ability to identify truth; it is also an important dimension of her *character*. Reflectiveness is one of a range of dispositions that we hope education will foster. I develop the more general point concerning character next.

Second, education is not merely a propositional matter; it aims at far more than fostering belief, whether true or rational. It is also fundamentally concerned with fostering *dispositions* in students, and, more generally, with helping students to become particular sorts of persons, with particular traits of character. Of course, there are many different sorts of dispositions and character traits that might be thought worthy of fostering; I will not here address the panoply of candidate dispositions and traits, although I think a strong case can be made for those associated with critical thinking (Siegel 1988, chs. 2–3). The important point in this context is that veritism misses this entire dimension of education. Even if Goldman is right that, so far as belief is concerned, true belief is the basic educational aim, and rational belief merely instrumentally valuable in its service to truth, it remains nonetheless that we want students to emerge from their education with more than a host of true beliefs and the skills required to capture more. We want them not only also to be reflective, but in addition to be disposed to base their beliefs upon reasons and evidence, to seek out reasons for candidate beliefs, to be open to both others' criticisms of their own beliefs and to others' contrary beliefs, to take seriously the reasons and points of view of others, and so on. While these can be seen by the veritist to be in service to the truth, and so compatible with veritism—which they are—it is important to see that these also have *moral* dimensions (involving respect for others, intellectual modesty and humility, etc.), and that these latter dispositions and traits can be justified independently of considerations of truth. Veritism's view of education is thus overly narrow in a way that the contrary view, that takes critical thinking to be equally fundamental educationally, is not.[18]

Third, a central dimension of critical thinking is its interrelationship with *autonomy*: insofar as a student is a critical thinker, she enjoys an *independence of judgment* that is of fundamental educational importance. That is, she is free to judge (and act) independently of external constraint, in accordance with her own reasoned appraisal of the matter at hand. As Israel Scheffler puts the point, we must "surrender the idea of shaping or molding the mind of the pupil. The function of education ... is rather to liberate the mind, strengthen its critical powers, [and] inform it with knowledge and the capacity for independent inquiry" (Scheffler 1989, p. 139). That is, a key aim of education is that of freeing students from the myriad of cognitive shackles that a myriad of sources— *including their education*—might place upon them. The idea that education aims at liberating the mind and fostering students' autonomy is a central dimension of the "Enlightenment" view that Goldman takes himself to be defending, but its desirability can be neither fully explained nor fully justified in veritistic terms. The explanatory and justificatory connections between autonomy, liberation, and critical thinking, on the other hand, are straightforward (Siegel 1988).

The points just made take for granted a set of "Enlightenment" values that can be and have been challenged from a variety of "post-Enlightenment" perspectives; both Goldman (1999) and I (1977, 1998) have responded to some of these challenges. Of course, our responses might be defective in various ways. But the issue on the table here concerns not these broad issues, but rather whether, from within the Enlightenment perspective we share, critical thinking is rightly seen as valuable merely instrumentally, in virtue of its tie to truth, or is rather better seen as of value also independently of that tie. I hope that the considerations just rehearsed make it clear that the former view is simply too narrow; that critical thinking's value, both cognitively and especially educationally, extends far beyond that tie. To link the value of critical thinking wholly to its instrumental tie to truth is unduly to narrow its scope. That value, even when considered from a narrowly epistemic perspective, exceeds critical thinking's fallible tendency to produce true belief. When a broader view of education is considered—one that takes into account education's central concern with the fostering of dispositions, the enhancement of autonomy, and the development of character—the narrowness of veritism's focus on true belief as the fundamental aim of education is manifest. I am happy to grant Goldman's claim that critical thinking is instrumentally valuable in virtue of its role in the production of true belief. Nevertheless, if the arguments above have merit, such thinking has epistemic value independently of its tie to truth. Moreover, it is valuable also in light of its place in the enhancement of autonomy and the fostering of dispositions and traits of character—matters which are themselves educationally fundamental, but which extend far beyond education's concern with the promotion of true belief. In all these respects, then, critical thinking is educationally fundamental, for both epistemology-related and epistemology-independent reasons, independently of its instrumental tie to truth.

3. Testimony and Trust

Goldman connects his argument that truth (rather than critical thinking) is the fundamental aim of education with his discussion of the roles of testimony and trust in educational contexts. His basic claim is that a thoroughgoing commitment to critical thinking is both educationally counterproductive and epistemologically suspect:

> A good bit of actual teaching consists of teachers "telling" things to students, that is, making statements or assertions without supporting reasons, evidence, or argument. Should students be expected to believe these statements? ... Not only students but all sorts of hearers encounter unsupported assertions or "testimony" from speakers. Under what circumstances are they justified in believing these statements? (pp. 363–364)

Goldman here links the problem of justified belief in teachers' testimonial assertions to the general problem of the epistemology of testimony, and suggests that it would be both educationally counterproductive to hold that students ought not to accept their teachers' testimonial assertions and epistemologically dubious to hold that students would not be justified in believing those assertions. He then argues—contrary to the view (associated with critical thinking) that students ought to believe only those teacher testimonial pronouncements that can be justified by testimony-independent good reasons, which Goldman labels "(GR)"—that students sometimes ought to believe such pronouncements despite the absence of justifying reasons/evidence. The just-cited passage continues:

> The good reasons approach would presumably answer with something like the following principle:
>
> (GR) A hearer is never justified in believing what a speaker (baldly) asserts unless the hearer has good, independent reasons to trust the speaker on that occasion. (p. 364)

Goldman proceeds to criticize (GR). His criticism depends partly on his doubts about "reductionism," according to which "a hearer is justified in believing speakers' assertions if and only if the hearer has good reasons to trust the speaker, reasons that do not ultimately rest on testimony itself but instead rest wholly on perception, memory and so forth" (p. 364; see also pp. 126–130; 1998, pp. 447–449). But Goldman does not declare himself on the ultimate non-acceptability of reductionism; although clearly inclined toward nonreductionism, he is uncharacteristically cagey in his unwillingness to take a definite stand on the matter (p. 127; 1998, pp. 447–449). His argument rather has the form: *if* reductionism is false, then (GR) is untenable. Below I will suggest some reasons for doubt concerning this antecedent.

But Goldman's case against (GR) does not rest entirely on his doubts concerning reductionism; it involves as well a suggestive discussion of Elizabeth Fricker's view of testimony. Fricker writes, "The thesis I advocate ... is that a hearer should always engage in some assessment of the speaker for trustworthiness. To believe what is asserted without doing so is to believe blindly, uncritically. This is gullibility" (p. 365, citing Fricker 1994, p. 145). As Goldman notes, this position is entirely in keeping with the spirit of (GR). However, in a later paper, Fricker "appears to soften her claim," and Goldman seizes upon this softening:

> Fricker appears to soften her claim. She distinguishes between the "developmental" and "mature" phases of the reception of testimony. "Simply-trusted testimony plays an inevitable role in the causal process by which we become masters of our commonsense scheme of things" ([Fricker] 1995: 403). In other words, young children cannot be expected to monitor for defeating evidence while they are still acquiring the kinds of common-sense knowledge that can be used to defeat presumptions of trust. This softer position seems to me more plausible. Notice, however, that when it is applied to the educational context, it cuts against a universal application of the critical-thinking approach. Very young children, at least, should not be expected or trained to monitor a teacher's utterances for untrustworthiness. Teachers' statements can be justifiably believed via unsupported trust, and it is not unreasonable for the educational system to expect young children to accept such statements without first subjecting them to critical scrutiny. (p. 365)

There are several points to note concerning this argument. First, even if correct, it applies only to very young children, and is in this respect only a minimal "softening" of Fricker's earlier-cited view. Fricker's "developmental phase" is not demarcated very precisely in her discussion, but it seems beyond doubt that, depending on the precise demarcation in question, many even very young children are already in possession of a "commonsense scheme of things." It would be foolhardy to try to identify the precise age or developmental (sub)stage at which the child achieves this possession, but it seems clear that it occurs before, and certainly by, the kindergarten years. (Recall conversations you have had with your three- or four- or five-year-old child, niece/nephew, or neighbor. Is it plausible that the child in question lacked "our commonsense scheme of things?") Goldman's point can and should be granted. It has little impact on the disagreement between us. The (GR) view remains (mainly) intact in the face of it. The point establishes only that "very young children" cannot be expected to monitor testimonial reports for trustworthiness. If they are really *very* young, who would disagree?[19]

Indeed, advocates of the (GR) position have typically embraced Goldman's point concerning very young children. Philosophers of education have routinely discussed it in the context of debate concerning *indoctrination*. In the "developmental" phase, in which young children acquire a host of concepts and learn (e.g.) the meanings of words, the mechanics of reference, basic facts about the world, and other basic items which together make up their "commonsense scheme of things," they are not yet in a position to be critical. This has suggested to many theorists that parents and other educators have no choice but to indoctrinate very young children into that commonsense scheme of things—that indoctrination, in other words, is inevitable. The problem has seemed to many to be especially acute for advocates of (GR), since it suggests that young children must be indoctrinated into the relevant beliefs, attitudes, and dispositions, and unreflectively master the relevant skills and abilities, in order to become critical thinkers—that they must, in short, be *indoctrinated into critical thinking*. This is a corner into which advocates of critical thinking are reluctant to be backed. Can they avoid being so backed, or escape the corner if they can't avoid being backed into it?

All sides agree that children cannot begin their cognitive lives as critical thinkers. They must learn to be critical thinkers—they must acquire the relevant concepts, and develop the relevant beliefs, skills, and abilities, and dispositions, values, and habits of mind, in the educational process of becoming critical thinkers. Whether this process requires indoctrination depends on one's account of indoctrination. Philosophical accounts of indoctrination have traditionally understood it in terms either of the *aim* or *intention* of the educator/indoctrinator, the *method* she utilizes, or the *content* he imparts to the student. These have in common that whether a student is a victim of indoctrination depends upon what Thomas F. Green called her *"style of belief"*: she has been indoctrinated to the extent that she has been led to hold beliefs in such a way that she cannot subject them to critical evaluation. In such a case, the student has a *non-evidential* style of belief. However, she can acquire all the relevant concepts, beliefs, skills, abilities, dispositions, etc. associated with critical thinking in a way that does not produce such a style of belief. What she acquires, by means of non-indoctrinative educational processes,[20] is, once acquired, open to critical assessment. In such a case, non-indoctrinative educational processes produce an *evidential* style of belief, and it is this that the advocate of (GR) prizes. In this way children can become critical thinkers without having to be indoctrinated into that status.[21]

Since children do not begin their cognitive lives as critical thinkers, they do not begin those lives able to monitor testimony for trustworthiness—as Fricker and Goldman rightly insist, they must first acquire their "commonsense scheme of things." In the "developmental phase," accepting the testimony of others, without monitoring it for trustworthiness, is at least largely inevitable. Here (GR) is indeed inapplicable, as Goldman rightly notes. However, this is a quite minor restriction on the application of (GR), since the developmental phase is essentially completed at a quite early point in the typical child's education. Beyond that point—that is, for most of a child's education, and the whole of her adult life—(GR) is, for all Goldman has said, completely applicable.

There are some further points to make concerning Goldman's case that students, contrary to advocates of critical thinking, are at least sometimes justified in believing what their teacher tells them, even when they lack independent reason to trust them on that occasion.

a. It is central to Goldman's analysis that students often, perhaps typically, do not have testimony-independent reasons for trusting their teachers. I believe, to the contrary, that students typically *do* have such reasons. Students generally have a variety of independent (of testimony) reasons for trusting their teachers: Teachers are in positions of authority; they possess relevant academic credentials; they are treated as experts by their colleagues, administrators, and other adults (including the students' parents); etc. All this is readily observable by students, and provides them with at least some non-testimony-based reasons for trusting their teachers. So the situation Goldman envisages, in which students have *no* non-testimony-based reasons for trusting their teachers, is much less common than might appear at first glance.

I have formulated the point in terms of students and teachers, but in fact it has application far beyond the educational context (although I cannot defend this broader point concerning the epistemology of testimony at length here). As Jonathan Adler (2002) argues, there is a wealth of indirect, background evidence for accepting as reliable (defeasibly, of course), without direct evidence of its reliability, the testimony of others. We all have lots of experience of such testimony (from strangers giving directions, from news reporters with whom we are not personally acquainted, from neighbors and friends, etc.); in the vast majority of cases such testimony proves trustworthy. If it didn't, our common practice of accepting testimony as reliable would be very different. The arguments Goldman advances against reductionism unduly ignore this vast repository of evidence we all have for the general reliability of testimony. (And it must again be noted that Goldman does not argue at length for the failure of reductionism and so of GR;

as noted above, his argument rather is of the form: *if* reductionism fails, *then* GR fails as well. I believe that the vast quantity of background evidence available to all of us for the general reliability of testimony, pointed to by Adler, upends the antecedent of this conditional.)

b. Even if we reject my claim that the general reasons for trust in the educational context given above (position of authority; relevant academic credentials; treatment by parents and other adults; etc.) are good, testimony-independent ones, other, more specific reasons are typically available. Consider, as an example, the algebra (or history) student. Let us suppose that on the first day of class the student has no independent reason to trust what her teacher tells her about the subject. But as the class proceeds, every day the student sees the teacher introducing material about which the student is ignorant, hears the teacher's explanations, observes the teacher answer her (and other students') questions, sees the teacher speak extemporaneously on tangents that (it is often apparent) were not part of the teacher's lecture/lesson plan, etc. All this provides the student with testimony-independent (defeasible) reasons for trusting the teacher's claims with respect to that subject matter. Consider: by the end of his first lecture in Introduction to Epistemology, don't his students have some testimony-independent reason to trust what Professor Goldman says about the conditions of knowledge or the history and character of the Gettier problem? In the same way, the algebra (or history) student has increasing testimony-independent reason for trusting her teacher's declarations concerning the subject matter at hand.

c. As noted above, it is important to be clear on which students we're discussing here. I agree with Goldman that very young children typically do not have testimony-independent reasons for trusting their teachers; among other reasons for this claim, they don't yet have a firm grasp of the relevant concepts or the required linguistic facility. So I'm happy to grant the point with respect to very young children. But education goes far beyond very young children who don't yet have a grasp of the relevant concepts, command of their native tongue, exposure to relevant evidence, or the basic knowledge that is a large part of our "commonsense scheme of things." For older children, and adult students, there is virtually always such independent reason for trust, of the sorts already mentioned. And even for quite young children such independent reason is sometimes available. For example, my daughter, when in second grade, was impressed with a number trick (concerning adding nines) her teacher taught her; she could see intuitively that the trick worked in the sense that it gave the right answers. When she saw that, she had independent reason for trusting that teacher in matters arithmetical (at least). If so, a second grader can have testimony-independent reason for trusting her teacher. Consequently, even quite young students needn't rely on trust. Goldman's point is highly *age- (and developmental stage-) sensitive*: it is most plausible at very young ages, but quite implausible at intermediate and higher ages.[22]

4. Conclusion

I have argued that Goldman's claims that true belief is the sole fundamental epistemic aim of education, and that critical thinking is of solely instrumental value with respect to the ultimate aim of truth, are problematic, as are his claims concerning the epistemic places of testimony and trust in education. Despite my disagreements with Goldman on these issues, I agree with him on the several specific matters noted at the outset. More important than these points of agreement/contention, in my view, is his taking these philosophical questions concerning education seriously. Goldman's work makes manifestly clear that epistemological reflection on education promises important philosophical insights, both for epistemology and for education. His discussions are important contributions to our broad theoretical understanding of the epistemology of education. Further work on these issues has enormous promise for the enhancement of the philosophy of education, as philosophers of education and epistemologists debate the desirability of conceiving the epistemological holy grail of education as truth, critical thinking, or something else.[23] I close by applauding Goldman, who has demonstrated the power of the philosophical insights that can be gleaned by applying the tools and theories of epistemology to the epistemological dimensions of education, and by encouraging other philosophers to join in the effort to shed philosophical light on the theory and practice of education.[24]

Notes

1. Happily, this situation is improving of late, as philosophers with increasing frequency address educational matters in their work. Well-known contemporary figures, e.g., Martha Nussbaum (1997), Hilary Putnam (1993), and Richard Rorty (1990, 1997), have addressed philosophical issues concerning education. Amélie Rorty's collection *Philosophers on Education* (1998) contains the work of many other prominent philosophers. Israel Scheffler (e.g., 1960, 1965, 1989) has for many years addressed such issues. The Eastern Division of the American Philosophical Association (APA) has in recent years recognized philosophy of education as a "special field" and has created an Advisory Committee to the Program Committee in philosophy of education. Philosophy of education as an area of philosophy is enjoying a period of increased activity and perceived legitimacy in the broader philosophical community. This is, in my view, a wholly good and welcome development.
2. Unless otherwise noted, all page references in the text are to this book. For a detailed descriptive (and laudatory) review of its contents, see Siegel 2002.

3. Frederick F. Schmitt insightfully notes that Goldman's book "is first and foremost a contribution to value theory – specifically, to the theory of cognitive or intellectual value" (2000, p. 259).
4. In my *Educating Reason* (1988, p. 32), I suggest that "critical thinking" is best understood as the "educational cognate" of rationality. I here assume this account of critical thinking, and so use "critical" and "rational" indifferently in the text. Obviously, much more can and should be said about these key notions and their relationship than I can say here.
5. I should acknowledge that in holding here that both true belief and rational belief (and so, relatedly, critical thinking) are rightly regarded as crucial epistemic aims of education, I have modified my earlier view according to which only the latter should be so regarded. This change is a result of sustained discussion with several of those acknowledged below, esp. Alvin Goldman and Israel Scheffler.
6. Although Goldman here equates them, philosophers of education often distinguish between education and schooling. I won't pursue this matter here.
7. I acknowledge that Goldman enjoys a dialectically strong position here, because he is in position always to say, in response to arguments that critical thinking/rational belief are valuable, that that value is instrumental with respect to truth. My task is to establish that *some* of that value is independent of that tie to truth, without denying the tie.
8. William Rehg (2000, pp. 298–299) makes a similar point about Goldman's treatment of argumentation.
9. I do not mean to suggest that rationality and justification are identical or equivalent epistemic notions. But as the quote from Goldman above (from pp. 362–363) suggests, any differences are irrelevant to the issues before us, so I will treat them indifferently here.
10. Thanks here to correspondence with Israel Scheffler. It is worth pointing out that many other philosophers have challenged the idea that the weak sense of knowledge is adequate for education, such as Mill (1981; cf. Scheffler 1989, pp. 64–65) and Ryle (1967, pp. 111–112; cf. Scheffler 1991, pp. 90–94). More recently, Jonathan Adler (2003) also endorses the strong sense as that most relevant for education, although much of his discussion stresses the importance of aspects of the weak sense.
11. Such an argument is a variant of what James Rachels (1986, pp. 111–114) has dubbed a "bare difference" argument. I am grateful to Graham Oddie for this reference, and to Oddie and Richard Feldman for helpful suggestions. (An earlier version of Rachels' discussion of such arguments, in which they are not so named, appears in Rachels 1979.) Oddie (2001a, 2001b) addresses a number of issues related to such arguments in a philosophically imaginative and technically sophisticated way.
12. As William Rehg puts the point, in the context of his discussion of a scientific controversy, "Although our goal is truth, good justificatory argumentation supplies the only means we have of determining which theory is most likely to be true" (2000, p. 300).
13. The passage continues: "The basic role of justification is that of a *means* to truth.... It is only if we have some reason for thinking that epistemic justification constitutes a path to truth that we as cognitive beings have any motive for preferring epistemically justified beliefs to epistemically unjustified ones. Epistemic justification is therefore in the final analysis only an instrumental value, not an intrinsic one" (BonJour 1985, pp. 7–8, emphasis in original). Like Goldman, BonJour here moves, illicitly in my view, from justification's having instrumental value to its having *only* instrumental value.
14. I should note that, as his use of "explore" in the quoted passage suggests, Goldman's discussion is uncharacteristically tentative: "I am not confidant I can make this doctrine [VVEU] stick in full and complete detail, but I want to explore how close one can come in defending its plausibility" (2002, p. 51).
15. Goldman makes the point himself, in discussing the alleged virtue of "generality": "Science has a distinctive intellectual mission.... The main point I wish to make is that epistemologists of science should not be allowed to persuade other epistemologists that distinctive goals and values of science are also goals of cognition and inquiry in general" (2002, p. 60; See also Feldman 2002, pp. 370–373).

16. Cf. Feldman 2001, pp. 165–167; Feldman 2002, pp. 377–380. Goldman acknowledges that some notions of justification—subjective justifiedness and metajustification—are not straightforwardly instrumental with respect to truth, but thinks that this is compatible with his "weak" version of veritistic unitarianism (2002, pp. 65–66).
17. Here I am indebted to conversation with Jonathan Adler and Israel Scheffler.
18. I am indebted here to correspondence with Don Arnstine and Israel Scheffler.
19. Moreover, granting the point about very young children, educators ought nonetheless to endeavor to develop the preconditions of critical thinking in them. Thanks here to Jonathan Adler.
20. Which I've termed "non-indoctrinating belief inculcation" (Siegel 1988, ch. 5).
21. There is of course much more to be said about all of this. For the fuller story, see Siegel 1988, ch. 5. The idea of "style of belief" originates, as far as I am aware, with Thomas F. Green (1971).
22. Scheffler has long emphasized the point that in teaching, reasons must be age-sensitive: a good reason—i.e., a reason which justifies, which renders belief rational—for a fourth-grader might not but need not meet the standard of goodness that reasons must meet for us (cf. Scheffler 1965, pp. 57–58).
23. For example, Catherine Z. Elgin suggests in her "Epistemology's Ends, Pedagogy's Prospects" (1999), a version of which was presented at the APA session mentioned in the next note, that *understanding* is the proper epistemic aim of education. See also her Elgin 1996.
24. This paper began as a commentary on papers presented by Catherine Z. Elgin and Alvin Goldman at an invited symposium on "Epistemology and Education" at the Eastern Division APA meeting in December 1998. I am grateful to the APA for organizing the session and inviting my participation, to Goldman and Elgin for their incisive criticisms of my commentary on that occasion, and to the audience for their excellent comments and suggestions. More recent versions have been presented at California State University, Fresno, in May 2002, the University of Rochester in April 2003, and the "IL@25" Informal Logic conference in Windsor in May 2003. I am grateful to Otávio Bueno for organizing the first of these recent events and to Bueno and the other participants, esp. Tim Black, for their challenging objections and illuminating suggestions on that occasion; to Rich Feldman for arranging the second of them and to Feldman and the members of the Rochester Philosophy Department, especially Andrew Cullison, for their tough criticisms and good suggestions; and to Alvin Goldman, who responded to the paper on the third occasion, for his gentle but clear and exceedingly helpful response then and for his supererogatorily generous help before and since. Thanks also to Jonathan Adler, Don Arnstine, Melissa Bergeron, Tim Black, Ed Erwin, Simon Evnine, and Michael Slote for their criticisms and suggestions on various drafts, to Graham Oddie for illuminating conversation, and to the students in my seminar on social epistemology, especially Shirong Luo, for their substantial contribution to my thinking on these topics. Special thanks to Israel Scheffler, who proposed and chaired the APA session, and whose important comments and suggestions on an earlier draft I have shamelessly incorporated throughout.

References

Adler, J. (2002). *Belief's Own Ethics*. Cambridge, MA: MIT Press.
Adler, J. (2003). "Knowledge, Truth, and Learning." In R. Curren (ed.), *A Companion to the Philosophy of Education* (pp. 285–304). Oxford: Blackwell.
BonJour, L. (1985). *The Structure of Empirical Knowledge*. Cambridge, MA: Harvard University Press.
Elgin, C. Z. (1996). *Considered Judgment*. Princeton, NJ: Princeton University Press.
Elgin, C. Z. (1999). "Epistemology's Ends, Pedagogy's Prospects." *Facta Philosophica* 1: 39–54.
Feldman, R. (2001). "Review of Alvin Goldman, *Knowledge in a Social World*." *British Journal for the Philosophy of Science* 52.1: 163–168.

Feldman, R. (2002). "Epistemological Duties." In P. Moser (ed.), *The Oxford Handbook of Epistemology* (pp. 362–384). Oxford: Oxford University Press.

Firth, R. (1981). "Epistemic Merit, Intrinsic and Instrumental." *Proceedings and Addresses of the American Philosophical Association* 55.1: 5–23.

Fricker, E. (1994). "Against Gullibility." In B. K. Matilal and A. Chakrabarti (eds.), *Knowing from Words* (pp. 125–161). Dordrecht, The Netherlands: Kluwer.

Fricker, E. (1995). "Telling and Trusting: Reductionism and Anti-Reductionism in the Epistemology of Testimony." *Mind* 104.414: 393–411.

Goldman, A. I. (1998). "Education and Social Epistemology." In Rorty 1998, pp. 439–450. Originally published (with minor changes) in A. Neiman (ed.) *Philosophy of Education 1995* (pp. 68–79). Urbana, IL: Philosophy of Education Society.

Goldman, A. I. (1999). *Knowledge in a Social World*. Oxford: Oxford University Press.

Goldman, A. I. (2002a). *Pathways to Knowledge: Public and Private*. Oxford: Oxford University Press.

Goldman, A. I. (2002b). "The Unity of the Epistemic Virtues." Originally published in A. Fairweather and L. Zagzebski (eds.), *Virtue Epistemology*. Oxford: Oxford University Press, 2001. Reprinted as chapter 3 of Goldman 2002a, pp. 51–70; page citations above are to the reprinted version.

Green, T. F. (1971). *The Activities of Teaching*. New York: McGraw-Hill.

Mill, J. S. (1981). "On Genius." In J. M. Robson and J. Stillinger (eds.), *The Collected Works of John Stuart Mill*. Vol. I (pp. 327–339). Originally published in 1832.

Nussbaum, M. (1997). *Cultivating Humanity: A Classic Defense of Reform in Liberal Education*. Cambridge, MA: Harvard University Press.

Oddie, G. (2001a): "Axiological Atomism." *Australasian Journal of Philosophy* 79.3: 313–332.

Oddie, G. (2001b). "Recombinant Values." *Philosophical Studies* 106.3: 259–292.

Putnam, H., and R. A. Putnam. (1993). "Education for Democracy." *Educational Theory* 43.4: 361–376.

Rachels, J. (1979). "Euthanasia, Killing, and Letting Die." In J. Ladd (ed.), *Ethical Issues Relating to Life and Death* (pp. 146–163). Oxford: Oxford University Press.

Rachels, J. (1986). *The End of Life: Euthanasia and Morality*. Oxford: Oxford University Press.

Rehg, W. (2000). "Goldman's Veritistic Rhetoric and the Tasks of Argumentation Theory." *Social Epistemology* 14.4: 293–303.

Rescher, N. (1988). *Rationality: A Philosophical Inquiry into the Nature and the Rationale of Reason*. Oxford: Clarendon.

Rorty, A. O. (ed.). (1998). *Philosophers on Education: New Historical Perspectives*. London: Routledge.

Rorty, R. (1990). "The Dangers of Over-Philosophication: Reply to Arcilla and Nicholson." *Educational Theory* 40.1: 41–44.

Rorty, R. (1997). "Hermeneutics, General Studies, and Teaching" In S. M. Cahn (ed.) *Classic and Contemporary Readings in the Philosophy of Education* (pp. 522–536). NY: McGraw-Hill. Originally published in *Selected Papers from the Synergos Seminars* 2 (George Mason University, 1982).

Ryle, G. (1967). "Teaching and Training." In R. S. Peters (ed.), *The Concept of Education* (pp. 105–119). London: Routledge & Kegan Paul.

Scheffler, I. (1960). *The Language of Education*. Springfield, IL: Charles C. Thomas.

Scheffler, I. (1965). *Conditions of Knowledge*. Glenview, IL: Scott, Foresman and Company.

Scheffler, I. (1989). *Reason and Teaching*. Indianapolis: Hackett. Originally published in 1973 by Routledge & Kegan Paul.

Scheffler, I. (1991). *In Praise of the Cognitive Emotions*. New York: Routledge.

Schmitt, F. F. (2000). "Veritistic Value." *Social Epistemology* 14.4: 259–280.

Siegel, H. (1988). *Educating Reason: Rationality, Critical Thinking, and Education*. London: Routledge.

Siegel, H. (1997). *Rationality Redeemed? Further Dialogues on an Educational Ideal*. New York: Routledge.

Siegel, H. (1998). "Knowledge, Truth and Education." In D. Carr (ed.), *Education, Knowledge and Truth: Beyond the Postmodern Impasse* (pp. 19–36). London: Routledge.

Siegel, H. (2002). "Review of Alvin I. Goldman, *Knowledge in a Social World*." *Argumentation* 16.3: 369–382.

11

Rationality and Judgment

1. Introduction

Philosophical/epistemic theories of rationality differ over the role of judgment in rational argumentation. According to what Harold I. Brown (1988) calls the "classical model" of rationality, rational justification is a matter of conformity with explicit *rules* or *principles*. On this view, a given belief, action, or decision is rational only insofar as it is rendered so by a relevant rule or principle. According to the classical model, judgment plays no role in the determination of rationality; whether a belief or action is rational is a matter, not of judgment, but of its relation to the appropriate rules.[1] Critics of the classical model, such as Brown and Trudy Govier (1999), argue that the model is subject to insuperable difficulties. They propose, instead, that rationality be understood in terms of *judgment* rather than (or in addition to) rules. Govier also criticizes some of my previous work on the subject for being overly committed to the classical model, and for equivocating on "judgment."

In this chapter I consider Brown's and Govier's criticisms of the classical model and their defense of what I will call their "judgment model" of rationality, as well as Govier's critique of my earlier discussions. While my own commitment to the classical model is (I think and hope) somewhat more nuanced than Govier alleges, and so avoids at least some of her criticisms, the main burden of the paper will be not so much to defend my view from those criticisms, but rather, first, to articulate what I think are two deep problems for the view that Brown and Govier advocate: (1) its inability to distinguish between rational and irrational judgment, and (2) its inability to avoid recourse to rules. These difficulties, I will argue, render the view inadequate as an account of rationality, critical thinking, or argument appraisal. Second, and more positively, I hope to show that, properly understood, an adequate account of rationality will centrally involve both rules *and* judgment.

2. The Classical Model and Its Problems

According to Brown (1988), it is basic to any acceptable account of rationality that "rational beliefs must be based on reasons" (p. 38; see also p. 183). That is, whatever else a given theory says about the character and constitution of rationality, it must at least include a provision according to which *reasons* are fundamental. The point is perfectly general and runs far beyond belief: for a belief, but also an action, a hope, a fear, a decision, a vote, or anything else, to be rational, it must in some sense be "based on reasons." It is endorsed by most contemporary theorists of rationality, including myself, and I will presume it in what follows.[2] Granting that rationality involves reasons, what else is needed for a belief, action, decision, or whatever to be rational?

On Brown's articulation of the classical model, there are three further necessary conditions on rationality: for X (a belief, action, decision, etc.) to be rational, it must be *universal*, in that a given body of evidence will render X rational (or not) universally, i.e., for any arbitrary individual agent; *necessary*, in that X must follow necessarily from the relevant body of reasons/evidence; and, finally, a matter of *rules*, in that X must both *conform to and be based on appropriate rules* (pp. 5–19). While all three conditions are worth extended discussion, I will focus on the last of them in what follows.

As Brown puts it, according to the classical model, "the rationality of any conclusion is determined by whether it conforms to the appropriate rules" (p. 17). Various sorts of rules can be employed here, according to the model: logical rules, inductive rules, methodological rules, evidential rules, etc. So, for example, according to the classical model, it is rational to conclude or believe that

>r: Amsterdam is in Europe

on the basis of

>p: Amsterdam is in The Netherlands

and

>q: The Netherlands is in Europe

along with the rule which can be stated as

>R: If a is in b, and b is in c, then a is in c.

Similarly, on the classical model it is rational to believe/conclude that

>q': Amsterdam is a beautiful city

on the basis of

>p': Amsterdam has many beautiful canals, buildings, and parks

and the rule which can be stated as

>R': If a city has many beautiful features, it is (probably) a beautiful city.

As a final example, according to the classical model, it is rational to believe/conclude that

  r'': Amsterdam is a more permissive city than any US city

on the basis of the reasons/premises

  p'': Amsterdam has a large and thriving "red light" district, and many cafes in which marijuana and hashish can be openly smoked

and

  q'': In US cities, prostitution and drug use are both illegal and actively discouraged by law enforcement officials

and the rule which can be stated as

  R'': If a city permits activities that other cities do not, the former city is, *ceteris paribus*, more permissive than the others.

These examples appeal to several different sorts of rules.[3] Although Brown provides illuminating discussions of these and other sorts of rules, I will pass over those discussions in order to focus directly on Brown's main point: the classical model's insistence that rationality is determined (in part) by conformity with relevant rules creates difficulties that it cannot satisfactorily resolve. The basic problem is that, in any given case in which we are concerned to determine the rationality of a given conclusion (or belief, action, etc.) by seeing whether it conforms to the appropriate rules—i.e., whether it can be rationally concluded from initial premises or information by appeal to such rules—we will have to answer two questions: (a) With what information/premises shall we begin?, and (b) To which rules shall we appeal? Brown argues that both questions can be answered only by appeal to further rules, thus launching an infinite regress (or a vicious circle or arbitrary decision). Let us focus for the moment on (b). How can we determine whether or not our appeals to, belief in, or acceptance of the rules R, R', and R'' in the examples above are *themselves* rational? There seem to be only two possibilities open to us, on the classical model, both of which are problematic: (1) appeal to further rules, which immediately raises the unsavory prospect of infinite regress; or (2) do not appeal to further rules, which seems to render our appeal to those rules arbitrary. As Brown summarizes his analysis:

> [T]he classical model of rationality faces serious problems when it is consistently developed. The model requires that rationally acceptable claims be justified, and that the justification proceed from rationally acceptable principles in accordance with rationally acceptable rules. Each of these demands leads to an infinite regress unless we can find some self-evident principles and rules from which to begin, but these have not yet been found, and there is no reason to expect that they will be forthcoming. (p. 77)

Brown's argument for this conclusion depends on his claim that "the classical model of rationality requires a foundational epistemology" (p. 58) in order to satisfy the requirements it places on rationality, coupled with a detailed critique of several types of foundationalism. I will not discuss the case Brown makes here because, while I agree with him that the versions of foundationalism he considers are defective, I think that the classical model—or at any rate the view that rationality is fundamentally a matter of rules—need not and should not be tied to foundationalism. Below I will suggest both that any successful account of rationality will perforce need to appeal to rules/principles, and that such rules/principles do not require a foundationalist epistemology. Before addressing these matters, however, it will be helpful first to consider the alternative to the classical model that Brown and Govier favor.

3. An Alternative to the Classical Model: The "Judgment Model" of Rationality

Central to the "judgment model" of rationality, of course, is the notion of *judgment*. So it is imperative that we be clear on how this notion is to be understood. Happily, Brown's and Govier's accounts of it are sufficiently similar—in fact, Govier on the whole simply embraces Brown's—that they can, for the moment, be treated together. Brown writes, "Judgement is the ability to evaluate a situation, assess evidence, and come to a reasonable decision without following rules" (p. 137). Govier writes, "What is judgment? It is what we exercise when we are able to make reasonable and sensible decisions without appealing to rules" (p. 129).[4] There are three elements of these accounts, as articulated in the passages just cited, to which we must attend: for both Brown and Govier, judgment (1) is an *ability*, something we *exercise*; (2) is *not* exercised by following or appealing to rules; and (3) results in *reasonable* decisions. All three elements will be addressed below. First, let us briefly consider some other features of Brown's and Govier's accounts.

For Brown (as for Govier, p. 127), the exercise of judgment is *fallible* (pp. 144–146). Brown emphasizes that neither this fallibility nor the fact that it is not rule-governed entail that judgment is arbitrary. A key reason Brown offers for thinking that judgment is not arbitrary is that, on his view, judgment cannot be made in ignorance: "judgment on a topic can only be made by those who have mastered the body of relevant information" (p. 146). He further emphasizes that, in addition to expertise, the exercise of judgment requires skill, that some people are more skilled at it than others, and, again, that its exercise does not require or involve an appeal to rules (pp. 156–165). Finally, Brown's new model of rationality differs from the classical model, and the foundationalism upon which Brown thinks the latter ultimately depends, by (1) making rational *agency* fundamental, and rational belief derivative; (2) taking the ability to make judgments in situations in which decisions cannot be determined by rules to be a basic feature of rational agency; and (3) requiring that candidate beliefs and judgments be submitted to the consideration of the relevant community of experts for their evaluation (pp. 185–187). Thus, on Brown's positive account, judgments—i.e., the results of the exercise of judgment—are not always rational. To be so they must be the result of the skilled exercise of judgment, reflect mastery of the relevant information, and "have been tested against the judgements of those who are also capable of exercising judgement in ... critical debate" (pp. 196–197).

Govier endorses and helpfully explains and develops Brown's account, in the context of her consideration of the place of rationality in the theory and practice of critical thinking and argument analysis. On Govier's view, "judgment is indispensable in critical thinking" (p. 123). She takes argument analysis and evaluation to be central to critical thinking and so to rationality (as do I). Her discussion begins with a basic observation concerning argumentation:

> In the analysis and evaluation of arguments there are many points where decisions have to be made which are not generated by algorithms. That is, we have to decide what to do or say, and there are no universal rules which we can call upon to generate or justify our decision. This is where judgment comes in. (p. 123)

On Govier's view, judgment is involved whenever our decisions are not guided—i.e., generated or justified—by algorithms or "universal" rules. She argues persuasively that judgment is required more or less throughout the activity of argument analysis and evaluation—it is involved in argument interpretation, reconstruction, and throughout the process of evaluation (pp. 123–125). But she (like Brown, p. 138) is not a skeptic about rules; she denies neither their existence nor their applicability to real cases of argument analysis/evaluation. Her view, rather, is that rules cannot be the whole story:

> I am not saying we should never use rules, or that we should seldom use rules, and I am not denying that it is often useful and appropriate to articulate possible rules and try to test their applicability. I am merely saying that abiding by universal rules is not all there is to rationality. Rules are bound to run out at some point, whatever the endeavor. (p. 125)[5]

If rules are not sufficient for rationality, what is? Govier's alternative account of rationality centers, of course, on judgment. She endorses Brown's account, according to which judgment is "the ability to evaluate a situation, assess evidence, and come to a reasonable decision without following rules." (p. 127, citing Brown, p. 137) She develops her view of judgment in ways that will be considered below. But we are now in position to consider some problematic aspects of the judgment model, to which I turn next.

4. Problems with the Judgment Model

Earlier I identified three features common to Brown's and Govier's versions of the judgment model: on both their accounts, judgment is an ability which persons exercise, it results in reasonable decisions (as we have now seen, for Brown, only if the additional constraints of expertise, skill, and social testing/evaluation are met), and its exercise does not involve following or appealing to rules. Let us consider these elements in turn.

A. Judgment Is an Ability That Persons Exercise

According to the judgment model, "judgment" refers to an ability that people exercise, rather than the products produced by the exercise of that ability. It is important to realize that very often the term is used to refer to the latter rather than the former. For example, when we utter sentences like "I judge that it will be more efficient to take the southern rather than the northern route," or "she judged that Jones would be a better prime minister than Smith"—indeed, whenever we use, or utter sentences which presuppose, the expression *"judge that"*— we refer to the product of the exercise of the ability, rather than the process in which the ability is exercised.

This point will perhaps be clearer if we consider some utterances or sentences that, I think, are unproblematically regarded as judgments. To all of them the expression "I judge that" can be prefixed:

a. "Amsterdam and Miami are both culturally heterogeneous."
b. "This stock has performed well in the past, so it is worth buying today" (Suggested by Govier, p. 129).
c. "Physicists will unify quantum mechanics and general relativity by 2020."
d. "The tyranny of evolutionary theory will be overcome in my lifetime" (asserted by Philip Johnson).
e. "Chocolate ice cream tastes better than pecan butter crunch" (asserted by my daughter).

f. "Chocolate stains are harder to remove from white blouses than pecan butter crunch stains" (asserted by one of my daughter's parents).
g. "Nine-year-old children cannot handle the following assignment: 'Write an essay evaluating your own character, accomplishments, and goals'" (asserted by Govier, p. 130 [not cited *verbatim*]).
h. "Deliberation, options, and the weighing of pros and cons all enter into judgment" (asserted by Govier, p. 129 [not cited *verbatim*]).
i. "The classical model of rationality requires a foundational epistemology" (asserted by Brown, p. 58).

These are all examples of judgments, as the term is often used in ordinary discourse. They are clearly not instances of the exercise of the ability the judgment model points to, but are rather examples of the outcome, or product, of that exercise. For those making them, these judgments are *estimates of truth value*, or of *worthiness of belief*. For example, it is my judgment that (a) both Amsterdam and Miami are culturally heterogeneous—I judge it to be true, and as worthy of belief—just as Brown judges it to be true that (i) the classical model of rationality requires a foundational epistemology, and Govier that (g) nine-year-old children cannot reasonably be thought capable of writing an essay in which they evaluate their own characters, accomplishments, and goals.

Below I'll raise the question of what makes judgments like these rational, or reasonable.[6] For the moment I want simply to make it clear that the term "judgment" can be used to refer either to the exercise of the ability, as Brown and Govier urge, or to the product of that exercise. Now this ambiguity is not necessarily a problem for the judgment model; Brown and Govier are certainly within their rights to use the term to refer to the ability, rather than the result of its exercise. But we should be aware of the shift in usage that the judgment model requires. It will be especially relevant below, when I address Govier's suggestion that my earlier discussions use the term equivocally.

Notice also that the classical model appears to be concerned with the rationality of the products of the exercise of judgment, rather than the rationality of the process in which that exercise occurs, and in that sense the judgment model might with some justice be thought to be a change of subject, rather than a new account of the subject matter of concern to the classical model.[7]

B. Judgment Results in Reasonable Decisions

As we saw above in citations from both Brown and Govier, the judgment model seems committed to the view that the exercise of judgment must, apparently by definition, result in reasonable decisions. But this seems problematic.

Notice first that on the account of judgment Brown and Govier endorse—"the ability to evaluate a situation, assess evidence, and come to a reasonable decision without following rules"—judgment is a *success* term; the exercise of judgment automatically or necessarily results in "reasonable" decisions. All judgments, on this account, are *good*, i.e., *normatively appropriate*, judgments. Two questions immediately arise. First, are all judgments necessarily good ones? Don't/can't we make *bad*, e.g., unreasonable or irrational, judgments? Second, when our judgments are indeed good, what is it about them that renders them so? On what basis are good/rational judgments distinguished from bad/irrational ones? I address them in turn.

1. *Are judgments necessarily good?* Of course, proponents of the judgment model can simply stipulate that judgments are always good. In that case we'll need to introduce a new term for attempted or pseudo-judgments and decisions that appear to be judgments but are not, because they fail to meet the relevant standards and/or criteria of goodness. Let us call all such failures "shmudgments." Our problem now becomes how, on the judgment model, we are to distinguish judgments from shmudgments.

On Brown's view, as we have seen, there are additional constraints that must be satisfied if judgments are to be rational: they must be informed, skilled, and "submitted to the community of competent individuals for evaluation and criticism" (p. viii).[8] But when these additional constraints are met, judgments will be, on his view, rational:

> If the subject is one in which we have the relevant expertise, we gather information, apply whatever rules are available, weigh alternatives, and arrive at a judgement; then we discuss our judgement and the reasons for it with our peers, and re-evaluate that judgement on the basis of their recommendations and critiques. The outcome of this process is a rational decision or belief. (p. 226)

As this passage makes clear, on Brown's account of it, the rationality of judgment is guaranteed, whatever decision is made or outcome reached, so long as the exercise of judgment follows the procedure and meets the constraints that the model imposes. Whatever the content of the judgment reached—e.g., whether or not Amsterdam and Miami are judged to be culturally heterogeneous, whether or not the classical model of rationality is judged to require a foundational epistemology, whether or not nine-year-olds are judged to be capable of writing essays in which they assess their characters, accomplishments, and goals—the judgment will be, on Brown's view, rational. Whatever the outcome of the process—whatever content, conclusion, or decision is reached—its rationality is guaranteed.

The view Brown here defends, that the rationality of a judgment is guaranteed by the procedure followed, and is independent of the content of its outcome, is problematic. First, an adequate theory of rationality will perforce declare itself not only on matters of procedure, but also on matters of content. That is, it will recognize the legitimacy and importance of questions concerning the rational status of the conclusions, decisions, and judgments reached through the exercise of our ability to judge. Is the judgment that *(a)* Amsterdam and Miami are both culturally heterogeneous rational? Suppose that we judge that *(¬a)* these cities are not both culturally heterogeneous. Would *that* judgment be rational, too—whatever the evidence? The view that the rationality of a given judgment is independent of its content is problematic because it simply ignores a central concern for any theory of rationality, namely the rationality of the *content* of judgments. Second, this independence of content makes a mystery of Brown's insistence that rationality be a matter of *reasons*. Why must rational decisions be based on reasons, if not because the rationality of those decisions depends on their content, and basing them on reasons helps to establish the rational status of that content?[9] These problems suggest that the judgment model *is incapable of distinguishing rational from irrational judgments*— or, to put it more generally, of speaking to the *epistemic status* of judgments reached by way of the process of judgment Brown articulates—and thus fails to accomplish a task basic for a theory of rationality. Following the procedure and satisfying the constraints Brown recommends, however salutary, cannot be *sufficient* for rationality, since the rational status of the content of judgments reached by it is left unaddressed.

Interestingly, Govier also (albeit indirectly) raises questions about the adequacy of Brown's "automatically rational" view. She does so by pointing out that judgments admit of normative appraisal, and, far from being automatically rational, can be made well or badly (in the following passages the emphases are added):

> A rational person, he [that is, Brown] proposes, is one who can exercise *good sense* and *good judgment* in difficult cases.... He or she can ... decide and act *sensibly* in cases where there are no rules. (p. 128)

> We will fall back on judgment when there are no rules to guide us— when we have to devise or amend rules, choose between rules, handle an unusual case, or decide whether other things are equal. To do this, *and do it well*, is to be rational. (p. 129)

> *Good* judgment ... requires sensitivity, good sense, ... a sense of what is realistic ... [and] a sense of proportion, of what is more or less significant.... A person with good judgment will be able to recognize what is relevant, what rules and principles bear on a case, what if anything is exceptional about that case, what the consequences or implications of various decisions are likely to be, and so on and so forth. (p. 130)

Rationality and Judgment

[J]udgment can ... be *reasonable or unreasonable*. (p. 132)

[P]eople often need *good* judgment, but have *bad* judgment. (p. 133)

We should try to *improve* our judgment in whatever ways we can. (p. 135)

Govier is, in my view, clearly correct that judgments—whether exercises of ability (processes) or products—admit of normative evaluation in this way. This poses a problem for Brown, since, as we have seen, on his view judgments that satisfy his (contentless) constraints are automatically rational. But I leave this as an in-house dispute for Brown and Govier to resolve as they see fit. Supposing that Govier is correct that judgments admit of normative evaluation, how can/do we evaluate them? Here we come to the second question posed above.

2. *When our judgments are indeed good, what is it about them that renders them so? On what basis are good/rational judgments distinguished from bad/irrational ones?* The answers to these questions seem clear: It is the satisfying of relevant *standards* or *criteria*—concerning strength of evidence, argument adequacy, etc.—that renders judgments good; we distinguish the good ones from the bad by seeing whether or not candidate judgments meet them. But now a new question, of considerable moment for proponents of the judgment model, arises: Can this be done without appeal to rules or principles? If not, Brown and Govier seem to be forced back to the classical view they wish to reject. If so, how? Presumably, the answer will be: By using one's judgment. But now the problems that plague the classical model—i.e., circularity, regress, or arbitrariness—seem to plague the judgment model as well. These problems might be avoided by simply insisting that we can use our judgment to tell whether a candidate judgment is good or bad, reasonable or unreasonable, a judgment or a shmudgment. But this way of avoiding the problems seems clearly enough either to settle the philosophical issue by stipulative definition, or to beg the question against all those, like Govier, who deny—quite reasonably, it seems to me—that all judgments are good, or rational.

So, the normative evaluation of judgments requires appeal to criteria. Can we so appeal without invoking rules or principles? Here we come to a decisive issue for the judgment model.

C. The Exercise of Judgment Does Not Involve Following or Appealing to Rules

Brown and Govier are clearly right that when we judge well, and use our judgment appropriately, we needn't appeal *explicitly* to rules or principles. Such explicit appeal cannot be required, on pain of the regress Brown exposes: If I had to appeal explicitly to a rule in order to exercise my judgment, and I had to appeal explicitly to another rule in order to exercise my judgment concerning, e.g., the appropriateness or proper application of the first rule, I would never be able to exercise my judgment completely or successfully at all. So the judgment model's insistence that judgment is a skill that can be exercised well or badly—and which, like most skills, is not properly exercised by explicit attention to rules guiding its proper exercise—is a perfectly correct claim concerning one important sense of "judgment." For Govier (as for Brown), it is inevitable that the exercise of judgment does not involve following or appealing to rules, because rules "are bound to run out at some point" (p. 125), and when they do, "there is no alternative to judgment" (p. 135). And she is surely right that the *exercise* of judgment does not require following or appealing to rules, since, as we've seen, each attempt to so follow or appeal would itself require the exercise of judgment (concerning, e.g., which rule to appeal to or how to follow it).

But the normative evaluation of the exercise of judgment (and of judgments) is central to Govier's view, and it requires appeal to a range of criteria, several of which (sensitivity, a sense of what is realistic, a sense of proportion and of what is more or less significant, etc.) she articulates in the passage cited above. If judgment admits of normative evaluation, then its *proper* exercise—that is, *good* judgment—is such because it satisfies relevant criteria. (The parallel point applies to the evaluation of judgments [products].) In general, judgment's being exercised well (or badly) is a matter of its satisfying (or failing to satisfy) relevant criteria. Moreover, the normative evaluation of either a given exercise of judgment or the product of that exercise (i.e., the belief, decision or action to which judgment gives rise) *as* good/bad inevitably requires appeal to such criteria. If so, can rules be avoided in its proper exercise?

The classical model is wrong insofar as it bans judgment from rationality. As Brown and Govier insist, judgment is inevitable. Even to determine that a given rule is applicable to a given case, judgment is required. But, as Brown insists, any adequate account of rationality will render it as dependent upon *reasons*. The rationality of beliefs or judgments depends (in part) upon the adequacy of their supporting reasons. That adequacy, like the goodness of judgment more generally, is a matter of satisfying relevant criteria (here of *epistemic* goodness). Thus, judgments, even if made without criteria in mind, are, if rational, supportable by reasons which themselves satisfy criteria of epistemic quality. Conformity with or appeal to reasons, moreover, like conformity with or appeal to relevant criteria, requires *consistency*: if p is a good reason for q in circumstances C, it will be so in all relevantly similar circumstances (Scheffler, 1989, p. 76, cited by Govier, p. 126). Consider Govier's own example of a (bad) judgment, i.e., that concerning (g) nine-year-old children being assigned an essay in which they are asked to evaluate their own characters, accomplishments, and goals. If Govier's own judgment, that the teacher's judgment in assigning the essay was bad, is itself good, its goodness will be consistency-dependent—e.g., it will concern nine-year-old children generally, not just her daughter; will not depend on the characters, accomplishments, and goals (or gender or cultural identity, etc.) of any particular child; will not be altered by changes in her (Govier's) mood or her work schedule; etc. That is, if Govier's judgment is good, it will be so in virtue of the quality of her reasons for it, and those reasons will in turn be good (i.e., epistemically forceful) only insofar as they can be consistently invoked and evaluated across the range of relevantly similar cases. Consistency, in turn, is a matter of conformity with *rules* and *principles* (e.g., "treat like cases alike"; "no difference in judgments without a relevant difference in reasons for them"; "if a is a reason for p and p is relevantly similar to q, then a is a reason for q"; etc.).[10] As Brown and Govier insist, one may judge rationally without appealing to rules. But that judgment's status, *as* rational, depends upon its satisfying relevant criteria. We needn't consciously follow rules to be rational, but our judgments must meet criteria in order to be, and to be certifiable as, rational. The normative evaluation of judgment hinges upon the satisfaction of criteria. Rationality is more generally a matter of satisfying criteria, at least insofar as rationality is *normative*, telling us what is *worthy* of belief, decision, or action. But then judgment—or at least *rational* judgment—is also a matter of criteria, and so of consistency, and so also of rules and principles. In short:

judgment → *normative evaluation* → *criteria* → *consistency* → *rules*.

And so, the view that judgment is innocent of rules fails. While Brown and Govier are right that particular exercises of judgment do not require explicit or conscious appeals to rules,[11] they are wrong to think that *good*, i.e., *normatively appropriate*, judgment is so independently of rules. The satisfaction of relevant criteria is fundamental to normative appropriateness, and that satisfaction requires consistency, which in turn requires rules. Exercising judgment might be "what we do when rules won't help," but exercising it *well* is nevertheless a function of reasons, criteria, consistency, and (so) rules.

It is important to note that my claim is that the normative evaluation of judgment requires, in the end, rules. I am *not* claiming that all instances of rational judgment are, as Govier puts it, "resolvable by appeals to rules" (p. 132). Whether available rules will suffice to *resolve* particular issues will depend very much on the issues, and rules, involved. There are obviously hard cases—in philosophy, in matters of pressing social concern, and in ordinary life—in which available evidence, criteria, and rules are insufficient to secure rational resolution. But resolution is a red herring here. The question before us is not whether reason can resolve all outstanding issues, but whether rational judgments are such independently of relevant criteria (and so, in the end, rules). A given issue may well be irresolvable by appeal to rules, as Govier and Brown insist, yet judgments about it will be rational in virtue of their being sanctioned by relevant criteria (and associated rules, for example, concerning the application of those criteria and the evaluation of the relevant evidence). I am content to let resolution fall where it may. It is rather the point about rationality's dependence on criteria, and so rules, that I am concerned to make.

5. The Place of Judgment in the Theory of Rationality

If the points made above are correct, what should an acceptable theory of rationality say about judgment? It should say at least the following:

First, the "classical model" of rationality, as articulated by Brown, is wrong in holding that rationality does not in any way involve judgment. The reason is straightforward and compelling: to tell whether a given rule/principle is applicable and correctly applied to a given belief, decision, or action, which applicability and correct application are essential to the determination of rationality on that model, judgment is required.

But the "judgment model," according to which rationality is a matter of rule/principle-independent judgment, and according to which rules and principles play no role in the determination of the rationality of beliefs, judgments, or decisions, is also mistaken. Here, too, the reason is straightforward and compelling: if judgments admit of normative evaluation, as Brown and Govier as well as other theorists of rationality agree, such evaluation depends upon criteria of normative appraisal, which in turn involves rules and/or principles. So an adequate theory of rationality needs both rules *and* judgment. (And so the Brown/Govier definition of "judgment" as something wholly innocent of rules forces their arguments against the classical model to rest on a false "judgment/rule" dichotomy.)

Thus, I do not embrace the "classical model" as Brown delineates it, but rather a hybrid model that includes both judgment and rules/principles. On my view (1988, 1997), as on Brown's,[12] (good) *reasons* are the key to rationality—as Scheffler puts it, "Rationality ... is a matter of *reasons*" (Scheffler, 1989, p. 62, emphasis in original)—and this in turn requires consistency, which in turn requires rules/principles. This is the part of my view that conforms to the classical model. But I also embrace judgment.

The "unresolved tension" in my view (p. 132) that Govier detects is genuine, and problematic, only insofar as (a) the quality of reasons is a matter of their satisfying epistemic criteria; (b) such satisfaction involves consistency, and so rules; and (c) judgment has nothing to do with rules. But since (c) is false—or at least not a part of my view—the tension Govier detects is actually neither genuine nor problematic. If "judgment" in (c)—and in particular, its *normative evaluation*—is understood to be totally independent of criteria, then the problem of distinguishing rational from irrational judgment is irresolvable. If understood rather in a way that acknowledges that the quality of judgment is a matter of the satisfaction of criteria, and that the normative evaluation of judgment as good/bad, or reasonable/unreasonable, requires at least implicit appeal to criteria, and so, *via* consistency, to rules, the "tension" to which Govier points disappears.

Govier also suggests that I equivocate, sometimes using "judgment" as she and Brown do, "to allude to a human ability to make deliberative decisions about cases not resolvable by appeals to rules" (p. 132), and other times using it to refer to the product, or outcome, of the exercise of that ability. Here I plead guilty (although the reservation concerning "resolvability" mentioned above must here be kept in mind), but think it a mistake to regard it as a criticizable offense. As noted above, "judgment" is used in ordinary discourse in both senses, and an account of judgment must include both. More importantly, the theory of rationality is vitally concerned with the rational status of those products/outcomes/conclusions. To banish that concern is to render the theory inert with respect to the epistemic evaluation of those products. My "equivocation" is thus correctly seen not as a mistake, but rather as an effort to address both senses of "judgment" in a way that retains the theory of rationality's central concern with the epistemic status of such products. I believe that all the passages Govier cites and discusses in which I use the words "judge" or "judgment" (pp. 126–133) are readily, and unequivocally, so interpreted.

We should think of judgment not as necessarily rule- or criterion-innocent, but rather as (a) the exercise of our capacity to evaluate, assess, consider, and decide; and/or (b) the results of such exercise. In either case, criteria are essential, and so, therefore, are rules. If this is correct, we should also hold that:

1. If we are to distinguish rational from irrational judgment—which is basic for an adequate account of rationality—there is no alternative to doing so by appealing to relevant criteria and/or standards.
2. Since doing so requires appeal to rules or principles, that aspect of the classical model needs to be retained by any adequate view of rationality.
3. The sting of this last point is entirely removed by recognizing that explicit appeal to rules is not required for the exercise of judgment, but rather for its normative evaluation, and by embracing—as all parties (including Govier (p. 127) and Brown (p. 144) to this discussion do—a thoroughgoing fallibilism: all our judgments, including every aspect of our theory of rationality, might be mistaken. Of course, that our judgments *might* be mistaken does not entail that they are in fact, or are likely to be, mistaken. (Brown emphasizes this point as well, pp. 144–146; see Evnine, 2001; Siegel, 1997.)
4. There is no need to fear that any view other than the Brown/Govier view must founder due to infinite regress. Fallibilism requires that every belief and judgment be regarded as possibly mistaken; any can be called into question,

and reasons can be demanded which purport to render continued belief justified. Vicious regress needn't follow, because at every point the demand for further reasons can, in principle, be met (as Brown agrees, p. 186). This is the way that Brown endeavors to avoid the regress; it is open to theorists who acknowledge that rules have a place in a fallibilistic theory of rationality as well. Acknowledging the places of criteria, consistency and so rules in an account of rationality that permits the normative evaluation of judgment is thus completely in keeping with the rejection of "foundationalism."

5. Finally, if the classical model is correct that the normative evaluation of judgments requires appeal to criteria, and so to rules, it must also be granted that the judgment model is also correct: as far as rationality is concerned, judgment is also required. In the end, we needn't reject either view; the task, rather, is to integrate them in an adequate account of rationality. I hope to have taken some small steps in that direction here.[13]

Notes

1. As well as the person's *recognition* of that relation (Brown, 1988, p. 19). (All page references to Brown in the text are to Brown 1988.)
2. For extended discussion, see Siegel, 1988, 1997; particularly explicit statements by Laudan and Scheffler are cited at the head of Siegel 1988, p. 32. It is endorsed by Rescher (1988) and Nozick (1993) as well, both of whom would I think be considered by Brown to be advocates of the classical model.
3. In fact, the notion of rules is much trickier than has been indicated thus far, and has been the subject of intense philosophical scrutiny in recent years. I regret that I cannot address this matter squarely here.
4. All page references to Govier in the text are to Govier 1999. I should note that Brown spells "judgement" with two occurrences of the letter "e," while Govier spells it with one occurrence of "e." I will quote them accurately, but otherwise use the shorter spelling. (According to the *Oxford English Dictionary*, both spellings are legitimate.)
5. Govier is clear that, on her view, this thesis about rules is not restricted to matters of rationality, but is rather "ubiquitous in human life" (p. 127).
6. Sometimes these terms are treated as synonymous, sometimes not. I treat them as equivalent here, since Brown and Govier seem to in their texts. For a more detailed consideration of them, see Siegel 1997, ch. 7.
7. As we saw above, on Brown's view, the classical model holds that "the rationality of any conclusion is determined by whether it conforms to the appropriate rules" (p. 17).
8. Notice that satisfying these additional constraints is also a matter of meeting relevant criteria (as discussed below).
9. Brown writes, "Our model requires that rational beliefs be based on judgement, and judgement requires assessment of evidence and arguments" (p. 192). But surely what is required is (not "mere" assessment, but) *competent, accurate* assessment of the probative force of the evidence and arguments assessed (i.e., assessment that meets relevant criteria/ standards).
10. Consistency in application of relevant empirical generalizations, e.g., concerning the cognitive and emotional abilities of nine-year-old children, is also necessary.
11. But Govier is wrong to attribute to me the contrary view (p. 126). On my view, critical thinking/rationality is fundamentally a matter of evaluation in accordance with reasons.

Rules and/or principles may be explicitly invoked when the reasons themselves become the object of critical scrutiny, but this is not itself inevitable.
12. "[R]ationality provides *reasons* for accepting claims, i.e., it provides grounds for considering propositions to be worthy of belief and for acting on decisions" (p. 226, emphasis Brown's).
13. An earlier version of this paper was presented at Fresno City College in April 2002; I am grateful to Robert Boyd for arranging that presentation, and to the audience on that occasion, and in particular to Boyd and Otávio Bueno, for their very helpful criticisms and suggestions. Subsequent versions were presented at the International Society for the Study of Argumentation (ISSA) Fifth International Conference, Amsterdam, June 2002; the International Network of Philosophers of Education (INPE) Biennial Conference, Oslo, August 2002; and the annual meeting of the California Association for Philosophy of Education (CAPE), Sacramento, November 2002. (The earlier ISSA version appears as chapter 3 of F. H. van Eemeren, J. A. Blair, C. A. Willard, and A. F. Snoeck Henkemans, eds., *Anyone Who Has a View: Theoretical Contributions to the Study of Argumentation* (Dordrecht, The Netherlands: Kluwer, Argumentation Library Series, 2004), pp. 27–40.) I am grateful to all those who heard and commented on those presentations. I want also to thank Simon Evnine, Michael Slote, Hal Brown, and Trudy Govier for helpful criticisms of and suggestions concerning the penultimate draft; Govier for her close attention to my work in her "Rosebuds, Judgment and Critical Thinking" (1999); and Hal Brown for extensive correspondence on these matters when he kindly sent me draft chapters of what became his *Rationality* (1988). Many of the points I made in that correspondence are made here, but it was only when I read Govier's paper that I decided to pursue these issues in print.

References

Brown, H. I. (1988). *Rationality*. London: Routledge.
Evnine, S. (2001). "Learning from One's Mistakes: Epistemic Modesty and the Nature of Belief." *Pacific Philosophical Quarterly* 82.2: 157–177.
Govier, T. (1999). "Rosebuds, Judgment and Critical Thinking." In *The Philosophy of Argument* (pp. 123–136). Newport News, VA: Vale Press.
Nozick, R. (1993). *The Nature of Rationality*. Princeton, NJ: Princeton University Press.
Rescher, N. (1988). *Rationality: A Philosophical Inquiry into the Nature and the Rationale of Reason*. Oxford: Clarendon.
Scheffler, I. (1989). *Reason and Teaching*. Indianapolis: Hackett. First published in 1973 by Routledge and Kegan Paul.
Siegel, H. (1988). *Educating Reason: Rationality, Critical Thinking, and Education*. London: Routledge.
Siegel, H. (1997). *Rationality Redeemed?: Further Dialogues on an Educational Ideal*. New York: Routledge.

12

Epistemology in Excess?

A Response to a Heideggerian Reconceptualizing of Critical Thinking

1. Introduction

Emma Williams' "In Excess of Epistemology" (2015[1]) admirably endeavors to "open up" the way to an account of critical thinking that "goes beyond" the one I have defended in recent decades by developing, via the work of Charles Taylor and Martin Heidegger, "a radically different conception of thinking and the human being who thinks," one which "does more justice to receptive and responsible conditions of human thought" (p. 142). In this response I hope to show that much of Williams' alternative approach is compatible with my own; that, where incompatible, that alternative is problematic; and, finally, that there is a risk of talking past one another, of talking at cross-purposes, that all sides must work to overcome. Williams has succeeded in addressing a tradition other than her own; I compliment her both for trying—too few of us do—and to a considerable extent succeeding. I will try, too, but I doubt I'll be as successful as Williams has been.

Williams is careful to make clear that she does not take herself to have offered either a fully developed alternative account of critical thinking or a fully developed critique of my own account (p. 144). She does not claim to have defended Taylor from my criticism of his claim to "overcome epistemology" (Taylor 1987), but rather to have offered an alternative reading of Taylor's paper that is considered below. She argues that the work of Taylor and Heidegger can be utilized in the development of a deeper, richer, "radically different conception of thinking and the human being who thinks" (p. 142). I am happy to concede that my account is not so ambitious as that, and to grant that such a deeper, richer account would be a good thing to have. The new account aims to "exceed the epistemological"; I address this below as well.

It is perhaps worth noting that the radically different account Williams hopes to develop, drawing on Taylor and Heidegger—henceforth the WTH account—actually has a fair bit in common with my "reasons" account. In what follows I hope to draw attention to such commonalities, and to critically evaluate some of the differences.

2. Too Much Epistemology?

Williams is concerned that my account of critical thinking is overly tied to epistemology; that it places too much weight on matters epistemological and neglects allegedly problematic "metaphysical assumptions" underlying that epistemology. As this is a crucial part of her discussion, I will address it fairly systematically.

I begin with a preliminary point: my account does not offer a pedagogical recipe for becoming a critical thinker. Williams correctly describes my view as putting the competent assessment of reasons at the heart of critical thinking; it is one of two components (the other is the "critical spirit") that are individually necessary and jointly sufficient for being a critical thinker. But she suggests that I "turn to epistemology" "[i]n order to explain how we might become so proficient, and master the rules and principles of reason assessment" (p. 142). This is a small point, perhaps, but it is worth making: I don't turn to epistemology in order to explain how we might develop the ability to assess reasons. Rather, I hold that the ability to engage well in reason assessment is *part of what it is* to be a critical thinker. For insight on how to help students develop the ability we must look elsewhere.

That said, Williams is quite correct about the strong link between critical thinking and epistemology in my account. The link is straightforward: the competent assessment of reasons is central to critical thinking; such assessment is competent insofar as it meets relevant criteria concerning the strength of candidate reasons; and it falls to epistemology—construed broadly enough to include other loci of relevant criteria such as logic, probability theory, and the like—to determine the status of such criteria, and thus the strength/weakness of the reasons that fall under their purview. Epistemology likewise provides the general account (or meta-account, if you prefer) of all this: what it is to be a reason; the way in which good reasons provide support for the items for which they are reasons; the nature of that support; etc. Here some of the main questions of epistemology enter in: epistemic support is closely related to justification; justification is in turn closely related to rationality; both have contentious connections to truth; the character of the normativity involved in epistemic evaluation stands in need of clarification; etc. So an account of critical thinking must perforce concern itself with the meat and potatoes of epistemology. This is the link between critical thinking and epistemology.

Williams does not argue that this link, or the account of critical thinking that places it center stage, is defective. Instead, she sets herself the task of showing that "Siegel's epistemologically-orientated account of critical thinking is *incomplete*—a task that will be achieved by articulating a conception of critical thinking that goes *beyond* that defended by Siegel" (p. 143, emphases in original). This suggests that Williams thinks that my account is acceptable as far as it goes, but just doesn't go far enough. But her subsequent Taylor-based critique of the "metaphysical assumptions," the "epistemological tradition," and the related "*prioritisation* of the epistemological project within philosophy" (p. 143, emphasis in original), along with her subsequent treatment of Heidegger, suggest rather that she thinks my account is not simply incomplete, but rather defective because of its embrace of those problematic metaphysical assumptions. Let us then look next to her discussion of Taylor and my criticism[2] of Taylor's "Overcoming Epistemology."

3. Charles Taylor and the "Overcoming" of Epistemology

According to Williams, Taylor's 1987 paper aims to show "how Heideggerian philosophy works to undermine the epistemological tradition by challenging the ideals that lie at its very root," by challenging the "*metaphysical assumptions*" on which that tradition rests (p. 143, emphasis in original). What is that tradition, and what are those ideals and assumptions?

As it turns out, Williams does not articulate the epistemological tradition in question, also called the "epistemological project" (p. 145), in any detail.[3] (It is hard for me to understand the tradition in question as anything other than the tradition of Western philosophy beginning in Greece, since issues concerning knowledge and our ability to know, along with fundamental metaphysical issues, have been central to it since before Socrates, but I will not pursue this point further here.) Rather, she centers her critique on three particular claims I have defended, which constitute for Williams the "*particular version* of epistemology" (p.144, emphasis in original) I advocate: (i) truth is independent of rational justification, in that highly justified beliefs can be false; justification does not entail truth; (ii) truth is to be understood in "realist" or "absolutist" and non-epistemic terms, such that the truth of a given claim or proposition is independent of us;[4] and (iii) justification is a fallible indicator of truth (p. 145).[5]

These particular epistemological theses, Williams argues, presuppose (1) "a *representational* account of thinking" and "of *thought* itself" (p.145, emphases in original), one of the metaphysical assumptions WTH problematizes. WTH also challenges (2) "a stress on methodology as the means through which we might reach truth" and (3) "a conception of the human being as a self-reflective, autonomous subject" (p. 145). Williams does not argue that these assumptions are false, but rather that they are not necessary, and that very different conceptions of critical thinking and of thought itself which reject them are available on the WTH view. We will consider those different conceptions, and the alternative assumptions they embrace, below.

Williams' explicit criticism of my view is that my verdict concerning Taylor— that his "overcoming" of epistemology "leave[s] epistemology 'pretty much as it is'" (p. 144, quoting Siegel, 1998, p. 28) is

> *too hasty*—for there is much more at stake in the account opened by Taylor via Heidegger than Siegel himself realizes. It is important to understand the claim being made here carefully. What I am seeking to challenge is not Siegel's defence of critical thinking *per se*. Neither am I attempting to engage directly with the issue of whether Taylor and Heidegger do, in fact, succeed [in?] undermining the entire epistemological enterprise. What I *am* seeking to challenge, however, is Siegel's inference that Taylor and Heidegger's conceptions do not go *beyond* his own view and leaves the epistemological perspective "pretty much as it is." As we shall come to see, far from leaving Siegel's position untouched, I would argue that Taylor and Heidegger open the way towards an account of critical thinking which radically *exceeds* the epistemological version propounded by Siegel. (p. 144, emphases in original; cf. also p. 147)

Williams argues, against my claim about Taylor "leaving epistemology pretty much as it is," that my reading of Taylor's case is flawed in that I mistake *causes* for *conditions*: that is, that I misunderstand Taylor to be making causal claims concerning agency's role in forming representations, when in fact he is offering *conditions of the possibility of thought or experience*—and that once this point is grasped, it is no longer clear that his analysis "leaves epistemology pretty much as it is" (pp. 146–149). As Williams puts it, "the account Taylor and Heidegger present cuts deeper than a causal claim—since it is a claim about the *conditions* that allow us to have a thought or an experience in the first place" (pp. 148–149, emphasis in original).

I am certainly no expert on the work of either Taylor or Heidegger, and happily bow to Williams' expertise with respect to Taylor and Heidegger interpretation.[6] So let me simply grant Williams' point: Taylor, like Heidegger, Merleau-Ponty, and Wittgenstein, is "seeking to examine ... not the *causes* of our taken-for-granted representations, but rather the *conditions of possibility* of our having thoughts or experience of the world at all" (p. 149, emphases in original). How does this insight get us to "an account of critical thinking which radically *exceeds* the epistemological version propounded by Siegel?" To answer this we must continue to follow Williams' discussion.

4. The WTH View of Language and Thought

Williams argues next that Taylor draws upon Heidegger's "examination [that] works to re-describe *some of the key conceptions that underpin the epistemological enterprise*" (p. 149, emphasis in original). First, Williams explains Taylor's appropriation of Heidegger's "argument from transcendental conditions," which, she points out, is importantly unlike a Kantian transcendental argument because "[i]t does not begin from the perspective of the *subject*, but rather seeks to examine what it is for there to be something like subjectivity in the first place" (pp. 149–150, emphasis in original). She then introduces two Heideggerian tropes, the "clearing" (*Lichtung*) and the "background," from which emerges "a level of 'non-explicit engagement with the world,' a horizon through which and against which all of our experience takes place" (p. 150, citing Taylor, p. 11).[7] From consideration of the background, and the suggestion

> that there is a horizon of engagement through which our experience of the world is opened up, thought itself comes to be re-described. More particularly, our account of thinking comes to be less a matter of disengaged representation, more an engaged and contextual practice. (p. 150)

From here Williams turns to Heidegger himself, who "works to foreground the *engaged* nature of thought, rather than the disengaged representation focused on in epistemology" (p. 150, emphasis in original). Heidegger emphasizes, by way of the "background," our "thrownness": "As Heidegger describes it, we are 'thrown' into the world—and hence are affected by a context *prior* to any wilful act of comprehension or representation" (p. 150, emphasis in original)—which not only highlights the engaged nature of thinking, but also allows us to see the ways that language both *reveals* and *conceals* the world. As Williams articulates the key Heideggerian points:

> [O]n account of the background, human beings find themselves in a world that is not primarily of their own making. Put otherwise, we find ourselves in a world that is *already* populated with meanings and significances. Hence ... we relate to things with "fore-sight"—finding them not as abstracted, singular objects, but rather as things that are already interpreted in terms of a web of possibilities.... Crucially, however, through our own dealings with the world, *we* also engage in producing

the world as meaningful and significant. This is because ... human existence is itself *disclosive*; we take things *as such and such* and hence lay the world open in terms of certain possibilities. A key mechanism of this disclosure is ... our use of *language*. Of course in traditional philosophical terms ... language is understood as a tool for communicating preformed ideas in the head. Yet, through a more careful meditation on the ways language actually works, Heidegger refers us to the way language, far from simply *representing* thought, rather appears to *produce* and *institute* our ways of thinking. Language, to put it otherwise, is a productive power that opens up the world.... [A]longside *opening up* the world in certain ways, our processes of revealing are at the same time processes of *concealing*. Put otherwise, our interpretive dealings with the world, by conditioning certain ways of showing up, also cause other ways to be hidden or covered over. This concealing is, importantly, part and parcel of what it means to reveal something in the first place—for bringing certain aspects of a thing to light necessarily means that other aspects will fade into the background. (p. 151, emphases in original)

Williams illustrates this revealing/concealing feature of language with the example of the utterance "the chair in the dining room is sturdy" to someone looking for something to help reach a pair of shoes on top of a wardrobe. The utterance reveals "the nature of the chair" as something that can help reach the shoes; at the same time it conceals "other aspects of the chair (its colour or its style for example) [that] fade into the background" (p. 151). And this is sufficient, Williams argues, to distinguish the WTH account she favors from my own:

Crucially, through this point, I would suggest that we come to see more fully how Heidegger's account offers us quite a *different* perspective to that assimilated by Siegel. We may recall that Siegel himself adhered to a certain conception of thinking (the representational conception) and a certain conception of the human being (as a self-sufficient, autonomous subject) within his account of critical thinking. Yet what we have just seen from Heidegger opens quite a different conception *of at least one of these notions*. More specifically, it opens a conception of human thought as [a?] process that reveals and conceals the world, rather than simply represents it.... [W]hat Heidegger's conception does draw our attention to is the way that there is a *productivity* within human thinking, in relating to the world, we open it up in certain crucial ways. There is, we might say, an "as-structure" to our thinking—a taking of things *as* this and not that, in *this* way rather than in that way.... [This] is [a?] process that takes place against a background of a world that has already been opened to us. (pp. 151–152, emphases in original)

Moving to the trope of the "clearing," Williams urges that an important lesson from Heidegger's work is that as language use both reveals and conceals, language users "open up the world in ways that *they do not control* . . . [and] that go beyond themselves" (p. 152, emphasis in original). She illustrates this phenomenon of language with the example of the utterance "my friend is fun but she is untrustworthy" (p. 153), which enables the speaker to reveal the world in a certain way to the hearer, but which is not fully under the speaker's control, since the hearer may not only have a different understanding of "fun" or "trustworthiness" than the speaker's understanding of them, but may also reveal something to the hearer that the speaker did not intend, for example "that perhaps I am not a very nice person to be speaking about my friend in this way!" (p. 153). Thus, the Heideggerian claim that "'*language* speaks'—which does not suggest that human beings do *not* speak, but rather attests to the way that, in using language, we acts [sic] in ways we do not control" (p. 153, emphases in original). In this way the second trope

> refers us to the way that our processes of revealing and concealing go beyond ourselves in a twofold sense: they are not only *conditioned* by a prior opening of the world to us, they also constitutively *produce* an opening up of the world that is beyond us. And yet, from here, we start to see that Heidegger's philosophy is offering us not only a re-description of the nature of human thinking—it also offers us a re-formulation of the human being *who* thinks. (p. 153, emphases in original)

This enables Williams to attempt to draw a sharp contrast between the Heidegger-inspired account and my own. Whereas mine focuses on "that self-sufficient, autonomous 'subject' who strove for 'independence of judgement' and 'liberation,'" WTH holds that "human thought is not the result of a solely *individual* achievement—it is not a power that *we* exercise or a process that *we* actively bring about in a self-sufficient manner" (p. 153, emphases in original). In doing so,

> Heidegger jettisons such conceptions of the human being. What Heidegger refers us to *instead*, we might say, is a view of the human being as a *receptive* and *responsible* agent. We are *receptive* insofar as our opening up and revealing of the world is, at the same time, conditioned upon the world's being opened and presented *to us*. Hence receptivity bears witness to the *co-dependency* between us and the world's coming to light . . . Our responsibility stems from the fact that, since we *do* open up the world through our ways of revealing, our thinking is *accountable* for the way the world is. (pp. 153–154, emphases in original)

I apologize for what must seem like excessive quotation from Williams' article; I worry about getting Williams wrong—after all, this literature is not where I normally hang out, philosophically speaking—and so have tried to stick close to her own words in depicting both her criticisms and her positive position. Let us now consider them.

5. Two Initial, Small-ish Matters

I begin by noting that even if WTH succeeds in articulating and defending an alternative view of "the nature of thinking and the human being *who* thinks" (p. 144, emphasis in original), this "re-description," whatever it is, will not constitute an alternative account of *critical* thinking for the simple reason that critical thinking is thinking that is responsive to, and appropriately reflective of, *reasons* and the criteria governing their quality. There is plenty of thinking that can be good in various ways without being critical: imaginative thinking, creative thinking, poetic thinking, artistic thinking, plodding, flat-footed[8] thinking, algorithmic thinking (if you'll allow that there can be such a thing), stodgy thinking, bureaucratic thinking, etc.[9] In this sense the specific content of the WTH re-description is neither here nor there. Whatever that content, an episode of thinking's being critical depends on its answering well to relevant epistemological criteria. We will return to this point below.

I note as well that Williams misdescribes my view when she claims, after discussing the three allegedly problematic claims that constitute my "particular version of epistemology," that I characterize critical thinking "as a practice concerned with the justification of our beliefs, for the purpose of arriving at or 'striving' after truth" (p. 145). Critical thinking often involves striving after truth, but this shouldn't be conceived as its *purpose*. If I have reasons to make pasta rather than salad for dinner tonight (we had salad last night, and right now the assembled eaters all fancy pasta), my thinking counts as critical if it properly estimates the force of those reasons (in conjunction with the estimation of the force of whatever other reasons are in play). Assessing reasons well is, on my account, part of what it is to think critically. It is not part of that account that the purpose of critical thinking is to arrive at or strive after truth. This may or may not be part of one's purpose in a given episode of thinking. Often it is, especially in deliberation concerning what to believe. (Should I believe that Trump really believes that Mexico will pay for the wall? Should I think that Britain's exit from the EU will be good for Britain's economy?) But even in such a case, the purpose is not part of the account of the thinking's—i.e., the thinking that results in the arrived-at belief—being (or not) an instance of critical thinking.[10]

But these points, though I think them correct, are insufficient to settle anything of importance in the present context. What, then, is the WTH view of thinking in general, and of critical thinking in particular, such that that view "exceeds the epistemological version" I defend?

6. "A Conception That Exceeds the Epistemological"

The contrast Williams draws between the two views certainly seems like a sharp contrast. How sharp is it in fact? In particular, how does WTH open the way to a new account of critical thinking that "exceeds the epistemological?"

On Williams' view of it, my account of critical thinking conceives of such thinking as "detached and disengaged," "so that we might come to judge our beliefs objectively, according to criteria that have been specified in advance," and so that "we fit what we experience into predefined conceptual frameworks" (p.154). Although Williams thinks I would find this articulation of my view "*uncontentious*" (p. 154, emphasis in original), it suggests a kind of straightjacketed, constrained thinking that is not part of my view. For one thing, our conceptual frameworks are, on my view, themselves subject to critical scrutiny (Siegel 1997, ch. 12; 2004). For another, the criteria that have allegedly "been specified in advance" are themselves open to critical analysis and improvement (1997, chs. 1, 5). Perhaps most importantly, our thinking is *ours*—so how can it be "detached and disengaged?" WTH seems to conflate two quite distinct claims:

1. Truth is independent of us.
2. Our judgments/estimates of the truth are disengaged or independent of us.

I affirm the first of these; it is the "realist"/"absolutist"/non-epistemic account of truth discussed earlier. While I acknowledge philosophical disagreement on this point, I don't myself see any plausible way to reject it. Consider, as an example, "Williams endorses Heidegger's account of language and the way it both reveals and conceals." Isn't this sentence (or the proposition it expresses) true exactly when Williams in fact endorses that account? If a playful Nietzschean named Paul whispers to me at the bar, "You know Emma doesn't really believe it; she's just saying it to get through the program," I may have a new reason to question its truth, but its truth is not a matter of what I (or Paul) say or think, but rather of her endorsement. It is, as metaphysicians and philosophers of language say, the *truth-maker* that makes the sentence (and the proposition it expresses) true.

But I reject the second claim, and in particular the suggestion that our judgments are somehow independent of us. How can they be? They're *ours*, after all. So of course they're not independent of us. Our thinking (and our judgments) is (are) inevitably influenced by our languages, our conceptual schemes, our backgrounds and horizons, our histories and cultures, our identities, etc.[11] WTH and I are agreed about the influence of such things. But once that influence is acknowledged, all sides endeavor to achieve some measure of critical distance from these influences, and some critical leverage over them, in order to say defensible things about them. Isn't this in fact what Williams, Taylor, and Heidegger themselves strive to do? Surely Heidegger's view doesn't come down to "Language speaks, and reveals/conceals, and I say this because language speaks, and reveals and conceals to me in such a way that this is the only view of language I can conceive or accommodate—I think language works this way because language itself tells me that this is how language itself works." Actually, being a neophyte with respect to Heidegger scholarship, I should not say that with confidence. Perhaps his view really does come down to that. But if so, we might be forgiven some measure of skepticism, since many in the history of philosophy (not to mention psychology and linguistics), equally under the influence of language, have accommodated rather different views of language and its influence on our thought. A more charitable interpretation of Heidegger's project, I would have thought, is that it seeks to offer a radically new understanding of the ways language works and influences our thinking and our thoughts, one that is not itself dictated by language. This is how Williams seems to take it, in her insistence on both our responsibility as language-users and our codependency with the world (p. 153). If so, we are agreed on the rejection of the second claim, despite her apparent embrace of it. In any case, lumping the two claims together and arguing that since our judgments are not independent of us, the truth itself is equally not, is a mistake. The truth may be independent of us, but our judgments of it surely are not.[12]

7. Worries about Representation

Williams' main complaint seems to be that my view

> goes hand-in-hand, not only with a particular version of epistemology, but with the estimation of a particular view of *thought* itself. For indeed, by arguing that critical thinking is the process of seeking a greater fit between our beliefs and knowledge claims and the world, Siegel's account works to foreground a *representational* account of thinking. (p. 145, emphases in original)

As we have seen, the preferred WTH view rejects this representational account of thinking in favor of the allegedly nonrepresentational account of thinking, and of thought, inspired by Heidegger and developed by Taylor and by Williams herself.

Does my account "foreground a representational account of thinking?" There are several things to say here. First, and perhaps foremost, that account is not an account of thinking in general, but rather of *critical* thinking. While I'm happy to admit that on my view lots of thinking—especially that involved in deliberation—is representational, I do not think it all must be. More importantly, my account is not about "thought itself," but rather about that subset of thinking that is rightly analyzed in responsiveness-to-reasons terms.

Second, it is worth considering the target of the objection carefully. Is it *thinking* (or "*thought itself*") that is (allegedly) problematically representational, or *belief*, or *truth*? Suppose Jan thinks through an argument of the familiar "Socrates is mortal" variety. Her reasoning carries her from a consideration of the premises/reasons to a judgment about the conclusion. When Jan concludes that the conclusion follows deductively from the premises, is she committed either to believing that a particular individual, Socrates, was in fact mortal, or that the proposition (or sentence expressing it) that he was mortal is true? Having reached the end of this bit of reasoning, must she believe it? So far, no. The standard analysis is that the argument is *valid* (i.e., the truth of the premises guarantees the truth of the conclusion); the conclusion follows deductively from the premises. Whether or not either it or the premises that entail it are true is another matter. Jan can reason well about this case without believing the conclusion or being committed to its truth—that is, without regarding the conclusion as an accurate representation of the world.

I suspect that Williams' worry is not so much about the representational character of thinking, but rather about both the representational character of *thoughts* (understood as manifested in beliefs, claims, sentences, or propositions) and the "realist" or non-epistemic understanding of truth that my account incorporates. That this view of truth is philosophically contentious is an understatement; Williams is in very good company in her reluctance to embrace it. But as Williams herself insists (p. 144), she does not argue that her nonrepresentational account of thinking (or her epistemic, non-"realist," non-"absolutist" view of truth, if that is indeed her view) is correct, or philosophically superior to its alternatives, but only that it is indeed an alternative. Of course. We must next consider why we should prefer it to its alternatives.

Consider a thought, then—for example, Williams' thought that I am mistaken in thinking that Taylor and Heidegger leave epistemology pretty much as it is. I hope it is uncontroversial that this is a thought expressed in her paper. The thought can be taken to be, and analyzed as, a sentence ("Siegel is mistaken ..."), a belief, a claim, or the proposition the sentence expresses. In any of these forms, doesn't it represent me as being mistaken about that particular claim, and doesn't it represent that claim as itself misrepresenting the actual impact of Taylor's and Heidegger's analyses of the "epistemological tradition?" It is difficult, for me at least, to see how a proper treatment of this thought can be nonrepresentational. In saying this, I do not deny our own contribution to whatever it is we think is representing and being represented here. I do not deny that all our judgments are made from particular, located points of view; nor do I deny the revealing/concealing powers of language or the other Heideggerian tropes Williams discusses. Still, while accepting all that, it seems that the thought (or the belief/sentence/claim/proposition) in question has a representational character: it represents something (in this case, yours truly) as being a certain way (in this case, being mistaken about a particular matter). It is difficult to see how this can be denied while continuing to regard the thought *as a thought*. The same point can be made for more or less any thought, it seems ("Syrian refugees are suffering needlessly"; "Trump is a proto-fascist"; "Light cannot escape from a black hole"; "There is no highest prime number"; "Broccoli is good for you"; "This student's work is better than that one's work"; "Heidegger is a great philosopher"; "The chair in the dining room is sturdy"; "My friend is fun but she is untrustworthy"; etc.). True or false, justified or not, all are thoughts that represent something or other as being some way or other. Thoughts are *about* their objects or contents. This "aboutness"— what philosophers often call *intentionality*[13]—seems both unavoidable and completely in keeping with the Heideggerian insights Williams emphasizes. Those insights do not upend either the need for representation in our analyses of thought or the representational nature of language. Intentionality appears to be inherently representational. If so, the Heideggerian analysis of language, even if correct, is not so radical as it may at first appear. If not, I look forward to reading an account of the thought considered above, that I'm mistaken about WTH leaving epistemology pretty much as it is, that does not represent me as being mistaken![14]

Moreover, I wonder how the WTH picture is meant to differ from or challenge an account that emphasizes reasons. Accept that our judgments take place against the "background," that language both reveals and conceals, etc. John utters, "The chair in the dining room is sturdy," and Patricia points out that the utterance both reveals the chair as something that can be stood on to reach the shoes and conceals other features or properties of the chair. Doesn't John's utterance give Patricia a reason to go to the dining room and get the chair, assuming she wants to reach the shoes, despite the concealed features of the chair? Perhaps a meatier example: Donald says, "Those refugees are crazy to risk their lives on those rickety boats just to get to Lesbos; I'd never do that. We should leave them to it and let them take their chances," and Hillary points out that Donald's utterance reveals something important about his background, worldview, or conceptual scheme, namely that his privilege is such that he can't even imagine the lives of poverty, oppression, and desperation lived by those refugees. Supposing that Hillary is right, doesn't her remark give us a reason, for example, to reject Donald's racist and isolationist policy proposals? In other words, isn't the WTH account compatible with an account that gives pride of place to the role of reasons in thought and deliberation?

My "foregrounding" the representational character of much of our thought, I should note, is compatible with acknowledging that not all our thought is best understood in representational terms. Moreover, as was acknowledged above, it is not to deny the contributions to our thinking made by our backgrounds, horizons, conceptual schemes, fundamental presuppositions, and the like. WTH may well be right (along with many other theorists, before and since) that it is this background that enables us to represent things in particular ways in the first place. (I can hardly represent the chair as sturdy without having mastered the concept "chair," and without seeing the thing in question *as* a chair.) Thus is acknowledged WTH's emphasis on our "thrownness" and dependence on our conceptual backgrounds and schemes.[15] We judge from the particular, located points of view we uncritically inherit. Nevertheless, once inherited, we do our best to gain critical leverage over them. At least, so I will argue below. Here the point is simply this: The acknowledgement of this non- or pre-representational dimension to our thinking does not "exceed" or "go beyond" the account of thinking Williams seeks to challenge. That dimension is already built into and acknowledged by the challenged account—though in fairness to Williams, it is not always emphasized in that account, as Williams rightly points out.

What about the WTH account of *critical* thinking? Does it "go beyond" my account, or is that account and its underlying epistemological commitments left pretty much as they are?

8. The WTH View of Critical Thinking

Why should we think that my claim that Taylor's analysis leaves epistemology pretty much as it is "too hasty?" Williams' answer is that Taylor and Heidegger "open the way" toward a different account of critical thinking that "exceeds" my epistemological view. Of course, opening up an alternative is not the same as establishing that that newly opened alternative is superior to the one it exceeds; for that we'll have to consider that newly opened-up alternative. What is it?

Williams begins her articulation of the alternative as follows:

> At the end of "Overcoming Epistemology," Taylor argues that, after Heidegger, the position at which we stand is one where we recognise the dimension of fallibility and limitation within epistemological enterprises. Put otherwise, what Heidegger's account positively succeeds in showing us is that, insofar as human thought is grounded in conceptual frameworks, it can be limited by our own interests and concerns.... [T]his recognition does not so much jettison the epistemological project, but rather offers us a more "critically defensible notion of what this entails" (p. 14). This is because it reveals to us that, when seeking

truth or congruence between our beliefs and the world, our interests and concerns may cause our conclusions to be fallible. Hence ... after Heidegger, it is important to recognise that our ways of describing the world do not constitute a complete story of the world; they do not provide us with one story of reality, which is universally true for all time. (p. 155, quoting Taylor)

Of course. As Williams acknowledges, fallibilism has been part of my story since the beginning, as has the changing, and in the good case improving, character of our "stories" of reality/the world. So far, then, this does not amount to an alternative account of critical thinking, let alone one that "exceeds epistemology."[16] What then is the excess? Williams helpfully "schematise[s] the demarcation as follows" (p. 156):

1. Whereas Siegel's conception of critical thinking emphasised the process of seeking to assess whether our representations of the world (occurring in the form of knowledge or belief-claims) are accurate, Heidegger's account refers us to the processes of revealing and concealing that take place through human thought—which are not simply representational reflections of the world, but rather open up and produce the world we have.
2. Whereas Siegel's conception of critical thinking emphasised the practice of coming to judge beliefs or propositions objectively, Heidegger's account refers us to the responsibility in human thought—to the way that, in and through our processes of revealing and concealing, we play a role in making things show up in the way they do and hence contribute to what gains access to thought and to what thought gains access to.
3. Finally, whereas Siegel's conception of critical thinking emphasised the disengaged activity of the autonomous thinking subject, Heidegger's account refers us to the receptivity and co-dependency of human thought—to the way that our thinking is not a self-sufficient, self-determined activity, but is rather conditioned by something that is *beyond* ourselves. (156, emphasis in original)

What should we make of these differences?

The first draws upon a sharp represent/produce-open up distinction that is untenable. As argued above, WTH does not escape representation; both my account and the WTH account are in the relevant respects representational. Both acknowledge that our thinking is not free from the influence of language, history, culture, or conceptual scheme. All parties are agreed that thinking, in its reliance on language, both represents and produces/opens up the world. There are differences of emphasis, of course. But the argument that

1. Language and thought reveal/conceal and open up/produce the world, therefore
2. Language and thought are not representational

is a non sequitur. Language and thought do and are both.

The second draws an equally untenable dichotomy between objective judgment and responsible judgment. Surely judgments can be and often are both. Let us suppose that Williams is judging responsibly when she argues that the WTH account exceeds the epistemological. Doesn't she also want that judgment to be correct, and objectively so? There is perhaps a lack of clarity here concerning the meaning of "objective." Williams seems to take it to mean "independent of us," but, as argued above, our judgments are not objective in *that* sense. There is much to say about the character of objectivity that I haven't the space to say here.[17] But insofar as we want our judgments to be informed, reflective of evidence, and free from pernicious bias (which does not require complete freedom from the influence of the background, language, or scheme from which we judge), we want them to be objective—as we want them to be responsible and appropriately acknowledging of (and critical of, to the extent possible and appropriate) the background from which they are made. Objectivity is an ideal we strive for in our judging; to reject the ideal is to give up the thought that our judgments (for example, that Heidegger's work is important, or that it "exceeds the epistemological") are in any way worth making and having. This, I trust, is something the defender of WTH should not be willing to give up, at least insofar as she takes herself to be *defending* that view.

The third, as we saw above, rests on an inadequate understanding of thinking as "disengaged." Our judgments are not and cannot be disengaged when that is understood as freedom from the influence of language, background, conceptual scheme, and the like. But they should be disengaged in the sense that they are free from the undue influence of those dimensions of those influences that are rationally indefensible: for example, that certain groups of people are inferior to others, which is, sadly, part of many people's backgrounds. Of course, we always judge from where we are; we cannot judge from "nowhere," free of all conceptual schemes, for there is no such viewpoint available to us. But that doesn't mean that we can't, or shouldn't, do our best to escape from those judgments and influences that we have reason to think do not deserve our allegiance. This is the continuous process of *improvement* of our beliefs, theories, and commitments. It does not require freedom from unavoidable influences, but rather that we strive, to the extent we are able, to exercise critical leverage over them.[18]

It should also be noted that although Williams presents them as alternative conceptions of critical thinking, the three differences she points to seem to involve thinking more generally. Why think that these are conceptions of critical thinking specifically, rather than thinking more generally?

Williams seeks to offer "an alternative conception of critical thinking" (p. 146), conceiving it "in the broad sense of the term, that is, as a notion of what it means to think well" (p. 144). This is a broad sense of the term indeed, making "thinking critically" equivalent in meaning to "thinking well." We can, of course, opt to adopt this broader meaning of "critical thinking," thereby giving up an explicit focus on responsiveness to reasons. If we do understand the meaning of the term in this way, then Williams is clearly right that there is more to critical thinking (understood in this new way) than what my account, or any other extant account I am aware of, treats.[19] But should we? It seems to me more helpful to reserve the expression to refer to a specific kind of thinking—namely, the responsive-to-reasons kind. I hypothesize that Williams wants to broaden it in order to distance herself from critical thinking "in the technical sense of the curriculum project that has developed in recent years" (p. 144).[20] I trust it is clear that my account of critical thinking is independent of the curriculum project she deplores.

Williams offers another reason for understanding "critical thinking" as "thinking well":

> In what sense are we entitled to call this Heideggerian-inspired account of thinking an account of *critical* thinking?.... [I]f we take "critical thinking" in the broader sense, that is, as a notion that is concerned with what it means to *think well*, then let us indeed call our account one of "critical" thinking. For this account itself directs us towards aspects of our thinking that can be improved—aspects that, moreover, are not called attention to in Siegel's epistemological account. For the recognition that human thought is a process of opening up and producing the world suggests to us that we should examine our thinking not only for how well it captures the world (as Siegel would suggest via his representational account), but also for what we are doing in and through our thinking as expressed in speech. Indeed, this is precisely what is at stake in the "responsibility" of human thinking that Heidegger's account refers us to ... [which] calls us to investigate what we are *doing* through our thinking and speaking; hence it directs our attention to the *performative* rather than purely *representative* aspects of our thought. (pp. 156–157, emphases in original)

This is, I think, an important point. Williams is right that my account does not emphasize the performative. But if I may be permitted three quick points in reply: (1) As Williams herself seems to concede in this passage, the WTH account also embraces representation. (2) I welcome Williams' suggestion that the educational task is to *improve* thinking. But how is such improvement to be judged, if not in terms of reasons and the satisfying of relevant criteria? This seems unavoidable. If so, it is another instance of agreement between the two accounts.[21] Finally, (3) while Williams is right that my account does not "call attention" to or emphasize the performative aspects of our thinking and speaking, it certainly does not exclude them. From the beginning my account has emphasized the importance of reasons in guiding believing, thinking, *and acting*.[22] Insofar as performatives are actions—things we do—they are straightforwardly included in my account. And insofar as thinking is something we do, it too is performative. That it is performative in this way is completely in keeping with evaluating the fruits of such performances in the epistemic terms I favor.

Williams' examples of the sorts of performatives my account does not call attention to are telling. She offers two: whiteness theory, in which theorists have identified "white talk"—white people speaking to each other in ways that insulate them from examining the role of such talk in perpetuating racism; and what might be called "Derridean criticality," a way of "calling to attention those presuppositions and categories that make possible and structure our ways of thinking" (p. 157). The first is a straightforward appeal to reasons in order to combat racism (racism is morally indefensible, white talk perpetuates racism, so white folks should notice that their way of talking is morally regressive and should work to change this pernicious way of talking—and education can help by drawing students' attention to this phenomenon and its role in perpetuating racism).[23] The second is a call to scrutinize even our most fundamental assumptions and presuppositions, insofar as they are scrutinizable—a call that has been central to my account from the beginning. So while Williams' call to attend to the performative dimensions of our thinking succeeds in drawing the spotlight to a point I haven't emphasized, it does not succeed in "going beyond" my account, which includes those dimensions. There may well be good reasons to emphasize them, in which case we should—just as my account suggests.

Williams ends her paper by noting that WTH points out that "judgement is not only the kind of thing that is settled by the application of criteria" and that it is "a complex and fluid affair that recognises new interpretations can be brought to light and revisions and re-arrangements can be made"; that it can "make sense of 'truth' ... not just [as] a matter of the epistemologist's 'correctness'— there is truth as a revealing and concealing of the world"; and that it can reach conclusions, albeit conclusions "that are provisional and open" (p. 158). I won't worry here over the idea that "concealing[s]" are "true"—if my utterance conceals some properties of the chair, isn't it still the case that they are properties of the chair?[24]—but other than that one, all these points are readily accommodated by, and indeed already included in, my account: actions, beliefs, theories, etc., as well as judgments, can be evaluated in light of (fallible, criticizable, improvable) criteria; new interpretations are always possible, and revisions to them, when backed by good reasons, welcomed; being fallible, our conclusions are always provisional, open, and subject to reasoned evaluation and improvement. There does not seem to be much here that exceeds the "reasons" account I favor.

So, does WTH "go beyond" my account, or does it "leave epistemology pretty much as it is"? Other than the salutary suggestion of attending to the performative nature of our thinking and speaking, there doesn't seem to be much to WTH that goes beyond that account. WTH's emphasis on language, revealing/concealing, the clearing and the background, and receptivity do indeed go beyond my account in the sense that I don't emphasize these things. But it doesn't "go beyond" that account—let alone go beyond epistemology—because, as I've argued above, all such WTH-inspired and -informed thinking is still subject to epistemic evaluation, as are the thoughts produced by such thinking.[25]

9. Autonomy, Self-Directedness, and Self-Sufficiency

Williams also objects to my account's incorporating "a conception of the human being as a self-reflective, autonomous subject" (p. 145). To this charge I plead guilty: I have in many places embraced an "Enlightenment" conception according to which humans are, ideally, self-reflective and autonomous. This conception is, like that concerning truth above, highly contentious. This is not the place to defend it at length.[26] I content myself here with pointing out that it is, on my account, an ideal to be pursued, both in and outside of education. I do not claim that we are in fact perfectly "self-reflective, autonomous subjects"; we are all to varying degrees self-reflective/unreflective and autonomous/heteronomous, as our thinking is to varying degrees critical/uncritical. I rest my case for the ideal on the moral imperative to treat students (and everyone else) with respect: to fail to do our best to foster their critical thinking ability and autonomy is to fail to treat them with respect as persons.[27] Of course, my argument for this is criticizable, but Williams doesn't offer a criticism of that argument. Instead she points to our dependence on language, the background, etc. We are agreed about that dependence. But we are apparently not agreed on what follows from it. I claim that despite our dependence, we can try, and sometimes succeed, in gaining critical perspective on even such fundamental presuppositions, thereby offering us the opportunity to modify and improve them. Obviously I might be mistaken about this too. But I see nothing in Williams' discussion that suggests that my claims about either the moral requirement concerning respect or the possibility of such critical leverage are mistaken.

10. Philosophizing across Boundaries

There is, I fear, a goodly amount of talking past one another going on. In addition to the points made above, when Williams suggests that, on my view, human thought is, contrary to WTH, "a *solely individual* achievement" (p. 153, first emphasis added), and that such thought is "a process that *we* actively bring about *in a self-sufficient* manner" (p. 153, second emphasis added), she misrepresents that view. Despite my efforts to be fair to her discussion, I'm sure Williams will think that I have similarly misrepresented her view, and will chastise me for my inability to escape the "rationalistic conception of thinking" (2016, p. 11) that she does her best to problematize. That "conception," and Williams' case against it, are worth a brief comment.

Williams is clear that she has something very general in mind by the "rationalistic conception": "[W]e shall be using this as a term of art, to designate conceptions of thinking that, while not reducible to each other, foreground a *certain range of general characteristics*" (2016, p. 11, emphasis in original). These general characteristics—thought as disengaged and representational; subjects as autonomous, self-directed, and self-sufficient; generic, transferable general skills/procedures of reason assessment/thinking; objective, "realist," "correct" truth; impartial evaluation; a schematic, *a priori*, deterministic, particular way of approaching the world; etc.—are ones we have been discussing throughout. As I hope to have shown, Williams locates them in my own account imperfectly: representation and objective truth are parts of both our views, and attempts to do away with them face insuperable difficulties; autonomy and self-sufficiency are ideals to strive after, not factual states of all actual persons; critical thinking aims at disengaged and impartial judgment, but not in the sense of judgment from "nowhere," free of the influences of language, conceptual scheme, and the like; principles of reason assessment are mixed, with some being general and others subject-specific; etc. The "term of art" in play here is far too underspecified to be helpful, as are the general characteristics: it is as if all non-Heideggerians are doomed to be closet Cartesians. All these characteristics need to be handled with care. Williams' discussion of them in the work of the authors she favors is indeed careful in this way. But her discussion of the opposition, collected together under the umbrella "rationalistic conception," is not. I have tried to show how my view in some ways fits under that umbrella and in other ways does not. I have defended the ways in which it does, and explained the ways in which it does not. For example, I have tried to explain that while I favor "impartial," "disengaged" judgment, I do not understand these terms as requiring freedom from all outside influence. As Williams herself might put it, we *always already* judge from the conceptual scheme we inhabit. But this does not preclude impartial, disengaged, objective judgments, including judgments concerning that scheme itself. By the same token, much of the WTH account—and in particular, the openness, conditionality, and productive character of thought—does not "exceed" my account but is rather at home in it.

Perhaps such mischaracterization is an inevitable feature of attempts at communication across our respective philosophical traditions. Perhaps—but I really hope it is not. It is clear that those traditions have, to a considerable extent, different literatures, languages, and problematics—different fundamental problems, issues, and ways of tackling them. Perhaps the best thing would be for the traditions to go their own ways, pursuing their problems and projects as they will, safely insulated from the distraction of other approaches. Perhaps—but again, I hope not. For the differences among our existing traditions, imposing though they are, ought not to preclude thoughtful engagement across their boundaries. I end as I began, by congratulating Williams on her attempt to engage what for her must seem an alien tradition. Despite my complaints above, I congratulate her on her partial success as well. Philosophy of education as practiced today, at least in English, is far too insular and clubby; too many of us simply can't understand what others of us are saying. (I certainly do not exempt myself from this charge; as the reviewers have suggested and discerning readers will readily detect, my lack of familiarity with and understanding of Heidegger is alas all too evident.) Let us all do our best to communicate across the boundaries of our traditions.[28]

Notes

1. Untethered page references in the text are to Williams 2015. Williams' *The Ways We Think* (2016) is an impressive, elegantly written demonstration of the possibilities of working across philosophical traditions, integrating discussions of Ryle and Heidegger, Austin and Derrida, and a broad range of other thinkers. Her treatment is, as Paul Standish declares in the book's preface, clear (at least insofar as the texts she discusses permit), careful, and rigorous. In what follows I make occasional reference to the book, but concentrate on the paper. I recommend the book, which develops in considerable depth and detail many of the points made in the paper.
2. In Siegel 1998.
3. Williams apparently thinks that that tradition—"epistemology as it is formally practiced"—consists in "the practice of making knowledge claims" (p. 145). This is not a successful characterization of either epistemology or "the epistemological tradition." We all make claims to know all the time, as do all the academic disciplines taught in schools, colleges, and universities. Epistemology concerns itself with philosophical questions concerning such claims—for example, are any of them justified or true?; if so, what is it for such claims to be justified or true, and how can we tell?; do any of them actually constitute knowledge, and if so, how do we distinguish the genuine articles from the pretenders?; etc.—not with the making of such claims, except those concerning those philosophical topics themselves. "Emma Williams is the author of the paper I'm here discussing" is a knowledge claim I am here and now making; it is hardly the sort of claim that counts as epistemological—any more than "It's sunny and hot here in Miami as I write" so counts.
4. For more detailed discussion, see Siegel 1997, ch. 1; Siegel 1998. There are hardly more controversial issues in philosophy than the nature of truth, and I certainly can't claim to have advanced the general discussion other than to argue that this sort of conception of truth is essential to the proper conceptualization and defense of the educational ideal of critical thinking. For a systematic discussion of truth and a defense of the weak version of the correspondence theory I favor, see Goldman 1999, ch. 2, and my review of Goldman's book (Siegel 2002). Whether or not this claim about truth is itself epistemological, rather than metaphysical, I set aside here.

5. It is perhaps worth pointing out that the phrase Williams attributes to me on p. 145—"mind-independent order of objective reality"—is actually quoted by me from Carr 1994, p. 236. For the text and subsequent discussion, see Siegel 1998, pp. 22–23.
6. Although in rereading the relevant portions of Taylor's famous paper and my discussion of them, my interpretation seems to me well justified by the text.
7. To avoid confusion it is perhaps worth mentioning that Williams and I have quoted from two different printed versions of Taylor's paper "Overcoming Epistemology," she from Taylor's collection *Philosophical Arguments* (Harvard University Press, 1997), me from what I think is the original publication in K. Baynes, J. Bohman, and T. McCarthy (eds.), *After Philosophy: End or Transformation?* (MIT Press, 1987). Since I'm here quoting Williams quoting Taylor, the reader should note that page references to Taylor's paper are to the first of these. In the discussion of Taylor in my "Knowledge, Truth and Education" (1998), the page references are to the second.
8. With apologies to Nelson Goodman.
9. I don't suppose that these are non-overlapping types. The point is simply that thinking can be good in lots of ways, at least some of which don't require that the thinking be critical in the sense of being appropriately responsive to reasons. If so, then—to anticipate and respond to a reviewer's worry—valorizing critical thinking need not and does not run the risk of excluding or demeaning other ways of thinking (or, for that matter, ways of acting or living). While critical thinking typically involves judgment (e.g., of the goodness of candidate reasons), whether or not some other way of thinking should be deemed inferior in a given context depends on many factors; there may well be good reasons to not be critical on a given occasion. For example, sometimes we do well to brainstorm—deliberately refrain from judging while trying to generate novel thoughts, ideas, and solutions. Such thinking is not critical, or judgmental, but is not for that reason inferior.
10. Williams' worry here concerning the purpose of critical thinking is not unlike my reaction to Alvin Goldman's claim that critical thinking is valuable only instrumentally, that is, in its reliable production of truth/true belief. I challenge his claim, that critical thinking is of instrumental value only, in Siegel 2005. Williams and I are agreed (though she doesn't put it this way) that critical thinking's epistemic value is not limited to its tie to truth.
11. For consideration of the epistemological ramifications of this point, cf. (among several other places) Siegel 2004; 1997, ch. 12.
12. It is still hard to do better than Israel Scheffler's (1965) pellucid discussion of the definition/test of truth distinction. Williams helpfully discusses Heidegger's distinction between truth as "correctness" (*adequatio*) and truth as "revealing" or "uncovering" (*aletheia*) (p. 158; 2016, pp. 79–82). The former sense is legitimate, according to Heidegger, but should not be prioritized over the latter, as it has been by the "epistemological tradition." Rather, "it is better to say that the notion of *aletheia* comes *before* the notion of *adequatio*, since it is only on the basis of things being disclosed to us that we can then go on to think about statements as corresponding to states of affairs within the world" (2016, p. 81, emphases in original). Whether or not *aletheia* is rightly thought of as another sense of "truth" or kind of truth I'm happy to leave to Heidegger scholars. But it seems to me problematic for the reason Williams emphasizes elsewhere: revealings also conceal. First, if what is revealed is true, is what is concealed also true? (When the utterance conceals the color of the chair, is it true that the chair is colorless?) Second, and more importantly, why think that what is revealed/uncovered is *true*, given human propensities for error, prejudice, and distortion?
13. As the *Stanford Encyclopedia of Philosophy* has it, "Intentionality is the power of minds to be about, to represent, or to stand for, things, properties and states of affairs" (cf. Jacob 2014).
14. Williams often writes as if she opposes representational accounts of language, thinking, and thoughts (e.g., 2016, pp. 128, 180, 233), although she also acknowledges its place in her and Heidegger's views as well (e.g., 152, 157). A reviewer suggests that my discussion of intentionality incorrectly attributes to Heidegger a view of it more appropriately attributed to Husserl, one that Heidegger challenged. The reviewer may well be right about that. But I don't think that point upends the one made in the text—that thoughts are about their

objects or contents, and as such represent those objects or contents as being (or not) in particular ways.

15. As a reviewer helpfully points out, one might understand this in terms of Heidegger's distinction between "ready-to-hand" (tacit, background-given meaning) and "present-to-hand" (available for explicit, reflective thinking). Both are operative in both the WTH and my accounts, although Heidegger's focus on the phenomenology of thinking and the role of the tacit/implicit in it clearly exceeds my own.

16. If I may be permitted two pedantic points: First, fallibilism has been widely acknowledged in epistemology since Peirce at least; it is hard to see why the credit for it should fall to Heidegger. Second, strictly speaking, it is not that "our interests and concerns may cause our conclusions to be fallible"; they are that in any case. It is rather that our interests and concerns (and misconceptions, false beliefs, etc.) may cause those conclusions to be *false*. I should here acknowledge David Bakhurst (2013, pp. 192–193), who chastises me for claiming that it is our beliefs or claims, rather than we ourselves, that are fallible. On Bakhurst's McDowellian view, strictly speaking it is *we* who are fallible, not our beliefs or claims. This is not the place to enter into a lengthy discussion of the matter, but I should say that I think McDowell's "conditional principle," on which Bakhurst here relies, is much more problematic than his discussion acknowledges.

17. Cf. Neiman and Siegel 1993. There is, of course, much more to say than is said in that paper.

18. I have tried to articulate and defend such a view in many places. See, e.g., Siegel 1997 and 2004. Emily Robertson (2009) provides a very helpful discussion that emphasizes the importance of doing our best to "exercise a controlling intelligence" over our beliefs and commitments and those influences that admit of it, while fully acknowledging our dependence both on others and the "background" from which we judge. The phrase is taken from Coady 1994.

19. For discussions of a range of alternative accounts, cf. Siegel 1988; Winch 2006; and my review of Winch's book (Siegel 2008).

20. This seems especially clear in Williams 2016, ch. 8.

21. In her book (Williams 2016, e.g., pp. 235–246) as in her paper, Williams speaks expansively in evaluative terms: "more adequate conceptions" of education and educated persons, "*the best way*" (emphasis in original) of approaching the world, "improve our judgement," etc. At the same time, she joins Wittgenstein in condemning us to be "perpetually 'disappointed' with criteria" (2016, p. 235). Criteria—fallible, criticizable, improvable criteria—are necessary for such evaluative projects as her own. They are completely in keeping with the "openness" and "productivity" that her account of thinking valorizes.

22. A representative articulation of the view: "[T]o say that one is *appropriately* moved by reasons is to say that one believes, judges, *and acts* in accordance with the probative force with which one's reasons support one's beliefs, judgments, *and actions*" (Siegel 1997, p. 2, last two emphases added).

23. This should not be taken to imply or suggest that people become racist "as a result of rational debate or argument," as a reviewer reads it, but rather that, according to whiteness theorists, white talk has the effect of perpetuating racism, and that such theorists are motivated in part by the imperative of combating racism and the need to understand the role of white talk in perpetuating it.

24. See note 12 above.

25. When we do the revealing/concealing thing in our understanding of both particular utterances and language more generally, can't we do it well or badly—that is, can't we be either correct or mistaken in particular analyses of instances of language's revealing and concealing? If so, we're going to need to appeal to reasons to evaluate those analyses, in order to establish that a given case really is a case of revealing or concealing of the sort the analyses urge. So we'll need to evaluate reasons—i.e., engage in epistemic evaluation in the way my account emphasizes.

26. Cf., among other places, Siegel 1988, 1997, 1998, 2005.

27. Here we have another reason for keeping in place the narrower, responsiveness-to-reasons conception of critical thinking, rather than the broader "thinking well" conception favored by Williams.
28. Thanks to two anonymous reviewers for their helpful suggestions. I regret that lack of both space and ability prevent me from addressing them all.

References

Bakhurst, D. (2013). "Learning from Others." *Journal of Philosophy of Education* 47.2: 187–203.
Carr, D. (1994). "Knowledge and Truth in Religious Education." *Journal of Philosophy of Education* 28.2: 221–238.
Coady, C. A. J. (1994). "Testimony, Observation, and 'Autonomous Knowledge.'" In B. K. Matilal and A. Chakrabarti (eds.), *Knowing from Words: Western and Indian Philosophical Analysis of Understanding and Testimony* (pp. 225–250). Dordrecht, The Netherlands: Kluwer.
Goldman, A. (1999). *Knowledge in a Social World*. Oxford: Oxford University Press.
Jacob, P. (2014). "Intentionality." In E. Zalta (ed.), *The Stanford Encyclopedia of Philosophy*. Stanford, CA: Center for Study of Language and Information, Stanford University. http://plato.stanford.edu/archives/win2014/entries/intentionality/.
Neiman, A., and H. Siegel. (1993). "Objectivity and Rationality in Epistemology and Education: Scheffler's Middle Road." *Synthese* 94.1: 55–83.
Robertson, E. (2009). "The Epistemic Aims of Education." In H. Siegel (ed.), *The Oxford Handbook of Philosophy of Education* (pp. 11–34). Oxford: Oxford University Press.
Scheffler, I. (1965). *Conditions of Knowledge*. Glenview, IL: Scott, Foresman and Company.
Siegel, H. (1988). *Educating Reason: Rationality, Critical Thinking, and Education*. London: Routledge.
Siegel, H. (1997). *Rationality Redeemed?: Further Dialogues on an Educational Ideal*. New York: Routledge.
Siegel, H. (1998). "Knowledge, Truth and Education." In D. Carr (ed.), *Education, Knowledge and Truth: Beyond the Postmodern Impasse* (pp. 19–36). London: Routledge.
Siegel, H. (2002). "Essay Review of Alvin Goldman, *Knowledge in a Social World*." *Argumentation* 16.3: 369–382.
Siegel, H. (2004). "Relativism." In I. Niiniluoto, M. Sintonen, and J. Woleński (eds.), *Handbook of Epistemology* (pp. 747–780). Dordrecht, The Netherlands: Kluwer.
Siegel, H. (2005). "Truth, Thinking, Testimony and Trust: Alvin Goldman on Epistemology and Education." *Philosophy and Phenomenological Research* 71.2: 345–366.
Siegel, H. (2008). "Autonomy, Critical Thinking and the Wittgensteinian Legacy: Reflections on C. Winch, *Education, Autonomy and Critical Thinking*." *Journal of Philosophy of Education* 42.1: 165–184.
Taylor, C. (1997). "Overcoming Epistemology." In *Philosophical Arguments* (pp. 1–19). Cambridge, MA: Harvard University Press. Originally published in K. Baynes, J. Bohman, and T. McCarthy (eds.), *After Philosophy: End or Transformation?* 1987, (pp. 464–488). Cambridge, MA: MIT Press.
Williams, E. (2015). "In Excess of Epistemology: Siegel, Taylor, Heidegger and the Conditions of Thought." *Journal of Philosophy of Education* 49.1: 142–160.
Williams, E. (2016). *The Ways We Think: From the Straits of Reason to the Possibilities of Thought*. Chichester, UK: Wiley.
Winch, C. (2006). *Education, Autonomy and Critical Thinking*. London: Routledge.

PART FOUR

RATIONALITY AND CULTURAL DIVERSITY

13

Multiculturalism and the Possibility of Transcultural Educational and Philosophical Ideals

1. Introduction: Can Educational and/or Philosophical Ideals Transcend Particular Cultures?

Are educational and/or (other) philosophical ideals relevant only to the cultures in which they are acknowledged and embraced, or can their legitimacy extend beyond the bounds of those cultures? By "*educational* ideals" I intend to refer to those ideals which have been thought to characterize (ideally) educated persons and (ideal) educational arrangements and efforts: ideals such as growth, self-realization, creativity, rationality, caring, freedom, obedience, discipline, conscientious citizenship, democratic (or authoritarian) social organization of schools, and so on. By "*philosophical* ideals" I intend to refer to moral and social/political ideals thought to characterize (ideally) moral persons and social/political arrangements, epistemic ideals such as those characterizing (ideal) knowers and believers, etc. In what sense, if any, can such ideals be thought of as *transcultural*? What is their relevance to cultures that reject them in favor of alternative educational or philosophical ideals?

I hope, in what follows, to establish the legitimacy of regarding ideals such as these as genuinely transcultural. I will endeavor to do so by consideration of a notion which might at first glance be thought to point in the opposite direction—that of *multiculturalism*. I will argue that, appearances to the contrary notwithstanding, multiculturalism does not entail that educational and philosophical ideals are relative to culture; and that it is possible, and desirable, to embrace both the moral and political directives of multiculturalism and a "universalistic" or culture-transcendent view of genuine educational and philosophical ideals.

2. What Is Multiculturalism?

Multiculturalism is often used to refer to the contemporary "educational reform movement that aims to equalize educational opportunities for diverse racial and ethnic groups" (Perez y Mena 1996, p. 415), which movement "incorporates the idea that all students—regardless of their gender and social class, and their ethnic, racial or cultural characteristics—should have an equal opportunity to learn in school" (Banks 1992, p. 2). It typically refers also to the more general ideas that schools, and people and institutions more generally, should acknowledge, value, and respect cultural differences and the alternative experiences and perspectives of members of different cultures; and that members of "minority" cultures should not be required to assimilate into, nor to adopt the alien cultural commitments or identities of, nor be marginalized, silenced, or oppressed by, a dominant, hegemonic, "majority" culture.[1]

Even a cursory review of the literature reveals that the term is used in a wide range of ways, to pick out a variety of ideas and practices.[2] In addition, many different forms of multiculturalism—"conservative," "corporate," "critical," "difference," "liberal," "insurgent," "managed," "resistance," "weak," etc.—have been identified and defended/criticized by various authors.[3] In view of these different meanings of "multiculturalism," and the different forms of it individuated in the literature, it is difficult to settle on a single conception. Nonetheless, my purposes here require that I do so. For better or worse, then, and in explicit recognition of the alternative conceptions of and distinctions among the various forms of it extant in contemporary discussions, in what follows I will understand *multiculturalism* to refer to that movement in contemporary social/political/educational thought, and the claims, theses, and values which characterize it, that celebrates cultural differences; that insists upon the just, respectful treatment of members of all cultures, especially those which have historically been the victims of domination and oppression; and that emphasizes the integrity of historically marginalized cultures.[4]

3. Why Value Multiculturalism?

If we ask *why* we should embrace multiculturalism—why we should think that students with diverse cultural backgrounds should have equal educational opportunities; why students should (at a minimum) not be penalized for their cultural identities and commitments; and, more generally, why cultural differences ought to be acknowledged, valued, and respected rather than denied, trivialized, ignored, or decried, or the members of minority cultures oppressed by the hegemonic dominant culture—the answer given by advocates of multiculturalism is straightforward: it is *morally* required that we treat students with justice and respect, in ways that do not demean, marginalize, or silence them; and education that provides such opportunities—that respects cultural differences, and (minimally) does not penalize students for being culturally different—is the only sort of education that meets this requirement. Contemporary discussion of multiculturalism involves many other complex issues, of course. But that the justification of multiculturalism, in education and in general, is at bottom *moral*—in that hegemonic monoculturalism is in various ways morally problematic, and that a multiculturalism that respects cultural differences is in various ways morally superior to such monoculturalism—is widely presumed in the relevant literature.

For example, all the essays in Charles Taylor's *Multiculturalism and "The Politics of Recognition"* (1992)—a highly visible and widely cited volume—take for granted that multiculturalism is justified on moral grounds. Taylor's lead essay, which provides a penetrating historical and analytical discussion of "the politics of recognition," focuses on the complex character of the moral requirements, emphasized by "liberal" social theory, to recognize and respect (members of) cultures other than one's own (and the moral complexities involved in determining failure to do so). Susan Wolf (1992, p. 85) says of "a conscientious recognition of cultural diversity" that "justice requires it." Amy Gutmann (1992, p. 3) asks whether it is "morally troubling" when "major institutions fail to take account of our particular identities", and criticizes "hate speech" directed at those outside one's culture—and, presumably by extension, other ways of failing to live up to the demands of multiculturalism as characterized above—for "violat[ing] the most elementary moral injunction to respect the dignity of all human beings" (p. 23). While the contributors to this volume differ on the exact character of the moral obligation to respect (members of) non-dominant cultures, and on the related issues of the cultural contribution to personal identity and the degree to which the maintenance of vibrant cultural identities might interfere with the health and well-being of the broader polity, they are agreed that the issues raised by the circumstances to which multiculturalism is the response are primarily moral (and morally charged political) ones, and that the primary reasons to embrace multiculturalism are moral reasons.

Similar remarks apply to the contributors to the collections edited by Arthur and Shapiro (1995), Fullinwider (1996), and Goldberg (1994b). To mention just a couple of prominent examples, Henry Giroux emphasizes the centrality of "the notion of social justice" and "the primacy of the ethical" (1994, p. 332) to an adequate consideration of the wide range of issues that multiculturalist initiatives seek to address. Peter McLaren likewise stresses the (resistance) multiculturalist's "commitment to social justice" (1994, p. 53), and urges the struggle for "a solidarity ... [that] develops out of the imperatives of freedom, liberation, democracy, and critical citizenship" (p. 57). He urges efforts "to change the material conditions that allow relations of domination to prevail over relations of equality and social justice" and that function to sustain "oppression, injustice, and human suffering" (p. 58) rather than "emancipation" (p. 63). McLaren's emphasis on justice, freedom, democracy, equality, emancipation, the importance of "liberation from oppression for all suffering peoples" and the ("contingent") "universality of human rights" (p. 66) clearly indicate the moral basis of his analyses and recommendations. Although Giroux and McLaren consistently and insistently position themselves at the "radical" end of the political spectrum, and in that respect are not representative of multiculturalists generally, their resting the case for multiculturalism on moral considerations is entirely representative. In sum, it is the moral evil and political injustice of cultural oppression, marginalization, and hegemony which are thought, by the advocates of multiculturalism, to justify multiculturalist conceptions and initiatives, in education and in general.[5]

4. Does the Embrace of Multiculturalism Preclude Transcultural Ideals?

I accept the view just rehearsed; that is, I agree that cultural domination and oppression, when they occur, are morally noxious, and that multiculturalist initiatives in response to morally objectionable relationships among cultures are, on such moral grounds, justified. I have defended this view of multiculturalism and the moral arguments for it elsewhere (Siegel 1997a, chs. 9–12); I will not do so again here. The question I want to pursue in what follows, rather, is this: Supposing that this understanding of multiculturalism, and of the moral reasons for embracing it, is correct, what follows concerning the status of educational and philosophical ideals? Can they be coherently thought of as "transcultural" or "universal"[6] alongside the embrace of multiculturalism? Educational and philosophical advocates of multiculturalism—understood, as above, as the thesis that all cultures (and their members) enjoy a sort of integrity, deserve a sort of respect, and are not to be marginalized, silenced, or otherwise oppressed by hegemonic, dominant cultures—often cast doubt upon the very possibility of transcultural ideals, i.e., ideals whose validity extends beyond the bounds of individual cultures. In their view, all ideals—of persons, societies, or whatever—are the ideals of particular cultures. Given a commitment to multiculturalism, and a recognition of the moral requirement to acknowledge and respect cultural differences—including, presumably, those which concern educational and philosophical ideals—such culturally specific ideals seem to have no relevance to other cultures, which have their own equally specific ideals—ideals which are legitimate within, but not beyond, the bounds of the particular culture in which they are acknowledged and embraced.

This challenge to transcultural ideals is trenchantly articulated (though not endorsed) by Susan Khin Zaw:

> The ... cultural relativist argument runs as follows. Values are meaningful only within a particular culture. Therefore the conception of absolute, or culture-neutral, value is a contradiction in terms. It follows that the value-system of one culture cannot be rationally regarded as absolutely better than that of another, since no culture-neutral standpoint is philosophically available from which the values of different cultures are intelligible, let alone susceptible of impartial comparison and rational judgment by the standards of absolute value. But if reason cannot show why one value-system is absolutely better than another, imposition of monocultural value hegemony on other cultures cannot be morally justified. Reason therefore requires that each value system tolerate the others. Multiculturalism, understood as the acceptance of other cultures living by their own values, thus becomes ... a rational requirement. (1996, p. 128)

Khin Zaw talks here about *values* rather than *ideals*, and values being *meaningful* rather than *applicable* or *relevant*, but the parallel is clear: just as cultures differ in their values, they differ in their ideals—which, after all, involve primarily those things which are held to be supremely valuable—and since they do so differ, and their differing ideals cannot be themselves ranked on some fair, absolute scale, multiculturalism seems to counsel that cultural ideals be regarded as relative to the cultures which recognize and embrace them. It seems equally to deny that such ideals can transcend individual cultures and have application to all. The argument, in a nutshell, then, is this:

1. Educational/philosophical ideals are meaningful, applicable, or relevant only within the particular cultures that acknowledge and embrace them.
2. Therefore, there can be no absolute, universal, or transcultural ideals.
3. There can be no culture-neutral standpoint—none is "philosophically available"—from which fairly and impartially to evaluate alternative, culturally relative ideals.
4. Therefore, the imposition or hegemony of culturally specific ideals upon other cultures that do not recognize the legitimacy of those ideals cannot be morally justified.
5. Reason therefore requires that cultures tolerate, and recognize the culture-specific legitimacy of, the ideals of other cultures. This commitment to

multiculturalism demands that all cultures accept the legitimacy of all other cultures living in accordance with their own, culturally specific, ideals.

There are several things worth noting about this argument. Most importantly for present purposes, the conclusion equivocates on two senses of "legitimacy." To say that

> (i) educational and philosophical ideals are necessarily culture-specific—legitimate only intraculturally—in that the legitimacy or force of such ideals does not extend beyond the bounds of the cultures that embrace them

is one thing; to say that

> (ii) all cultures must accept the legitimacy of all other cultures living in accordance with their own, culturally specific, ideals

is quite another. The first denies the possibility of transcultural legitimacy, while the second propounds the transcultural duty to accept every culture's right to live in accordance with its own ideals. That is, there are in play here both culture-specific and transcultural senses of "legitimacy." Despite this equivocation, though, the multiculturalist is strongly motivated by her own argument to embrace both (i) and (ii); understanding why will provide the key to reconciling commitments to both multiculturalism and transcultural ideals.

It is easy to see why the advocate of multiculturalism is inclined to embrace (i). After all, her advocacy flows from her moral outrage over the patent injustices perpetrated by indefensible cultural hegemony. Testing children from minority cultures with instruments biased against them, and deeming them failures when they test less well than their dominant-culture counterparts; "tracking" them in ways which effectively guarantee second-class (or worse) economic status upon their entering the workforce and adult life; failing to respect, or even to take seriously, alternative histories, values, and patterns and modes of speech, and denying the members of such cultures the opportunity to live in ways which honor those histories, values, and patterns; reflecting "a confining or demeaning or contemptible picture of themselves" back to members of marginalized groups, and in that way undermining their self-respect and thereby oppressing them and imprisoning them in "false, distorted, and reduced mode[s] of being" (Taylor 1992, p. 25); and, more generally, harming irrevocably whole ways of life and the people who live them—all these sins against the children and adult members of minority cultures, in schools and in general, lead her to conclude, naturally enough, that the basic problem here is that one culture is unjustifiably dictating the terms of cultural adequacy to all other cultures. In response, she says, in effect, "Your (dominant, hegemonic) cultural values and ideals are no better than those of other cultures. Yours are perhaps legitimate in your own culture, but they should not be thought to constitute the only legitimate cultural values and ideals; they have no legitimacy in cultures that eschew them in favor of their own. This imposition of values and ideals is the root of objectionable hegemony. To avoid such hegemony, we must recognize that your cultural values have no legitimacy beyond the bounds of your own culture." Hence (i).

As just articulated, the multiculturalist's response—which appears to be an argument for (i)—incorporates both (i) and (ii): it asserts both that cultural values and ideals have force only within the particular cultures in which they are recognized; and that all cultures—and in particular, the dominant one—must accept the legitimacy of all other cultures living in accordance with their own, culturally specific, ideals. As recently noted, however, these two claims do not sit happily with one another, since the second asserts a transcultural value—indeed, a universal moral obligation—the legitimacy of which the former denies, in principle. In this circumstance, what is the advocate of multiculturalism to do? Her choices are limited. She can give up (i), or (ii), or both, but she cannot embrace both. She cannot give up both if she wishes to remain an advocate of multiculturalism. So which should she give up? If she gives up (ii), she gives up the heart of her position. For if (ii) is rejected, there is no reason to be bothered by the sorts of cultural hegemony enumerated above—and, in particular, there is nothing to underwrite the multiculturalist's sense of moral outrage over what she perceives to be the patent injustices perpetrated by an indefensible cultural hegemony. But to give up this claim to moral outrage is to give up multiculturalism. Thus, the multiculturalist's only viable option is to maintain (ii), and reject (i).

Further reflection permits a deeper understanding of the multiculturalist's need to give up (i). We saw earlier that advocates of multiculturalism typically justify their position in moral terms. They hold—rightly, in my view—that the evils visited upon marginalized cultures and their members by a hegemonic dominant culture that marginalizes, silences, and devalues them are genuine evils, in which dominant cultures can engage only in violation of their moral obligations. As multiculturalists claim, all persons and cultures are morally obliged to treat cultures other than their own, and the members of those cultures, justly, with respect, in ways that do not silence, marginalize, or oppress. As educators, we are obliged to embrace multiculturalism—irrespective of the cultural context in which we find ourselves—simply because we are morally obliged to treat cultures other than our own, and the members of those cultures, justly and with respect.

It is significant, though, that this moral obligation is not itself limited to cultures that recognize it; it applies even to cultures that do not acknowledge that it does. That is why advocates of multiculturalism can coherently urge monoculturalists to embrace it. After all, if members of dominant, majority cultures were not erring in neglecting the views and interests of members of other cultures, there would be no reason for them to change their views, or their educational or social/political agendas, in order to respect and incorporate the views and interests of those other cultures. It is because those persons and cultures that fail to treat other cultures and their members properly are mistaken in their treatment—because, that is, there is something morally wrong with such treatment—that multiculturalists can compellingly make their case.

Moreover, that cultural domination is indeed a moral mistake is not something that can be claimed only from the perspective of some particular culture; it cannot be regarded as a culturally relative truth that cultural domination, marginalization, and oppression are wrong. If it were to be regarded in this way, the monoculturalist would have an obvious reply: "Perhaps this domination and marginalization is wrong from the perspective of *your* culture, but it is fine from the perspective of mine." The multiculturalist has no response to this, *if* she sees the multiculturalist imperative as a legitimate imperative, a moral truth, only from the perspective of her own culture. Consequently, the advocate of multiculturalism must see the requirements of avoiding cultural domination and hegemony, and of treating cultures and their members justly and respectfully, as themselves *culturally transcendent* or *transcultural* moral requirements. She must in fact see them as *universal* in the strong sense that they are applicable to all cultures, including those that do not recognize them as moral truths or imperatives. In this sense, multiculturalism (and its attendant rights and obligations) is *itself* a transcultural educational and philosophical ideal: it tells us how students, and persons generally, are ideally to be treated; and how cultures must and must not be treated in educational and other contexts.[7]

The multiculturalist, therefore, must embrace (ii) and give up (i); that is, she must reject the idea that cultural values and ideals have legitimacy only within cultures, and instead embrace the idea that certain values and ideals—in particular, those constitutive of multiculturalism itself—enjoy transcultural legitimacy. From this it follows further that (ii) must be reformulated somewhat in order to acknowledge this sort of transcultural legitimacy, and thereby to acknowledge that the advocate of multiculturalism need not (and ought not) regard as legitimate *all* culturally specific ideals and practices, but only those which do not violate the multiculturalist ideal itself (and whatever other genuine transcultural ideals and imperatives there happen to be). Accordingly, (ii) must be reformulated as

(iii) all cultures must accept the legitimacy of all other cultures living in accordance with their own, culturally specific, ideals, insofar as those culturally specific ideals and attendant practices are consistent with the moral imperatives of multiculturalism itself.

This reformulation is required because without it the commitment to a transcultural multiculturalist ideal is incoherent: one would be committed to the legitimacy of all culture-specific ideals and practices, including those which explicitly reject such legitimacy—in which case one is not committed to the ideal after all. For example, if my embrace of the multiculturalist ideal requires me to regard as legitimate the specific ideals and practices of Culture C, which rejects as illegitimate the values and ideals of Culture D and acts in order to stamp out D's values and ideals (or even D itself), then my acknowledgement of the legitimacy of C's ideals forces me to accept as legitimate their rejection of their own obligation to apply the principles of multiculturalism to D—and thus my embrace of multiculturalism (as it applies to C) requires my rejection of multiculturalism (as it applies to D). Many real world examples, from notorious historical cases to a range of current cultural conflicts around the globe, could easily be supplied. The reformulation of (ii) as (iii) is required simply in order to maintain the coherence of the multiculturalist ideal, when understood as a transcultural ideal—as the argument above shows it must. It is a necessary condition of the multiculturalist reply to the monoculturalist one paragraph back, without which the multiculturalist has no adequate reply.

My claim, then, is that multiculturalism is itself a culturally transcendent or universal moral, educational, and social ideal in the sense that it is applicable to all cultures, even those that do not recognize or embrace it; and that it rests upon other, equally transcendent, moral imperatives and values.[8] It is important that this claim not be misunderstood, and so I close this section with the following clarification: By "culturally transcendent" I do not mean "can exist or be recognized apart from all culture." I happily grant that, prior to culture and language, it would not be possible to conceive or articulate educational or philosophical ideals; nor can there in fact exist actual, flesh-and-blood people, capable of formulating and affirming such ideals, who are not in significant ways shaped by the culture(s) in which they are embedded. I mean rather to argue that such ideals can "transcend culture" in the more modest sense that they can be legitimately applied to (the members of) cultures other than those that explicitly recognize them, and even to those that explicitly reject them—and that multiculturalism is itself one such ideal.

5. "With Friends Like This, Who Needs Enemies?": Further Clarification and Defense

I have been arguing that there are values, obligations, and ideals that may be legitimately applied to cultures (and their members) even when they *reject* those ideals as inapplicable to themselves. The reader might well react to this claim with horror—after all, isn't this suggestion that cultures are subject to sanction in virtue of their failure to live up to the ideals of others the very essence of objectionable cultural hegemony? Moreover, how can someone be bound by an ideal that she doesn't even understand—for example, one that can be expressed only with concepts alien to her and her culture—or for which she has no reason, limited as she is by the language and traditions of her culture (as we all are), to regard as justified?

These are important objections[9] that demand a direct response. There are three points to make that I believe jointly suffice to reply to them, and that provide the opportunity for a further spelling out of the position defended thus far.

First, as argued above, it must be acknowledged that multiculturalism makes sense only when understood transculturally. When one *advocates* multiculturalism, one claims that it is right, indeed obligatory, to treat members of "minority" cultures in accordance with the dictates of that ideal, and that it is wrong to fail to do so. To shy away from such claims—to be unwilling, for example, to criticize a majority culture that marginalizes or oppresses members of minority (sub) cultures within it—is in effect to give up one's commitment to multiculturalism. Such unwillingness renders multiculturalism a toothless tiger, unable to criticize offensive cultural domination or to defend interventions aimed at ending such domination. No such toothless version of multiculturalism would suffice to accomplish the aims of its advocates. Taking the moral/political directives of multiculturalism seriously, in other words, *requires* that it be understood transculturally, with teeth enough to criticize effectively objectionable cultural hegemony and to justify advocating and working toward the establishment of institutions that respect the integrity of all cultures (insofar as their ideals and practices are consistent with the multiculturalist ideal itself). Far from being "the very essence of objectionable cultural hegemony," regarding multiculturalism as itself a transcultural ideal is the only way in which that ideal can be seen as having the moral/political implications to which its advocates are committed. Advocates of multiculturalism are *taking a stand* that will undoubtedly be rejected by (members of) some cultures—in particular, by those that are dominant and exert hegemonic control over others. To say that it does not apply to such cultures is to give up that advocacy; to maintain it is to hold that it applies to those cultures, despite their rejection of it. This is simply what the advocacy of multiculturalism involves.[10]

Second, to say that an ideal is *applicable* to a given culture, as I am understanding that term, is not to say either that a member of that culture is morally *obliged* to accept it, or that such a person is necessarily *blameworthy* for failing to conduct herself in accordance with it. To illustrate with a trivial example: suppose that the best way to remove wallpaper of a certain sort from a wall of a certain sort is to steam it off, rather than to scrape it off or remove it with chemicals. (Steaming, let us suppose, approaches the ideal in that it is easier, leaves the wall ready to be painted or repapered with minimal additional preparation, is environmentally friendly, requires an easier cleanup, etc.) Joe Apprentice-Wallpaper-Remover may well be found blameworthy by his supervisor, Janet Expert-Wallpaper-Remover, for attempting to remove it in one of those less-than-ideal ways. But Jane Novice-Wallpaper-Remover, who has no reason to think there is a better way of removing the offending wallpaper than by scraping it, and who may not even know of the existence of steamers and may have no idea that that is a possible way of removing wallpaper, is in no way obliged to use a steamer, or blameworthy for removing it with a scraper—even though it would have been better had she used a steamer. Ideally, she would have used a steamer; but failure to live up to the wallpaper-removal ideal is in no way blameworthy, since she had neither the knowledge nor the concepts (e.g., that of "steaming" wallpaper) necessary to understand and justify the ideal. Similarly, a person whose culture does not have the conceptual resources to articulate and justify the multiculturalist ideal, or whose culture explicitly rejects that ideal, may well not be blameworthy for failing to live up to it; nor, in those circumstances, can she be thought to be obliged to accept and act in accordance with the ideal. ("Ought," as philosophers often put it, implies "can"; if a person cannot grasp or accept the ideal, she cannot be obliged to act in accordance with it.) Nevertheless, the advocate of multiculturalism must regard it as a *mistake* to so fail. Otherwise, her "advocacy" is empty, and is clearly unable to ground the sorts of social changes that multiculturalists call for. In short, we must distinguish the *belief in* or *acceptance of* a norm or ideal, and the *blameworthiness* of failure to live up to an ideal, from the *applicability* of that ideal. My claim is that its advocates must understand the ideal as transculturally applicable. Whether or not failure to live up to the ideal is blameworthy is another matter entirely: sometimes it will be, sometimes not.[11]

Finally, we must clearly distinguish *genuine* from *putative* norms and ideals; both fallibilism and modesty are appropriately applied to our own judgments of the genuineness of ideals, including that of multiculturalism. Still, the advocate of that ideal is asserting its correctness and applicability, as well as the concomitant incorrectness and unjustifiability of those views and practices that countenance or exemplify what she deems to be oppressive cultural domination. How else could she understand her own condemnation of (e.g.) the marginalization or mistreatment of the members of minority cultures in schools?

I hope that these remarks are sufficient to quiet the complaint that regarding multiculturalism as a transcultural ideal it itself an instance of objectionable cultural hegemony. I turn now to another aspect of the transcultural character of that ideal.

6. Transcultural Normative Reach

The multiculturalist argument we have been considering also presupposes another sort of transculturalism, which might be called "transcultural normative reach." It proceeds from premises to a conclusion that is said to follow from those premises. That it does so is not dependent on the cultural affiliation of the person contemplating the argument. The argument is taken to provide good reasons for embracing its conclusion, reasons which should be found compelling by any person who fair-mindedly considers it. In this sense, the argument's force—the ability of its premises to justify its conclusion—is what it is, independently of the culture of either the arguer or her audience.

Such transcultural normative reach must be accepted by any advocate of multiculturalism who thinks that that advocacy is not only non-arbitrary, but *rational*—warranted by the reasons offered in its support. For an advocate who rejects such reach cannot regard herself as advancing reasons that ought to persuade a fair-minded opponent, e.g., an imagined rational monoculturalist. She cannot regard her embrace of multiculturalism as more rational than her opponent's embrace of monoculturalism. But this leaves her in a troubling position. If she can't offer such reasons, why should her opponent, or anyone else, agree with her? If she regards multiculturalism as in any way rationally preferable to its alternatives, she must accept that that view is supported by reasons that have force beyond the bounds of those who happen to share her cultural presuppositions and commitments. In short, the *rational* advocacy of and commitment to multiculturalism presupposes a further sort of transculturalism, that of transcultural normative reach. In particular, such advocacy presupposes the transcultural character of the normative force of arguments as such.

This point raises many deep questions concerning the nature of rationality that I cannot consider here.[12] But I do want to reply to a response often made to this line of argument. Many advocates of multiculturalism and related positions seem to reject the idea of transcultural normative reach, in concert with a rejection of the claim, developed above, that multiculturalism is itself a transcultural ideal justified in universal (moral) terms. Such thinkers offer, instead, accounts of multiculturalism that explicitly or implicitly reject the idea of a reason's "normative reach" extending beyond communities and cultures, and that reject as well the case for transcultural ideals presented thus far. Let us turn, then, to a consideration of one such account. In considering it, we will be in position to appreciate further both the character of transcultural normative reach and the character of transcultural ideals more generally.

The view I want to explore rejects the possibility of transcultural ideals on the grounds that such ideals are conceptually impossible, in that they necessarily are (or rely upon) culturally specific ideals that are mistakenly regarded as universal. It holds, that is, that cultural ideals and values, and judgments concerning the goodness or normative force of reasons and arguments, are *necessarily* culture-specific. Perhaps the most visible systematic defense of this view, and denial of the possibility of transcultural ideals, is that developed by Richard Rorty. Rorty's favored version of pragmatism famously rejects the search for "an Archimedean point from which to survey culture" (Rorty 1982, p. 150), in favor of a frank embrace of ethnocentricity or "solidarity," according to which there is no non-circular or non-question-begging way to justify our own ideals, values, and commitments to those who reject them in favor of their own, equally ethnocentric alternatives: "We pragmatists ... should say that we must, in practice, privilege our own group, *even though there can be no noncircular justification for doing so*" (Rorty 1989b, p. 44, emphasis added). David Theo Goldberg helpfully summarizes and develops Rorty's view as follows:

> The traditional historical commitment of philosophical liberalism to universal principles of reason and (moral) value presupposes universal ideas like intrinsic humanity, human dignity, and human rights—values, that is, that are thought to mark individuals in virtue of their very humanity. As Rorty insists, there is no transhistorical or super-social Godly view on which such universal (moral) principles can be grounded or from which they can be derived. Axiological concepts and values are necessarily those of some historically specific community.... Thus, any insistence on the universalism of values must be no more than the projected imposition of local values—those especially of some ethnoracial and gendered particularity—universalized. The supposed universalism of epistemological politics reduces to the political epistemology of an imposed universality. (Goldberg 1994a, p. 17–18)

Is Goldberg correct that values cannot be universal, but only local; that any proposed universal value (such as that minority cultures ought to be respected rather than silenced) "must be no more than the projected imposition of local values ... universalized"? Must it be that any proclamation of universal value is in the end merely "the projection of local values as neutrally universal ones, the globalizing of ethnocentric values" (Goldberg 1994a, p. 19)? I see three difficulties with this position.

First, it rests on a problematic "universal/local" dichotomy. In claiming that some particular value or ideal is "universal"—like that of human dignity, or those constitutive of multiculturalism—the universalist need not, and ought not, reject the completely compatible claim that these ideals are also "local" in the sense that they have been formulated and advanced in particular historical/cultural locations, and that they are recognized and endorsed only by some, but not all, cultures. In holding these ideals to be universal or transcultural, the universalist is completely free to acknowledge their locality/particularity. Goldberg here presumes that "local" and "universal" are contradictories, and so that "local" entails "non-universal," but this is simply an error. The correct point Goldberg makes, with Rorty, is that all proclamations of universal principle emanate from and are championed in particular locations. It does not follow from this, though, that such principles have no legitimacy or force beyond the bounds of the locations from within which they are proclaimed. All principles, values, and ideals—indeed, all beliefs, theories, and judgments more generally—are conceived and embraced (if at all) only in particular locales; whether or not any of them enjoy legitimacy beyond the bounds of those locales is an independent matter. When such legitimacy extends across all local boundaries, they are both local *and* universal. This dichotomy is a false one—and so one cannot reject universality on the grounds that all ideals are local, either in origin or in current acknowledgement and acceptance.[13]

Second, Goldberg's (and Rorty's) denial of universality relies upon the presupposition that values, in order to be "universal" or "transcultural," must be grounded in some impossibly neutral perspective. He argues, in effect, as follows:

1. Universal (moral) principles and values must be grounded on, or derived from, a "transhistorical or supersocial Godly" perspective.
2. There is no such perspective.
3. Therefore, there can be no universal principles or values.

If "universal" is understood in this way, then Goldberg and Rorty are right that there can be no such universal values, principles, or ideals. But we need not and should not understand the term in this way. Let us grant that there are no universal (or transcultural) values in the sense that they are grounded in, or derived from, a perspective outside of history and culture, for there simply is no such "Godly" perspective available to us. This is not the sense of "universal" relevant here. In the more modest sense noted above, according to which a principle, value, or ideal is universal insofar as it has application across all cultural boundaries, the first premise is simply false—Godly perspectives or perspectives outside of history are not required in order for universal status to be achieved—and so this argument against the very possibility of universal principles or values fails.

Third, this argument fails because *it itself presupposes the viability of transcultural normative reach*. As noted above, the argument is presented by its proponents as one that is forceful, that establishes its conclusion concerning the impossibility of transcultural ideals, independently of the cultural location of the arguer or her audience. It therefore presupposes just the sort of transcultural legitimacy it seeks to deny.

Goldberg attempts to defuse this last point by pointing to the formal, contentless character of logic:

> Axiological relativism [i.e., the contrary of "axiological universalism"] is bound to deny neither some basic formal principles of thinking—call them universal, if necessary—nor generalizable value judgments concerning especially pernicious social conditions and practices. So,

owning up to formal principles of logical relation implies nothing about the assertive content of thought.... Logical formalism enables only that inconsistent and incoherent claims for the most part can be ruled out; it is thoroughly incapable of assertively promoting some coherent or consistent standard over another. It is equally incapable of fashioning rules for interpreting metaphors or of choosing one reasonable interpretation over another.[14]

Goldberg is right, I think, to acknowledge the universality of "basic formal principles of thinking"; he is right as well that formal logic itself typically will not suffice to enable us to choose "one reasonable interpretation over another." But it is important to be clear here. First, if logical formalism can indeed enable us to rule out inconsistent and incoherent claims, that is no trivial matter. In particular, if it allows us to rule out, as inconsistent or incoherent, the joint assertion of "all ought to endorse the values and ideals of multiculturalism" and "no values or ideals have legitimacy for all," this is an important result, since—assuming the success of the moral case for the first assertion just mentioned—it establishes the transcultural status of multiculturalism itself. If the arguments presented above are successful, universalistic formal principles of logic contribute importantly to (even if they are not by themselves sufficient to establish) the case for choosing a transcultural view of multiculturalism over a culturally relative view of it.[15]

Second, and more importantly, Goldberg's argument here fails to acknowledge that it is itself resting on a stronger universality than that of logic. After all, his arguments defend and criticize a wide range of theses, concerning the status of various versions of multiculturalism; they rely on historical narratives and claims, political values and assessments, and scholarly analyses of various sorts. If logic can't make his case for these various claims and theses, something else must—or else his case is not made. So his acceptance of the universality of logic, alongside his claim that logic is "incapable of ... choosing one reasonable interpretation over another," leaves it unclear why his interpretations and conclusions ought to be embraced by the fair-minded reader. The answer is, of course, clear: she ought to embrace those conclusions because he has made a compelling case for them; that is, he has provided reasons for them which are or should be found persuasive by a fair-minded consideration of them. In other words, if we are rightly to regard Goldberg's case as having been made, then not just formal logic, but contentful reasons more generally, must be presumed to have transcultural force or reach. Otherwise, there is no reason to think that his case has been made—and indeed, the very point of his (or anyone) arguing for his or her favored conclusions is lost. Transcultural normative reach, in other words, is not just a matter of formal logic, but of (contentful) reasons more generally.[16] Those who accept Rorty/Goldberg-like arguments against the possibility of transcultural ideals are themselves committed, by that acceptance, to the transcultural normative reach of reasons. The universality of argumentative force—what I have been calling "transcultural normative reach"—involves, contra Goldberg, not just "formal principles of logical relation," but "the assertive content of thought" as well.

We can appreciate the importance of these several points intended to discredit the Goldberg/Rorty argument against universality by relating them to Goldberg's positive claims. Goldberg argues, for example, that "multicultural pedagogy be concerned also self-critically with questioning the grounds of the knowledge claims and truth values being advanced, and with challenging the dominant interpretation and underlying structures of institutional and ideological power represented in prevailing pedagogical narratives" (1994a, p. 17). I think that Goldberg is importantly right here, that "questioning the grounds of ... knowledge claims" and "challenging the dominant interpretation and underlying structures of institutional and ideological power represented in prevailing pedagogical narratives" are important aspects of "multicultural pedagogy"—and of education more generally. But how are we to understand such "questioning" and "challenging"? At a minimum, questioning and challenging requires the ability—fallible, to be sure—to distinguish successful questionings and challenges from unsuccessful ones. If it is thought not to be possible to so distinguish, there is no point to such questioning and challenging. And given that there is contention on such controversial matters that parallels alternative cultural allegiances, this ability of multicultural education presupposes a rich domain in which reasons—not just logic—can have force, which domain cuts across the boundaries of those cultural allegiances. That is, multicultural education as Goldberg here envisions it requires the kind of transcultural normative reach for which I have been arguing. Without it, the vision of multicultural education offered by Goldberg (and Giroux, McLaren, and the others cited above) collapses: there cannot, without it, be the sort of questioning of knowledge claims or challenges to institutional or ideological authority that gives that vision life.

Finally, it should be noted once again that the sort of universality or transculturalism defended here does not depend upon the legitimacy of any "view from nowhere," beyond or outside of history. Rorty (1989a) emphasizes the *contingency* of language and value; nothing said here is incompatible with that contingency. But the contingency of a culture's beliefs, values, and ideals does not entail that those beliefs, values, and ideals have no legitimacy or force beyond the bounds of that culture. Humans cannot attain a view from nowhere; Goldberg and Rorty are right that, as Goldberg says, "there is no transhistorical or supersocial Godly view [available to the likes of us, at any rate] on which such universal (moral) principles can be grounded or from which they can be derived" and that "[a]xiological concepts and values are necessarily those of some historically specific community." But they are wrong to think that from this it follows that such values are relevant or applicable only to the historically specific community in which they contingently arise and flourish. That is, we can and should embrace both contingency and the possibility, and actuality, of transcultural and even universal values and ideals.

6. Conclusion: On Valuing Transcultural Ideals

I have argued that multiculturalism, as a value informing and governing our educational and social/political endeavors, is rightly thought of as a transcultural educational and social/political ideal. If my arguments have succeeded, we may conclude not only that such transcultural ideals are possible, but that certain ideals are actual or genuine. Multiculturalism, and the principle of respect for persons and "minority," "dominated" cultures intrinsic to it, is itself one such genuine, culturally transcendent ideal.

Embracing multiculturalism, therefore, is completely compatible with acknowledging the possibility of culturally transcendent philosophical and educational ideals. While, as a matter of fact, cultures do not converge on a universally held set of ideals, it is nevertheless the case that some ideals are universal in the strong sense that they are applicable to all cultures, even to those cultures that do not recognize them as such. To say they are universal is not to say they are from God or from Nowhere, but only that they transcend individual cultures in that they are legitimately applicable, and have force, not only beyond the bounds of the particular cultures in which they are acknowledged, but also beyond all such cultural boundaries.

I have endeavored to establish the possibility and actuality of transcultural ideals, but not, I trust it is clear, at the expense of the commitment to multiculturalism. On the contrary, I have endorsed multiculturalism as a key moral and sociopolitical value, on grounds that are widely shared by its advocates.[17] I hope then to have offered a case for multiculturalism while at the same time rejecting the anti-universality with which it is often accompanied. My endorsement of universality extends beyond the ideal of multiculturalism, though; I hope to have indicated how other ideals can with equal legitimacy be regarded as universal. If so, my conclusion has implications beyond the context of multiculturalism and establishes the legitimacy of both transcultural and universal educational and philosophical ideals generally.

In claiming this broad relevance of my conclusion—especially in light of my reliance on the viability of the notions of rationality, fair-mindedness, and the like at key junctures in my arguments—I may be accused of offering little more than an apologetic for "Western" values and ideals. Haven't my arguments for transcultural ideals simply begged the question against those who challenge those ideals? I have indeed tried to defend some of the traditional ideals that characterize Western, "Enlightenment" thought; in so doing, I might be thought to have biased my case against those cultural traditions that do not embrace those ideals. But if my arguments have succeeded, I will have provided not *just* an apologetic. Rather, I will have pointed to features of the particular ideals in question, and to features of arguments for and against them, that establish the unavoidability of these ideals.[18] That is, I will have shown that these particular ideals, which are endorsed by some but by no means all extant cultures, can be justified to all who are inclined, in the name of multiculturalism, to call them into question, but who agree that their status as transcultural ideals is open to fair-minded assessment—as advocates of the culture-specificity of such ideals must.[19]

Notes

1. Cf. Appiah 1996, p. 74; Blum 1996, pp. 24, 32–34; Khin Zaw 1996, p. 123; Goldberg 1994a, pp. 4–5, 30. Fullinwider 1996a is a very helpful guide to the literature and the issues concerning multicultural education.
2. Concerning this range, see Chicago Cultural Studies Group 1994, pp. 114 ff.
3. On these various sorts of multiculturalism, see especially Chicago Cultural Studies Group 1994; Giroux 1994; Goldberg 1994a; and McLaren 1994. At the risk of oversimplification, while these versions of multiculturalism differ conceptually in terms of how deeply they analyze existing patterns, conditions, and presuppositions of domination, their main divergence is political, i.e., a function of how explicitly and committedly they call for revising those patterns of domination and relationships of power/powerlessness. I will not explore the strengths and weaknesses of these various versions of multiculturalism here.
4. I have said nothing here about the vexed questions of the meaning of "culture" and the individuation of cultures. Like virtually all the authors cited herein, I am understanding "culture" in a very general way, and taking for granted its intersection with other classificatory categories, especially those of race, gender, and class.
5. Having just mentioned the controversy, within the community of advocates of multiculturalism, concerning the extent to which such advocacy requires the concomitant embrace of a radical political posture, I should note that this controversy does not undermine my characterization of the case for multiculturalism as primarily moral in nature. In particular, those authors who urge multiculturalists to embrace a radical political agenda also base that recommendation on the presupposition of ("universal") moral values, e.g., of dignity, freedom, and justice. There does not seem to be any other possible basis for their promulgation of that political agenda. For further discussion of this point, see Siegel 1997a, ch. 10; Howe 1998.
6. I have been treating these two terms as equivalent, but they are not: "transcultural" refers to ideals, etc., which apply to more than one culture; "universal" to those which apply to all. Since the arguments against transcultural/universal ideals are critical of both, it seems harmless enough to treat them this way here. Where the distinction matters, I have tried to use the appropriate term in the text.
7. The preceding two paragraphs are taken (with changes and additions) from Siegel 1997b, pp. 97–98.
8. Of course, this claim is not original with me. Robert K. Fullinwider, for example, notes well the ways in which multicultural education depends for its rationale upon transcultural values such as the fostering of critical judgment and of equality, justice, and human dignity

(1996b, pp. 9, 13–16). Amy Gutmann argues for the rightful place in multiculturalist education of "universalist values such as equal liberty, opportunity, and mutual respect among citizens" (1996, p. 162). Charles Taylor relatedly notes the "universalist basis" of the "politics of difference" that is a key political expression of the multiculturalist ideal (for compelling analysis, see Taylor 1992, pp. 38 ff.).

9. Raised independently by Donald Arnstine and Denis Phillips. In this section I respond mainly to Phillips' (1997) incisive and detailed criticism, from which I have shamelessly adapted the title of this section.

10. I hope it is clear that my argument is not that the multiculturalist should embrace my proposed view of multiculturalism because it has the consequence of enabling her to defend herself from critics. It is rather that the version of multiculturalism that holds both that ideals have force only within the cultures that sanction them *and* that certain cultural practices (i.e., those that dominate and oppress) are objectionable even when not seen to be so by the members of that culture is self-inconsistent. The version of multiculturalism defended here is intended as the best way to remove the inconsistency while honoring the multiculturalist opposition to objectionable domination and oppression.

11. I note in passing that often, perhaps typically, members of cultures that engage in objectionable cultural domination *do* have the requisite conceptual resources to recognize the objectionable character of their domination: Nazis *could* have seen their treatment of Jews, Gypsies, and homosexuals as violating their own moral commitments; similar remarks apply to slave owners in the US South, and perhaps our own current treatment of minority inner-city residents in the public schools. Whether or not members of such dominating cultures do have the requisite conceptual resources—and, more generally, whether or not they should be deemed blameworthy for their failure to live up to the multiculturalist ideal—the point remains that multiculturalists must see such failure *as failure* (to live up to a *bona fide* ideal), whether blameworthy or not.

The same point applies to scientific claims: one cannot blame members of cultures with no access to or familiarity with Western science for not knowing that water molecules are composed of hydrogen and oxygen atoms. Nevertheless, the claim that water molecules are so composed (is true of, and) applies to their water as much as it does to (is true of) ours.

Finally, I trust it is clear that I am not suggesting that removing wallpaper is akin in moral seriousness to objectionable cultural hegemony. The wallpaper example is meant simply to illustrate the distinction between *applicability*, on the one hand, and *obligation/blameworthiness*, on the other. Thanks here to audience members at the Ljubljana conference (see below, note 19), whose comments prompted this paragraph.

12. For extended discussion see Siegel 1997a and references therein.

13. For further discussion of this point, see Siegel 1997a, pp. 174–178.

14. Goldberg 1994a, pp. 16–17, note omitted.

15. I note in passing that, even if Goldberg is right that "logical formalism ... is thoroughly incapable of assertively promoting some coherent or consistent standard over another," he fails here to acknowledge that logic, in enabling us to rule out inconsistent and incoherent claims, in fact *constitutes* just such a standard.

16. Here the growing literature in informal logic and argumentation theory is relevant. See Siegel and Biro (1997) for discussion and references. The new-ish journals *Informal Logic* and *Argumentation* are important loci of discussion. On the limitations of logic and the need for a broader normativity of reasons, see Siegel 1997a, ch. 7.

17. That defense relies centrally, if sometimes implicitly, on the Kantian moral imperative of *respect*, here extended both to persons as individuals and to cultures more broadly. An important question is whether Kant's insistence that all persons be treated with respect, as ends rather than mere means, can be applied to cultures in this direct way, since cultures, after all, are not persons and so are not obviously the sorts of entities to which Kant's dictums apply. I regret that I cannot pursue this question here.

18. For the argument concerning the unavoidability of the ideal of rationality, see Siegel 1997a, ch. 5.

19. I am grateful to the Spencer Foundation, the National Endowment for the Humanities, and the University of Miami for their support of this project. The views expressed are, of course, solely my own responsibility. Ancestors of this paper were presented at a conference on Philosophy, Education and Culture in Edinburgh in September 1997, at Simon Fraser University in October 1997, at the European Conference on Educational Research (ECER 98) in Ljubljana, Slovenia, in September 1998, and at Western Michigan University in February 1999. (One such ancestor was published, in conjunction with the Ljubljana conference, in the Slovenian journal *The School Field* (1998, 9.1/2: 5–31). I am grateful to the audiences on those occasions for their insightful comments and suggestions. I want also to thank Donald Arnstine, Stephen Campbell, and especially Denis Phillips, whose challenging response to the paper at Simon Fraser (Phillips 1997) prompted significant clarifications and emendations.

References

Arthur, J., and A. Shapiro (eds.). (1995). *Campus Wars: Multiculturalism and the Politics of Difference*. Boulder, CO: Westview Press.
Appiah, K. A. (1996). "Culture, Subculture, Multiculturalism: Educational Options." In Fullinwider 1996b, pp. 65–89.
Banks, J. A. (1992). "Multicultural Education: Characteristics and Goals." In J. A. Banks and C. A. McGee Banks (eds.), *Multicultural Education: Issues and Perspectives* (3–32). Boston: Allyn & Bacon.
Blum, L. A. (1996). "Antiracist Civic Education in the California History-Social Science Framework." In Fullinwider 1996b, pp. 23–48.
Chicago Cultural Studies Group. (1994). "Critical Multiculturalism." In Goldberg 1994b, pp. 114–139. Originally published in *Critical Inquiry* 18.3 (1992): 530–555.
Fullinwider, R. K. (1996a). "Multicultural Education: Concepts, Policies, and Controversies." In Fullinwider 1996b, pp. 3–22.
Fullinwider, R. K. (ed.). (1996b). *Public Education in a Multicultural Society: Policy, Theory, Critique*. Cambridge: Cambridge University Press
Giroux, H. A. (1994). "Insurgent Multiculturalism and the Promise of Pedagogy." In Goldberg 1994b, pp. 325–343
Goldberg, D. T. (1994a). "Introduction: Multicultural Conditions." In Goldberg 1994b, pp. 1–41.
Goldberg, D. T. (ed.). (1994b). *Multiculturalism: A Critical Reader*. Oxford: Blackwell.
Gutmann, A. (1992). "Introduction." In Taylor 1992, pp. 3–24.
Gutmann, A. (1996). "Challenges of Multiculturalism in Democratic Education." In Fullinwider 1996b, pp. 156–179.
Howe, K. (1998). "The Interpretive Turn and the New Debate in Education." *Educational Researcher* 27.8: 13–20.
Khin Zaw, S. (1996). "Locke and Multiculturalism: Toleration, Relativism, and Reason." In Fullinwider 1996b, pp. 121–155.
McLaren, P. (1994). "White Terror and Oppositional Agency: Towards a Critical Multiculturalism." In Goldberg 1994b, pp. 45–74.
Perez y Mena, A. I. (1996). "Multiculturalism." In J. J. Chambliss (ed.) *Philosophy of Education: An Encyclopedia* (pp. 415–417). New York: Garland.
Phillips, D. C. (1997). "Harvey Siegel's Strengthening of Multiculturalism, or With Friends Like This You Don't Need Enemies." Paper presented at Simon Fraser University, October 1997.
Rorty, R. (1982). *Consequences of Pragmatism*. Minneapolis: University of Minnesota Press.
Rorty, R. (1989a). *Contingency, Irony, and Solidarity*. Cambridge: Cambridge University Press.
Rorty, R. (1989b). "Solidarity or Objectivity?" In M. Krausz (ed.), *Relativism: Interpretation and Confrontation* (pp. 35–50). Notre Dame, IN: University of Notre Dame Press, 1989.

Siegel H. (1997a). *Rationality Redeemed?: Further Dialogues on an Educational Ideal.* New York: Routledge.
Siegel, H. (1997b). "Science Education: Multicultural *and* Universal." *Interchange* 28.2: 97–98.
Siegel, H. and J. Biro. (1997). "Epistemic Normativity, Argumentation, and Fallacies." *Argumentation* 11.3: 277–292.
Taylor, C. (1992). *Multiculturalism and "The Politics of Recognition,"* with commentary by Amy Gutmann (ed.), Steven C. Rockefeller, Michael Walzer, and Susan Wolf. Princeton, NJ: Princeton University Press.
Wolf, S. (1992) "Comment." In Taylor 1992, pp. 75–85.

14

Argument Quality and Cultural Difference

1. Argument Quality as Impersonally and Transculturally Conceived

Central to argumentation theory is the matter of the normative evaluation of argument quality: that is, of argument *normativity*. Argumentation theorists are concerned, among other things, with explaining why some arguments are *good*, or at least better than others, in the sense that they provide reasons for embracing their conclusions which are such that a fair-minded appraisal of the arguments yields the judgment that those conclusions ought to be accepted—are *worthy* of acceptance—by all who so appraise them.

Such goodness is an *epistemic* matter. Argument normativity is a variety of epistemic normativity, in that what makes an argument good is that its premises provide reasons for accepting its conclusion. That is, the conclusion ought to be accepted, on the basis of the support provided that conclusion by those premises: the premises *justify* the conclusion, rendering it worthy of belief.[1]

The feature of this view of argument normativity that is of concern in what follows is its impersonal and transcultural character. The quality of a given argument is *impersonal*, on this view, in the sense that its normative status is *independent* of the person(s) evaluating that status.[2] This is not to say that the argument could be evaluated without a person to conduct the evaluation (although some arguments can be successfully evaluated by machine). It is to say, rather, that the quality of the argument is a feature of the argument itself, rather than of the person(s) assessing its quality. Moreover, the quality of an argument is *transcultural* in the sense that its normative status is independent of the cultural locations and perspectives of its evaluators. It is the character of such impersonal and transcultural evaluation, such that the quality of an argument is as it would appear to a hypothetical "fair-minded" evaluator—rather than as it actually appears to actual, flesh and blood evaluators, with their own cultural locations and perspectives—that will occupy us in what follows.

2. Argument Quality as Culturally Contextualized: Preliminary Considerations

This impersonal, transcultural conception of argument normativity makes no reference either to the attributes of the persons appraising the argument and judging its normative force or to the characteristics of the culture(s) to which such persons belong or the cultural context in which the appraisal occurs. The premises of the argument provide whatever support for its conclusion that they do—from no support whatsoever in the case of a really bad argument, to extremely strong support in the case of a really good argument, with every degree of support in between for arguments of every degree of quality—*whoever* is conducting the evaluation, in *whatever* cultural context.

But recent work by a wide range of philosophers, argumentation theorists, and social theorists rejects such an abstract, decontextualized notion of argument goodness. Instead, these theorists insist upon taking seriously, in the evaluation of arguments, the features and perspectives—and in particular, the cultural locations—of the evaluators. That is, such theorists emphasize the importance of *cultural differences* in argument appraisal. Often locating themselves under the banner of *multiculturalism*, they argue that the quality of an argument depends upon culturally specific beliefs, values, and presuppositions. Consequently, they contend, no acontextual[3], culture-independent characterization of argumentative goodness can succeed.

A considerable range of writers advocate the view that judgments concerning the goodness or normative force of reasons and arguments (and cultural ideals and values more generally) are inevitably, and perhaps necessarily, culture-specific. Alasdair MacIntyre's celebrated *Whose Justice? Which Rationality?* (1988) announces in its very title the doctrine that rationality—and so the probative force of reasons, and so argument quality—is in some sense relative to cultural/historical tradition, and is in that sense neither impersonal nor transcultural. MacIntyre writes that all rational activity is "inescapably historically and socially context-bound" (1988, p. 4); elsewhere he suggests that one "cannot find ... any genuinely neutral and independent standard of rational justification" (MacIntyre 1989, p. 198)—and so, presumably, any context- or tradition-independent standard of argument quality.[4] Jean-Francois Lyotard is said to champion "the irreducibly local character of all discourse, argumentation, and legitimation" (Baynes, Bohman, and McCarthy 1987, p. 70); he holds, clearly enough, that what counts as knowledge and as justification is itself relative to local, cultural context, and he rejects any sort of transcultural "metanarrative" that sets out standards of argument quality as "terroristic." (Lyotard 1987) More generally, those thinkers generally classified as "postmodernists" are typically regarded as holding that "rationality is always relative to time and place," implying that argument quality is similarly relative.[5]

Perhaps the most visible writer in that somewhat vague classification is Richard Rorty, who also rejects the possibility of personally or culturally transcendent evaluation of arguments, and of cultures more generally.[6] His favored version of pragmatism famously rejects the search for "an Archimedean point from which to survey culture" (Rorty 1982, p. 150), in favor of a frank embrace of ethnocentricity or "solidarity," according to which there is no noncircular or non-question-begging way to justify our own ideals, values, and commitments to those who reject them in favor of their own, equally ethnocentric alternatives: "We pragmatists ... should say that we must, in practice, privilege our own group, even though there can be no noncircular justification for doing so" (Rorty 1989, p. 44)—including, presumably, our own group's judgments and standards of argument goodness. David Theo Goldberg helpfully summarizes and develops Rorty's view as follows:

> The traditional historical commitment of philosophical liberalism to universal principles of reason and (moral) value presupposes universal ideas like intrinsic humanity, human dignity, and human rights—values, that is, that are thought to mark individuals in virtue of their very humanity. As Rorty insists, there is no transhistorical or supersocial Godly view on which such universal (moral) principles can be grounded or from which they can be derived. Axiological concepts and values are necessarily those of some historically specific community.... Thus, any insistence on the universalism of values must be no more than the projected imposition of local values—those especially of some ethnoracial and gendered particularity—universalized. (Goldberg 1994, pp. 17–18)

As Goldberg here suggests, Rorty's ethnocentrism rejects the possibility of "universal principles of reason" in accordance with which arguments can be impersonally evaluated. While Rorty's denial of the possibility of impersonal, transcultural beliefs, values, and ideals is in the first instance directed to moral values and principles rather than to principles of "reason" or of argument evaluation, it is readily extended there, as Goldberg suggests:

> Axiological relativism is bound to deny neither some basic formal principles of thinking—call them universal, if necessary—nor generalizable value judgments concerning especially pernicious social conditions and practices. So, owning up to formal principles of logical relation implies nothing about the assertive content of thought.... Logical formalism enables only that inconsistent and incoherent claims for the most part can be ruled out; it is thoroughly incapable of assertively promoting some coherent or consistent standard over another. (1994, pp. 16–17)

So, on the Rorty/Goldberg view, there may be universal "formal principles" both of "thinking" and of "logical relation," but these will be insufficient to determine the quality of "the assertive content of thought." With respect to the quality of thought—and, in particular, the quality of particular arguments—such determinations of argumentative quality cannot be other than the judgments of "some historically specific community," which may well differ from the judgments of argumentative quality of other specific communities. How good is a given argument, then? It appears that the Rorty/Goldberg answer to this question can only be that it depends on the cultural identities and commitments of its evaluators, and on the cultural circumstances in which the evaluation takes place. But appearances here *may* be deceiving.

As Rorty and Goldberg both acknowledge, their view suggests a problematic form of epistemological relativism. Rorty explicitly rejects relativism, although it remains unclear whether he is nonetheless committed to it.[7] Goldberg defends "a more robustly nuanced," "multicultural" relativism, as the following two passages indicate:

> If the truth is relative simplistically to the group proclaiming it, then all claims to truth, no matter how much they lack substantiation, are on an equal footing. Pat Lauderdale has noted recently that the critique of "objectivity" as veiling the imputation of Eurocentric value has buried justifiable concerns about accuracy. A more robust and more robustly nuanced conception of relativism underpinning the multicultural project will enable distinctions to be drawn between more or less accurate truth claims and more or less justifiable values (in contrast to claims to *the* truth or *the* good). (1994, p. 15, emphases in original)

Here Goldberg seems clearly to reject epistemological relativism—at least the "simplistic" form of it according to which "the truth is relative simplistically to the group proclaiming it"—in favor of an epistemology that explicitly and legitimately distinguishes "between more or less accurate truth claims and more or less justifiable values." There is nothing here that the epistemological "absolutist" need reject. His version of relativism is spelled out further as follows:

> [T]he relativism upon which a sophisticated form of critical multiculturalism rests is not restricted to value particularism. Multicultural relativism is ready and able to fashion general judgments, that is, revisable inductive generalizations as the specificity of (particular) circumstances and relations warrant. These circumstances and relations will include often, though not necessarily always, racial, class, and gendered articulation. Thus multiculturalists are able to condemn a specific form of racism, say, apartheid, in terms of a general judgment that racist exclusions are unacceptable because they are unwarranted in a specifiable scheme of social value to which we do or should adhere for specifiable (and, perhaps, generalizable) reasons. But there is no transcendental proof or grounds, no universal foundation, for this scheme or any other. (1994, p. 19)

Here again, what Goldberg calls "multicultural relativism" seems not particularly relativistic: it accepts that general judgments, e.g., that "racist exclusions are unacceptable," can be warranted within "a specifiable scheme of social value to which we do *or should* adhere for specifiable (and, perhaps, generalizable) reasons" (emphasis added). The "scheme of social value" is one to which we should adhere for specifiable reasons, even if we (or some of us) do not in fact so adhere: we would be *wrong* not to adhere to it, given the reasons which can be offered for it. This seems not only not relativistic, but the very definition of "absolutism" (Siegel 1987, 2004).

Why then, given his willingness to distinguish between more or less "accurate" (1994, p. 15) or warranted claims, does Goldberg consider his view to be a "relativistic" one? I can only speculate here, but there is considerable textual support for the hypothesis that Goldberg regards his view as relativist because he rejects all claims to "*the* truth" and "*the* good" (p. 15), to "transcendental proof or grounds," and to "universal foundation[s]," for any particular scheme (p. 19). That is, it appears that Goldberg is concerned mainly to reject foundationalism, certainty, necessity, and transhistorical and supersocial Godly perspectives from which claims to the truth or the good might be made, and to embrace a thoroughgoing epistemological fallibilism. With all this the nonrelativist can happily concur. Whether or not this hypothesis is correct, the important point for present purposes is that Goldberg's "robustly nuanced multicultural relativism" appears not in the end to hold that argument quality is relative to culture; it holds, rather, that some cultural beliefs, values, and practices can be legitimately criticized on the basis of reasons which, while neither necessary nor certain, are nevertheless good ones which we *should* acknowledge as probatively telling, even if we in fact do not. (Only thus are we (on Goldberg's view) within our epistemic rights to condemn racist exclusions as "unacceptable"—i.e., as *wrong*—not just for us, who are already convinced of the wrongness of racism, but for everyone, including the racist who does not, but *should*, accept our scheme of social value on the basis of the reasons that can be offered for it and that itself provides us with reasons adequate to establish the unacceptability of such exclusions.)

If this analysis of Goldberg's view is correct, that view in the end does not, despite initial appearances, support a culturally relative view of argument quality. But I hasten to acknowledge that other passages in Goldberg's discussion do seem to recommend such a view. I consider some of those passages further below.

As is already clear, the thesis that argument goodness depends upon cultural commitments and differences raises problems that also arise in the context of discussions of epistemological relativism; in contemplating the former it will prove necessary to consider the latter as well. In what follows, then, I will discuss difficulties with the view that argument quality depends upon culture that accrue to that view in virtue of its apparent embrace of a problematic epistemological relativism; but I will consider other difficulties as well, namely difficulties that befall it even if it avoids relativistic ones. While I hope in what follows to acknowledge the genuine insights of a multiculturalist approach to argument quality, I will argue that that quality is not rightly understood as dependent upon cultural difference.

3. Four Difficulties with a Culturally Contextual View of Argument Quality

A. Transcendence

Central to the view that argument quality depends upon culture is the claim, embraced by the view's defenders—and, as we will see, by its critics as well—that there is no possibility of "transcending," no escape from, whatever specific historical/cultural[8] location argument evaluators happen to occupy. I consider next a version of the argument that defends that view by appeal to this premise.[9]

One case for a personal, culturally sensitive—rather than an impersonal, acultural—conception of argument quality depends upon a rejection of culturally "transcendent" principles of argument evaluation and criteria of argument quality. According to it, all such principles and criteria, however much they are made to look universal or transcendent, are local; their status varies from locale to locale. As Goldberg puts the point, "As Rorty insists, there is no transhistorical or supersocial Godly view on which such universal (moral) principles can be grounded or from which they can be derived.... any insistence on the universalism of values must be no more than the projected imposition of local values ... universalized" (1994, p. 18). If the values in question are those relating to argument quality, this claim seems to lead directly to the culturally relative conception of argument quality we are considering.

The point, it must be admitted, is widely acknowledged in contemporary discussion: one can never completely escape one's historical/cultural location, with its associated perspective, framework, or conceptual scheme, and achieve a "God's eye view" or a "view from nowhere" (Nagel 1986); all cognitive activity—including, of course, the evaluation of arguments—is inevitably conducted from some ongoing perspective or point of view. A typical expression of the thesis is Quine's:

> The philosopher's task differs from the others', then, in detail; but in no such drastic way as those suppose who imagine for the philosopher a vantage point outside the conceptual scheme that he takes in charge. There is no such cosmic exile. He cannot study and revise the fundamental conceptual scheme of science and common sense without having some conceptual scheme, whether the same or another no less in need of philosophical scrutiny, in which to work. (1960, pp. 275–276)

Philosophers generally grant Quine's point: there is no "cosmic exile" from all conceptual schemes; one cannot cognize except from within the confines of some scheme or other. As Goldberg puts it, there is no "transhistorical or supersocial Godly view" from which human judgments—and in particular, judgments concerning argument quality—can be made. But from the relatively uncontroversial claim that we cannot escape all perspectives and achieve a "view from nowhere," it seems a short step to the conclusion that principles of argument evaluation and criteria of argument quality are themselves relative to the cultural frameworks which inevitably limit our judgment—that, since there is no "perspectiveless" judgment, there is no possibility of achieving a perspective which would allow us to judge the quality of arguments in a culturally transcendent way. That is, the uncontroversial claim that all judgments of argument quality inevitably occur in the context of some cultural location or other might be thought to entail that all such judgments are therefore *bound* or *determined* by such *inescapable* locations—and so that what counts as a good argument is problematically *limited* by cultural context in such a way, or to such an extent, that a culturally relativistic view of argument quality inevitably results.

However, it does not—or so I will argue. The alleged entailment just mentioned fails. Even though we cannot attain a culturally transcendent perspective, in the relevant sense we *can* nevertheless "transcend" such perspectives in judging argument quality. The key is to distinguish between transcending or escaping *any particular* perspective from transcending *all* such perspectives. Once this distinction is drawn, the "no transcendence, therefore argument quality is relative to culture" argument collapses.

Consider the question first in general terms, i.e., without regard to the specific case of judgments concerning argument quality, and without restricting ourselves to *cultural* frameworks or perspectives. Are we limited by our perspectives, such that we cannot achieve any critical perspective on them? Are we really "trapped" within our perspectives in this way? Common sense and everyday experience indicate the contrary. Perhaps the most obvious counterexamples involve the cognitive activities of children. Children of a certain age, for example, can count and have a reasonable grasp of whole numbers, but have no understanding of fractions or decimals, i.e., parts of whole numbers. If asked "is there a number between 1 and 2?," they will answer in the negative, and will be unable to comprehend any suggestion to the contrary. But, given normal psychological/cognitive development, within a few years such children will answer affirmatively; they will have no problem recognizing that, e.g., 1.5 is a number between 1 and 2, and, more generally, that there are non-whole numbers. This seems a perfectly straightforward case of the modification of a framework (or of the abandonment of one framework for another) that belies the claim that we are trapped in, bound by, or limited to our frameworks.[10] Scientific examples can equally easily be given, e.g., of the recognition of the existence of things too small to see with the naked eye, or of the interanimation of space and time and of the large-scale non-Euclidean geometry of the universe.

Very different sorts of examples can also be given. Consider, for example, the "male sexist pig" who has no awareness or understanding of women other than as (sex) objects, but who in the course of his experience comes to realize (if only dimly) that he does treat women as objects, that many women want not to be so treated, and that there might well be something objectionable about treating women in that way. Suppose that this benighted male comes eventually to a full(er) awareness of the injustice of his earlier treatment of women; he comes to believe that it is wrong to treat women as objects and, over a considerable period of time and with the help of many women (and perhaps some courses in the Women's Studies Department), he develops a radically different and more respectful view of women and (hallelujah!) treats them accordingly. (Surely many men have had their consciousnesses raised to some extent in this way in recent decades.) Here again, it seems that our subject has had his perspective altered and, indeed, improved; that is, he has "transcended" his old sexist perspective for another.

In these examples, not only have perspectives altered, but the cognizers considered also regard their later perspectives as *improvements*, i.e., as better than, superior to, their earlier ones. If asked, these cognizers will be able to offer reasons that purport to justify those judgments of superiority. Those reasons, and the judgment that they are good ones which offer justification for the superiority of those later perspectives, are of course made from the perspective of those later perspectives or frameworks; they are not outside of all frameworks or issued from a perspectiveless perspective. Thus is acknowledged the uncontroversial premise of the argument under consideration. But the conclusion is undermined by the several counterexamples offered: epistemic agents always judge from some perspective or other, but there is no reason to think that they are trapped in or bound by their perspectives such that they cannot subject them to critical scrutiny. In this sense, we *can* "transcend" our perspectives, and this sense is sufficient to defeat the general argument for the relativity of judgment to perspectives that we have been considering. As Popper puts the point:

> I do admit that at any moment we are prisoners caught in the framework of our theories; our expectations; our past experiences; our language. But we are prisoners in a Pickwickian sense: if we try, we can break out of our frameworks at any time. Admittedly, we shall find ourselves again in a framework, but it will be a better and roomier one; and we can at any moment break out of it again.
>
> The central point is that a critical discussion and a comparison of the various frameworks is always possible. (1970, p. 56)

Here Popper clearly draws the crucial distinction that undermines this path to relativism. While the Quinean point that there is no "cosmic exile" from all perspectives—that we inevitably judge from some framework or other, and that we cannot judge from a perspectiveless perspective—must be granted, it does not follow that our judgments are necessarily tainted by the fact that they are made from some framework or other, or are "good" only relative to that framework. On the contrary, we can and regularly do "transcend" our frameworks from the perspective of other, "roomier" ones, in which can fit both our earlier one and relevant rivals to it—and in this way fair, nonrelative evaluations of both our judgments and the frameworks/perspectives from which they are made are possible.[11]

I have to this point been treating the general question of the degree to which our judgments are determined by, and therefore relative to, our conceptual schemes/frameworks/perspectives. The conclusion to which these musings have led is that, while it is clearly correct that we cannot attain or judge from a "perspectiveless perspective," we nevertheless not only can but regularly do attain sufficient critical leverage on our perspectives that we can criticize, evaluate, and improve them—and, consequently, that judgment is not inevitably determined by or trapped within those perspectives. This general point is directly applicable to the special case involving judgments of argument quality.[12] When we evaluate arguments, we inevitably do so from some perspective or other. In particular, we do so from the particular historical/cultural perspective in which we are embedded, with its own particular principles of argument evaluation and criteria of argument quality. Nevertheless, we are not "trapped" within that perspective; our judgments of argument quality are not wholly determined by it. Indeed, during the long history of the development of principles of argument evaluation within Western/European culture, many such principles have been altered as theorists gained critical perspective on them. Particularly salient examples involve the impact of the development of probability theory on principles of argument evaluation and criteria of argument quality that touch upon probabilistic matters, e.g., principles and criteria relevant to what are now taken to be the gambler's fallacy, the fallacy of hasty generalization, and arguments whose cogency depends upon representative sampling.[13] The moral of the story is clear: while there is a clear sense in which judgments of argument quality are embedded in particular historical/cultural locations, that sense is not such as to challenge the impersonal and transcultural conception of argument normativity with which we began. The argument in question—we cannot transcend our historical/cultural locations, therefore argument quality depends upon the features of and is relative to those locations—founders on the failure to distinguish between "transcending" all perspectives at once (and in doing so judging from a perspectiveless perspective) and transcending any particular perspective. The former is not possible, but the latter is not only possible but quite common. In particular, judgments of argument quality admit of this latter sort of transcendence. Consequently, this route to a culturally relative conception of argument quality does not succeed.

The argument we have been considering rests upon a failure to distinguish between transcending all perspectives and transcending any particular one. A related argument suffers from the opposite failing: it draws a sharp, but ultimately untenable, distinction between the *locatedness* or particularity of principles of argument evaluation and criteria of argument quality, on the one hand, and the possibility of any "universal" status for such principles and criteria, on the other. It moreover regards these as contraries, and consequently holds that principles and criteria relevant to argumentation, being particular, cannot also be thought to be universal. I turn to this argument next.

B. Universality and Particularity

Here, as we have already seen, Goldberg clearly articulates the problematic dichotomy in question: "Axiological concepts and values are necessarily those of some historically specific community.... Thus, any insistence on the universalism of values must be no more than the projected imposition of local values ... universalized." On this view, all principles and values are local and particular; any claim to universality is nothing more than "the imposition of [the] local values ... of some ethnoracial and gendered particularity" (1994, p. 18). The application of this view to principles and criteria concerning argumentation is straightforward: they too are particular, not universal; argument quality is dependent upon the particular location in which evaluation takes place. So a given argument may (for example) beg the question, and be judged to be of poor quality in a locale that takes a dim view of that particular argument form, but be judged to be of high quality in a locale in which that form is regarded with equanimity. To take a real example: any argument of the form that we now call "the gambler's fallacy" was thought to be a good argument in the environs of the Harvard logicians of the 1870s, but is thought to be a bad argument in the rarefied atmosphere of the Emerson Hall (where the Harvard Philosophy Department is housed) of today.[14]

Let us grant that all principles of argument evaluation and criteria of argument quality are local and particular,[15] in the sense that they are inevitably articulated and endorsed in particular historical/cultural circumstances—just (as granted above) as they are inevitably endorsed from some perspective or other. Does it follow that they are therefore not universal? Two contemporary denizens of Emerson Hall suggest not. Israel Scheffler writes, "I have always supposed that the universal and the particular are compatible, that grounding in a particular historical and cultural matrix is inevitable and could not conceivably be in conflict with universal principles" (1995, p. 14). Hilary Putnam, in commenting on this passage, agrees:

> When we argue about the universal applicability of principles ... we are not claiming to stand outside of our own tradition, let alone outside of space and time, as some fear; we are standing within a tradition, and trying simultaneously to learn what in that tradition we are prepared to recommend to other traditions *and* to see what in that tradition may be inferior—inferior either to what other traditions have to offer, or to the best we may be capable of. ...
>
> ... [W]e are not forced to choose between scientism and skepticism [or between "universalism" and "particularism"]. ... The third possibility is to accept the position we are fated to occupy in any case, the position of beings who cannot have a view of the world that does not reflect our interests and values, but who are, for all that, committed to regarding some views of the world—and, for that matter, some interests and values—as better than others. This may mean giving up a certain metaphysical picture of objectivity, but it does not mean giving up the idea that there are what Dewey called "objective resolutions of problematical situations"—objective resolutions to problems which are *situated* in a place, at a time, as opposed to an "absolute" answer to "perspective-independent" questions. And that is objectivity enough. (Putnam 1990, p. 178, emphases in original)

Putnam is here discussing principles of ethics rather than of argument evaluation, and matters metaphysical as well as epistemological, but the relevance of his remarks to our topic is clear. In regarding argument quality as "impersonal," "transcultural," or "universal," we are not denying that our principles of argument evaluation and criteria of argument quality are local and particular, in the sense that they are *ours*: articulated and endorsed by us, in our particular historical/cultural context. But acknowledging their particularity does not preclude us from proclaiming their universality—that is, their legitimate applicability to arguments, considered independently of their location.

In holding these principles and criteria to be "universal" or transcultural, we need not deny their locality/particularity. Goldberg and Rorty are correct in holding that all proclamations of universal principle emanate from particular locales. It does not follow from this, though, that such values have no legitimacy or force beyond the bounds from within which they are proclaimed or embraced. The problematic move is to regard "particularity" and "universality" as contraries, such that a principle or criterion's being one precludes it from being the other. Elsewhere (Siegel 1997, pp. 174–178; Siegel 2004) I have offered general arguments against regarding these as contraries, as well as a range of examples, from mathematics, science, and morality, of claims, theses, principles and criteria which are both particular and universal. I will not repeat these arguments and examples here. I will instead content myself with suggesting that, for the reasons given both here and there, this argumentative path—principles of argument evaluation and criteria of argument quality are particular and local; therefore they cannot be "universal" or "transcend" their locales; therefore argument quality is relative to historical/cultural location or context—does not succeed.

C. "Transcultural Normative Reach"

I believe that the two problems facing culturally relative conceptions of argument quality just rehearsed are formidable. The main difficulty with conceiving of argument quality in culturally relative terms, however, is that any argument for that conception must presuppose the impersonal, transcultural conception of such quality with which it contrasts. As I will call it, any such argument must presuppose "transcultural normative reach."[16] For any such argument will proceed from premises to a conclusion which is said by its proponents to follow from those premises. That it does so, if it does, will not be dependent on the cultural characteristics or commitments of those either advancing or contemplating the argument. The argument is taken by its proponents to provide good reasons for embracing its conclusion, reasons which should be found compelling by any person who fair-mindedly considers it. In this sense, the argument's quality—the ability of its premises to justify its conclusion—is what it is, independently of the culture of either the arguer or her audience.

Such transcultural normative reach must be accepted by any advocate of a culturally relative conception of argument quality who thinks that her advocacy is not only non-arbitrary, but *rational*—warranted by the reasons offered in its support. For an advocate who rejects such reach cannot regard herself as advancing reasons which ought to persuade a fair-minded opponent, i.e., an imagined rational and open-minded person interested in determining for herself which conception of argument quality is more worthy of embrace. Neither can she regard her embrace of the culturally relative view as more rational than her opponent's embrace of its rival. But this leaves her in a troubling position: if she can't offer such reasons, why should her opponent, or anyone else, agree with her? If she regards her favored view of argument quality as in any way rationally preferable to its alternatives, she must hold that that view is supported by reasons which have force beyond the bounds of those who happen to share her own presuppositions and commitments. In short, the *rational* advocacy of and commitment to the culturally relative view of argument quality presupposes the transcultural character of the normative standing of arguments (and reasons) as such.[17]

It is important to recognize that this "transcultural normative reach," which I am claiming must be acknowledged by all parties to the debate concerning argument quality, does not depend upon the presumption that judgments enjoying such reach must be issued from some impossibly neutral perspective. Earlier we saw that Goldberg and Rorty reject the possibility of universal principles or values—including those concerned with argument quality—on the grounds that any such principles must stem from a "transhistorical or supersocial Godly" perspective, and there simply is no such perspective available, at least to the likes of us. Goldberg and Rorty are right about the unavailability of such a perspective, and, if such a perspective were to prove necessary for arguments to enjoy transcultural normative reach, they would be right to reject such reach. But it is not. Let us grant that there are no universal or transcultural values in the sense that they are grounded in, or derived from, a perspective outside of history and culture, for there simply is no such "Godly" perspective available. This is not the sense of "transcultural" relevant here. All that is required for argumentative principles and criteria to be, in the relevant sense, transcultural is that it is possible that reasons offered for particular conclusions be such that a fair-minded contemplation of those reasons will result in such conclusions being deemed worthy of acceptance on the basis of that contemplation, independently of the cultural heritage and commitments of those doing the contemplating. And this possibility, we have seen, is presupposed by any argumentative advocate of any conclusion whatsoever—and *a fortiori* by the advocate of the culturally relative view of argument quality. Consequently, that advocate, like every other, must accept the viability of what I have been calling "transcultural normative reach"—and must therefore reject the culturally relative view of argument quality, which is incompatible with it.

A parallel point is powerfully made by Robert Fullinwider:

> Consider the case of Christopher Columbus: did he discover America or invade it? From the perspective of fifteenth century Europe, he discovered it. From the perspective of the Arawak and other indigenous American populations, he invaded it. As descendants of the European immigrants of America most of us take (or took) the perspective of Europe. Why should we give it up or modify it? Because it is inadequate in some way? Saying it is amounts to measuring it against something outside itself, some more comprehensive and better point of view.
>
> However, the strong separatist denies there are any overarching perspectives, just *other* perspectives. Now, no other perspective can claim to supercede our own merely by being *other*. If an Arawak-centered perspective is no better than a Eurocentric perspective or no part of a more comprehensive synthesis, why bother to re-write the books on poor Columbus? The ironic implication of strong perspectivism is that the label "Eurocentric" ceases to be a charge, complaint or criticism; it becomes a mere description. (Fullinwider 1991, p. 14, emphases in original)

Fullinwider's "strong perspectivist" may for present purposes be identified with the advocate of a culturally relative view of argument quality; the lesson of the example is the same for both. Since the strong perspectivist denies the possibility of overarching perspectives in terms of which particular, local perspectives can be evaluated, she denies herself the ability to criticize any such particular perspectives. More tellingly for present purposes, in doing so she likewise denies herself the ability to criticize alternatives to her favored "strong perspectivist" view, and to defend as rationally superior to its alternatives that view itself.

Similarly, by denying the possibility of overarching, transcultural principles of argument evaluation and criteria of argument quality, the advocate of a culturally relative view of argument quality denies herself the ability to criticize particular, culture-bound, argument-related principles and criteria; and, in doing so, likewise denies herself the ability to criticize alternatives to her favored culturally relative view, and to defend as rationally superior to its alternatives that view itself. But her whole purpose, *qua* advocate of that view, is to establish its superiority. Consequently she must, in order to advocate it, *accept* rather than deny the possibility—and indeed the actuality—of overarching, transcultural principles of argument evaluation and criteria of argument quality. That is, she must accept "transcultural normative reach," and, as above, must therefore reject the culturally relative view of argument quality that is incompatible with it.[18]

D. Argumentation, Rhetoric, and Power

A final worry, which I can treat only briefly here, concerns a kind of skepticism toward the very idea of argumentative or epistemic normativity. The claim that a given argument is a good one, in that its premises provide justification for its conclusion, is (it may be said) not really a claim about normative status at all, since there is "in the world" no such thing. Such claims, rather, are simply rhetorical devices, which serve to mask the exercise of power. My persuading you that you ought to believe a conclusion C because it is well supported by its premises P, or that certain standards of probative support (which I endorse) are the standards by which you should judge such support, is simply an exercise of my power over you. That certain principles and criteria of argument quality are seen as legitimate is itself no more than a reflection of the power enjoyed by those able to establish them as such. That some items are thought to be "good reasons" while others are not is—as van Eemeren, Grootendorst, and Henkemans put it in their helpful review[19] of recent work on argumentation, communication, and rhetoric—"systematically to privilege certain kinds of claims over others" (1996, p. 209). As they point out, this claim

> points to the nexus between argumentation and power. It is power, whether political, social, or intellectual, that permits one to stipulate what sorts of claims "count" in any argumentative situation. Power enables those who hold it to impose a partial perspective as if it were holistic—the definition usually given for the term *hegemony*. The most recent wave of argumentation studies seeks to explore and expose the tendency of power to foreclose discourse, and it seeks emancipation by opening up alternatives. This project focuses on marginalized arguers and arguments, and is given impetus by the widespread concern for matters of race, gender and class.
>
> The intellectual underpinning of argument-as-critique is "postmodernism." . . . There are many varieties of postmodernism, but the central core seems to be the denial that there are any verities or standards of judgment, and the claim that what passes for such standards really is socially constructed. In its . . . location of argument in communities, this perspective is in some measure consistent with the others we have discussed. But it goes on to argue that only *a part* of the relevant community has defined the standards, then hegemonically imposed them on the whole. The goal of critique is thus to shed light on this practice and to promote emancipatory potential by posing alternatives. (p. 209, emphases in original)

As these authors point out, one "implication . . . of the postmodern project . . . is the denial that there can be any such thing as communal norms or standards for argument" (p. 209).[20]

The claim, and the argument for it, can perhaps be summarized as follows: "Rational argument" is really just a form of rhetoric. The use of rhetoric is the exercise of power. Judgments of argument quality are likewise rhetorical exercises of power. Thus the impersonal, transcultural view of argument quality defended above can be seen only as an equally rhetorical, power-laden construct; it can be no more than a tool of power wielded to further marginalize those not involved in its construction but expected to judge in accordance with its dictates.

This is a fundamental charge; as such, adequate treatment of it requires more attention than I can give it here.[21] But three points in reply seem in order. First, this skepticism concerning the very idea of argument quality (other than as an exercise in power) plagues culture-relative as well as transcultural views of argument quality, since according to it the former as well as the latter are mere rhetorical exercises of power. Consequently, it does not offer a reason for preferring the former to the latter (or vice versa). Second, it is unclear why this view of argumentation should be itself embraced. If the application of standards of argument quality is *just* a rhetorical exercise, with no genuinely normative epistemic force (which renders the conclusions of some arguments *worthy* of belief), there seems to be no reason to embrace this rhetorical view of argumentation and judgments of argument quality either. The rational *defense* of the view requires that some rhetorical efforts are more probatively forceful, and some exercises of rhetorical power more legitimate, than others—and so, that argument quality is not *merely* a matter of rhetoric and power.

Of course, the "advocate" of the view might simply shrug off the debate concerning the relative merits of her view versus opposing views, regarding all such "rational" debate as merely rhetorical exercise; she may, in denying any sense of "rational superiority" other than the rhetorical/power one here being considered, be flatly uninterested in establishing the rational superiority of her view. This stance embodies an admirable consistency, but it comes at a high price: in adopting it, and so rejecting the very possibility of rational advocacy of her view, this "advocate" seems clearly enough not to be engaging the issue with which this paper is concerned. Indeed, taking this stance would render its defense logically impossible; it would make it impossible either to advocate the view in question as rationally preferable to its alternatives, or to engage the general issue of the relative merits of the rival views of argument quality we have been considering. Consequently, while the stance in question appears at first blush to constitute a possible position to take with respect to that issue, taking it not only renders that position indefensible, it renders the issue itself incapable of being coherently posed—in which case it cannot be seen as an adequate stance to take with respect to that issue.[22]

There is, obviously enough, much more to be said here. Nevertheless, I hope to have said enough to make it clear that the view of argumentation as rhetorical, and as fundamentally the exercise of power, has no tendency either to upend a transcultural view of argument quality or to support a culturally relative view of it.

4. Conclusion

I have argued that while there is much merit in the general multiculturalist perspective on argumentation—it rightly warns us against impossible "perspectiveless" perspectives and "Godly" perspectives outside of time, space, and culture; and rightly reminds us that argument evaluation is conducted by flesh-and-blood people in specific historical/cultural locations, that it takes place in a context—the multiculturalist argument against impersonal, transcultural conceptions of argumentative quality fails. It fails, first, because its criticism of the possibility of "transcendence" depends upon a conception of transcendence that, although rightly rejected, is far stronger than that required by a transcultural view of argument quality. It fails, second, because it depends upon a sharp "universal/particular" dichotomy that is in the end untenable. Most fundamentally, it fails because it itself presupposes just the impersonal sort of argumentative quality it seeks to reject: that of *transcultural normative reach*. Finally, it gains no support from regarding argumentation as the rhetorical exercise of power.

I conclude that the transcultural conception of argument quality survives at least the multiculturalist challenges to it discussed here.[23]

Notes

1. For further articulation and defense of this epistemic conception of argumentation, see Feldman 1994; Lumer 1991; Wreen 1997; Biro and Siegel 1992; Siegel and Biro 1997; for criticism see Adler 1997a, 1997b. For more general consideration of epistemic normativity in the context of consideration of "naturalized" epistemology, see Siegel 1996a and Siegel 1996b and references therein.
2. Feldman (1994) appears to disagree, as his treatment relativizes argument goodness to persons: the same argument, on Feldman's view, can be a good one for you but a bad one for me. But I believe that this apparent relativization to persons is in fact relativization to the *evidence* that a given argument evaluator has at the time of evaluation. The latter sort of relativization, according to which the quality of an argument depends upon the probative strength of the relevant, available evidence utilized in its premises, is the very hallmark of the epistemic view. Thanks to Richard Feldman for helpful conversation and correspondence on this point.
3. Such theorists can thus also be categorized as "contextualists," who hold that standards of argument quality differ from context to context, culture being one such context-type. For references and critical discussion, see Combs 1995. For insightful discussion of possible cultural bias inherent in critical thinking itself, see Ennis 1998.
4. Although I must immediately concede that on MacIntyre's view relativism *can* be "transcended." For discussion of MacIntyre's view of rationality and relativism, see Siegel 2004.
5. The quoted passage is taken from Carr 1995, p. 80, which offers a general and plausible characterization of the central themes of postmodernism. For critical discussion see Siegel 1998.

6. This paragraph borrows from Siegel 1999.
7. For discussion of Rorty and relativism, see Siegel 2004.
8. There is, presumably, equally no ready escape from our gendered, class, and other locations. For ease of exposition I will treat these further dimensions of our locations and identities as understood. I also acknowledge the vexed problem of the constitution and individuation of "cultures," which I make no effort to address here.
9. What follows is adapted from Siegel 2004, to which the reader is referred for further discussion.
10. Children typically attain "a reasonable grasp of whole numbers" by age three or four. Grasp of fractions and decimals usually involves a process which extends over several years and is presumably in part a function of what is taught, when. The classic work in this area is Gelman and Gallistel 1978; it (including its account of what counts as a "reasonable grasp" of numbers) is summarized briefly and lucidly in Moshman, Glover, and Bruning 1987, pp. 420–423. Thanks to David Moshman for helpful advice on matters concerning psychological development.
11. For critical discussion of Popper's view, and of "framework relativism" more generally, see Siegel 1987, ch. 2; for consideration of this issue in the context of arguments for and against naturalized epistemology, see Siegel 1995, esp. pp. 50–51; for more general discussion of the possibility of "transcendence," see Siegel 1997.
12. It is equally applicable to the special case involving specifically *cultural* context. The example involving a sexist perspective I trust makes this clear.
13. For discussion of the epistemic status of these and other examples, including a sharp change of judgment concerning the legitimacy of the gambler's fallacy, see Siegel 1992.
14. For discussion and references, see Siegel 1992, p. 33.
15. Of course, *persons* are also particular; all people are, in Seyla Benhabib's words, "embodied and embedded" (1992, p. 6), and have to be understood as such by philosophers if they are to avoid "the metaphysical illusions of the Enlightenment" (p. 4). Benhabib strives to reformulate "the universalist tradition in ethics" (p. 9) in such a way that it respects the "concrete other" as well as the "generalized other" (pp. 158 ff.); she too rejects the universal/particular dichotomy I am challenging in this section.
16. This section is adapted from and builds upon the discussion of "transcultural normative reach" in Siegel 1999.
17. This parallels the analysis of (and argument against) epistemological relativism offered in Siegel 1987, ch. 1, and rehearsed in Siegel 2004.
18. She must, moreover, argue that from the perspective of those transcultural principles and criteria, her favored view of argument quality proves to be superior to its rivals. Here she runs into the well-rehearsed incoherence arguments against the relativism implicit in her view, since that view centrally denies the possibility of "transcultural superiority" that it must nevertheless claim for itself. I will not rehearse again those arguments here. They are laid out in some detail in Siegel 1987 and Siegel 2004.
19. The review in question appears as chapter 7 of van Eemeren et al.1996. They are here reviewing the literature concerning this point, not endorsing it.
20. For detailed discussions pro and con, see the several essays collected in Simons and Billig 1995 and Cherwitz and Hikins 1995.
21. I have addressed various aspects of it, though not in the context of argumentation theory, in Siegel 1997.
22. This point is developed further in Siegel 1987, Siegel 2004, and Siegel 1997, ch. 5.
23. I am grateful to the Spencer Foundation, the National Endowment for the Humanities, and the University of Miami for their support. The views expressed are, of course, solely my own responsibility. This paper was presented at a session sponsored by the Association for Informal Logic and Critical Thinking (AILACT) at the World Congress of Philosophy in Boston, August 1998; I am grateful to Jonathan Adler for the invitation to participate in the session and to those in attendance for their stimulating reactions.

References

Adler, J. (1997a). "Fallacies Not Fallacious: Not!" *Philosophy and Rhetoric* 30.4: 333–350.
Adler, J. (1997b). "Reply by Repetition and Reminder." *Philosophy and Rhetoric* 30.4: 367–375.
Baynes, K., J. Bohman, and T. McCarthy (eds.). (1987). *After Philosophy: End or Transformation?* Cambridge, MA: MIT Press.
Benhabib, S. (1992). *Situating the Self: Gender, Community and Postmodernism in Contemporary Ethics*. New York: Routledge.
Biro, J., and H. Siegel. (1992). "Normativity, Argumentation, and an Epistemic Theory of Fallacies." In F. H. van Eemeren et al. (eds.), *Argumentation Illuminated: Selected Papers from the 1990 International Conference on Argumentation* (pp. 85–103). Dordrecht, The Netherlands: Foris.
Carr, W. (1995). "Education and Democracy: Confronting the Postmodernist Challenge." *Journal of Philosophy of Education* 29.1: 75–92.
Cherwitz, R. A., and J. W. Hikins (eds.). (1995). "The Role of Argument in the Postmodern World and Beyond." *Argumentation* 9.1.
Combs, S. C. (1995). "The Evocativeness Standard for Argument Quality." In F. H. van Eemeren, R. Grootendorst, J. A. Blair, and C. A. Willard (eds.), *Perspectives and Approaches: Proceedings of the Third ISSA Conference on Argumentation/* Vol. 1 (439–451). Amsterdam: Sicsat.
Ennis, R. H. (1998). "Is Critical Thinking Culturally Biased?" *Teaching Philosophy* 21.1: 15–33.
Feldman, R. (1994). "Good Arguments." In F. F. Schmitt (ed.), *Socializing Epistemology: The Social Dimensions of Knowledge* (pp. 159–188). Lanham, MD: Roman & Littlefield.
Fullinwider, R. (1991). "Multicultural Education." *Report from the Institute for Philosophy & Public Policy* 11.3: 12–14.
Gelman, R., and C. R. Gallistel. (1978). *The Child's Understanding of Number*. Cambridge, MA: Harvard University Press.
Goldberg, D. T. (1994). "Introduction: Multicultural Conditions." In D. T. Goldberg (ed.), *Multiculturalism: A Critical Reader* (pp. 1–41). Oxford: Blackwell.
Lumer, C. (1991). "Structure and Function of Argumentations—An Epistemological Approach to Determining Criteria for the Validity and Adequacy of Argumentations." In F. H. van Eemeren, R. Grootendorst, J. A. Blair, and C. A. Willard (eds.), *Proceedings of the Second International Conference on Argumentation*. Vol. 1A (pp. 98–107). Amsterdam: SICSAT.
Lyotard, J. -F. (1987). "The Postmodern Condition." In Baynes, Bohman, and McCarthy 1987, pp. 73–94.
MacIntyre, A. (1988). *Whose Justice? Which Rationality?* Notre Dame, IN: University of Notre Dame Press.
MacIntyre, A. (1989). "Relativism, Power, and Philosophy." In M. Krausz (ed.), *Relativism: Interpretation and Confrontation* (pp. 182–204). Notre Dame, IN: University of Notre Dame Press. Originally published in *Proceedings and Addresses of the American Philosophical Association* (1985), pp. 5–22.
Moshman, D., J. A. Glover, and R. H. Bruning. (1987). *Developmental Psychology: A Topical Approach*. Boston, MA: Little, Brown.
Nagel, T. (1986). *The View from Nowhere*. Oxford: Oxford University Press.
Popper, K. R. (1970). "Normal Science and Its Dangers." In I. Lakatos and A. Musgrave (eds.), *Criticism and the Growth of Knowledge* (pp. 51–58). Cambridge: Cambridge University Press.
Putnam, H. (1990). *Realism with a Human Face*. Cambridge, MA: Harvard University Press.
Quine, W. V. (1960). *Word and Object*. Cambridge, MA: MIT Press.
Rorty, R. (1982). *Consequences of Pragmatism*. Minneapolis: University of Minnesota Press.
Rorty, R. (1989). "Solidarity or Objectivity?" In Michael Krausz (ed.), *Relativism: Interpretation and Confrontation* (pp. 35–50). Notre Dame, IN: University of Notre Dame Press.
Scheffler, I. (1995). *Teachers of My Youth: An American Jewish Experience*. Dordrecht, The Netherlands: Kluwer.
Siegel, H. (1987). *Relativism Refuted: A Critique of Contemporary Epistemological Relativism*. Dordrecht, The Netherlands: D. Reidel.
Siegel, H. (1992). "Justification by Balance." *Philosophy and Phenomenological Research* 52.1: 27–46.

Siegel, H. (1995). "Naturalized Epistemology and 'First Philosophy.'" *Metaphilosophy* 26.1: 46–62.
Siegel, H. (1996a). "Naturalism and the Abandonment of Normativity." In W. O'Donohue and R. Kitchener (eds.), *The Philosophy of Psychology* (pp. 4–18). London: Sage.
Siegel, H. (1996b). "Naturalism, Instrumental Rationality, and the Normativity of Epistemology."*Proto Sociology* 8/9: 97–110.
Siegel, H. (1997). *Rationality Redeemed? Further Dialogues on an Educational Ideal.* New York: Routledge.
Siegel, H. (1998). "Knowledge, Truth and Education." In D. Carr (ed.), *Knowledge, Truth and Education: Beyond the Postmodern Impasse.* (pp. 19–36). London: Routledge.
Siegel, H. (1999). "Multiculturalism and the Possibility of Transcultural Educational and Philosophical Ideals." *Philosophy* 74: 387–409.
Siegel, H. (2004). "Relativism." In I. Niiniluoto, M. Sintonin, and J. Woleński (eds.), *Handbook of Epistemology* (pp. 747–780). Dordrecht, The Netherlands: Kluwer.
Siegel, H., and J. Biro. (1997). "Epistemic Normativity, Argumentation, and Fallacies." *Argumentation* 11.3: 277–292.
Simons, H. W., and M. Billig (eds.). (1995). "In Search of a Postmodern Rhetoric of Criticism." *Argumentation* 9.1.
van Eemeren, F. H., R. Grootendorst, F. S. Henkemans, et. al. (1996). *Fundamentals of Argumentation Theory: A Handbook of Historical Backgrounds and Contemporary Developments.* Mahwah, NJ: Lawrence Erlbaum.
Wreen, M. (1997). "Absent Thee from Fallacy a While?" *Philosophy and Rhetoric* 30.4: 351–366.

15

Multiculturalism and Rationality

1. Introduction: Cultural Difference and Judgments of Rationality

Do cultures differ with respect to judgments of rationality? Insofar as we can generalize about cultures and their members in this way, and given a sufficiently generous understanding of "culture," the answer seems, trivially, to be *yes*: a belief, claim, or inference can be judged by the members of a given culture to be rational, while the members of a different culture might judge that same belief, claim, or inference to be irrational.

Examples of such judgments are legion. Consider, for example, the *gambler's fallacy*. Today there is more or less universal agreement among philosophers, logicians, probability theorists, and other relevant scholars that reasoning in accordance with the gambler's fallacy—that is, reasoning that "in a fair game of chance, the probability of a given sort of outcome occurring after $n + 1$ consecutive instances of non-occurrence is greater than the probability of its occurrence after n consecutive instances of non-occurrence" (Stich and Nisbett 1980, p. 192)—is fallacious, in that it fails to take into account the probabilistic independence of such outcomes. But logicians of the late nineteenth century apparently did not so regard it. One of them, Henry Coppée, depicted the alleged cogency of this form of reasoning as follows:

> Thus, in throwing dice, we cannot be sure that any single face or combination of faces will appear; but if, in very many throws, some particular face has not appeared, the chances of its coming up are stronger and stronger, until they approach very near to certainty. It must come; and as each throw is made and it fails to appear, the certainty of its coming draws nearer and nearer. (Coppée 1874, p. 162, cited in Stich and Nisbett 1980, p. 193)[1]

Coppée (and presumably his fellow late nineteenth-century logicians) and we clearly differ in our judgments of the rationality of reasoning in accordance with the gambler's fallacy.[2]

Consider next examples of divergence of opinion concerning the rationality of alternative explanations of natural phenomena. The ancient Greeks, we are told, explained storms, sneezes, and many other phenomena in terms of the desires, attitudes, and dispositions of one or another of the gods, and judged such explanations to be rational; today "scientifically literate Westerners" typically judge otherwise. In our own day, some groups, in their "local," "indigenous sciences," explain natural phenomena in spiritual, magical, or animistic terms, and judge it to be perfectly rational to do so, while those same scientifically literate Westerners demur.[3] Richard Shweder (1986, pp. 170–171) briefly reviews similarly divergent explanations of illness in different "ideological regions" to similar effect, and notes that "in some non-Western cultures ... [i]t is animism, not mechanism, that dominates the intellectual scene" (p. 175). Here too judgments of rationality seem clearly enough to differ.[4]

Do these differences in judgments of rationality track differences of *culture*? Here we must be cautious, not least because of the vagueness of that notion. It may well be objected that late nineteenth-century logicians and probability theorists do not constitute a culture at all, and so not a different culture from that of early twenty-first-century logicians and probability theorists, though we do often speak of different groups of academics constituting different cultures.[5] But several of the other geographical or temporal locations and groups just mentioned or referred to—ancient Greece, the Nisga'a people of northwest Canada, the Yupiaq of southwest Alaska, the Maori of northern Australia, particular Islamic and African groups, and the broad "Western" group that endorses "Western modern science"—seem straightforwardly to constitute distinct cultural locations or groups. In what follows I utilize a very generous understanding of *culture*; I won't try to settle the murky matters of the definition of *culture* or the constitution or individuation of cultures here.[6] However conceived or individuated, it seems clear enough that such groups as those just mentioned do indeed differ systematically with respect to judgments of rationality.[7] And that is sufficient for my purposes here.

So far, we have been considering *judgments* of rationality. What about "rationality itself": do cultures differ with respect to *it*? That is, does "rationality itself" differ from culture to culture? Here we must unpack the relevant sense of rationality.[8] But before we address these questions, we must first attend to the notion of *multiculturalism*.

2. What Is Multiculturalism?

Multiculturalism is, like many philosophical notions, contested. Authors use it in a bewildering variety of senses, and it is important to be clear on the sense intended in this paper. I will not here attempt a systematic review of the many senses of the term in use in the philosophical and educational literatures.[9] Instead, I will briefly discuss one such sense, after which I will introduce the one to be adopted in what follows.

In the Introduction to their valuable collection, Arthur M. Melzer, Jerry Weinberger, and M. Richard Zinman offer the following "working definition":

> In sum, and with all due trepidation, we suggest the following working definition for multiculturalism: it is a movement that radicalizes and Nietzscheanizes the liberal ideal of tolerance—thus turning that ideal against liberalism—by tending to deny the possibility of universal truth as well as of nonoppressive power and by seeking, through this very denial, a comprehensive redistribution, not so much of wealth as of self-esteem, and not so much to individuals as to various marginalized groups. (Melzer, Weinberger, and Zinman 1998, p. 4)

Despite its various strengths, this definition is, I think, problematic, because it builds into the very notion of multiculturalism a contentious epistemological thesis. Why should the (Nietzschean) denial of the possibility of universal truth be thought to be part of the very meaning of multiculturalism? On this understanding of the term, it would be impossible to be a multiculturalist and at the same time a fan of such truth.[10] This seems to place an arbitrary limit on the class of multiculturalists, since, given the contentious and controversial nature of truth, one would expect—and in any case it should be possible for—the members of that class to agree on the character and importance of multiculturalism, yet also disagree about truth. More significantly, it rules out as a conceptual impossibility the clear possibility that a member of that class could assert, as universal truths, claims involving multiculturalism itself—for example, that we should all embrace, and our social/political institutions and arrangements reflect, the values and norms constitutive of multiculturalism. I offer myself as one such multiculturalist, and so as a counterexample to the Nietzschean working definition of the term.

The basic problem with that working definition is that it renders multiculturalism as (at least in part) an epistemological notion, whereas it is usually, and in my view rightly, understood in moral terms.[11] So in what follows I will understand multiculturalism rather to refer to "that movement in contemporary social/political/educational thought—and the claims, theses and values which characterize it—[that] celebrates cultural differences; insists upon the just, respectful treatment of members of all cultures, especially those which have historically been the victims of domination and oppression; and emphasizes the integrity of historically marginalized cultures" (Siegel 1999b, p. 389). Is such an understanding of multiculturalism tenable? According to Stanley Fish, it is not.

3. Stanley Fish on the Impossibility of Multiculturalism

Stanley Fish (1998)[12] argues that any version of multiculturalism serious enough to be worthy of the name is untenable. He distinguishes between "boutique multiculturalism" and "strong multiculturalism." Boutique multiculturalism "is the multiculturalism of ethnic restaurants, weekend festivals, and high-profile flirtations with the 'other' ... [which is] characterized by its superficial or cosmetic relationship to the objects of its affection" (p. 69). Fish argues that it is inadequate as a version of multiculturalism because of this superficiality:

> [T]he boutique multiculturalist resists the force of the appreciated culture at precisely the point at which it matters most to its strongly committed members: the point at which the African American tries to make the content of his culture the content of his children's education, the point at which a Native American wants to practice his religion as its ancient rituals direct him to, the point at which antiabortionists directly confront the evil that they believe is destroying the moral fiber of the country, the point at which Mormons seek to be faithful to the word and practices of their prophets and elders. (p. 70)[13]

In so "resisting the force" of the allegedly appreciated culture, boutique multiculturalism reveals its superficiality: it appreciates only those aspects of other cultures that it can appreciate without cost or challenge to itself or its underlying commitment to transcultural or universal values. As Fish puts it,

> [A] boutique multiculturalist does not and cannot take seriously the core values of the cultures he tolerates. The reason he cannot is that he does not see those values as truly "core" but as overlays on a substratum of essential humanity. That is the true core, and the differences that mark us externally—differences in language, clothing, religious practices, race, gender, class, and so on—are for the boutique multiculturalist only an *accidental* aspect of their beings. (p. 70, emphasis in original)

Because the boutique multiculturalist cannot take sufficiently seriously the core values of cultures other than her own, when they conflict either with the core values of her own culture or with the "substratum of essential humanity" which (it is alleged) members of all cultures share *qua* human beings, hers is not a serious form of multiculturalism at all. This is because a strong form of multiculturalism must be "committed to the ... flourishing ... [and] active fostering of the unique distinctiveness of particular cultures" (p. 72) and cultural traditions, something to which (as we have seen) the boutique multiculturalist cannot commit herself.

Consequently, Fish turns to "strong multiculturalism," according to which the "unique distinctiveness" of *all* cultures and cultural traditions is to be fostered, and the cultures themselves regarded as worthy of flourishing. For Fish, strong multiculturalism "is strong because it values difference in and for itself rather than as a manifestation of something more basically constitutive" (p. 73). Accordingly, "a strong multiculturalist will want to accord a *deep* respect to all cultures at their core, for he believes that each has the right to form its own identity and nourish its own sense of what is rational and humane. For the strong multiculturalist the first principle is not rationality or some other supracultural universal, but tolerance" (p. 73, emphasis in original).

But Fish identifies a seemingly crushing problem for strong multiculturalism:

> But the trouble with stipulating tolerance as your first principle is that you cannot possibly be faithful to it because sooner or later the culture whose core values you are tolerating will reveal itself to be intolerant at that same core; that is, the distinctiveness that marks it as unique and self-defining will resist the appeal of moderation or incorporation into a larger whole. Confronted with a demand that it surrender its viewpoint or enlarge it to include the practices of its natural enemies—other religions, other races, other genders, other classes—a beleaguered culture will fight back with everything from discriminatory legislation to violence.

> At this point the strong multiculturalist faces a dilemma: either he stretches his toleration so that it extends to the intolerance residing at the heart of a culture he would honor, in which case tolerance is no longer his guiding principle, or he condemns the core intolerance of that culture (recoiling in horror when Khomeini calls for the death of Rushdie), in which case he is no longer according it respect at the point where its distinctiveness is most obviously at stake. Typically, the strong multiculturalist will grab the second handle of this dilemma (usually in the name of some supracultural universal now seen to have been hiding up his sleeve from the beginning) and thereby reveal himself not to be a strong multiculturalist at all. Indeed it turns out that strong multiculturalism is not a distinct position, but a somewhat deeper instance of the shallow category of boutique multiculturalism. (pp. 73–74)

I am somewhat surprised to find myself in substantial agreement with Fish. But I think that he takes the wrong lesson from his discussion of this difficulty with "strong multiculturalism." Let me explain.

Fish is right, I think, that the advocate of "strong" multiculturalism faces a deep difficulty concerning cultures that themselves reject multiculturalist principles, such as that concerning tolerance. Let us suppose, as above, that a multiculturalism worthy of the name holds that all cultures and cultural traditions are to be fostered and regarded as valuable and worthy of flourishing. Now consider a culture *C* that does not endorse this view, but rather holds that some other cultures are not so worthy. What should an advocate of multiculturalism say about *C*? If she says that *C*, like all other cultures, should be valued, and its traditions fostered and regarded as worthy of flourishing, then she has compromised her commitment to multiculturalism, since she thereby endorses as valuable and worthy *C*'s refusal to value and regard as worthy some other cultures. On the other hand, if she says that *C* is not to be valued or regarded as worthy because of its unwillingness to so value and regard as worthy some other cultures, she fails to regard *C* in the way that her commitment to multiculturalism says she should. Either way, it seems impossible for her to honor her commitment to multiculturalism.

Fish concludes that multiculturalism is impossible, or not a coherent position, at all (p. 75, see below). I think a more appropriate conclusion is that while the view Fish calls "strong multiculturalism" is indeed incoherent, this incoherence demonstrates the need for an alternative formulation of multiculturalism, one that is limited in such a way that the incoherence is avoided. Multiculturalism should be understood as holding *not* that all cultures should be valued and regarded as worthy—or as I have put it elsewhere, that "all cultures must accept the legitimacy of all other cultures living in accordance with their own, culturally-specific ideals" (Siegel 1999b, p. 393)—but rather as holding that all cultures should be valued and regarded as worthy *only if they extend that value and regard to other cultures*, i.e., that "all cultures must accept the legitimacy of all other cultures living in accordance with their own, culturally-specific ideals, *insofar as those culturally-specific ideals and attendant practices are consistent with the moral imperatives of multiculturalism itself*" (Siegel 1999b, p. 396, emphasis added). That is, a consistent multiculturalism should hold not that all cultures be viewed, valued, and treated in accordance with its dictates no matter what, but rather that particular cultures should be so viewed, valued, and treated only if they endorse the moral imperatives of multiculturalism themselves and view, value, and treat other cultures accordingly.

This, I submit, is simply what a consistent, coherent conception of multiculturalism requires.[14] Fish demurs; the limitation on it that I urge as a matter of ensuring that the doctrine is coherent, Fish regards as a matter of abandoning multiculturalism altogether:

> It may at first seem counterintuitive, but given the alternative modes of multiculturalism—boutique multiculturalism, which honors diversity only in its most superficial aspects because its deeper loyalty is to a universal potential for rational choice; strong multiculturalism, which honors diversity in general, but cannot honor a particular instance of diversity insofar as it refuses (as it always will) to be generous in its turn; and really strong multiculturalism, which goes to the wall with a particular instance of diversity and is therefore not multiculturalism at all—no one could possibly *be* a multiculturalist in any interesting and coherent sense. (p. 75, emphasis in original)

In one respect Fish is right: we are both urging the abandonment of multiculturalism, and denying that anyone could actually be a multiculturalist "in any interesting and coherent sense," *as that doctrine is incoherently formulated*. But the proposed reformulation seems to me to be not an abandonment of multiculturalism, but rather a reformulation that removes the incoherence. The limitation is simply what is required for the coherent formulation of multiculturalism.

Of course, Fish could grant that, as reformulated, multiculturalism is coherent, but deny that it is "interesting." But this denial would be warranted only if the only "interesting" sense of multiculturalism is the incoherent one. Why think this? As reformulated, multiculturalism prohibits the blanket celebration of all cultures, and in particular those inclined "to stamp out the distinctiveness of some other culture" (p. 75), but it is nevertheless able to endorse much of what multiculturalists are typically interested in urging in its name. In particular, it leaves multiculturalists free to urge the celebration of cultural difference and distinctiveness (insofar as they are compatible with the multiculturalist imperative itself); to insist upon the just, respectful treatment of members of all cultures, especially those that have historically been the victims of domination and oppression; and to emphasize the integrity of historically marginalized cultures.[15] This seems to me to leave multiculturalism plenty interesting.

But Fish's criticism has not yet been fully discharged. For he could, and presumably would, charge that the reformulation simply reveals a commitment to a "supracultural universal" that is incompatible with both the spirit and letter of multiculturalism. Recall the dilemma Fish poses:

> At this point the strong multiculturalist faces a dilemma: either he stretches his toleration so that it extends to the intolerance residing at the heart of a culture he would honor, in which case tolerance is no longer his guiding principle, or he condemns the core intolerance of that culture . . ., in which case he is no longer according it respect at the point where its distinctiveness is most obviously at stake. Typically, the strong multiculturalist will grab the second handle of this dilemma

(usually in the name of some supracultural universal now seen to have been hiding up his sleeve from the beginning) and thereby reveal himself not to be a strong multiculturalist at all. (pp. 73–74)

Fish is correct that the reformulation is indebted to a commitment to a "supracultural universal." While in this passage the "universal" on the table is tolerance, the reformulation does not take tolerance to be such a universal, since on it multiculturalism extends tolerance just to cultures that honor its principles and directives. The heart of Fish's objection here is rather that multiculturalism, as he formulates it, is incoherent, since it espouses principles it cannot honor without rendering itself incoherent. ("As a multiculturalist, I should tolerate all cultures, but I can't tolerate that one because it is itself intolerant. If I tolerate it I tolerate intolerance; if I don't tolerate it I am intolerant. Either way I can't coherently endorse universal toleration.") The reformulation does not embrace tolerance as a "supracultural universal," but rather embraces the universal of *coherence*: it is alleged by its advocates to be superior to Fish's formulation precisely because it is coherent, while Fish's formulation (as Fish himself correctly points out) is not. So Fish's objection remains, insofar as he is right that an alleged multiculturalist who embraces a "supracultural universal" is not a multiculturalist at all. Is he right about this? Is commitment to the "supracultural universal" of coherence an abandonment of multiculturalism? In a word: no. Here is why:

First, Fish's argument rests on his presupposition of a sharp, exclusive particular/universal dichotomy, according to which a claim, principle or value can be either particular or universal, but not both. As argued elsewhere, this is a mistake: claims and theses, and principles and values, including that of multiculturalism, can be and often are both particular *and* universal (Siegel 1997, ch. 12; 1999b). So establishing that the multiculturalist has "some supracultural universal . . . hiding up his sleeve" does nothing, in and of itself, to undermine his right to the title "multiculturalist." Fish's criticism presupposes that the multiculturalist cannot avail herself of any "supracultural universal" consistently with her continuing commitment to multiculturalism. This is simply a mistake.[16]

Second, multiculturalism—like any other doctrine, position, or directive, including the claim that it is incoherent—is, if offered as a correct or recommended position, subject to all the "supracultural universals" required by the advocacy of any such position: it is subject to "universals" involving not simply consistency and coherence, but also those involving the proper evaluation of arguments, reasons, evidence, criticisms, probative or evidential force, etc. And it is neither trivial nor irrelevant that Fish's criticism is itself open to evaluation on the basis of just these "universals." Fish is offering us reasons to think that "no one could possibly *be* a multiculturalist in any interesting and coherent sense" (p. 75); his success depends upon the strength of his reasons and arguments, and that strength is not itself a culturally particular matter that varies from culture to culture, on pain of an in-principle inability of his reasons to establish, or even support, his conclusion (Siegel 1999a, 1999b).

Moreover, Fish explicitly relies on exactly such "supracultural universals" in mounting his case. For example, his criticisms of multiculturalism rest on its inability to grasp successfully either horn of the dilemma he poses for it, since both horns lead to incoherence. This manifestly relies upon the "universal" of *coherence*[17] that Fish is unwilling to allow the multiculturalist to violate. Fish's criticisms of a host of key players in the multiculturalism literature, including Amy Gutmann, Jürgen Habermas, and Will Kymlicka (pp. 78–86), also depend on this same reliance on the "supracultural universal" of coherence, and indeed on the panoply of "universals" relevant to the criticism and defense of scholarly theses and claims. For example, Fish provides arguments against the views of those three worthies, and for his own thesis that "no one could possibly *be* a multiculturalist in any interesting and coherent sense." In so arguing, Fish is relying upon all the "universals" relevant to academic argumentation and disputation, and he is engaged in the project of establishing that his positive thesis, and his arguments in support of that thesis and against the theses of his opponents, are stronger, better justified, and more likely to be correct than the theses and arguments of those opponents. And such quality cannot, for him, be something to be judged solely from his own "uniculturalist" (p. 75) point of view, for going "uniculturalist" at this point results in a standoff: Fish's arguments might be stronger from *his* point of view, but Gutmann's, Habermas' and Kymlicka's will be stronger from *their* points of view. This result is not compatible with Fish's strenuous efforts to establish his view as correct (or at least better justified than theirs), and theirs as incorrect (or at least not as well justified as his). The lesson: again, "supracultural universals" are not something that *any* parties to this (or any other genuine) dispute can do without (Siegel 1999a, 199b).

Fish attempts to deflect this line of criticism by resisting the move of containing fundamental disagreements "to matters that can be debated within the decorums of Enlightenment rationalism"; he argues that "fundamental" disagreements, i.e., conflicts between "deeply antithetical positions" of the sort that characterize "disagreements between groups that want not to talk to one another but to exterminate one another" (p. 79), cannot be so contained. I have already suggested that advocates of the coherent multiculturalist position outlined above need not and ought not extend their multiculturalist tolerance to groups (or their cultures) that deny it to others. But whether or not Fish is correct that certain "fundamental" disagreements, like that concerning (his example of) abortion, cannot fruitfully be rationally or intellectually addressed, it is clear that his own disputes with Gutmann, Habermas, and Kymlicka *can* be so addressed. So this line of deflection does not succeed.[18]

If the arguments to this point are on target, it is a mistake to think that multiculturalism—that is, the coherent version of it formulated above, not the incoherent version rightly criticized by Fish—is incompatible with "supracultural universals." What about the particular "supracultural universal" with which we began? What should the coherent multiculturalist say about *rationality*?

4. The Case for "Divergent Rationality"

Many authors conceive of rationality as specific (or relative) to particular cultures. Consider, for example, the following passages from the science education scholar Masakata Ogawa (1995), discussing the work of the historian and philosopher of science Yehuda Elkana:

> Elkana claims that every culture has its science and adds: "By science, I mean a rational (i.e. purposeful, good, directed) explanation of the physical world surrounding man" (Elkana, 1971, p. 1437).... I agree that every culture has its own science and I shall refer to the science in a certain culture as its "indigenous science." (Ogawa 1995, p. 585)

> In Elkana's definition of science mentioned above, you can find the word "rational." I shall claim that this rationality never means Western modern rationality alone. It is also possible to view rationality in a relativistic perspective. This idea may be difficult for most Western science educators to accept, because they are so accustomed to regarding Western modern rationality as *the* rationality. (p. 586, emphasis in original)

In discussing the philosopher Hajime Nakamura (1964), Ogawa writes:

> Although the Chinese seem to be indifferent to logical exactitude and in fact have never developed formal logic, to be indifferent to rules of formal logic is not necessarily to be irrational. And, he [Nakamura] insists that if rational means thinking in a practical utilitarian way, then it is the Chinese rather than Westerners who are far more rationalistic. Such a stance toward rationality supports the idea of "relativization of rationality." (p. 587)

> I shall postulate that each indigenous science as well as Western modern science is accompanied by its respective rationality. (p. 588)

Ogawa is, of course, not the only writer to claim that rationality varies with culture. Fish himself seems to be partial to the thesis that rationality varies from culture to culture: on his view, a strong multiculturalist "will want to accord a *deep* respect to all cultures at their core, for he believes that each has the right to form its own identity and nourish *its own sense of what is rational*" (p. 73, second emphasis added); he writes as well that "if rationality is always differential, always an engine of exclusion and boundary-making, the opposition is never between the rational and the irrational, but between *opposing rationalities*, each of which is equally, but differently, intolerant" (p. 82, emphasis added). Citations could here be readily multiplied; the view that rationality is culturally or otherwise variable is not uncommon in contemporary scholarly discussion.

But the argument I want to consider here is that offered by the anthropologist Richard Shweder, who argues on both conceptual and anthropological grounds that rationality is indeed culture-specific. Shweder's paper is wide-ranging and ambitious, arguing for the development of "[a] 'science of subjectivity' [that] requires a broadened conception of rationality" (1986, p. 178). I cannot here treat all the many issues addressed by Shweder's paper,[19] but instead concentrate on his argument for what he calls *divergent rationality*.[20] I quote Shweder at length to give the full flavor of his challenging and engaging case:

> I think what we have come to realize is that if rational thought is restricted to inductive and deductive logic, we will have very little of a rational sort to say to each other. No presuppositions. No analogies. No semantic or pragmatic implications.... Yet if rational thought requires a "third sort" of logic or a nonlogical necessity, it is not the kind of constraint that anchors us to a unitary external world of objects. It is more likely the kind of thing that makes it possible for two Marxists, two psychoanalysts, two radical behaviorists, two Muslim fundamentalists to have rational discussions within their respective versions of reality but not across them. Rationality seems to have that peculiar bounded quality; it requires deductive and inductive logic, but deductive and inductive reasoning goes on within the framework of a third sort of logic that is bound to something neither uniform nor unitary. What we seem to need is a concept of divergent rationality.

> In defining the concept of "divergent rationality," it is useful to consider a minitaxonomy of the processes underlying subjective experience. These processes can be grouped in a rough-and-ready way into those that are rational, nonrational, and irrational. A rational process is a self-regulating process controlled by, or at least guided by, impersonal criteria, reason and evidence. It can be distinguished, on the one hand, from nonrational processes, where reason and evidence are irrelevant to subjective experience. The processes that account for taste preferences, likes or dislikes in food are prototypical examples of nonrational processes. On the other hand, rational processes can be distinguished from irrational processes, where there is a breakdown or degradation of the capacities that support rationality. Examples from our own culture

include the loss of voluntary control, the failure to distinguish self from other or to discriminate past, present and future.

Some rational processes are universally distributed across our species. As far as we know, all peoples respect certain elementary logical principles (negation, the law of the excluded middle) and adopt certain common patterns of hypothetical reasoning, means-ends analysis, causal analysis, and experimental reasoning. Things that vary together are connected by the human mind. So are things that are contiguous in space and time, and so on.

At the same time, there are certain rational processes that are not universal. These include, for example, the presuppositions and premises from which a person reasons; the metaphors, analogies, and models used for generating explanations; the categories or classifications used for partitioning objects and events into kinds; and the types of evidence that are viewed as authoritative—intuition, introspection, external observation, meditation, scriptural evidence, evidence from seers, monks, prophets, or elders. The version of reality we construct is a product of both the universal and the nonuniversal rational processes, but it is because not all rational processes are universal that we need a concept of divergent rationality.

For example, there are several hundred million people in that "ideological region" known as South Asia who believe in the transmigration of the soul and the continuity of identity across lifetimes (see Shweder 1985). Let us try to step inside their world for a moment. Perhaps one reason for the near universal acceptance of the idea of the soul is that it helps conceptualize the intuitive experience of what we in our secular culture call the "self," that direct contact we all have with our own "observing ego." In South Asia, among Hindus, that observing ego is conceptualized as a soul or spirit, and all sorts of searching questions are asked about where it came from, where it's going, and why it is now occupying the body it happens to occupy (Sivananda 1979). It is at this point in the reflective process that the concept of a reincarnating soul is postulated to exist behind or within experience, and the concept is used to explain or make sense of various facts of life.... The explanation by reference to reincarnation is especially powerful for those who are willing to accept as evidence the pervasive intuitive experience of one's own observing ego and for those who have already adopted a conceptual reference point from which souls exist, for whom reincarnation and the transmission of prior experiences across lifetimes is at least a theoretical possibility.... For the believer, the concept of reincarnation is not without explanatory appeal, and within certain communities in South Asia, rationality and objectivity are not inconsistent with its use. (Shweder 1986, pp. 180–182)

This is a powerful and suggestive passage. Nevertheless, despite its strengths, in the end Shweder's case for "divergent rationality" does not succeed—or at least, so I argue next.

There are several preliminary points to make concerning the claims articulated in the cited passage. Consider, first, the claim that "rational thought" is such that "rational discussions" are possible "within . . . versions of reality but not across them." Is it correct that two Marxists, psychoanalysts, radical behaviorists, or Muslim fundamentalists can converse rationally with each other but not with others? This seems clearly incorrect, given the many well-known academic conversations involving Marxists and liberals, behaviorists and Freudians, etc. Shweder's own discussion seems to be an example of the very sort of rational discussion across "versions of reality" about which he suggests that rational thought cannot engage: a nonmember of the "'ideological region' known as South Asia" engaging with interested others, including members of that "ideological region," concerning the rationality of the "ideology" of that region. I shall say more about this example below. For now, the point to note is that it is, at a minimum, *controversial* (and so in need of further defense) that rational thought is limited to, and rational discussions engaged in only within, particular "versions of reality."

Consider next Shweder's discussion of rationality in terms of *processes*. Notice, first, that most of the items on Shweder's list of non-universal rational processes—"the *presuppositions* and *premises* from which a person reasons; the *metaphors, analogies,* and *models* used for generating explanations; the *categories* or *classifications* used for portioning objects and events into kinds; and the *types of evidence* that are viewed as authoritative" (p. 181, emphases added)—are not processes at all. Rather, they are various sorts of "cognitive entities" that play a variety of roles in a variety of processes of reasoning and explanation.

It is also important to distinguish the rationality of a process from that of the product of that process. When a particular reasoning or belief-forming process results in some particular belief, questions about rationality typically involve the status of the belief rather than the process that gave rise to it. Suppose I come to believe that Cheney intentionally shot Whittington, that evolutionary theory provides a better explanation of the variety of shapes of finch beaks in a particular geographical region than does "intelligent design," or that my soul, i.e., the soul currently inhabiting my present body, inhabited the body of a Scottish distiller of illicit Campbeltown whisky eight generations ago. Questions about the rationality of such beliefs involve not the processes by which they arose or are maintained, but the evidential or probative support they enjoy. Of course, we can and do ask questions about the *reliability* of such processes, and advocates of the "externalist" view of epistemic justification called *reliabilism* analyze such justification in terms of such reliability: to oversimplify, on this view, a belief's justificatory status is a function of the reliability of the process that produced it, where "reliability" is in turn understood in terms of the ratio of the production of true to false beliefs. Pursuing this theory and attendant issues would take us far from our present topic.[21] Still, we can and should say here that the rationality of a belief is quite a different matter than the reliability of the process that produced it; that the relationship between such reliability and the rationality of that process—assuming that it makes sense to speak about the "rationality," as opposed to the reliability, of such processes—is far from clear; and that, as far as rationality is concerned, it is the belief and the evidence for/against it, rather than the process, that is key.[22]

It is equally important to be clear about the character of the relevant diversity pointed to in Shweder's claim that rationality is divergent or, as he also puts it, that "rationality is compatible with diversity" (Shweder 1986, p. 191). There are clear and innocuous senses in which rationality is indeed compatible with diversity, other than the sense for which Shweder argues. One obvious way that rationality diverges involves access to evidence. If you have very strong evidence that I lack that Cheney intentionally shot Whittington, then your belief to that effect may well be rational, yet mine not. Here the divergence is a straightforward consequence of the differences in our available evidence sets. Similarly, your belief in an esoteric logical or mathematical claim may be rational, while my belief in that same claim is not, if you can follow the proof but I cannot. Here too rationality diverges in the sense that your belief that p is rational but mine is not. But this sort of divergence is epistemologically innocuous and not the sort for which Shweder argues. These are cases in which rationality diverges due to differences in access to, possession of, or ability to appreciate the probative force of relevant evidence.[23] It does not in such cases diverge along cultural lines; nor is multiculturalism implicated in such divergence.

It should also be noted that the "rational processes that are not universal" mentioned in the cited passage themselves admit of rational evaluation, and so it is unclear that we should grant at the outset that they are in fact *rational* processes. For example, not all presuppositions and premises are rational: some are, others not. The same can be said for the other items on Shweder's list, such as analogies, category and classification schemes, types of evidence deemed authoritative, etc. This is not a point about universality. Nor does it involve the idea, questioned above, that such things as premises and presuppositions are rightly thought of as processes. Rather, the point is just that all these items can be subjected to critical scrutiny, and evaluated on a variety of dimensions, including those related to rationality, and found wanting—in which case it seems unwarranted to regard them as "automatically" rational, however non-universal they might be.

Finally, it is worth noting that while Shweder's discussion focuses on *explanation* and "explanatory appeal," the relations between these and rationality are far from clear. For example, "intelligent design" appears to have a significant amount of explanatory appeal to many people, although it manifestly fails to explain particular biological phenomena. Similarly, while we should grant Shweder's claim that some explanations have appeal in some "ideological regions" but not others—a good example of which is explanation in terms of reincarnation and the transmigration of souls—it is unclear what if anything follows concerning either the explanatory force or the rationality of such explanations. To put the point tendentiously: explanatory *appeal* is one thing, explanatory *power* quite another, and the *rational status* of a given explanation yet another (although the latter two are presumably importantly related). Moreover, our *taking* something to be a good explanation is one thing; its *being* a good explanation is quite another. This is not the place to engage in a systematic discussion of the character and vicissitudes of philosophical theories of explanation. Still, we should be wary of granting without further consideration Shweder's claims about explanation, and especially his apparent view of the relation between explanation and rationality. Matters are not so straightforward here as Shweder's remarks suggest.[24]

These several considerations might show that Shweder's argument for the thesis that rationality is divergent is unsuccessful. But they do not by themselves establish that that thesis is false, or otherwise problematic. I turn next to the task of offering an argument to that effect.[25]

5. Is Rationality Divergent?

Suppose that we are justified in thinking that rationality is indeed divergent, for the reasons that Shweder offers. If so, those reasons provide justification for that thesis—that is, they are good reasons, sufficient in quantity and quality to justify the thesis that rationality is divergent. Call the latter "The Thesis":

The Thesis: Rationality is divergent.

We are supposing that *The Thesis* is justified on the basis of the reasons offered by Shweder (or, alternatively, that we are justified in so believing[26]). Call this "The Claim":

The Claim: *The Thesis* is justified on the basis of Shweder's reasons.

From what "rationality"—or, perhaps better, perspective involving rationality— might *The Claim* be established? Does the advocate of *The Claim* hold that

The Claim is correct and so *The Thesis* justified or rendered rational only in some "ideological regions" but not others; or rather that *The Claim* is correct, and *The Thesis* rational, *universally*, i.e., across all such regions, or independently of region? Here the defender of *The Claim* faces a choice: she can hold that *The Claim* is correct either in some particular (set of) "ideological region(s)," i.e., from the perspective of some particular and "divergent" rationality, or rather from the perspective of a nondivergent, "supracultural," universal (perspective concerning) rationality. If she chooses the first, her defense is limited in a way that she herself should find unsatisfying, since she would, in so choosing, render her claim far less applicable and so interesting than it otherwise would be. After all, if she holds that *The Claim* is correct only within some particular ideological region, she thereby grants that it might nevertheless be incorrect in other such regions. Presumably, Shweder himself would not be satisfied with this result: while on his view the belief in reincarnation might be rational in the ideological region of South Asia but non- or irrational in the ideological region of (say) North America, his argument for *The Thesis* seems clearly intended to persuade anthropologists, philosophers, and others from both these regions. It would be disappointing, from his own point of view, if *The Claim* could be judged to be correct, and *The Thesis* justified, only within particular such regions. In this case anthropology and philosophy themselves would have to be understood to be "ideologically regionalized" in a way that would vitiate his case, and his project.

The alternative is to regard *The Claim* as correct nondivergently, i.e., independently of ideological region. But this seems clearly enough to require (or be equivalent to) the invocation of a "supracultural," universal (perspective concerning) rationality, according to which *The Thesis*' truth and the epistemic ability of the reasons for thinking it true (referred to in *The Claim*) to justify or render it rational are so independent. That is, to avoid the problem just noted, the defender of *The Thesis* must defend it from a position or perspective that transcends particular "ideological regions." But this is just to say that "rationality itself"—at least the rationality involved in sanctioning both *The Thesis* and *The Claim*—is not divergent.[27]

6. Conclusions

Multiculturalism can and should be understood in a way that renders it, and its advocacy, coherent. So understood, it is primarily a moral and/or social/political matter, rather than an epistemological one, and its criticism and defense depends upon the epistemological presuppositions that make the criticism and defense of all such claims (including those presuppositions themselves) possible.

We should be doubtful of the claims that cultures have their own rationalities, that rationality is relative to culture, and that a commitment to multiculturalism requires a commitment to any such claims about rationality. Cultures are diverse and divergent, but rationality is not. And in any case, such claims as these concerning multiculturalism and rationality cannot themselves be rationally established if it is.[28]

Notes

1. For discussion see Siegel 1992.
2. The history of the development of probability theory is full of such examples. See Hacking 1975, esp. chs. 6–7.
3. For discussion and references, see Siegel 2001.
4. Other, more obvious examples of group differences with respect to judgments of rationality involve moral and social/political matters. Some groups regard particular practices—abortion, infanticide, torture, enslavement, and the like—to be not just immoral but irrational as well, while other groups, in particular those who engage in such practices, judge them to be unproblematic as far as rationality is concerned.
5. For example, Barry Barnes and David Bloor (1982, p. 39) speak of the "received culture of epistemologists."
6. Although I won't try to settle the matter here, I have great sympathy with Seyla Benhabib's (2002, pp. ix, 4, 24–6, and *passim*) conception of cultures as hybrid, multifaceted, fluid, porous, polyvocal, interdependent, and mutually influential, and (as will be evident below) with her view of the compatibility of multiculturalism and universalism (on which see also Sen 2000); and I applaud Pradeep Dhillon and J. Mark Halstead's criticism of "the assumption that cultures are hermetically sealed" (2003, p. 157).
7. And, according to Richard Nisbett (2003), some of them differ with respect to reasoning and cognition more generally. I cannot here undertake systematic consideration of Nisbett's challenging claims concerning differences between "Eastern" and "Western" thinking, but his discussion seems clearly enough to endorse the idea that judgments of rationality are culturally specific, at least insofar as "East" and "West" constitute cultures. Whether or not they lend credence to the further idea that rationality itself is culturally specific I must leave for another occasion.
8. As I hope will become clear, as I use the term, *rationality* is a matter of believing, judging, and acting on the basis of *reasons* and *evidence* whose probative force is properly assessed and whose influence on belief, judgment, and action reflects that assessment. As such it is at bottom an *epistemological* notion. (See Siegel 1987, 1988, 1997) Many authors use "rationality" and "reason" (sometimes with upper case R's) in radically different ways. Cynthia Willett writes of "European Reason" in Hegelian spirit; here "Reason" is understood in metaphysical, historical, cultural, economic, and emancipatory terms (Willett 1998a, pp. 10–11). Lucius Outlaw Jr. similarly writes (critically) of "the universality of a singular rationality unfolding in the historical *telos* of the leading nations of the white race of Europe" (Outlaw 1998, p. 389, emphasis in original). Scott L. Pratt defends the Haudenosaunee (Iroquois) tradition's equation of rational thinking and responsible thinking, and contrasts "European conceptions of rationality as a process of acquisition" with the Haudenosaunee view, according to which "'responsible thinking' or rationality … may be understood as a process of conversation and responsive action" (Pratt 1998, p. 401). While I have some sympathy with many such efforts, I mention them here just to make clear that I do not use the central terms *rationality* and *reason* as these authors do. There are, of course, many important challenges to the epistemological conception of rationality that I favor, launched from a variety of ("radical" [see Gottlieb 1993], feminist, postmodernist) philosophical perspectives that I cannot consider here. For consideration of some of them see Siegel 1997.
9. Many of them are documented in Siegel 1999b, pp. 387–389, and references therein.

10. I here set aside questions concerning the meaning of "universal truth" and the character of such truths.
11. I argue for this view of the matter in Siegel 1999b.
12. All references to Fish below are to this article.
13. It is perhaps unfortunate that Fish's examples here are limited to the US scene, but it is clear that a broader range of examples would work just as well to illustrate his point.
14. A similar and, in my view, compelling analysis, in terms of the "politics of difference," is offered in Callan 1998 (see esp. p. 150). Henry Louis Gates Jr. (1994, p. 212) makes a related point in terms of the unavoidability of "universalizing theory." See also Dhillon and Halstead's discussion of "deep humanism" (2003, pp. 159–161), Caws 1994, esp. pp. 371–372 and 379–380, and Siegel 1997, chs. 9–12.
15. This characterization is taken from Siegel 1999b, p. 389. The view of multiculturalism briefly defended here is treated at much greater length in this article and the other pieces referred to therein.
16. Indeed, multiculturalism itself constitutes just such a "supracultural universal." At least, so I argue in Siegel 1999b.
17. Or more simply, *logic*. Let MC = (strong) multiculturalism; A = the first horn of Fish's dilemma; B = the second horn. Fish's argument has the straightforward logical form:
    1. If MC, then either A or B.
    2. If A, then not-MC.
    3. If B, then not-MC.
    4. Therefore, If MC, then either not-MC or not-MC.
    5. Therefore, If MC, then not-MC.
    6. Therefore, not-MC.
    (I leave out the assumed premises "Either MC or not-MC," "If either not-MC or not-MC, then not-MC," and "If not-MC, then not-MC," which are, strictly speaking, required for the argument as formulated to go through. I should also note that the argument can also be reconstructed as a *reductio*; so reconstructed, the assumption of MC leads to a contradiction.) So, insofar as he takes his argument to be compelling, Fish is himself committed to at least the claim that logic is a "supracultural universal." My critique takes issue not with the logic of the argument, but with the first premise and the notion of multiculturalism it assumes. On my preferred, more restricted account of that notion, that premise is false.
18. It is also worth pointing out that Fish's characterization of "fundamental disagreements" is problematic. As Fish puts it, "In an intellectual disagreement the parties can talk to one another because they share a set of basic assumptions; but in a fundamental disagreement, basic assumptions are precisely what is in dispute. Either you can have 'fundamental' or you can have 'intellectual,' but you can't have both; and if … you privilege 'intellectual,' you have not honored the level of fundamental disagreement but evaded it" (p. 79). This way of characterizing fundamental disagreements renders them intellectually irresolvable by stipulation. But parties to such disagreements always share *some* "basic assumptions"; if they don't, it is unclear why such situations are rightly characterized as *disagreements*. In any case, whether the parties to actual disagreements share any basic assumptions, and whether their disagreements can be intellectually resolved, cannot be resolved in so neat, stipulative, and a priori a way.
19. I particularly recommend Shweder's criticisms of a sharp objective/subjective distinction and his related discussions of ontology, especially Goodman's "irrealism."
20. While my basic argument against "divergent" rationality (offered in section 5 below) is not dependent on Shweder's case for it, his is the most plausible and sympathetic discussion of it of which I am aware, which is why I concentrate on that case here.
21. For elementary but nevertheless sophisticated "dueling essays" on the internalism/externalism controversy, and references to Alvin Goldman's pioneering essays on reliabilism, see Feldman 2005 and Greco 2005. For discussion of related issues concerning naturalism and instrumental rationality, see Siegel 1996.
22. I grant, of course, that we do sometimes criticize such processes as irrational; for example, we would normally deem the processes of forming beliefs by choosing randomly or

arbitrarily from among a given set of alternative candidate beliefs, choosing the candidate with the smallest number of letters (in English), or consulting the Ouija board, as irrational. But it seems clear that we regard such processes as irrational because we have no reason to think that beliefs so formed will enjoy, because so formed, any more evidential or probative support than alternative beliefs (including the negations of the targeted beliefs) formed by either those same or other processes.

23. There are also, of course, cases in which "reasonable people may differ" concerning the proper evaluation of candidate pieces of evidence. I leave the difficult issues involved in these sorts of cases aside here.
24. Thanks to Graham Haydon for reminding me of this cluster of problems concerning explanation and helping me to see the need to note it here.
25. Thanks to Michael Hand for clarifying the need to distinguish the preceding remarks from the argument that immediately follows.
26. The distinction between a belief/claim/sentence/proposition's being justified, on the one hand, and our being justified in so believing, on the other hand, is epistemologically fundamental. But it does not, as far as I can see, affect the present point, so I ignore it here.
27. As noted earlier, Shweder holds that rationality is not completely divergent; that some rational processes are universal. But that concession to universality is not sufficient to avoid the problem just rehearsed. For further consideration of such "transcendental" arguments concerning rationality, see Siegel 1987, 1988, and 1997. For a more empirical and textual argument to the same conclusion, see Sen 2000, especially pp. 36–37.

    I trust it is clear that I am *not* arguing that the denizens of the "ideological region" of South Asia are irrational—their beliefs in transmigration and reincarnation may well be rational. I am arguing, rather, that if those beliefs are rational, they are so in the same (ideological region-independent) sense that all rational beliefs are rational.
28. Versions of this paper were presented at the University of London, Institute of Education in October 2005, and at Hong Kong University and the annual Philosophy of Education Society of Australasia conference at the Hong Kong Institute of Education in November 2005. I am grateful to Mark Mason for inviting my participation in the two Hong Kong presentations, to my gracious PESA and HKIE hosts on those occasions, and to the audience members at all three presentations for their comments and criticisms. Thanks also to an anonymous reviewer and especially to Randy Curren for insightful criticisms and suggestions for improvement.

References

Barnes, B., and D. Bloor. (1982). "Relativism, Rationalism and the Sociology of Knowledge." In M. Hollis and D. Lukes (eds.), *Rationality and Relativism* (pp. 21–47). Cambridge, MA: MIT Press.

Benhabib, S. (2002). *The Claims of Culture: Equality and Diversity in the Global Era*. Princeton, NJ: Princeton University Press.

Callan, E. (1998). "The Politics of Difference and Common Education." In D. Carr (ed.), *Education, Knowledge and Truth: Beyond the Postmodern Impasse* (pp. 145–158). London: Routledge.

Caws, P. (1994). "Identity: Cultural, Transcultural, and Multicultural." In Goldberg 1994, pp. 371–387.

Coppée, H. (1874). *Elements of Logic*. Rev ed. Philadelphia: J. H. Butler & Company.

Dhillon, P. A., and M. Halstead. (2003). "Multicultural Education." In N. Blake, P. Smeyers, R. Smith, and P. Standish (eds.), *The Blackwell Guide to the Philosophy of Education* (pp. 146–161). Oxford: Blackwell.

Elkana, Y. (1971). "The Problem of Knowledge." *Studium Generale* 24: 1426–1439.

Feldman, R. (2005). "Justification Is Internal." In M. Steup and E. Sosa (eds.), *Contemporary Debates in Epistemology* (pp. 270–284). Oxford: Blackwell.

Fish, S. (1998). "Boutique Multiculturalism." In Melzer, Weinberger, and Zinman 1998, pp. 69–88. Originally appeared as "Boutique Multiculturalism, or Why Liberals Are Incapable of Thinking about Hate Speech." *Critical Inquiry* 23.2 (Winter 1997): 378–395.

Gates, H. L., Jr. (1994). "Good-Bye, Columbus? Notes on the Culture of Criticism." In Goldberg 1994, pp. 203–217. Originally published in *American Literary History* 3.4 (1991): 711–727.

Goldberg, D. T. (ed.). (1994). *Multiculturalism: A Critical Reader*. Oxford: Blackwell.

Gottlieb, R. S. (ed.). (1993). *Radical Philosophy: Tradition, Counter-Tradition, Politics*. Philadelphia: Temple University Press.

Greco, J. (2005). "Justification Is Not Internal." In M. Steup and E. Sosa (eds.), *Contemporary Debates in Epistemology* (pp. 257–270). Oxford: Blackwell.

Hacking, I. (1975). *The Emergence of Probability*. Cambridge: Cambridge University Press.

Melzer, A. M., J. Weinberger, and M. R. Zinman (eds.). (1998). *Multiculturalism and American Democracy*. Lawrence: University Press of Kansas.

Nakamura, H. (1964). *Ways of Thinking of Eastern Peoples: India—China—Tibet—Japan*. Honolulu, HI: East-West Center Press.

Nisbett, R. E. (2003). *The Geography of Thought: How Asians and Westerners Think Differently ... and Why*. New York: Free Press.

Ogawa, M. (1995). "Science Education in a Multiscience Perspective." *Science Education* 79.5: 583–593.

Outlaw, L., Jr. (1998). "'Multiculturalism,' Citizenship, Education, and American Liberal Democracy." In Willett 1998b, pp. 382–397.

Pratt, S. L. (1998). "Ceremony and Rationality in the Haudenosaunee Tradition." In Willett 1998b, pp. 401–421.

Sen, A. (2000). "East and West: The Reach of Reason." *New York Review of Books* 47 (July 20): 33–38.

Shweder, R. A. (1985). "Menstrual Pollution, Soul Loss, and the Comparative Study of Emotions." In A. Kleinman and B. Good (eds.), *Culture and Depression: Studies in the Anthropology and Cross-Cultural Psychiatry of Affect and Disorder* (pp. 182–215). Berkeley: University of California Press.

Shweder, R. A. (1986). "Divergent Rationalities." In D. W. Fiske and R. A. Shweder (eds.), *Metatheory in Social Science: Pluralisms and Subjectivities* (pp. 163–196). Chicago: University of Chicago Press.

Siegel, H. (1987). *Relativism Refuted: A Critique of Contemporary Epistemological Relativism*. Dordrecht, The Netherlands: Kluwer/Springer.

Siegel, H. (1988). *Educating Reason: Rationality, Critical Thinking, and Education*. London: Routledge.

Siegel, H. (1992). "Justification by Balance." *Philosophy and Phenomenological Research* 52.1: 27–46.

Siegel, H. (1996). "Instrumental Rationality and Naturalized Philosophy of Science." *Philosophy of Science* 63.3: 116–124. Supplement (PSA 1996 Proceedings, Part 1).

Siegel, H. (1997). *Rationality Redeemed?: Further Dialogues on an Educational Ideal*. New York: Routledge.

Siegel, H. (1999a). "Argument Quality and Cultural Difference." *Argumentation* 13.2: 183–201.

Siegel, H. (1999b). "Multiculturalism and the Possibility of Transcultural Educational and Philosophical Ideals." *Philosophy* 74: 387–409.

Siegel, H. (2001). "Incommensurability, Rationality and Relativism: In Science, Culture, and Science Education." In P. Hoyningen-Huene and H. Sankey (eds.), *Incommensurability and Related Matters* (pp. 207–224). Dordrecht, The Netherlands: Kluwer/Springer.

Sivananda, Swami. (1979). *What Becomes of the Soul after Death?* Shivanandanagar, India: Divine Life Society.

Stich, S. P., and Nisbett, R. E. (1980). "Justification and the Psychology of Human Reasoning." *Philosophy of Science* 47. 2: 188–202.

Willett, C. (1998a). "Introduction." In Willett 1998b, pp. 1–15.

Willett, C. (ed.). (1998b). *Theorizing Multiculturalism: A Guide to the Current Debate*. Oxford: Blackwell.

16

Epistemological Diversity and Educational Research

Much Ado about Nothing Much?

1. Introduction

Research in education, and thus the training of future educational researchers in graduate schools of education, is often said to require attention to *epistemological diversity*. Future researchers ought, it is claimed, to be familiar with many different ways of knowing, alternative methods of inquiry, diverse epistemological perspectives, and distinct cultural or group epistemologies.

An impressive range of scholars defend the idea that different groups and/or cultures have their own distinct epistemologies. For example, Dolores Delgado Bernal, in advancing a "Chicana feminist epistemological framework," argues that

> [e]pistemological concerns in schools are inseparable from cultural hegemonic domination in educational research.... Therefore, "endarkened" feminist epistemologies are crucial, as they speak to the failures of traditional patriarchal and liberal educational scholarship and examine the intersection of race, class, gender, and sexuality. (Bernal 1998, p. 556)

James Scheurich and Michelle Young report that

> [r]espected scholars of color have suggested ... that the epistemologies we typically use in educational research may be racially biased. They have argued that our epistemologies—not our use of them, but the epistemologies themselves—are racially biased ways of knowing, implicitly proposing, thus, a new category of racism that could be labeled *epistemological racism*. (Scheurich and Young, 1997, p. 4, emphasis in original)

Molefi Kete Asante, discussing the "quest for truth in the Afrocentric enterprise," argues that in that enterprise,

> language, myth, ancestral memory, dance-music-art, and science provide the sources of knowledge, the canons of proof and the structures of truth. (Asante, 1990, p. 10)

In these passages the clear suggestion is that cultural or group membership has epistemological consequences, that culture impacts epistemology. But how epistemology might be so influenced is unclear. In this paper I will address some basic issues raised by this suggestion, in a way that emphasizes its relevance to educational research and the graduate education/training of future educational researchers. These issues are insightfully addressed in a 2001 symposium in the journal *Educational Researcher*,[1] which will serve as a touchstone in pursuing them. What ought we to say about such diversity? Ought we, as Lauren Jones Young suggests, "rethink and expand our conceptions of ways of knowing and modes of inquiry" (2001, p. 5)? If so, in what specific ways ought we to do this?

At first glance, the call to respect (and train future researchers to interact competently with) epistemological diversity seems as innocent and obvious as a call for researchers to be open-minded, broad-minded, and tolerant when dealing with unfamiliar practices and views concerning knowledge and inquiry. So understood, it captures the anti-dogmatic spirit of the Enlightenment and is uncontroversial. But advocates of epistemological diversity typically have more than this in mind. What more is not always clear, however. But if our efforts to make such diversity central to the graduate training of educational researchers are to be worthwhile, such clarity is required. In what follows, then, I will explore that notion in an effort to answer the following questions: What is "epistemological diversity"? What exactly is the *epistemological* dimension and significance of such diversity? Why is it important for educational researchers to be well trained with respect to it? In what specific ways ought we to "expand our conceptions of ways of knowing and modes of inquiry"? In answering these questions, I will suggest that the call for epistemological diversity is not, where justified, as radical or significant as it is often taken to be; and that, where it is radical or significant, it is, alas, not justified.

2. What Is "Epistemological Diversity"?

What does "epistemological diversity" mean? To what does the expression refer? What sort of diversity is at issue? The candidates for diversity include at least the following: beliefs and belief systems; research methodologies/methods of inquiry; research questions; researchers; cultures and "cultural epistemologies"; views of knowledge; ways of knowing; and "epistemologies," "epistemological assumptions," "epistemological premises," and "epistemological perspectives." Let us consider these candidates for/versions of epistemological diversity.

A. Beliefs/Belief Systems

Some prominent authors in the multicultural education arena use "knowledge" as a synonym for "belief," thus rendering "epistemological diversity" as a matter of systematic differences in belief. For example, James Banks writes,

> I am using knowledge in this article to mean the way a person explains or interprets reality.... My conceptualization of knowledge is broad and is used the way in which it is usually used in the sociology of knowledge literature to include ideas, values, and interpretations.... Although many complex factors influence the knowledge that is created by an individual or group, including the actuality of what occurred, the knowledge that people create is heavily influenced by their interpretations of their experiences and their positions within particular social, economic, and political systems and structures of a society. (Banks 1993, p. 5)

This sense of "epistemological diversity" is uncontroversial. Different people have different beliefs and systems of belief, to which they appeal in explaining and interpreting reality, and particular groups of people share belief systems that often differ in systematic ways from other such systems. For example, some extant belief systems hold that some natural phenomena are best explained in spiritual or supernatural terms, while other belief systems eschew such explanations, holding rather that legitimate explanations of natural phenomena must be couched in naturalistic terms.[2] Insofar as "epistemological diversity" refers to diversity of beliefs and belief systems, it is uncontroversial. No one disputes the diversity of beliefs believed by the wide range of epistemic agents (i.e., believers), and Banks is surely correct that the factors that give rise to particular beliefs, and so explanations and interpretations of reality, include not just "the actuality of what occurred," but also believers' "interpretations of their experiences and their positions within particular social, economic, and political systems and structures of a society."

Philosophers do not typically understand "epistemology" in this way, taking it to refer rather to theories of *knowledge* (or more broadly, to that area of philosophy that takes such theories, and the issues they address, as its subject matter). There is no need to argue here about which meaning of "epistemology"—that is, as referring to beliefs, or to theories of knowledge or a central area of philosophy—is more appropriate. The main point to note is that if "epistemological diversity" is taken to refer to alternative beliefs or belief systems, the phenomenon in question is uncontroversial, since all are agreed that beliefs/belief systems do indeed differ.[3]

B. Research Methodologies/Methods of Inquiry

It is also widely agreed that researchers inquire in many different ways, that they use a wide variety of different methods or techniques as they go about their work. Some biologists rely upon naked-eye observation, others use microscopes. Some physicists use tunneling electron microscopes, others use infrared telescopes. Some sociologists and anthropologists rely upon sophisticated statistical techniques, others endeavor to gain a more qualitative understanding of their subjects. This sort of "technique diversity" characterizes natural and social scientific research generally. As is well known, educational research is also diverse in this way, as scholars often conceive of themselves as either "quantitative" or "qualitative" researchers. Within these two broad categories, there is a wide variety of more specific approaches.[4]

This sort of methodological diversity is both undeniable and uncontroversial. If we (educational researchers) want to discover the attitudes of a given population toward a proposed revision of school boundaries, we have to ask, by way of survey, interview, or the like. If we want to predict the consequences of those attitudes for the success of the proposal, we cannot rely solely on those surveys or interviews, but also have to consider (among other things) patterns of attitudes and outcomes in earlier, similar events. If we want to predict the likely effects of a proposed hot lunch program on student learning in a given student population, we have to consider a broad range of information, which will have to be gathered, processed, and manipulated in a variety of (statistical and other) ways. If we want to estimate the probability of success of a new approach to teaching reading on the development of student reading ability, we have to engage in (among other things) careful observation and data collection, and sophisticated statistical manipulation of that data. If we want to understand differences in different local communities' understandings of the meaning and significance of a new policy concerning, e.g., admissions requirements for a newly designed arts or science magnet school, we have to engage in systematic, comparative ethnographic study of the interpretations of that policy held by the various members of those communities. And so on. The general thesis that there are many legitimate ways to conduct research is unexceptionable.[5]

Notice that this *methodological pluralism* is, on the whole, benign. While it grants that there are many ways in which research can legitimately be conducted, it does not follow from it that all research efforts are equally legitimate or that any approach to (or product of) research is as good as any other. That is, methodological *pluralism* does not entail either methodological *skepticism* or methodological *relativism*. This is a good thing for all those concerned with the education of educational researchers. For such skepticism or relativism would render graduate education in educational research pointless. What would we teach future researchers, how would we train them, if no ways of conducting research could yield knowledge or justified belief (skepticism), or if all ways of conducting research, and so the fruits of all research, were equally legitimate or good (relativism)? Worse, what would be the point of such long and arduous graduate education if the results of all research were either worthless or equally legitimate? In these circumstances, there would be no point in conducting research, since any result would either be worthless or stand on an equal epistemological footing with any alternative result.[6]

Of course, if we can distinguish between legitimate and illegitimate research, or between better and worse research, we must do so with reference to relevant *criteria* in accordance with which such discriminations of quality or legitimacy can be made. A set of key epistemological questions concerning research involves such criteria; central among these questions are: What are these criteria? How are they themselves legitimated or justified? Do they apply to all instances or types of research equally? We shall return to these questions, which are among those routinely addressed by epistemologists, below.

C. Research Questions

This sort of diversity is also uncontroversial. Just as researchers in different disciplines pursue many different, worthwhile research agendas, so do researchers within the same discipline. This is especially true of educational researchers, who pursue issues of many different sorts—from understanding the cognitive processes underlying learning to devising efficient and fair ways of organizing, administering, and funding schools and school systems; from innovative ways of promoting equal educational opportunities to effective ways of teaching reading and of enhancing student self-esteem; from understanding the nature, value, and legitimate demands of multiculturalism to determining the best ways to meet those demands. There is no special new kind of epistemological diversity introduced here.

Many scholars note the importance of culture/group membership in the determination of research questions actually pursued (and funded) or not. For example, Patricia Hill Collins writes,

> Because elite white men and their representatives control structures of knowledge and validation, white male interests pervade the thematic

content of traditional scholarship. As a result, Black women's experiences with work, family, motherhood, political activism, and sexual politics have routinely been distorted in or excluded from traditional academic discourse. (Collins 1990, p. 201)

James Banks similarly urges that

[t]he biographical journeys of researchers greatly influence their values, their research questions, and the knowledge they construct. (Banks 1998, p. 5; original emphasis deleted)

And Sandra Harding writes that

both "women's experiences" and "what women say" certainly are good places to begin generating research projects. (Harding 1990, p. 142)

While these citations include important differences, they are agreed that the research questions one asks, deems important, and pursues are influenced by one's cultural, racial, gender, etc. location. The point is undeniable, as (for example) the history of federal funding for breast cancer research in the United States makes clear (Braun 2003, p. S101). But that there are a wide variety of research questions that could be pursued, and that researchers' and funding agencies' decisions concerning research pursuits are so influenced, leaves open the further question of the epistemic status of the findings produced by and conclusions drawn from the results of research actually conducted. No special new kind of epistemological diversity is introduced by these important considerations concerning cultural and other influences on decisions concerning research agendas.

D. Researchers and Their Cultures

There is considerable, and increasing, diversity in the community of educational researchers (which is not to say that more wouldn't be better). Researchers differ in interests, education, temperament, curiosity, ambition, originality, beliefs, values, etc. In these respects, at least, diversity among researchers is much like diversity among people in general. Are there *epistemological* dimensions or ramifications of such diversity?

Many theorists have argued that specific sorts of diversity among researchers—in particular, diversity with respect to race, gender, sexual orientation, class, and the like—are indeed epistemologically significant. The inclusion in the educational research community of those whose groups have traditionally been the victims of exclusion or marginalization has brought new issues to the fore, and has provided new voices, approaches, and substantive and methodological presuppositions to the conversations in which both new and more familiar issues are addressed. That inclusion—of large numbers of nontraditional (i.e., not white, male, middle class, heterosexual, able-bodied) new and future researchers, who can be separated into distinct groups on the basis of such categories—has suggested to many that such groups can and should be distinguished on the basis of their respective epistemological orientations. For example, Young urges that graduate students in educational research doctoral programs "bring with them their own cultural histories and ways of knowing and being in the world" (2001, p. 4), and that,

> [i]n the same ways that we acknowledge epistemological diversity across practices of research, we also see a diversity of epistemology among the practitioners, the community groups, and the family members we and our students study. We need only look at our students to see how values and cultures influence the sense we make of our observations and the meanings that we give them. (pp. 4–5)

Aaron M. Pallas likewise suggests that "traditionally subordinated groups" have their own "epistemologies" (2001, p. 7).

While sympathetic toward the sociological point, my own situation as a member of the traditionally dominating group—white, male, middle class, heterosexual, able-bodied, and, more generally, privileged—leads me to doubt the idea that one's group significantly influences (let alone determines) one's epistemology, since the "bad guys," i.e., those in that dominating group, have a terrifically broad range of epistemological commitments and predilections. While I won't argue the case in any detail, the thesis that groups systematically share epistemological outlooks or presuppositions seems to me dubious. There is just too much within-group difference in epistemological orientation. Within my own group, advocates and critics can be found of more or less every epistemological stance yet articulated—as a casual glance at *The Journal of Philosophy, Philosophical Studies, The Philosophical Review, Philosophy and Phenomenological Research*, or any of the other leading philosophy journals that regularly publish important work in epistemology will reveal.[7]

But I think my dissent from the view here articulated by Young and Pallas hinges crucially on our respective understandings of the key terms of our claims. What exactly does it mean to say that the new voices in the educational research community provide that community with new "ways of knowing" or "epistemologies" or "epistemological perspectives"? What exactly is an *epistemology* or *epistemological perspective*, such that previously excluded individuals and groups bring new ones to the table?

E. Epistemologies/Epistemological Perspectives

The essays under discussion are, I think, obscure on just this crucial point. Young, for example, seems to equate "research methodology" and "epistemology," such that every different approach to research has, or amounts to, its own epistemology:

> Metz, for example, writes of the importance of researchers learning to "read each others' work across different kinds of research" and of researchers learning "to build on work from traditions other than the one in which they find their intellectual home base." Yet significant caveats to constructing such opportunities remain. For example, how many epistemologies should students encounter, which ones, at what point in the doctoral experience should these be introduced, and to what level of expertise should students be prepared? (Young 2001, p. 4)

In her paper (an earlier version of which Young here cites), Metz is clearly discussing alternative research methodologies—"deductive" vs. "inductive," quantitative vs. qualitative, those involving rules vs. those that don't, etc.—that Young here calls "epistemologies." As already noted, it is uncontroversial that there is a broad range of alternative ways of conducting educational research, i.e., different research methodologies. If this is what it means for educational research to involve different epistemologies, the existence of these differences is obvious and unproblematic. In this sense, making a fuss about "alternative epistemologies" is indeed much ado about nothing much. Here the question is not a deep philosophical one, but only the practical (although nonetheless difficult) one of the desirability of education for students' breadth versus depth: should their graduate education be such that they should become deeply competent in one research tradition, at the risk of narrowness; or should they rather be exposed to a broad range of research methodologies, at the risk of superficiality? This is the familiar "depth versus breadth" trade-off familiar to all fields. Insofar as "epistemological diversity" refers to the range of extant methodologies in use in the education research community, worrying about how to deal with it in the graduate education of future educational researchers is nothing new.

Similarly, Pallas engagingly speaks of "the cacophony of diverse epistemologies" (2001, p. 6). But his discussion makes clear that he does not mean by that phrase to refer to alternative research methodologies, but rather to the key epistemological assumptions underlying those methodological approaches.[8] He defines "epistemologies" as "beliefs about what counts as knowledge ..., what is evidence for a claim, and what counts as a warrant for that evidence" (p. 6). Noting the intimidating range of these present in contemporary educational research, Pallas addresses himself to "the consequences of this diversity" for educational research and for the education of future researchers. These consequences are far from trivial:

> Epistemologies are central to the production and consumption of educational research. Since epistemologies undergird all phases of the research process, engaging with epistemology is integral to learning the craft of research. Moreover, epistemologies shape scholars' abilities to apprehend and appreciate the research of others. Such an appreciation is a prerequisite for the scholarly conversations that signify a field's collective learning. (p. 6)

In light of this centrality of epistemology to the education of researchers and the conduct of research, and the diversity of epistemologies among communities of researchers, how should graduate education in educational research be conducted? Pallas' answer is eloquent and clear:

> If educational researchers cannot understand and engage with one another, both within and across at least some educational research communities, the enterprise is doomed to failure. Thus, to prevent a recurring pattern of epistemological single-mindedness, educational researchers will need to engage with multiple epistemological perspectives to the point that members of different communities of educational research practice can understand one another, despite, or perhaps through, their differences. Preparing novice educational researchers for such epistemological diversity is one of the most important things that the faculties of research universities can do. (p. 7)

How should this preparation for epistemological diversity be accomplished? Pallas analyzes the situation in terms of Etienne Wenger's (1998) notion of "community of practice," thus reformulating the problem of epistemological diversity into that of enabling graduate students to interact successfully across diverse communities of practice of educational research, since "the preparation of educational researchers largely takes place within local communities of research practice" (Pallas 2001, p. 9). Significantly, on Pallas' analysis, these local communities—several of which live side by side in graduate schools of education, the main sites of the education of future researchers—are united by their own epistemologies, and diverge from the others, which also have their own epistemologies, thus providing a model of epistemological diversity in graduate schools of education.[9] As Pallas puts it,

> Novices who are learning educational research through participation in a particular local community are destined to negotiate *the*

meaning of what counts as knowledge through interactions with others in the same community, as well as through exposure to reifications (e.g., books and articles), which are often interpreted in local terms. If there is a connection between community and epistemology, then a local community of research practice is not likely to reflect *within itself* a deep understanding of multiple epistemological perspectives. The more a newcomer is drawn toward the center of such a community, the less likely he/she is to develop a more variegated understanding of the epistemologies of educational research. This is largely because being drawn to a community's center is at odds with the possibility of being drawn into other communities whose practices are defined in different epistemological terms. A novice who, over time, deepens his or her understandings of educational research practice in the terms of a particular epistemology in a particular community—as we usually expect doctoral students to do—is unlikely to develop a first-hand feel for diverse epistemological framings of educational research. (p. 9, first emphasis added)

In other words, new students apprentice and experience "intense participation" (p. 9) in a community of research practice—e.g., the community of quantitative educational psychology, or of qualitative anthropologically oriented educational ethnography, etc.—and embrace the epistemology of that community of practice, while getting relatively little and only superficial exposure to the alternative epistemologies of other communities of practice. On the basis of this analysis of epistemological diversity in the graduate education of future educational researchers, Pallas offers several promising practical recommendations for the reform of that education, including (a) elevating the consideration of epistemology by both faculty and graduate students, (b) making the discussion of epistemology the responsibility of the entire faculty, (c) linking discussions of epistemology to the practice of educational research, (d) placing discussions of epistemology in historical context, (e) designing social spaces in which epistemological experimentation is safe and encouraged, and (f) acknowledging the inevitability that some doctoral students will not be deeply engaged in reflection concerning alternative epistemological perspectives (pp. 9–10). These suggestions are, I think, to be applauded.

3. Epistemology and Diversity: The Heart of the Matter

However, Pallas' suggestions, and his discussion more generally (as well as those of Young, Metz, and Page), treat epistemological diversity itself somewhat uncritically, as if the critical evaluation of these diverse epistemological perspectives is impossible, undesirable, or inappropriate. The idea seems to be that the many epistemologies available—those of diverse research traditions/communities of practice, and those of particular, traditionally subordinated social groups—are held by actual persons and groups, and therefore are not to be held up to the light of critical scrutiny. Rather, they are to be accepted at face value as legitimate, and integrated into the graduate study of future researchers. To champion epistemological diversity, apparently, is to strive to enable graduate students to understand and interact meaningfully with as many alternative epistemologies as they can manage.

Why think that the epistemologies of all such groups are worthy of curricular inclusion and the attention of all future researchers? The possibilities here seem to be three: criticizing the epistemology of a particular community of practice or subordinated group is either *epistemologically*, *morally*, or *pragmatically* suspect. The authors being considered here do not say this, but their discussions I think presume it. For consider: why is it important that we strive "to prevent a recurring pattern of epistemological single-mindedness" (Pallas 2001, p. 7) in our students? Presumably, because such "epistemological single-mindedness" is a bad thing; something to be deplored and avoided in our graduate students. But why? Presumably, because the many alternative epistemologies available and in use are, because in use, worthy of the serious consideration of graduate students/future researchers, whatever their own epistemological outlook might be. But why does the fact they are in use by some relevant group render these alternatives worthy of attention, or beyond critical rejection as unworthy of the attention of future researchers? Let us consider each possibility in turn.

A. Is It *Epistemologically* Suspect to Criticize the Epistemology of a Particular Community of Practice/Approach to Research/Subordinated Group?

At first blush it seems not, since the philosophical subdisciplines of epistemology and philosophy of science do just this. Courses in epistemology and philosophy of science routinely subject alternative epistemological positions and theses to critical scrutiny; some survive rather well, while others do not. For example, contemporary theoretically and methodologically oriented educational researchers routinely bash "foundationalism" and "positivism." This bashing may well be justified. But it is somewhat troubling that the views being bashed are often rather badly mischaracterized by the bashers.[10] Epistemological positions such as these are complex and multifaceted; one cannot address a plethora of them in a one-semester course and expect theoretical sophistication to result. More to the point, they cannot be adequately grasped without at least a bit of philosophical training. Understanding and criticizing epistemological/methodological positions takes time, effort, and expertise; the serious coming to grips with "alternative epistemologies" requires the serious inclusion of philosophy in the graduate educational research curriculum.

But the more important point is this: epistemologies are not all born equal; those that deserve to count as legitimate epistemological alternatives must prove their mettle in the give and take of scholarly disputation. Some proposals will survive such disputation; others will not. As suggested above, the scholarly educational research community should endorse *pluralism*, not relativism.

When it comes to research methodologies, this point is readily accepted. It is uncontroversial that there are legitimate forms of "qualitative" as well as "quantitative" research; of "inductive" as well as "deductive" research; of efforts aimed at nonquantitative understanding as well as those aimed at deriving significant findings from the sophisticated statistical manipulation of large sets of data. It is equally uncontroversial that some approaches to research are illegitimate or otherwise problematic—e.g., those that pretend to be thoroughgoingly value neutral;[11] that fail to place adequate controls on key variables; that fail to control for placebo, halo, and other well-known effects; that fail to protect against experimenter bias; etc. Consequently, it is a mistake to think that criticism of "alternative epistemologies"—understood either as research methodologies or their basic underlying assumptions—is in any way epistemologically suspect.

My claim here is that "alternative epistemologies" themselves admit of critical evaluation. As noted above, such evaluation will itself be conducted in terms of relevant *criteria*, such criteria being the property not of any given epistemology, but rather of an overarching epistemological/philosophical perspective (or "meta-perspective") that is *neutral* with respect to them all.

I can well understand the incredulity that this boldfaced appeal to neutrality will undoubtedly provoke. How can *any* perspective be neutral? After all, contemporary research across the humanities and social sciences has unambiguously rejected any sort of "view from nowhere" or "God's-eye perspective" that is alleged to be free of the influence of the language, culture, conceptual scheme, gender, race, class, etc. of the person or group whose perspective it is. Any such allegedly neutral perspective, it is commonly held, is nothing more than a cover for the hegemonic imposition of the perspective of the dominant group upon dominated others.

There is much in this commonly held rejection of neutrality that I endorse. I agree, of course, that any such hegemonic imposition is to be rejected. I agree as well that there is no God's-eye view, no "perspective-less perspective," from which we can judge. But such a *global* neutrality, suggested by a God's-eye perspective, is not required for the sort of neutrality in question. All that is needed is a *local* neutrality, i.e., one that affords the possibility of fair-minded, non-question-begging evaluation of the issue, or epistemology, in question. Consider "positivism," an epistemological orientation widely rejected by the contemporary educational research community. Is that rejection warranted?

Are we right to reject it? If so, it is because we have good reasons for thinking it defective. But these good reasons must themselves be neutral in that they do not beg the question or otherwise prejudice the case against the rejected view. That is, they must be such as to establish the deficiencies, and so the rational rejection, of positivism, and moreover to do so in a way that would in principle incline a fair-minded advocate of that view to agree that rejection is indeed rational and appropriate. Such neutrality is a necessary condition of both fair, effective evaluation of alternative epistemological presuppositions and theses in particular, and of any sort of serious scholarly inquiry more generally. Insofar as educational researchers of any epistemological orientation actually establish any research findings, their doing so requires that those findings are in fact supported by reasons and evidence that are neutral in this sense. Any researchers who take themselves to have established any such finding—most of them/us, I dare say—are committed to the possibility of such neutrality.[12]

It is perhaps worth noting that the neutrality just defended receives support from what may at first blush seem an unlikely source: *standpoint epistemology*. The basic idea of standpoint theories is that "in a socially stratified society, different social positions yield distinctive epistemic positions, and some are better than others" (Antony 2002, p. 472). Sandra Harding's important account of what she calls "strong objectivity" argues that "a feminist standpoint theory can direct the production of less partial and less distorted beliefs" (1991, p. 138). As Harding puts the crucial point,

> A feminist standpoint epistemology requires strengthened standards of objectivity. The standpoint epistemologies call for recognition of a historical or sociological or cultural relativism—but not for a judgmental or epistemological relativism. They call for the acknowledgment that all human beliefs—including our best scientific beliefs—are socially situated, but *they also require a critical evaluation to determine which social situations tend to generate the most objective knowledge claims*. They require, as judgmental relativism does not, a scientific account of the relationships between historically located belief and maximally objective belief. So they demand what I shall call *strong objectivity* in contrast to the weak objectivity of objectivism and its mirror-linked twin, judgmental relativism. (p. 142, first emphasis added)

There is much in this passage, and in Harding's work more generally, that deserves extended consideration; I regret that I cannot consider it further here.[13] But the central point is clear: on Harding's view, feminist standpoint theories require and insist upon the possibility of a robust (though not "perspectiveless" or "unsituated") objectivity, and the possibility of fair critical evaluation of competing knowledge claims, in order to establish that particular social situations do in fact "tend to generate the most objective knowledge claims." Such determinations of objectivity depend upon fair critical evaluation of the relevant evidence, and so depend upon the sort of neutrality argued for above, for without such neutrality we would have no reason to think either that a given social situation does in fact yield (or not) less distorted, more objective knowledge, or that claims to that effect are themselves sufficiently objective. In this way, Harding's call for "strong objectivity" both supports and requires the possibility (and actuality) of locally neutral, fair-minded evaluation of claims and the reasons and evidence alleged to support them.

Among the criteria, neutral in the "local" sense just specified, in terms of which alternative epistemologies can be critically evaluated are those mentioned in the following questions: Does the epistemology in question utilize research methods that reliably produce reliable evidence? Do its methods require evidence sufficient in quantity, quality, and variety to warrant the conclusions/findings it produces? Do those methods require adequate sample size? Do they control for subject and experimenter bias? Does the epistemology in question possess the conceptual resources to afford adequate explanations of the phenomena it addresses? Does it take adequate note of counter-evidence and of criticism? And so on. The proper understanding and application of such criteria are complex, requiring not only statistics and qualitative methods courses, but also epistemology courses in which the careful articulation and critique of such criteria are themselves a focus of concern, and philosophy of science courses in which their place in a full understanding of scientific research and its appropriate methods and constraints is itself an object of study. I do not mean to suggest that these criteria are themselves unproblematic or uncontroversial; they are neither. Nevertheless, without an appeal to some such criteria, there can be no critical appreciation of the strengths and weaknesses either of diverse epistemological approaches or of the criteria in terms of which those approaches are evaluated. The anticipated result of such appeals is that some, but not all, "alternative epistemologies" will meet the criteria—that is, pluralism.

It is worth repeating that the criteria in question are neither unproblematic nor uncontroversial; such criteria are always in principle open to challenge, and in fact are often likely to be contested. They are manifestly not beyond criticism. But if such contestation can be even potentially effective, i.e., if it is possible in principle for the criticism to show a given criterion to be defective, that can only be because fair, legitimate appeal has been made to other criteria or "meta-criteria." Such criticism requires appeal to (meta-)criteria that are themselves applicable in a way that is locally neutral, and so does not beg the question against the criterion being criticized.

While the sort of epistemological criticism of alternative epistemologies just discussed is most obviously relevant to alternative research methodologies/approaches to research, it is equally relevant to the epistemologies of marginalized or traditionally subordinated groups. This leads directly to the next point.

B. Is It *Morally* Suspect to Criticize the Epistemology of a Particular Community of Practice/Approach to Research/ Subordinated Group?

I suspect that much of the call for incorporating "epistemological diversity" in the curriculum is motivated by this concern. Members of "traditionally subordinated groups" increasingly populate the communities of educational researchers and of graduate students in graduate schools of education (Pallas 2001, p. 7). It is often thought that criticizing the epistemologies of such groups is *morally* inappropriate, or a failure to treat the members of these groups with respect.

I have already expressed my reason for doubting the very idea that epistemologies can be ascribed to such groups in a straightforward, one-to-one way. There is simply too much within-group variation to think that each such group (women, people of color, nonheterosexuals, etc.), or even specific subgroups within such groups (Chicana feminists, African women, white Jewish gay men, etc.), can be neatly assigned their own epistemology. Indeed, such an assignment smacks of a problematic essentialism.

But even if we could correctly ascribe unique epistemologies to such groups, criticizing those epistemologies would not necessarily be morally problematic. To be sure, treating the members of such groups with respect is a moral requirement—as it is to so treat all persons. But treating the members of such groups with respect does not prohibit the criticism of their ideas in general, or of their epistemologies in particular. Treating people with respect requires taking their ideas seriously, rather than ignoring them or regarding them as unworthy of serious consideration. But it does not require regarding their ideas as correct, or correct "for them," or as good as any alternative ideas. This general point applies in particular to their epistemologies. There is nothing suspect about criticizing the epistemological views of the members of a subordinated group in terms of relevant criteria, including those mentioned in the previous section. Respecting the group and/or its members does not require making their epistemologies immune to criticism.[14]

Readers might well think that this answer, while perhaps good as far as it goes, does not go far enough, because it does not squarely address an issue that has been lurking just below the surface for some time now: that of the use/abuse of *power*. Let us address it squarely now.

C. Is Criticism of the Epistemology of a Particular Community of Practice/Approach to Research/Subordinated Group Inevitably a Hegemonic Abuse of Power?

I have argued that alternative epistemologies can be legitimately criticized by appeal to suitable, locally neutral criteria. But can such allegedly legitimate critique be distinguished from the imposition of the criteria of the dominant perspective on dominated alternative perspectives? If not, then criticism of alternative epistemologies appears to be nothing more than the hegemonic abuse of power.

This is a deep and serious problem that my position must be able to resolve. Happily, it can. The key is to realize that charges of hegemonic abuse of power, just like criticisms of alternative epistemologies, must be justified on the basis of reasons and evidence, and so must themselves appeal to relevant criteria.

I agree, of course, that the hegemonic abuse of power, in the guise of allegedly neutral criticism of alternative perspectives, must be rejected. This danger is real and must be avoided. Cases in which critique is indeed an abuse of power must be exposed and seen for what they are: not fair critique, but abuses of power. But this is not a flaw inherent in critique per se; it is rather a danger of dominating imposition masquerading as critique. The only way to expose and overcome such abuse is to deal with it by way of critique, i.e., by making the case (by way of appeal to legitimate criteria, locally and neutrally applied) that the "critique" in question does not stand up to critical evaluation, but is rather a matter of inappropriate imposition. What alternative is there? Isn't this precisely what critics of domination (e.g., feminists, antiracists, etc.) do? The feminist case is instructive: to establish that particular "male" criteria were in fact objectionable gendered impositions, feminist scholars offered compelling reasons/evidence/arguments that the criteria in question, or systematic applications of them, were objectionably biased in favor of "male" interests. In this way, illegitimate dominant impositions were made visible, subjected to fair critique, and eventually overcome (or are at least on the way to being overcome).[15]

To this line of response, it might be replied that it is itself an instance of hegemonic imposition, and so of abuse of power. The imposition in question is that of imposing "the very tools of mainstream philosophical thought as the standard for determining the merits . . . of alternative epistemologies."[16] According to this reply, if we are to make a serious attempt to make room for alternative epistemologies, we must not hold such alternatives captive to mainstream, dominant criteria of epistemic evaluation.

To the extent that such criteria are in fact wielded hegemonically, and so are abusively applied to alternative epistemological perspectives, the appeal to them is indeed inappropriate. But consider: To what criteria could we appeal in order to sustain such a charge? It is clear that such criticism depends upon appeal to the criteria embedded in directives, such as: Don't beg the question against the position you are attempting to criticize; Be fair in your criticism; Don't assume without justification what your opponent denies; etc. (That is, the critic is claiming that the imposition of dominant epistemological values upon dominated others problematically violates these very criteria, in finding fault with alternative epistemological perspectives by begging the question against them, criticizing them unfairly and prejudicially, assuming what they reject, etc.) Indeed, there is no logical alternative to so appealing. But notice that these are exactly "the tools of mainstream philosophical thought." It is not possible to defend alternative epistemologies from critiques that rest upon the illegitimate, hegemonic imposition of dominant criteria without appeal to such "tools." Advocates of alternative epistemologies must rely upon these very same tools in making their criticisms of "mainstream philosophical thought" and defending those alternatives from hegemonic imposition masquerading as legitimate critique. That is, the advocates of alternative epistemologies cannot coherently reject these aspects of mainstream thought (Siegel, 1987, 1997, 2004).

Educational research should indeed make room for alternative meanings, values, and ways of knowing. All this is captured by pluralism. But saying this, or indeed making any claim about educational research, requires appeal to those "very tools of mainstream philosophical thought." Consequently, the appeal to such tools is not necessarily or inevitably a hegemonic abuse of power. Sometimes it is; in these cases the appeal is flawed, and can be shown to be so by arguments that demonstrate the flawed nature of the appeal. In other cases the appeal can be shown to be legitimate, by way of arguments that establish the non-question-begging nature of the appeal, or the need of the proponent of the alternative perspective to appeal to those very same tools in order to make her case. To forbid or reject all such appeals is to embrace not pluralism but relativism, the difficulties of which have been noted above. The call for "epistemological diversity," therefore, is defensible only within limits: pluralism, but not relativism.

D. Is It *Pragmatically* Suspect to Criticize the Epistemology of a Particular Community of Practice/Approach to Research/ Subordinated Group?

Here the idea is straightforward: as a matter of fact, the alternative epistemologies in use are in fact in use; educational research as a field is the sum total of all the research conducted from these alternative perspectives; educational researchers should be able, to the greatest extent possible, to interact meaningfully with all available research. Given the general difficulty of uncontroversially showing a particular epistemology to be deficient, the pragmatic course is simply to take all those currently in use as legitimate, so that present and future researchers will be able to communicate maximally effectively, thus maximizing the research output of the educational research community as a whole. This will have the added significant benefit of enhancing all research, from whatever perspective, by allowing it to benefit from the insights of all other perspectives (Pallas 2001, pp. 6–7).

With this pragmatic point I am in considerable sympathy. The more communication and understanding across diverse communities of research practice we can get, the better. Insofar as the motivation for enhancing epistemological diversity in the educational research community is this pragmatic one, it is difficult to see any reason for rejecting it, other than equally pragmatic considerations, e.g., the multiplicity of extant epistemological perspectives and the shortage of time in a typical graduate student's schedule for mastering both the epistemologies of multiple communities of research practice and the philosophical knowledge and skills required to evaluate them. But I would be remiss not to note that this pragmatic point is itself somewhat superficial, amounting to little more than: "There are lots of ways to conduct good research; let's teach our students as many as we can, and help them to become open-minded with respect to the insights of those they do not themselves master, consistently with helping them to become skilled in conducting research themselves."

4. Conclusion

Young, in introducing the papers by Pallas, Metz and Page, writes,

> All three authors ... argue especially for thoughtful, intentional, and reflexive consideration of systematic experiences that prepare novice researchers in education to deal with epistemological diversity. Each author calls for rich occasions where students have opportunities to learn multiple epistemological perspectives in order to be able to engage meaningfully with members of other communities of education practice. (Young 2001, p. 4)

Understood as calls for students to have substantial familiarity with at least some of the many approaches to research utilized by the various members of the contemporary educational research community, such calls for epistemological diversity face practical objections concerning available time and the need for students to specialize in and master a particular approach to research, but are otherwise unproblematic. For scientific research, including educational research, has always been pluralistic in that researchers bring different knowledge bases to their work, appeal to many distinct types and sources of evidence, and utilize many legitimate ways to gather, evaluate, and infer from that evidence. Understood as calls for students to learn to see things from the perspectives of alternative communities of research practice and alternative cultural perspectives, such calls for epistemological diversity are likewise unproblematic, since this sort of tolerance—involving open-mindedness, openness to objections and alternative points of view, a willingness to take into account alternative points of view and to take seriously criticisms of one's own point of view, etc.—is part and parcel of the traditional, "Enlightenment" epistemology that calls for epistemological diversity are often intended to challenge.

The call for epistemological diversity and for students to engage multiple epistemological perspectives becomes problematic just at the point at which it suggests the sorts of skepticism or relativism disparaged earlier. The suggestion that there is no fair way of evaluating any given sort of research, so that any piece of research is as good as any other, is both incorrect philosophically and undermining of the very activity of educational research. The quite different suggestion that different cultures or communities have their own, unchallengeable "epistemological perspectives," such that what counts as knowledge or as acceptable research varies from group to group—so that a given research finding counts as knowledge, or as established, for men but not for women; or for African Americans but not for Anglo-Americans, Cuban Americans, Korean Americans or Haitian Americans; or for gay and lesbian but not heterosexual consumers of educational research—is equally incorrect philosophically and equally undermining of the very point of conducting or reading such research. So understood, the call for epistemological diversity is one that should be resisted by educational researchers.

To say this is not to call for the silencing of alternative voices or alternative approaches to research. On the contrary, openness to new voices and approaches should be both welcomed and encouraged by educational researchers and incorporated into the education of future researchers. But conflating epistemological pluralism and a problematic relativism or skepticism can only hamper the important project of rethinking the graduate education of future educational researchers. Keeping these distinct calls for epistemological diversity clear is a key step in the process of rethinking and ultimately enhancing the graduate education of current and future students of educational research.[17]

Notes

1. "Research for Doctoral Students in Education." *Educational Researcher* 30.5 (June/July 2001). (See Metz 2001; Page 2001; Pallas 2001; Young 2001.)
2. For examples, discussion, and references see Siegel 2001, 2002.
3. It is perhaps worth pointing out that philosophers' emphasis on knowledge allows them to regard epistemology as a *normative* domain, since it leaves room for consideration not only of what people in fact believe, but also of what they *should* believe, of what is *worthy* of belief.
4. For example, Mary Haywood Metz identifies "qualitative sociology" and "anthropologically inclined ethnography" as two sorts of qualitative approaches taken in her own department at the University of Wisconsin-Madison. She mentions "traditional experiments," "quasi-experiments," "survey research," "ethnography," "history," "critical theory" and "post-modernism" as approaches to research treated in the Research Education Program in that department (2001, p. 12).
5. Many philosophers of science take this sort of "technique diversity" to show that there is no such thing as *scientific method*, or no one method to follow in pursuing scientific research. Understood as either an algorithmic procedure or a universal technique, there is surely no such thing. My own view is that this is the wrong way to think about scientific method. That method is best understood in terms, not of a unique technique or procedure, but rather of its reflection of a systematic *commitment to evidence*. For the fuller story, see Siegel, 1985. Interestingly, Metz posits "an underlying research process common to very different kinds of work" (2001, p. 13), and Page refers to a common "logic of inquiry" consisting of basic "philosophical issues that inform any systematic inquiry" that different methodological approaches address in distinct ways (2001, p. 22). In these ways both Metz and Page acknowledge a commonality of both purpose and method (not technique) across the wide range of methodologies taught and practiced by researchers in graduate schools of education.
6. For more on relativism see Siegel 1987, 2004.
7. Much depends on the degree to which group membership is alleged to influence one's epistemology. All the authors discussed suggest that the one seriously influences the other. I offer my own case of within-group variation as a counterexample to any claim of significant influence; I suggest that other groups, e.g., women and people of color, also harbor extensive within-group variation, thus again undermining the claim of significant influence of group membership on epistemology. I intentionally leave "significant" and "serious" vague here.
8. In addition to her using it as an expression equivalent in meaning to "research methodology," Young also understands "epistemology" in this broader way when she writes of the call for faculty "to assume responsibility for explicating the assumptions, goals, and epistemologies that undergird their research, their courses, and their initiation of doctoral students into professional life in the field of education" (2001, p. 4).
9. Here Pallas, like Young, equates "epistemology" with something like "research methodology." That is, both authors use "epistemology" equivocally, using it sometimes to mean "research methodology" (or "research method"), and sometimes to refer to the epistemological assumptions or presuppositions underlying such methodologies.
10. I particularly recommend D. C. Phillips' (1987, 2000) documentation of the misunderstandings of "positivism" and other "epistemologies" in the educational research literature.
11. That is, that fail to acknowledge cognitive and/or contextual values that they presuppose and that guide their research agendas and trajectories.
12. There is obviously much more to be said about the character of such neutrality than I can say here. As the anonymous reviewers have forcefully reminded me, such "neutrality" is difficult to articulate. (For a recent attempt, see Siegel 2004, pp. 750–754; cf. also Siegel 1987, 1997.) My thanks to the reviewers, whose criticisms prompted the preceding two paragraphs. I borrow the "local/global" neutrality distinction from my former student Timothy

Mosteller, who introduced it in his PhD dissertation, *Epistemological Relativism: MacIntyre, Putnam and Rorty* (University of Miami, 2002), a revised version of which appeared as Mosteller 2006.
13. Harding develops her account of "strong objectivity" in several places; see particularly Harding 1991, chs. 5–7; Harding 1993; and Harding 1998, pp. 18–19 and ch. 8.
14. This point deserves much more attention than I can give it here. For further discussion, see Siegel 1997, 1999, 2001, and especially 2002, pp. 812–813. One further matter I have yet to address is the moral complexity of the classroom situation, and in particular the fact that the teacher's authority makes criticism of students' "alternative epistemologies" especially tricky. My thanks to Judith Suissa for this important point.
15. For further discussion, see Siegel 1997, esp. ch. 12.
16. As suggested by a reviewer.
17. An earlier version of this paper was presented as part of a Spencer Foundation–sponsored program on "Ways of Knowing in Educational Research and Practice" at Teachers College, Columbia University, in March 2003. I am grateful to Chris Higgins for the invitation to participate in this program, to the audience members for their probing questions, criticisms, and discussion, and to Aaron Pallas for his insightful and helpfully clarifying response on that occasion. A more recent version was presented to the Philosophy of Education Society of Great Britain in April 2004; my thanks to the participants on that occasion as well. Thanks also to Jon Levisohn and Denis Phillips for sharing their manuscript (subsequently published as Levisohn and Phillips 2011), from which I derived considerable benefit. Finally, my thanks to the anonymous reviewers and especially to Features Section Editor Stafford Hood, who labored long and hard to persuade me of the need for improvements and who made several excellent suggestions. I have taken their collective advice as often as I could, but probably not often enough.

References

Antony, L. M. (2002). "Embodiment and Epistemology." In P. K. Moser (ed.), *The Oxford Handbook of Epistemology*. Oxford: Oxford University Press, pp. 463–478.

Asante, M. K. (1990). *Kemet, Afrocentricity and Knowledge*. Trenton, NJ: Africa World Press.

Banks, J. (1993). "The Canon Debate, Knowledge Construction, and Multicultural Education." *Educational Researcher* 22.5: 4–14.

Banks, J. (1998). "The Lives and Values of Researchers: Implications for Educating Citizens in a Multicultural Society." *Educational Researcher* 27.7: 4–17.

Bernal, D. D. (1998). "Using a Chicana Feminist Epistemology in Educational Research." *Harvard Educational Review* 68.4: 555–582.

Braun, S. (2003). "The History of Breast Cancer Advocacy." *Breast Journal* 9 (Suppl. 2, May): S101–S103.

Collins, P. H. (1990). *Black Feminist Thought*. New York: Routledge.

Harding, S. (1990). "Starting Thought from Women's Lives: Eight Resources for Maximizing Objectivity." *Journal of Social Philosophy* 21.2–3: 140–149.

Harding, S. (1991). *Whose Science? Whose Knowledge?: Thinking from Women's Lives*. Ithaca, NY: Cornell University Press.

Harding, S. (1993). "Rethinking Standpoint Epistemology: What Is 'Strong Objectivity'?" In L. Alcoff and E. Potter (eds.), *Feminist Epistemologies* (pp. 49–82). New York: Routledge.

Harding, S. (1998). *Is Science Multicultural?: Postcolonialisms, Feminisms, and Epistemologies*. Bloomington: Indiana University Press.

Levisohn, J. A., and D. C. Phillips. (2011). "Charting the Reef: A Map of Multicultural Epistemology." In C. W. Ruitenberg and D. C. Phillips (eds.), *Education, Culture and Epistemological Diversity: Mapping a Disputed Terrain* (pp. 39–63). Dordrecht, The Netherlands: Springer.

Metz, M. H. (2001). "Intellectual Border Crossing in Graduate Education: A Report from the Field." *Educational Researcher* 30.5: 12–18.

Mosteller, T. (2006). *Relativism in Contemporary American Philosophy: MacIntyre, Putnam and Rorty*. London: Continuum.

Page, R. N. (2001). "Reshaping Graduate Preparation in Educational Research Methods: One School's Experience." *Educational Researcher* 30.5: 19–25.

Pallas, A. M. (2001). "Preparing Education Doctoral Students for Epistemological Diversity." *Educational Researcher* 30.5: 6–11.

Phillips, D. C. (1987). *Philosophy, Science, and Social Inquiry*. Oxford: Pergamon.

Phillips, D. C. (2000). *The Expanded Social Scientist's Bestiary: A Guide to Fabled Threats to, and Defenses of, Naturalistic Social Science*. Lanham, MD: Rowman & Littlefield.

Scheurich, J., and M. Young. (1997). "Coloring Epistemologies: Are Our Research Epistemologies Racially Biased?" *Educational Researcher* 26.4: 4–16.

Siegel, H. (1985). "What Is the Question Concerning the Rationality of Science?" *Philosophy of Science* 52.4: 517–537.

Siegel, H. (1987). *Relativism Refuted: A Critique of Contemporary Epistemological Relativism*. Synthese Library, vol. 189. Dordrecht, The Netherlands: D. Reidel/Springer.

Siegel, H. (1997). *Rationality Redeemed?: Further Dialogues on an Educational Ideal*. New York: Routledge.

Siegel, H. (1999). "Multiculturalism and the Possibility of Transcultural Educational and Philosophical Ideals." *Philosophy* 74: 387–409.

Siegel, H. (2001). "Incommensurability, Rationality, and Relativism: In Science, Culture, and Science Education." In P. Hoyningen-Huene and H. Sankey (eds.), *Incommensurability and Related Matters* (pp. 207–224). Boston Studies in Philosophy of Science. Dordrecht, The Netherlands: Kluwer/Springer.

Siegel, H. (2002). "Multiculturalism, Universalism, and Science Education: In Search of Common Ground." *Science Education* 86.6: 803–820.

Siegel, H. (2004). "Relativism." In I. Niiniluoto, M. Sintonen, and J. Woleński (eds.), *Handbook of Epistemology* (pp. 747–780). Dordrecht, The Netherlands: Kluwer.

Wenger, E. (1998). *Communities of Practice: Learning, Meaning, and Identity*. New York: Cambridge University Press.

Young, L. J. (2001). "Border Crossings and Other Journeys: Re-envisioning the Doctoral Preparation of Education Researchers." *Educational Researcher* 30.5: 3–5.

17

How Should We Educate Students Whose Cultures Frown upon Rational Disputation?

Cultural Difference and the Role of Reason in Multicultural Democratic Education

1. Democratic Public Education and Cultural Difference: The Problem

How should public education in democratic states deal with cultural differences among citizens?

This question gains importance and practical relevance from the increasingly diverse cultural constituencies that collectively constitute the citizenry of contemporary democratic states. However, to shed light on it, it is helpful to step back and consider the question without reference to culture. So, what should public education in democratic states be like (irrespective of the cultural make-up of their citizens)? At what should it aim?

One common answer, which I endorse, is that it should aim at fostering in students the skills and abilities, and attitudes and dispositions, needed to participate fully and successfully in democratic decision-making and, more generally, in democratic life. This may not be the only aim of public education in democratic states, but it is clearly a central one. Fostering these skills, abilities, attitudes, and dispositions amounts to helping students to become critical thinkers; that is, helping them to become rational or reasonable persons. Public education in democratic states should aim, in other words, at the cultivation of reason in its students (Siegel 1988, 1997, 2003; Bailin and Siegel 2003).[1]

Why should this be thought of as a central aim of public education in democratic states? There are two sets of reasons, the first having to do with education per se, the second with the nature of democracy. First, education must, for moral reasons, educate students in ways that treat them with respect as persons, and which further their own interests (as opposed to those of the school or the state, where the latter might conflict with the former). The Kantian principle of respect for persons is one that has relevance far beyond the bounds of education, but it is as applicable there, governing the treatment of students, as it is everywhere else. Education, moreover, has to prepare students for adulthood, where this is conceived not as preparation for a predetermined slot in the preexisting social/economic matrix, that slot being determined by the state, but rather as enabling students to determine for themselves, to the greatest extent possible, the character of their lives and their place in the social order in which they find themselves. Further, education must endeavor to provide students with a suitable introduction to, and understanding of, the many intellectual traditions developed during the long course of human history. In all these, the "cultivation of reason"—or, less prosaically, the fostering of rationality, reasonableness, and the abilities and dispositions of critical thinking—is central (Siegel 1988, ch. 3; Siegel 2003).

The second set of reasons for thinking that public education in democratic states should aim at fostering rationality, or critical thinking abilities and dispositions, in its students relates directly to the nature of democracy itself. It is a commonplace that democracy requires an educated citizenry. But what sort of "educated citizenry" is required? What is needed, I submit, is a *critical* citizenry; that is, citizens who are able, and disposed, to settle matters of public policy and concern by appeal to relevant reasons. For democratic states to flourish, their citizens must be able to conceive, consider, and properly evaluate reasons for and against alternative policies and practices concerning the many, varied matters that require public deliberation and decision. Citizens must be able to construct arguments imaginatively, and to assess their own arguments and those of others in accordance with the epistemic principles governing the assessment of reasons and arguments, in order to determine wisely the course of social policies and institutions. Without a critical citizenry, the state itself is threatened.

Worse than the situation of a democratic state peopled by an uncritical citizenry, in my view, are the situations of uncritical citizens themselves in a democratic state. Such a citizen has no adequate way to contribute to public discussion, to voice her concerns, to protect her and her community's interests, or to work for constructive political change. She is marginalized, left on the outside, unable to participate meaningfully in democratic life. Her lack of critical abilities and dispositions renders her unable to enjoy the fruits of that life. Insofar as we value democracy, and think it a good thing that states are democratic, we must deplore both an uncritical citizenry in such states in general, and the fate of the marginalized uncritical citizen in them in particular. In valuing democracy, we recognize the crucially important place of the critical citizen in democratic states, and the centrality of democratic public education's task of cultivating the reason of its students.²

With this view of democracy, and the place of reason in it, in place, we are in position to pursue our initial question. How, then, should public education in democratic states be conceived, in light of significant cultural differences among citizens? It is worth noting that the question is not of merely theoretical interest. Virtually all "First World" democratic states have large and growing numbers of immigrants, from a range of cultural groups. Around the globe, and perhaps especially in contemporary Western Europe and North America, the question is of pressing political moment. While the practical relevance of the matter is clear, in what follows I abstract away from such practical considerations and offer an answer to the question that depends rather on particular aspects of cultural difference and the demands of democratic education themselves.

2. The Solution?

A quick answer is: Cultural difference doesn't matter. The conception of democratic public education rehearsed above, as involving the fostering of the abilities and dispositions of reason/critical thinking, is the correct one for democratic states, whether or not citizens in those states are members of different cultures. In fact, it might plausibly be argued, the more culturally diverse citizens are, the more important it is that they be able to engage in rational, democratic decision-making. If cultural differences cannot be managed rationally and democratically, those differences might well render just, peaceful social existence impossible. (The recent and current state of various cultural conflicts around the globe seems to provide some evidence for this claim: where democratic institutions are in place and functioning, there appears to be at least a chance of peaceful, just resolution of conflict; where not, not.)

While this "quick" answer is plausible, it does not obviously resolve the most fundamental form of the problem, because it does not acknowledge two different sorts of cultural conflict. First, there can be conflict between cultures, both (or all) of which—despite their conflict—embrace democratic ideals, principles, and a commitment to endeavor to resolve their conflict through participation in reasoned discourse and in democratic institutions and procedures. The quick answer might well suffice for this sort of cultural conflict.

But a second, more difficult sort of cultural conflict involves cultures, some (or all) of which reject democratic ideals, principles, and practices, including those involving reasoned argumentation. In such a circumstance, it is difficult to see how the quick answer can succeed. For how can such conflicts be resolved when (at least some of) the parties to the conflict explicitly reject the value or worth of the sort of argumentation and reasoned deliberation required for democratic decision-making?³

This problem can seem particularly pressing in situations in which large numbers of recent immigrants originate in nondemocratic states, and so have no experience of, and/or lack cultural respect for, the reasoned deliberation characteristic of democratic decision-making at its best. There are, of course, many different sorts of nondemocratic states and cultures. A short list would include those characterized by forms of patriarchy in which women are denied access to the existing education system and are systematically excluded from participation in public life; overtly and covertly racist ones, in which certain groups are systematically excluded from meaningful participation in political life on the basis of race; those in which policy is determined not by citizens or their elected representatives, but by nondemocratically selected monarchs or oligarchs; and those governed by religious leaders according to religious precept. There are also those which are democratic but are nevertheless characterized by an antipathy toward the rough-and-tumble of open democratic deliberation and debate. As Alvin Goldman rather circumspectly puts the point:

> In almost every culture, and especially in certain cultures, there are norms that deter critical argumentation. It is widely said that in Japanese and other Asian cultures people are encouraged to conduct their discourse so as to preserve harmony. The expression of conflict, including verbally explicit disagreement, is said to be discouraged.... [S]tudies definitely reveal contrasts between different cultures in their toleration of critical discourse. (Goldman 1999, p. 147)

In such cases, the quick answer won't do. Or will it? There are actually two distinct possibilities here.

In the first possible scenario, members of cultures that reject the value or worth of reasoned deliberation in the context of democratic decision-making simply reject democratic values as incompatible with their culture or way of life. Here, democracy itself is rejected. In this case, the political/educational task is to persuade them—rationally, of course—of the value of democratic institutions and practices in the actual multicultural social context in which they find themselves. We may well fail in this task. If we cannot succeed, our question appears to be irresolvable: public education for democratic citizenship is itself, in such circumstances, impossible. Such citizens do not actually want to live in a democratic state.⁴

Alternatively, they might recognize the conflict between democratic values and institutions and their own undemocratic cultural values, but nevertheless value living in a democratic state. In such a case there seems to be no alternative to the compromising of their cultural values—i.e., their rejection of reasoned deliberation, etc.—insofar as such compromise is necessary for democracy to flourish, or, less ambitiously, for them to participate in their state's democratic life.

So, when democratic and non- or antidemocratic cultural values conflict, it is essential (a) to respect and allow cultural difference to flourish as much as possible, since this sort of respect is morally required (Siegel 1997, 1999). But it is also necessary that (b) in such cases of conflict, *democracy trumps cultural difference*. That is, when members of anti- or nondemocratic cultures become citizens of democratic states, the requirements of democratic participation must take precedence over their nondemocratic cultural values. When cultural values and attitudes and the requirements of democratic education conflict, the latter must prevail. Why must the requirements of democratic participation, and education for it, take precedence over conflicting nondemocratic cultural values? Because if it does not, educating for democratic citizenship—and thus the commitment to democracy itself—is abandoned.

3. Begging the Question?

But doesn't the argument just given beg the question against those who value their culture more highly than they do democratic citizenship? This is an important objection; I conclude by responding to it.

First, no question has been begged. The argument merely points out that its conclusion—"democracy trumps non- or antidemocratic cultural values"—is required for education for democratic citizenship to be possible in cases of such conflict. Rejecting the conclusion amounts to rejecting, in such cases, that sort of education, and so democracy itself. But since the question being addressed is that of the character of precisely that sort of education—i.e., education for democratic citizenship in democratic states—in multicultural contexts, such rejection seems clearly enough to amount to throwing the baby out with the bath water.

Second, the problem at hand is that of understanding how to maximize respect for and toleration of cultural difference, while at the same time educating new citizens for full participation in democratic life. A citizen who is unwilling to so participate not only, in effect, rejects democracy. She also marginalizes herself by rendering herself unable to participate fully in the life of the democratic state in which she finds herself. This inability must be discouraged by education for democratic citizenship, since any such education aims at preparation for precisely such participation. But the benefit of such education comes at a price, for it inevitably encourages the "relaxing" of her relationship to her original culture. This price might be judged by many to be too high a price to pay, although so judging amounts, as we have seen, to valuing that relationship more highly than democracy itself.

Moreover, such "relaxing" is not necessarily a bad thing, since cultures—in the contemporary world, at any rate—are not monolithic, but are rather fluid and changing. As Seyla Benhabib (2002, pp. ix, 4, 24–26, and *passim*) has characterized them, compellingly in my view, cultures are best conceived not as monolithic and static but rather as hybrid, multifaceted, fluid, porous, polyvocal, interdependent, and mutually influential. Relatedly, Pradeep Dhillon and J. Mark Halstead have criticized effectively "the assumption that cultures are hermetically sealed" (2003, p. 157). If this is correct—that is, if cultures are indeed fluid and changing rather than monolithic—then even members of cultures most concerned to cling to them have no alternative to negotiating such changes and the "outside" influences that bring them about. Closing off oneself and one's culture from the rest of the world is simply not a realistic option. If so, the kind of education called for above seems suitable even for such members. Preserving a citizen's relationship to her culture, in whatever state that culture happens to be in at the time in question and conceiving of that state as fixed, is thus both erroneously to conceive of that culture as fixed and static, and is moreover not obviously a good thing from the point of view of education. Enabling her to be open to positive cultural change, or even to judge stasis to be preferable to such change on the basis of relevant reasons and evidence, requires just the sort of education being called for.

In any case—and this is perhaps the most important point of all—democracy is a substantive matter with substantive values. There is no reason to think that all cultures, especially those with antidemocratic values, can thrive in a democratic state. Opting for democracy amounts to opting for its substantive values—including those animating its education—and so opting against incompatible cultural values. If a person values (e.g.) decision by religious leader or military dictator rather than decision by democratic institution, or if she disvalues reasoning, deliberation, argumentation, and public discussion, defense, and critique of proposed policies and practices—e.g. as disrespectful or disharmonious—she has yet to fully embrace democracy and its substantive values.[5]

If the foregoing considerations are correct, our problem is solved. Democracy requires democratic public education; such education must take precedence over respect for cultural traditions that reject it. It is, of course, crucially important to respect cultural differences. But when non- or antidemocratic cultural traditions conflict with democratic public education, the latter must prevail. If it does not, democracy itself is given up. If it is not to be given up, in actual cases of such conflict, culture must yield to its demands—including, especially, those of its public education.[6,7]

Notes

1. By "reason" I do not mean to refer to the cultivation of some metaphysically mysterious entity. Rather, as articulated in the works just cited, I mean to refer simply to the abilities and dispositions involved in constructing, evaluating, and being appropriately guided by reasons. (On this point, see Scheffler, 1989, p. 3.) It is obvious that this is an individualist, "Enlightenment" value/commitment; I defend this orientation in the works just cited.
2. It might be further suggested that in some circumstances the appropriate course is to relax our commitment to democracy in the name of tolerance and respect. However, such a course fails to respect, for it leaves such citizens marginalized in the ways just characterized. Thanks here to conversation with Michael Slote.
3. I here make the idealizing assumption that cultures can be monolithically anti-reason in order to sharply focus the problem being discussed. In fact, I doubt that there are any such cultures. As with individuals, being pro- or anti-reason (like being reasonable or unreasonable) is best seen as a matter of degree, and particular cultures are best seen as occupying some particular interval range along that continuum. Thanks here to conversation with Jennifer Uleman.
4. Public education for democratic citizenship could, of course, be imposed on such citizens. But this would clearly enough be contrary to the obligation to respect such cultures and their members, and contrary to the spirit of democratic citizenship as well. Thanks here to Michael Slote.
5. It is important to note that multicultural concerns may well, and rightly, impact the ways in which we put democratic ideals into practice. For example, in cases where disenfranchised and/or marginalized citizens are relatively unable or unwilling to advocate for themselves in public forums, such forums may well have to be redesigned in order to allow such citizens to participate fully, fairly, and effectively. Thanks here to Jennifer Uleman.
6. My discussion is obviously a "bare bones" one, without either real world examples, exploration of related issues (e.g., how democratic principles are best put into practice in culturally diverse democracies), or references to relevant philosophical discussion. My intention has been to avoid these in order to focus the basic issue more clearly. A more thorough, adequate discussion would need to include them all, and, in particular, references to and consideration of the important work on these matters of Amy Gutmann, Will Kymlicka, Iris Marion Young, and many other contemporary authors, as well as the agenda-setting work of John Dewey and other major historical figures.
7. An ancestor of this paper was presented at a conference on "Citizenship Education, Political Theory, and Their Reflection in Language" in Bled, Slovenia, November 2001, and appeared in *The School Field* 13.6 (2002): 33–39. I am indebted to the conference participants for their helpful comments and criticisms, and to Michael Slote and Jennifer Uleman for excellent suggestions on an earlier draft. The current version also borrows a bit from Siegel 2007.

References

Bailin, S., and H. Siegel. (2003). "Critical Thinking." In N. Blake, P. Smeyers, R. Smith, and P. Standish (eds.), *The Blackwell Guide to the Philosophy of Education* (pp. 181–193). Oxford: Blackwell.

Benhabib, S. (2002). *The Claims of Culture: Equality and Diversity in the Global Era*. Princeton, NJ: Princeton University Press.

Dhillon, P. A., and J. M. Halstead. (2003). "Multicultural Education." In N. Blake, P. Smeyers, R. Smith, and P. Standish, eds., *The Blackwell Guide to the Philosophy of Education* (pp. 146–161). Oxford: Blackwell.

Goldman, A. I. (1999). *Knowledge in a Social World*. Oxford: Oxford University Press.

Scheffler, I. (1989). *Reason and Teaching*. Indianapolis, IN: Hackett. First published in 1973 by Routledge & Kegan Paul.

Siegel, H. (1988). *Educating Reason: Rationality, Critical Thinking, and Education*. London: Routledge.

Siegel, H. (1997). *Rationality Redeemed?: Further Dialogues on an Educational Ideal*. New York: Routledge.

Siegel, H. (1999). "Multiculturalism and the Possibility of Transcultural Educational and Philosophical Ideals." *Philosophy* 74: 387–409.

Siegel, H. (2003). "Cultivating Reason." In R. Curren (ed.), *A Companion to the Philosophy of Education* (pp. 305–317). Oxford: Blackwell.

Siegel, H. (2007). "Multiculturalism and Rationality." *Theory and Research in Education* 5.2: 203–223.

INDEX

Note: References to tables are denoted by '*t*' in italics following the page number

actions, 4, 11, 26, 34, 53, 76, 78, 82–86, 94, 118n4
   beliefs and, 79, 83–84
   dispositions and, 63n19
   ends of, 44n4
   performatives as, 188
   of students, 54
   thoughts and, 24
   unreasonable, 10
   See also behaviors; belief; education
anthropology, xiii, 248, 253, 261, 267, 277n4.
   See also diversity; pluralism; sociology
argumentation, 153n12, 160, 227, 285
   epistemic conception of, 234n1
   multiculturalist perspective on, 234
   philosophical, 54
   power and, 232–34
   rational, 156
   reasoned, 282–83
   social practices and, 135
   theory of, 215n16, 218–20, 235n21
   universals relevant to academic, 246
   See also argument quality; philosophy; power; rational disputation; rhetoric
argument quality, xii, 113, 218–34, 234nn2–3, 235n18. *See also* argumentation
Aristotle, 23–24, 30n3, 80, 106n26, 135. *See also* education; habits; philosophy; virtue
Asante, Molefi Kete, 259. *See also* epistemology
Austin, J. L., 191n1. *See also* philosophy
autonomy, xi, 5, 7, 11, 33, 73, 124, 189–91
   Kantian, 39–43
   rational, 16, 26, 41–42
   of the space of reasons, 27

   student, 87n2, 102, 106n20, 146, 189
   See also critical thinking; rationality; self-sufficiency

Baehr, Jason, xiii, 91, 95–98, 100–3, 105nn4–15, 106n17, 132n3. *See also* philosophy
Bailin, Sharon, 7, 105n13, 128. *See also* critical thinking; philosophy of education
behaviors
   abilities and, 93
   correction of, 78
   dispositions and, 51, 52–55, 58, 60, 63n15, 63n25, 94
   modification of, 103
   rules and, 52–53, 61
   sensitivities and, 93
   virtue in a person's, 98
   See also actions; dispositions; rules
belief, 69–70, 78–79, 84–85
   education a necessary condition of justified, 126–27
   epistemological diversity and, 260–61
   lucky true, 140–41
   non-evidential style of, 109–11
   rational, 145–47
   style of, 111–16
   systems of, 260–61
   See also actions; doctrines; indoctrination; knowledge; truth
Benhabib, Seyla, 235n15, 254n6, 285. *See also* philosophy
Bernal, Dolores Delgado, 258. *See also* education; epistemology; feminism; philosophy of education
Brandom, Robert, 23, 30nn6–7, 30n12. *See also* philosophy

Brown, Harold, xiii, 156–70, 170n4, 170nn6–9, 168. *See also* philosophy
Burbules, Nicholas, 52–53. *See also* philosophy

caring, 80–82, 84, 91, 102, 197. *See also* character; empathy; ethics; sentiment
character, xiv, 3, 5, 21–29, 53, 77–78, 80–92, 104, 105nn2–3, 106n17, 126–29, 132n7, 162–67
   development of, 146
   dispositions and, 145–46
   ethical, 24
   failures of, 144
   intellectual, 105n10
   intellectual virtues as traits of, 103
   natural, 24
   virtues as excellences of, 96, 106n18
   See also dispositions; ethics; habits; sentiment; virtue
Christianity, 3, 71–72, 106n26. *See also* ethics; virtue
close-mindedness, 108–11, 115–17, 118n3. *See also* belief; critical thinking; fundamentality; indoctrination
compatibility, 25–28, 136
concept, 21, 28, 132n1, 149, 151, 184, 206–7
   axiological, 209, 212, 220, 227
   of close-mindedness, 111
   definition of a, 248
   of education, 123–32, 133n15
   epistemic, 123–32, 132n5
   of justification, 141
   Kantian, 39–40
   proper use of, 30n7
   of rationality, 249
   system of, 23
   "thick", xii, 123–32
   See also thinking
Coombs, Jerrold, 64n25. *See also* philosophy
critical thinking
   education and, xii–xiv, 5–13, 21–29, 35–54, 62n10, 67–79, 85–104, 108–17, 125–29, 136–52, 153nn4–5, 187, 191n4, 281–82
   Heideggerian reconceptualizing of, 172–91
   the intellectual virtues and, xii, 68, 77, 89–104, 129
   reasons conception of, xii–xiv, 40
   See also democracy; dispositions; education; intellectual virtues; open-mindedness; philosophy; reasoning; thinking
culture, 197, 218–34
   difference of, 238–39, 280–85
   education and, 280–85
   research and, 263–64

   See also argument quality; diversity; multiculturalism; universality
Cuypers, Stefaan, 33–44, 44nn1–5, 45n10. *See also* critical thinking; philosophy

democracy, xiii, 7, 135, 199–200, 280–85, 286n2. *See also* critical thinking; diversity; education; multiculturalism
Derrida, Jacques, 191n1. *See also* philosophy
Dewey, John, 3, 80, 228, 286n6. *See also* education; philosophy; philosophy of education
dispositions, xiv, 52–60, 86, 126
   critical, 67–74, 77, 79, 89–92
   of critical thinking, xii, 6–7, 92–100, 104, 113–15, 125, 128, 281–82
   of democracy, 280
   of education, 128–29, 133n14, 145–46, 149
   of the gods, 239
   reasons and, 4–5, 29, 35, 118n2, 118n4, 137, 286n1
   thinking, 49–61, 61nn1–5, 62nn6–11, 63nn14–25, 64nn26–27
   virtues and, xi, 103–4
   See also behaviors; critical thinking; habits; metaphysics; rules; thinking
diversity, xiv
   cultural, xiv, 199, 280–85
   discouragement of, 8
   in educational research, 263–64
   epistemological, xiii, 258–76
   methodological, 261
   multiculturalism and, 244
   rationality and, xii, 251
   technique, 261, 277n5
   See also culture; democracy; education; multiculturalism
doctrines, 67–74, 219, 243, 245
   the content of, 68
   the formulation of, 244
   the inculcation of, 69–70
   indoctrination and, 69
   the scope of, 70–72
   See also belief; indoctrination

education
   the aims of, 102–4, 116–17, 125, 138–40, 145–47
   "being educated" and, 126–28
   critical thinking and, xii–xiv, 5–13, 21–29, 35–54, 62n10, 67–79, 85–104, 108–17, 125–29, 136–52, 153nn4–5, 187, 191n4, 281–82
   as an epistemic concept, 123–32

and epistemic virtue, 128–30
the ideals of, 116–17
liberal civic, 68
moral, 76–86
multicultural democratic, 280–85
research in, 258–76
science, 87n2
as initiation into the space of
  reasons, 20–29
success in, 140–41
thinking dispositions and, 49–52
See also critical thinking; democracy;
  diversity; epistemology; knowledge;
  philosophy of education; reason;
  thinking
Elgin, Catherine, 99, 105n7, 106n20, 106n26, 125, 154n23. *See also* philosophy;
  philosophy of education
empathy, 80–82. *See also* caring; character;
  ethics; sentiment
epistemic dependence, xi, 11–13. *See also*
  epistemology
epistemology, xiii, 132n2, 135–52, 172–91,
  260, 277n9
  Chicana feminist, 258, 272
  diversity in, 258–76
  education and, 123–32, 135–52,
    258–76
  "Enlightenment" conception of, 136
  excessive, 172–91
  feminist, 270
  naturalized, 133n19, 234n1, 235n11
  perspectives of, 265–67
  political, 209
  social, 11, 123, 132, 135–36,
    138–39, 154n24
  "thick" pursuit of, 131–32
  veritistic, 136
  virtue, 128–30, 132, 132n7
  See also belief; epistemic dependence;
    ethics; knowledge; philosophy;
    philosophy of education; "thick"/"thin"
    distinction
ethics, 24
  care, 80–81
  epistemology and, 124–25
  principles of, 228
  reasons and, 24
  "thick"/"thin" distinction in, 124
  the universalist tradition in, 235n15
  See also epistemology; feminism;
    philosophy; "thick"/"thin"
    distinction; values
explanations
  dispositions in, 55–60, 63n19, 63n24

emptiness of, 57–59
epistemology and, 271
genuine, 61
of natural phenomena, 260
scientific, 239, 247, 250
See also epistemology; science

feminism, 13–16, 80–81, 270. *See also*
  epistemology; ethics; philosophy;
  philosophy of education
Feyerabend, Paul, xiii, 8–11. *See also*
  philosophy of science; relativism
Fish, Stanley, xiii, 241–48, 255nn17–18. *See
  also* philosophy
foundationalism, 159–60, 170, 222, 268. *See
  also* judgment; rationality; rules
Fricker, Elizabeth, 148, 150. *See also*
  philosophy
fundamentality, 80, 109, 111–17. *See also*
  close-mindedness

Gilligan, Carol, 81. *See also* feminism;
  philosophy
Goldberg, David Theo, xiii, 199, 209–12,
  215n15, 220–24, 227, 229–30. *See also*
  philosophy; relativism
Goldman, Alvin, xii–xiii, 125, 135–52,
  153nn3–15, 154n16, 154n24, 192n10,
  255n21, 283. *See also* education;
  epistemology; philosophy
Govier, Trudy, 159–62, 167, 170n6. *See also*
  philosophy
Gutmann, Amy, 199, 215n8, 246, 286n6. *See
  also* education; philosophy

Habermas, Jürgen, 246. *See also* philosophy
habits, 78, 80, 82, 84, 86, 149
  of mind, xiv, 5, 21, 29, 77, 89–91, 104,
    126–28, 137, 149
  proper, 80, 82
  See also Aristotle; character;
    dispositions; values
Hanks, Chris, xiii, 25–27, 29, 30n11. *See also*
  philosophy
Hare, William, 108, 112–17, 118nn5–8. *See
  also* philosophy
Heidegger, Martin, xii, 172–91, 191n1,
  192n12, 192n14, 193nn15–16. *See also*
  philosophy
Hoffman, Martin, 81. *See also* empathy; ethics
Hume, David, 3, 33–44, 44n2, 81–82. *See also*
  philosophy
Hutcheson, Francis, 81. *See also* philosophy
hypostatization, 56–57, 59, 63n24. *See also*
  dispositions

ideals, 6, 17, 26–27, 174, 190
   cultural, xiii, 219, 243
   democratic, 282, 286n5
   educational, xiv, 4, 29, 77, 102, 108, 116–17, 131, 197–214
   intellectual, 3
   philosophical, 197–214
   of rationality, 13
   of reason, 14
   transcultural, 197–214, 220
   universal, xii–xiii
   See also education; ethics; values
indoctrination, xi–xii, 79, 86n2, 108–17, 118n3, 149
   brainwashing and, 130, 139
   close-mindedness and, 109–11
   doctrines and, 67–74
   liberal civic education and, 68
   problem of, 30n11
   See also belief; doctrines
inquiry
   communities of, 7
   critical, 118n3
   knowledge and, 259
   methods of, 258, 260–62
   rational, 8
   scholarly, 270
   truth and, 136, 142
   See also research
intellectual virtues, xii, 67–68, 80, 144
   critical thinking and the, 89–104
   education and the, 77, 129, 132n7
   reliabilist account of the, 96–100
   responsibilist account of the, 96–100
   See also critical thinking; knowledge; reason; virtue

judgment, xiv, 156–70
   rationality and, 168–70, 238–39
   reasonable decisions and, 162–65
   rules and, 165–68
   See also rationality; rules

Kant, Immanuel, xi, 33–44. *See also* philosophy
Khin Zaw, Susan, 201. *See also* philosophy
knowledge, 7, 91, 174, 191n3, 207, 212, 259–63, 267, 270–71
   belief and, 12
   common-sense, 148, 151
   education and, 4, 123, 126–28, 130–31, 138–40
   feminism and, 14
   naturalized accounts of, 133n19
   social character of, 11, 135–36
   See also belief; epistemology; intellectual virtues

language, 30n7, 176–86, 189–91, 193n25
   culture and, 205–6, 241, 259, 269
   emotive, 53
   intentional contents of, 21
   learning of a, 28–29, 127
   normativity of, 24
   philosophy of, 22, 132n8, 180
   private, 127
   representational account of, 192n14
   thought and, 176–79, 181, 186
   value and, 212
   See also representation; rhetoric; thinking
lyrics, 72–74

MacIntyre, Alasdair, 219, 234n4. *See also* philosophy
McDowell, John, xi, 20, 23–29, 30nn6–8, 30n11, 30n14, 193n16. *See also* philosophy
metaphysics, 22, 30n11, 30n14, 49–52, 129. *See also* dispositions; philosophy
Metz, Mary Haywood, 265, 267, 275, 277nn4–5. *See also* anthropology; sociology
multiculturalism, 197–214, 218–34, 238–54, 280–85
   definition of, 240–41
   impossibility of, 241–47
   See also culture; diversity; rationality

naturalism, 22–25
   epistemological, 27–28
   instrumental rationality and, 255n21
   metaphysical, 27–28
   See also ethics; epistemology; metaphysics
Noddings, Nel, 80–82, 84–85. *See also* feminism; philosophy
normativity, 22–25, 92, 207–13
   argument, 218–19
   epistemic, xii, 22, 30n7, 38, 173, 218, 232, 234n1
   naturalistic view of, 22–25
   of reasons, 30n7, 37, 215n16
   transcultural, 229–31
   See also norms; epistemology; rationality
norms, 128, 240, 283
   communal, 232
   genuine, 207
   moral, 81
   putative, 207

scientific, 14
See also normativity
Nussbaum, Martha, 15–16, 152n1. *See also* philosophy

objectivity, 8–11, 119n8. *See also* rationality
open-mindedness, xii, 67, 77, 91, 95–98, 101–3, 105n5, 108–19, 129, 230, 275–76. *See also* close-mindedness; critical thinking; education; intellectual virtues; virtues

Pallas, Aaron, 264–68, 272, 275, 277n9. *See also* philosophy of education; sociology
particularity, 16, 209, 220, 227–29. *See also* universality
philosophy, 7–10, 20–22, 42, 135, 167, 174, 181, 260–61. *See also* argumentation; philosophy of education; philosophy of science; rational disputation; relativism; rhetoric
anthropology and, 253
philosophy of education, xii–xiii, 3, 20–29, 29n1, 45n12, 74, 108, 117, 123–32, 133n15, 152
analytic, 105n7, 126
contemporary, 191
science, 247
See also education; epistemology; philosophy; philosophy of science
philosophy of science, 8–11, 23, 39, 62n5, 268, 271, 277n5. *See also* philosophy; philosophy of education; science
pluralism, 143–44, 269, 271, 274
epistemological, 276
methodological, 261–62
See also philosophy; relativism
positivism, 268–70, 277n10. *See also* foundationalism; philosophy
postmodernism, xi, 13–16, 136, 220, 232, 234n5. *See also* philosophy; rationality
power, 13, 16, 29, 98, 232–34, 273–74
argumentation and, 232–34
critical, 146
explanatory, 55–60, 252
hegemonic abuse of, 273–74
ideological, 212
language as a, 177, 183
nonoppressive, 240
of philosophical insights, 152
relationships of, 214n3
rhetoric and, 232–34
See also argumentation; rhetoric
practical reason, 24, 33–44, 76–77, 83
Humean, 33–39, 43

Kantian, 39–40, 43
motivational character of, 45n12
See also philosophy; reason
Putnam, Hilary, 152n1, 228–29. *See also* philosophy

Quine, W. V. O., 22–23, 51–52, 61n2, 61n5, 62n9, 224, 226. *See also* metaphysics; philosophy

rational disputation, 246, 280–85. *See also* argumentation; education; philosophy; rationality; rhetoric
rationality, xiv, 3–7, 14, 23–28, 30n7, 81, 91, 113, 156–70, 197, 208, 213, 238–54, 254n8
autonomy and, 41
the classical model of, xii, 156–59, 162
critical thinking and, xii, 13, 25, 27–28, 33–37, 125, 153n4
criticism of, 3–17
cultivation of, 20–21, 25, 29, 281
cultural diversity and, 197–285
divergent, 247–54, 255n20, 256n27
epistemic, xii, xiv, 30n7
Humean conception of, 33–34, 38–40
instrumental, 23, 38–39, 255n21
the judgment model of, 156, 159–68
judgment and, 156–70
judgments of, 238–39, 254n4, 254n7
justification and, 138, 141, 153n9, 173
justified belief and, 99
multiculturalism and, 238–54
normativity of, 167
relativity of, 219–20, 234n4
of science, 8
truth and, 138
universal, 253, 254n8
the value of, 123–91
See also critical thinking; epistemology; judgment; normativity; objectivity; rational disputation; reason; thinking
reason
critiques of, xiv, 3–17
cultivation of, 3–17
cultural difference and, 280–86
virtue and, 100–2
See also education; practical reason; rationality; reasoning; reasons; virtue
reasoning, 26, 28, 36, 78–85, 91, 93, 97–98, 113, 182, 238, 248–50, 285
abstract, 14
good, 90
logical, 52

reasoning (Cont.)
  rationality of, 239
  valid form of, 25, 30n10
  See also critical thinking; rationality; reasons; thinking
reasons, xiv, 76–86
  education as the space of, 20–29
  examples of, 77t
  the logical space of, 21–22
  in moral education, 82–85
  motivation of, 43–44
  See also education; philosophy; rationality; reason; reasoning
relationships
  among cultures, 200
  among items of knowledge, 127
  multiple, 111–16
  of power/powerlessness, 214n3
relativism, 8–11, 221–23, 226, 235n7, 235n11, 235nn17–18, 262, 269, 274, 276
  axiological, 210, 221
  cultural, 133n20, 270
  epistemological, xi, 8, 21, 221, 223, 270
  judgmental, 270
  methodological, 262
  multicultural, 221–22
  rationality and, 234n4
  See also epistemology; normativity; philosophy; pluralism; skepticism
representation, 175–77
  agency's role in forming, 175
  disengaged, 176, 190
  mental, 132n1
  semantic, 132n1
  thinking and, 174, 182–87, 192n14
  of the world, 185
  worries about, 181–84
  See also epistemology; language; thinking
research, 13, 93, 277n11
  culture and, 263–64
  educational, 49–50, 55–56, 64n27, 258–76, 277n10
  methodologies of, 261–62, 269–72, 277nn8–9
  psychological, 95
  questions of, 262–63
  scientific, 13, 271, 276, 277n5
  See also education; inquiry; science
rhetoric, 232–34. See also argumentation; language; power
Robertson, Emily, 45n12, 125, 128, 193n18. See also education; philosophy; philosophy of education

Rorty, Richard, xii–xiii, 152n1, 208–12, 220–23, 229–30, 235n7. See also philosophy
rules, 55, 156–61, 163–70, 170n3, 170n5, 211, 265
  appropriate, 157–58, 170n7
  axiomatic, 81
  evidential, 157
  formal, 52–53, 55, 61, 62n11, 63n14
  inductive, 157
  judgment and, xii, xiv, 156, 160, 165–68
  logical, 62n11, 157, 247
  methodological, 157
  principles and, 167–68, 171n11, 173
  rationality a matter of, 159, 167
  universal, 160
  See also behaviors; dispositions; judgment; logic; philosophy; rationality; thinking
Ryle, Gilbert, 63n23, 191n1. See also philosophy

Scheffler, Israel, 3, 5–6, 53, 92, 105n13, 126, 128, 139–40, 146, 152n1, 168, 192n12, 228. See also philosophy
Scheffler, Samuel, 123–24. See also philosophy
Scheurich, James, 258. See also education; epistemology
science, 8, 14–15, 22, 30n7, 52, 70–71, 135–36, 144, 153n15, 215n11, 224, 229, 239, 247–48, 259. See also philosophy of science; research
self-sufficiency, 6, 189–90. See also autonomy
Sellars, Wilfrid, xi, 20–29, 30nn2–7, 30n14. See also philosophy
sentiment, 78, 80–82, 84–86. See also caring; character; education; empathy; ethics
sexual orientation, xiv, 215n11, 258, 263–64, 272, 276. See also diversity; epistemology; multiculturalism
Shweder, Richard, 239, 248, 250–53, 255nn19–20, 256n27. See also anthropology
Siegel, Harvey, 5, 7, 25–26, 35, 37–40, 90, 125, 128, 132n2, 137, 174–77, 181–82, 185, 187. See also education; epistemology; philosophy; philosophy of education
skepticism, 181, 228, 232–33
  methodological, 262
  relativism and, 262, 276
  rules and, 160
  See also philosophy; relativism
Slote, Michael, 80–82, 84–85. See also caring; education; empathy; ethics
social practices, 123, 131, 135, 138–39, 210, 221, 240. See also epistemology; ethics

sociology, 260–61, 264, 270, 277n4. *See also* anthropology; philosophy
Spiecker, Ben, 67–74, 74nn5–6. *See also* indoctrination
Steutel, Jan, 67–68, 74n6, 80. *See also* indoctrination; virtue

Taylor, Charles, 172, 174–76, 181–85, 192nn6–7, 199, 215n8. *See also* epistemology; multiculturalism; philosophy
testimony, 135–52
   epistemology of, 147, 150
   evidential status of, 123
   expert, 13
   of others, 11–12, 150
   reliability of, 13, 150–51
   trust and, 135–36, 147–52
   See also belief; education; epistemology; trust
"thick"/"thin" distinction, 124–25. *See also* epistemology; ethics
thinking, 24, 27–28, 123, 135–52, 176–79, 187–89, 192n9, 247
   conceptual, 21, 25
   creative, 7, 179
   deciding, 73
   dispositions of, 49–61, 62nn10–11, 63n14, 64nn26–27, 93
   episodes of, 63n19, 63n21, 63n25
   ethical, 23
   formal principles of, 210–11, 221
   good, 6
   independent, 7, 13
   judgment and, 86
   rationalistic conception of, 190
   reasoning and, 79–80, 83–85
   representational account of, 181–82, 184, 192n14
   responsible, 254n8
   truth and, 136–38
   See also concept; critical thinking; dispositions; education; language; reasoning; thought; truth
thought, 16, 22, 172, 174–79
   action and, 55, 60, 61n4, 62n13, 63n19
   assertive content of, 211–12, 221
   correctness of, 27–28
   critical, 6
   formal rules of, 52, 55, 62n11
   imaginative, 126
   language and, 21, 24, 176–79, 181, 185–86
   rational, 248, 250
   reasoned judgment in, 7

representation and, 181–84, 187, 190
   See also behaviors; language; thinking
transcendence, 22–27, 223–27, 234. *See also* argument quality; rationality
trust, 135–52
   of others, 11
   of teachers, 150–51
   testimony and, 12, 135–36, 147–52
   See also belief; epistemology; testimony
truth, 27, 99, 135–52, 173, 185, 188, 190, 192n12
   access to, 141–43
   account of, 180, 182
   aim of, 125, 128, 138, 144, 147, 152
   Aristotle's characterization of, 30n3
   culturally relative, 204, 221
   epistemological value of, xii
   intellectual virtues and, 89, 95
   justification and, 4, 138, 174
   love of, 67, 110
   moral, 204
   nature of, 191n4
   non-epistemic conception of, 21
   postmodern rejection of, 136
   representation and, 190
   striving after, 179
   structures of, 259
   thinking and, 136–38
   universal, 240, 255n10
   See also belief; education; epistemology; representation; thinking

ungeneralizability, 56, 59–60. *See also* dispositions
universality
   of argumentative force, 212
   of basic formal principles of thinking, 211
   denial of, 210
   of human rights, 200
   of logic, 211
   multiculturalism and, 213
   particularity and, 227–29
   political epistemology of imposed, 209
   rationality and, 254n8, 256n27
   of values, 209
   See also culture; multiculturalism; particularity

values, 11–13, 34, 62n10, 77, 86, 94, 103–4, 114, 149, 221, 228–29, 243–45, 263
   absolute, 201
   alternative, 274
   antidemocratic cultural, xiii, 285
   axiological, 220, 227
   of autonomy, 7, 11

values (Cont.)
  clarification of, 103
  cognitive, 277n11
  core, 241–42
  of critical thinking, 146
  cultural, 203–5, 208–9, 212, 219–20, 222, 243, 283–85
  democratic, xiii, 7, 281–83, 285
  diversity and, 264
  educational, 131, 137
  Enlightenment, 146, 286n1
  epistemic, xii, 123, 136, 140, 142–44, 146, 192n10
  epistemological, 274
  explanatory, 56
  instrumental, xii, 125, 138, 144, 152, 153n7, 153n13, 192n10
  intellectual, 153n3
  justificational, 143–44
  moral, 214n5
  of multiculturalism, 198–202, 211, 213, 240, 262
  non-instrumental, 145
  of rational belief, 140
  of rationality, xii, xiv, 282–83
  social, 222–23
  transcultural, 203, 210, 213, 214n8, 220, 230, 241
  truth, 140–42, 162, 212
  ultimate, 143
  universalism of, 209–10, 213, 215n8, 220, 223, 227, 230
  of women's perspectives, 16
  See also education; ethics
virtue, 3, 80, 84, 49–117
  epistemic, 95–96, 99, 123, 127–30, 143–44
  epistemology and, 92, 123, 129–30, 132, 132n7, 133n15
  of feminism, 16
  genuine, 98
  of humility, 106n26
  moral education and, 82
  natural, 98
  reason and, 100–2, 104
  theorists of, 42, 98
  See also Aristotle; character; dispositions; education; habits; intellectual virtues

Williams, Bernard, 124, 131. *See also* philosophy
Williams, Emma, 172–91, 191n1, 191n3, 192nn5–14, 193n21. *See also* philosophy
Williamson, Timothy, 132n1, 133n19. *See also* philosophy

Young, Lauren Jones, 259, 264–65, 267, 275, 277nn8–9. *See also* education; epistemology; philosophy of education
Young, Michelle, 258. *See also* education; philosophy of education

Ingram Content Group UK Ltd.
Milton Keynes UK
UKHW022312090423
419801UK00003B/55